Vampire State

Vampire State

The Rise and Fall of the
Chinese Economy

Ian Williams

BIRLINN

First published in 2024 by
Birlinn Limited
West Newington House
10 Newington Road
Edinburgh
EH9 1QS

www.birlinn.co.uk

ISBN: 978 1 78027 837 7

British Library Cataloguing-in-Publication Data
A catalogue record for this book is available from the British Library

Typeset by Initial Typesetting Services, Edinburgh

Papers used by Birlinn are from well-managed forests and
other responsible sources

Printed and bound by Clays Ltd, Elcograf S.p.A.

Contents

Acknowledgments

More credulous writers have predicted that rapid economic growth would propel the People's Republic of China inextricably towards world domination; others have forecast that the country is careering towards inevitable economic collapse – or years of stagnation. What can be said with more certainty is that the challenges facing the Chinese Communist Party are more serious than at any time since the country embarked on 'reform and opening' in the late 1970s, and there are severe doubts about whether the Party is capable of addressing them. In trying to reach my own understanding of those challenges and the nature of the Chinese economy, I have drawn on many years of travelling and reporting from China and across Asia. I am immensely grateful to those who have been so generous with their time, sharing with me their insights, knowledge and experience about the often addictive, but also dangerous, intimidating and frequently surreal beast that is the Chinese economy. Many of those are named in the pages that follow, though many more – particularly those still working in or with China – prefer anonymity. It is safer that way, since the Party is a capricious and vengeful organisation, and increasingly so under Xi Jinping. It is intolerant of criticism, wherever it comes from. Speaking out, even on seemingly innocuous subjects, can incur considerable cost. This book is dedicated to those with the courage to do so.

For inspiration for the title of this book, I am indebted to the German economist and writer Günter Reimann. In 1939, on the eve of the Second World War, he published a book entitled *The Vampire Economy: Doing Business Under Fascism,* in which he examined the chilling manner in which the Nazis ruthlessly bent the German economy to their will. This involved all manner of coercion, though many companies closed their eyes to tyranny and willingly collaborated. In reading his book today, it is remarkable how seamlessly the words 'Nazi Party' can be replaced with 'Chinese Communist Party'.

In many ways the themes of *Vampire State: the Rise and Fall of the Chinese Economy* build on those of my earlier study of the surveillance state, *Every Breath You Take: China's New Tyranny*, and *Fire of the Dragon: China's New Cold War*, which looks at China's global belligerence. I am especially grateful to Hugh Andrew of Birlinn for recognising the need to turn this into a trilogy by critically examining the economic dimension of China's rise and challenging the many myths that have grown around it. Many thanks to my editor, Andrew Simmons, for his deft touch and expertise throughout; and to my agent, Andrew Lownie, for his enthusiasm and encouragement. Lastly, a big thank you to my family for their support and feedback as this manuscript took shape.

Ian Williams
London, July 2024

CHAPTER 1

The Death Star Canteen

'China became the world's factory floor. Consumer
goods, which were hardly ever seen in the
country in 1981, are now abundant.

The Made-in-China list today grows ever longer,
its products more sophisticated . . . the world's factory
is now the world's laboratory and marketplace.'

President Xi Jinping, October 2017

Among the more seasoned traders, the lobby bar of the Sheraton
Hotel in the southern Chinese city of Dongguan was known as the
Death Star canteen on account of the dizzying number of languages
and dialects to be heard there. During the Canton Fair it was packed
day and night with buyers who came from every corner of the
planet to visit the world's largest trade show. Rather in the manner
of the fictional space station of the *Star Wars* movies, the bar did
have a common language of sorts, its own version of 'galactic basic',
with conversations punctuated by the universal commercial jargon
of 'lead times', 'MOQs' (minimum order quantities), 'costs', 'price'
and 'schedules'. The bar was to one side of the hotel's cavernous
lobby, which was lined with artificial palm trees, tall mirrors and
giant television screens looping kitschy videos – a log fire, coral
reef, mountains. Large chandeliers hung from a distant ceiling. The
traders huddled in excitable groups, barking loudly at each other
or into mobile phones that transmitted their deal-making across
multiple time zones. It was always a mystery to me why they preferred to discuss their business in the bar rather than in the privacy
of their rooms, to which they would only occasionally dash to collect or deposit documents or samples. The atmosphere was always

urgent, bordering on the neurotic, and when riding in the elevator with a group of traders it was wise to stand clear of the console as fingers stabbed manically at the door-close button at each stop, as if every micro-second lost was business forfeited. Perhaps it was.

An enormous fleet of minibuses stood ready to whisk the traders back and forth to the China Import and Export Fair Complex, the largest of its type in the world, consisting of forty-five hangar-like exhibition halls covering more than 1.6 million square metres.[1] That is roughly equivalent to 225 Wembley football pitches and is larger than London's Hyde Park. In the years before the Covid-19 pandemic hit travel and commerce, demand was so great that the event was split into two, one in the spring and one in the autumn, and together they regularly attracted around 400,000 buyers from more than 200 countries. Each fair lasted two weeks and was sub-divided into three phases. Phase one included electronics and home appliances, lighting, vehicles and accessories, machinery, hardware tools, building materials, chemical products and energy. Phase 2 was given over to daily consumer goods, gifts, toys and home decoration, while the third and final phase included textiles and clothing, footwear, office, luggage and leisure products, medicine and health care, and food items. The changeover seemed seamless as the stands and displays of one army of factories gave way to the next. As a buyer, planning and focus were essential, as was stamina. Navigating the vast and crowded complex could be exhausting, and even veteran buyers admitted they'd only ever explored a fraction of it. If a product wasn't on display it could be made to order, and some traders arrived armed with their own samples, marvelling at the ability of the factories to reverse engineer and then quickly reproduce the most complex of products at a fraction of the price. This truly was the workshop of the world, and it was easy to understand the buzz of the Death Star canteen as the buyers took in the enormity of it all as well as the raw and addictive power of 'Made in China'.

The 500-room Sheraton Dongguan was not the closest of the countless hotels that serviced the Canton Fair complex, which was set on an island in the Pearl River on the outskirts of Guangzhou, the regional capital. However, it was convenient for its proximity to the factories, which were concentrated in a vast arch around the Pearl River delta, to the north of Hong Kong and Shenzhen. To those who came by car or train from the former British colony, this journey too was a revelation. The landscape was one of endless sprawling factories, tens of thousands of them, mostly identikit low, squat buildings with walls of stained white, pale blue or peach tiles and surrounded by tall fences. The blocks that housed adjoining dormitories were distinguished only by the laundry hanging from windows, the meagre possessions of the migrant workers on whose backs China's economic miracle was built. Guangdong province, which hosts the Canton Fair, is China's most populous and has the country's largest transient population – more than a quarter of its 126 million people are migrants, mostly working in the factories.[2] Across China, the annual return of migrants to their home provinces for Chinese New Year has been described as the largest movement of humanity on the planet, with an estimated 2 billion journeys taken during the holiday period. It is not so much a workforce as an army, a force which turned China into the world's biggest exporter, dominating trade in everything from toys to textiles, mobile phones and other consumer electronics.

China even spawned a series of towns that traders less familiar with the Mandarin language named after their dominant product or service. There was 'zipper and button town' (Qiaotou in Zhejiang province), which dominated the international market in both; 'bra town' (Gurao in Guangdong province), which had an iron grip on global underwear; 'jeans town' (Xintang, also in Guangdong), which was built on denim; and 'rubbish town' (Guiyu, still in Guangdong), the world's largest electronic waste dump, where mountains of e-waste were imported for recycling. By the time Xi Jinping came to power in 2012, labour costs in China were rising and many buyers of lower-end products, such as shoes and textiles, were looking at cheaper locations, such as Cambodia, Bangladesh or Indonesia. But the word among the hard-nosed buyers in the Death Star canteen was that this was easier said than done. The would-be usurpers simply couldn't compete with the depth and sophistication of China's supply chains. Not only could just about every imaginable product be bought or made in China, but so could all the components that made up those products, and the components that made up those components – all to a schedule and of a quality that was hard, if not impossible, for others to compete with.

Where rising costs did drive low-end manufacturers away from China, the Chinese Communist Party (CCP) did not mourn their loss, at least not officially, since it became a Party mantra that China needed to go upmarket. It was not enough to be the world's factory, a manufacturing superpower, Xi Jinping wanted China to lead the world in innovation and the technologies of the future. In his eyes, Shenzhen, the gaudy high-rise gateway to southern China, was testament to the success of that policy. This was where China's economic reforms began, a laboratory for paramount leader Deng Xiaoping's 'reform and opening' policy, which we shall examine in more detail in the next chapter. It was China's first Special Economic Zone, established by Deng in 1980, and initially was fenced off from the rest of the country. Back then, it was a sleepy settlement with a population of barely 30,000; at the time of writing, it is the fifth most populous city in China, home to nearly 18 million people and a forest of glistening skyscrapers, just across the border from Hong Kong.

Shenzhen led the way from low-wage manufacturing to more 'value-added' businesses, in the jargon of economists – or 'high-quality growth' as Chinese leaders called it, the city becoming a symbol of their high-tech ambition. In 2020, Chen Rugui, the city's mayor, claimed it already hosted 70,000 tech companies and that the 'new economy' accounted for 60 per cent of GDP.[3] The city's Yue Hai district was the high-tech hub, boasting dozens of home-grown start-ups, nurtured with generous government support, and the mayor had a roll call of some of China's leading tech giants. Shenzhen was the base of Tencent, a gaming and social media giant and owner of WeChat (*Weixin* in Chinese), the app for everything, and DJI, the world's biggest manufacturer of consumer drones. Huawei, China's telecoms champion, had a sprawling campus – a city within a city – on the edge of town. Also here was BYD, now vying with Tesla as the world's top seller of electric vehicles. Shenzhen Inovance Technology, a big robot maker, aspired to supply the area's factories with humanoids, preparing for the day when the supply of cheap migrant labour dried up. Even the city's highways had a tech theme – including Science and Research Road and High Tech Road. The city was presented by officials as China's answer to Silicon Valley. It boasted of being the country's fastest growing metropolis, a city of youth and opportunity. A popular 2022 comedy drama, *Qi ji – Ben xiao hai* (*Nice View*), the story of a poor twenty-year-old who started out repairing mobile phones, overcoming numerous difficulties to achieve success, played to that legend.

Opening the Communist Party congress in October 2017, Xi Jinping boasted of how China had been transformed. 'China became the world's factory floor. Consumer goods, which were hardly ever seen in the country in 1981, are now abundant,' he boasted. 'The Made-in-China list today grows ever longer, its products more sophisticated . . . the world's factory is now the world's laboratory and marketplace.'[4] Whether it was viewed from the rostrum of the Great Hall of the People or the bar stools of the Death Star canteen, China was not only indispensable to the global economy, but its rise to global dominance seemed inevitable and unstoppable.

In late 2018, in a speech marking four decades since the country embarked on its economic transformation, Xi promised that the economy would continue to produce 'miracles that will impress the world'.[5] China's GDP per person grew by an average annual rate of 8.5 per cent over that period, faster than any other major economy, doubling incomes every nine years.[6] In 1979, national income per head was less than $200, roughly on a par with Bangladesh or Afghanistan; in 2018 it was about to surpass $10,000, close to the world average, and China was considered a 'middle income country' with a thriving 300 million-strong middle class.[7] In 1978, China's exports were valued at $10 billion, less than 1 per cent of world trade; forty years later, the country was by far the world's biggest exporter, shifting goods worth more than $4 trillion.[8] The World Bank marvelled at how China had pulled almost 800 million people out of 'extreme poverty', as defined by incomes below $1.90 per day. Such poverty was near universal in China in 1979, but forty years later afflicted just 5.5 million people. 'China's economic growth and poverty reduction over the past 40 years are historically unprecedented, both in speed and scale,' the World Bank said in a gushing report jointly published with the Chinese government.[9] As the size of China's economy closed in on that of the United States ($18 trillion for China against $25.5 trillion for the US in 2022) economists speculated as to when Beijing would take the psychologically important crown. For most it wasn't a matter of if, but when, with 2030 as a popular date. When adjusted for what economists call purchasing power parity – broadly speaking, what you can buy for your money in different countries – China was already ahead.[10]

By 2018, China had also become the world's biggest bilateral lender, with its giant state-owned banks issuing nearly $500 billion in international loans[11] – a figure that was to more than double again over the following five years. China was the world's largest source of overseas tourists, who were also the world's biggest spenders.[12] The country was also the largest source of international students.[13] This economic clout was rapidly transforming into political and strategic influence, and also bankrolling one of the biggest military expansions and modernisation ever seen during peacetime. *When China Rules the World*, gloated the title of a book by one credulous British author who argued that not only would China replace the United States as the world's dominant power, but that in the process the world would become more Chinese, not more Western.[14] The phrase 'the East is rising and the West is declining' gained currency after the 2008 global financial crisis, which China weathered better than most, and which bolstered the confidence of Chinese leaders in the fundamental superiority of their own system. Over the years that followed, it became a catchphrase of state-owned media and government officials in describing their vision of the future. Xi Jinping argued that China's model was not only superior, but one to be emulated, particularly by the Global South, a term used increasingly for the world's less developed counties, which China aspired to lead. 'The Chinese path to modernization is a sure path to build a stronger nation,' Xi said. 'Chinese-style modernization breaks the myth of "modernization equals Westernization".'[15]

Xi's 'model' has attracted many labels: 'state capitalism', a 'socialist market economy', 'socialism with Chinese characteristics', and numerous permutations, including the more recent and clunkier 'socialism with Chinese characteristics for the new era (guided by Xi Jinping thought)'. Some are empty slogans, while others attempt to describe an evolving blend of market and state control. It is a system in which private companies are the most dynamic and innovative players, responsible for 60 per cent of GDP and 80 per cent of urban employment,[16] but are kept on an increasingly tight leash, and where the market is supposed to do as the Party tells it. Among the characteristics of China's 'model' are a capitalism at times so raw that it would make Victorian factory owners blush, with limited worker rights, minimum social safety net and a wilful indifference to environmental degradation. The primary drivers of the economy have been the massed ranks of exporters who grace the Canton Fair, together with vast state-backed investment in infrastructure and property. By one estimate, during just three years between 2010 and 2013, China poured more concrete than the United States did in the entire twentieth century.[17] This has delivered apparently heady rates of growth, but the statistics need to be treated with caution; the system is still built around rigid five-year plans, with officials at all levels rewarded and penalised by their ability to hit growth targets – which have also provided an enormous incentive to cheat, and has resulted in the routine debasement of official statistics. Even China's own officials have described the economy as 'unbalanced' and 'unsustainable'.[18] This economy operates beneath an autocratic political system in which the Chinese Communist Party is increasingly intolerant of any dissent.

For all the attempts to pin a label on it, none seems adequately to capture an economy that can be highly addictive to outsiders, but also predatory and surreal. Nor does one label come close to capturing the often bruising and mind-bending experiences of many of those seeking to navigate its seemingly arbitrary twists and turns. Western admirers have characterised the economy as essentially technocratic, overseen by skilled pragmatists, planning for the long term unlike their skittish Western counterparts – something to be praised and emulated. However, the CCP's behaviour frequently resembles that of a mafia don and an international loan shark. At home, the economy is riddled with corruption and deceit, while globally China routinely uses its new economic muscle to bully and coerce, plundering foreign technology through all available means. Mao Zedong had a big thing about contradictions – they were the basis of life, driving it forward, he once mused.[19] Yet even he might have struggled to understand the muddled dynamics of the modern Chinese economy. What follows is a story of that economy, of what really lies behind the transformation of China into what I characterise as a vampire state. It is a story of the Party's single-minded efforts to bend economics and business to its own will and ambition – with the ultimate aim of ensuring its own survival, but which is now facing its biggest crisis since reforms began in the late 1970s.

The Covid-19 pandemic shut down the Canton Fair for three years, during which China closed its borders and imposed the world's most draconian restrictions on its population in an ultimately failed effort to completely eliminate the virus. A fair of sorts was held online, but the vast China Import and Export Fair Complex sat eerily empty like some sort of lost world or decaying film set. The nearby city of Guangzhou saw some of the most severe lockdowns, with millions confined to their homes for weeks on end. When the fair reopened its doors again in 2023, traders reported that business was much slower. State media tried to talk up the occasion, pointing to a record 35,000 exhibitors and the greater presence of China's burgeoning high-tech firms,[20] but the atmosphere was more subdued, and the cavernous halls lacked the energy and optimism that had once been their hallmark.

The more perceptive traders who travelled by road will have noticed the changes as soon as they crossed from Hong Kong to Shenzhen. More than a quarter of Shenzhen's office space was now empty, the highest rate of any major Chinese city, and the population had shrunk for the first time since reforms began as the tech giants cut their workforces.[21] The city's pioneering slogan had been 'time is money, efficiency is life', but now in the tech district, opposite the headquarters of Tencent, sat an artwork, a futuristic cube on which was etched a hammer and sickle and the words, 'Follow the Party, start your business' – the Party pointedly coming first.[22] One of the most prominent of the empty office blocks was the forty-three-storey Excellence Centre, the former headquarters of Evergrande, which the bankrupt property giant abandoned in 2022.[23] The world's most indebted property firm was the first casualty of a bursting property bubble, which battered the nation's developers and exposed a mountain of debt engulfing not only them, but also banks and local governments which had been swept along in the property mania.

Foreign investors were turning their backs on China, growth was stagnating, stock markets slumping and unemployment soaring among the young people on whom Shenzhen had once relied for its dynamism. The benign international environment that had abetted China's rise was over, amid an intensifying technology trade war with the United States and worsening relations with the West in general. Geopolitical tensions were soaring, notably around Taiwan and in the South China Sea. China's share of the global economy, which rose nearly twentyfold from 1 per cent in 1990 to 18.4 per cent in 2021, appeared to be going into reverse. After slipping slightly in 2022, it dropped by an estimated 1.4 per cent to 17 per cent in 2023.[24] More sympathetic commentators argued that China would inevitably bounce back, that it had weathered problems before, and that this was all a blip after the economic strictures of the pandemic. However, by early 2024 the bounce back looked increasingly illusive, and the economic problems far more deep-seated.

Traders can be a hard-nosed and unsentimental crowd, especially those who routinely prowled the alleyways of the Canton Fair, one of the least sentimental places on the planet. They were laser focused on price and profit, and in the view of most of the buyers I met over the years neither messy geopolitics nor concerns over human rights should interfere with the serious business of striking a deal. As the Canton Fair resumed, that was a view the CCP sought to encourage, telling the world that China was once again open for business and that it remained committed to further 'reform and opening'. Yet the policies pursued by Xi, his growing belligerence abroad and his strengthening of the role of the Party in every aspect of life at home, seemed to belie those assurances. The atmosphere in Xi's China was altogether more hostile to foreigners. China's openness and engagement with the Western-led global economic system seemed to have been opportunistic and temporary. Many of those gathered in the not-so-crowded Death Star canteen at the Sheraton concluded that China's economic miracle was over; others questioned whether the miracle had ever been for real and whether the days of 'Made in China' might be drawing to a close. 'Reform and opening' was looking increasingly like an empty slogan, and even the most hardened traders realised the economic ground was rapidly shifting beneath them.

Chapter 2

The Myth of 'Reform and Opening'

'Coolly observe, calmly deal with things, hold
your position, hide your capacities, bide your time,
accomplish things where possible.'

Deng Xiaoping

The circular plaque is made of metal and is about the size of a
saucer. At the centre is Deng Xiaoping's head in profile, around
which are etched the words in Chinese and English, OUR GENERAL
DESIGNER. COMRADE DENG XIAOPING. It was presented to me in 1995
by officials in the town of Guang'an, Deng's birthplace, at the end
of a lengthy dinner of mouth-numbingly spicy Sichuan food with
the local governor. The governor was a tall gregarious man with
more than a passing resemblance to Mao Zedong, and the meal
was punctuated by endless toasts in the local baijiu, a fiery sorghum liquor – to eternal friendship, brotherhood, and of course to
Deng. The governor insisted on toasting each member of my team
individually, and by the end of the meal, it was hard to know what
we were drinking to, since the governor's words were increasingly
slurred, and he eventually had to be helped from the restaurant by
his officials.

Guang'an lies around seventy miles to the north of the mega-city
of Chongqing in China's southwestern Sichuan province, and Deng
was born here in 1904. At the time of my visit, he had not been seen
in public for well over a year and was assumed to be close to death,
though he hung on for another year and a half before passing away
in February 1997, aged ninety-two. There was considerable speculation about whether the policies of 'reform and opening', so closely
associated with Deng, would outlive him, and I was there to make

a television news report speculating about that. Guang'an, whose population was barely 50,000 at the time, had clearly decided to cash in on Deng's fame, and much of the scrappy town resembled a building site – multiple 'development zones', as the governor described them, to which he was confident the world would soon flock. Slogans strung across their dusty entrances conveyed that optimism: 'Guang'an must go to the world and the world will know Guang'an well', 'Guang'an must be well constructed', they read. However, it was the bustle and noise of market day that gave a better picture of China's new energy. Vendors, many still wearing threadbare Mao-style suits, had come from miles around and just about everything and anything was for sale. Just walking a few metres was exhausting amid the hooting and shouting, the constant human traffic hauling bags and trollies laden with vegetables, fruit, ducks, pigs and chickens. One enterprising seller of rat poison had laid out in neat rows several dead rats, presumably to demonstrate the effectiveness of his product. Nearby, a traditional medicine seller hawking 'bear' and 'tiger' parts was being harangued by a farmer who clearly felt he knew a cow or buffalo bone when he saw one.

Deng's family home lay just over a hill from downtown Guang'an, in a township called Paifang. The slogans along the roadside here urged the newly empowered farmers to obey the law, pay taxes and not steal electricity. Another urged them to 'follow the socialist line'. The tax issue was particularly touchy in this region following riots a few months before my visit, which were blamed on corrupt officials extorting money from farmers, supposedly for new roads. 'There was a problem with the peasants, when a few people organised them to attack schools and government buildings, and to burn cars,' one official told me dismissively, assuring me that the troublemakers had been 'dealt with'.

Deng's family home was a sprawling seventeen-room farmhouse, built around an inner courtyard. The local authorities were turning it into a museum, with rooms devoted to different periods of his life, with pride of place given to a large bed made from lacquered wood. 'And this is where Comrade Deng Xiaoping was born, right here,' my guide said with evident pride. When I suggested the Deng family appeared to be quite well off, she quickly put me in my place. 'It was a big family,' she explained, uncomfortable with suggestions of bourgeois roots. 'But not very rich. Middle level. Only middle level.' For an additional fee I was invited to meet Deng Xiaoping's cousin, a man called Dan Wenquan. Only, he appeared to be a rather distant cousin, who had never met his illustrious relative and had never been to Beijing. 'Of course, if there's a way, I'd love to meet him. Though I'm sure he's very busy,' he told me. Dan was enthusiastic about plans by the authorities to build a new tourist centre on the ridge above, complete with restaurant, karaoke bar, teahouse, hotel and souvenir shop – at which he clearly hoped he could further leverage his distant connection.

In a compound next door, I was taken to meet Wu Wei Chang who told me how she had seized the new spirit of enterprise to set up a small business distilling liquor from sorghum and wheat. She shrugged when I asked whether the governor was among her customers, since he seemed rather keen on the product. 'Farmers are better off now. They can afford to buy more liquor,' she said, serving a steady stream of customers before showing me the motorcycle she had bought from the profits. I was then taken to a nearby primary school, which had been built in 1946 to replace the one where Deng studied and where I was assured that the spirit of the paramount leader lived on, the students telling me mechanically that it was their duty to carry out reform, with only the sketchiest idea of what that meant. One teacher said that after the 'glorious revolution' in 1949, the triumphant communists had turned the school into what he described as a facility for 'reform through labour', before quickly changing the subject under the withering look of my local government guide.

On the way back to the centre of Guang'an, our car was stuck for a while behind an overloaded truck that had shed half its load of pigs and chickens, and the driver was frantically trying to round up the traumatised animals. It was hard to know quite what to make of the town. Deng Xiaoping, the man they called their 'general designer', had left there when he was sixteen, never to return, even when he was Communist Party boss in nearby Chongqing during the early 1950s. To ask local officials why Deng had never come back was to invite a vacant look not dissimilar to that of the dazed animals on the road in front of me. Guang'an was a chaotic place that was for sure, but not without a certain entrepreneurial energy. I'd witnessed a frenetic farmers market, been introduced to a booze merchant as a model of enterprise, met the governor who'd got blotto on that very product, been to a school that was also for a while a prison and met a man who claimed to be a distant cousin of Deng Xiaoping, but didn't have much of a clue about him. The cousin and the school were very possibly both fakes. Yet in a way these very details said more about Deng and his reforms than a good many of the hagiographic profiles and empty platitudes produced over the years.

Who can forget the images of a smiling diminutive Deng, less than five feet tall, donning a ten-gallon cowboy hat at a Texas rodeo during a 1979 visit to the United States, proving, as one commentator put it at the time, 'that he was not only good-humoured, but, after all, less like one of "those Communists" and more like "us".'[1] Or as another noted: 'The whistling, cheering crowd watches with delight as Deng theatrically dons his new hat. And in one simple gesture, Deng seems to not only end thirty years of acrimony between China and America, but to give his own people permission to join him in imbibing American life and culture.'[2]

The visit came just weeks after Deng had supposedly seen off hardliners, consolidated control of the Communist Party and kicked off reforms at a key Party meeting. This followed a two-year power struggle following the death of Mao Zedong, and Deng would soon be telling the world that 'to get rich is glorious' and 'It doesn't matter whether a cat is black or white, as long as it catches mice' – both presented as evidence of Deng's pragmatism and lack of ideological baggage. This was, after all, a man who had been purged twice, once by Mao during the Cultural Revolution and later more briefly in 1976 as factions manoeuvred for power ahead of Mao's death. 'By orchestrating China's transition to a market economy, Deng Xiaoping has left a lasting legacy on China and the world . . . The outcomes of Deng's reforms have been without historical peer,' as one commentary put it.[3] In 1986, *Time* magazine named him its man of the year, hailing his 'audacious effort to create what amounts almost to a new form of society'.[4] It sometimes seemed that while Deng had eschewed a cult of personality at home, it was alive and well in the West.

The reality and the motives of 'reform and opening' were rather different. It is misleading to see the December 1978 leadership conference as a seminal moment, which is how it is presented in CCP propaganda. As noted by Bao Tong, a former aide to Party Secretary Zhao Ziyang, who was ousted after the 1989 Tiananmen Square massacre, 'To put a halo on this meeting as a conference of reform and opening up is to concoct a myth.'[5] The official communiqué of the meeting only referred twice to 'reform' and there was no mention of the market. Deng was reluctant to criticise Mao, and it would be six years before the term 'reform and opening' became more widely used.[6] The process of market reforms, reducing the role of the state and allowing more private enterprise, together with opening China to trade and investment, was a faltering process – as it has remained. The slogans attributed to Deng are of dubious provenance or have been taken out of context. The phrase 'To get rich is glorious' has been cited thousands of times, and as a slogan it seemed to capture the mood of the times, but there is no evidence he ever said it.[7] Deng's black-and-white cat quote is also not quite what it seems. Alexander V. Pantsov, a biographer of Deng, has traced it to a 1962 Party session examining rural work at which Deng said: 'In districts where the life of peasants is difficult, we can use various methods. The comrades from Anhui said, "It doesn't matter if the cat is black or yellow, as long as it can catch mice it is a good cat".'[8] The context was in regard to efforts to restore agricultural production, the yellow cat would later become white, and Deng is quoting someone else.

Deng's ten-gallon cowboy hat is now on display in a glass cabinet as part of 'The Road to Rejuvenation' exhibition in the National Museum of China on Tiananmen Square in Beijing. The museum, which opened in 2011, was plagued by infighting within the Party over what constituted 'correct' history. You will, for example, be hard-pressed to find any mention of the Great Leap Forward and Cultural Revolution, during which tens of millions of people died of starvation or abuse. The Great Leap, a campaign from 1958 to 1962 to transform the country's economy, which resulted in the most severe famine in recorded history, merits the briefest of mentions: 'The project of constructing socialism suffered severe complications.' The Cultural Revolution, a decade-long campaign of political persecution and turmoil from 1966 to 1976, is marked by a single photograph.

It was Deng who in 1989 sent the People's Liberation Army to murder hundreds, perhaps thousands, of protesting students in and around Tiananmen Square. The only reference in the museum to that period is a photograph of Deng meeting Mikhail Gorbachev, the then Soviet leader, who was visiting Beijing. Even the most ardent Western admirers of Deng accept that the massacre somewhat blotted his copy book – though he rehabilitated himself in the minds of many investors when he rebooted reforms three years later in what became known as his Southern Tour. He was ailing at the time, and his only title was honorary chairman of the China Bridge Association (the card game, that is), but he still wielded immense power and his visit to the places where reform began was seen as an endorsement of its continuation.[9]

Tiananmen Square was not the only dark and brutal episode in Deng's biography. Between 1949 and 1952 he was Party enforcer in southwest China, based out of Chongqing, and charged with supressing counter revolutionaries and introducing agrarian reforms. The wave of public executions on his watch was so large that even Mao found the barbarity excessive, writing to Deng that 'We should not kill too many people . . . If we kill too many, we will forfeit public sympathy and shortage of labour power will arise.'[10] In Deng's region the daily rate of killings then fell to nine or ten a day, as opposed to more than 400 previously. Called to Beijing, Deng would later lead a campaign against the intelligentsia, who had been encouraged to voice their opinions in what became known as the 'Hundred Flowers Campaign'. Having flushed them out, Deng was tasked to 'squeeze the pus out of the abscess', something he undertook with relish.[11] During this Anti-Rightist Campaign, which lasted from 1957 to 1959, beatings and torture were routine, and around half a million people were sent to 're-education through labour' – very possibly utilising the school I had visited in Deng's home town.

It has been argued that reforms in the countryside began not through CCP initiative, but spontaneously. After the death of Mao, the country was so impoverished and traumatised that many farmers took control of land from the hated communes. The household contract system, as it became known, whereby the land was in effect leased to farmers in return for a specified amount of harvest, proliferated locally before it was endorsed by Beijing.[12] In essence reform and opening was forced upon the CCP because the country was in such a dire state and the Party itself was facing an existential threat. 'It was in order to strengthen the Party. Deng Xiaoping realized that the Party on its then trajectory was doomed,' Bilahari Kausikan, Singapore's former top diplomat, told me. Or as China scholar Yasheng Huang has written, 'The history of Chinese reforms is one of central leaders acknowledging and approving of fait accompli on the ground, not one of a wise ruler designing and micro-managing each reform measure.'[13]

Mao presided over three decades of endless campaigns, purges and persecution. While the Great Leap Forward and Cultural Revolution are usually given prominence by Western scholars, underground Chinese historians believe the silencing of critical thinking during the earlier Anti-Rightist Campaign, overseen by Deng, paved the way for the later madness since it gave Mao a free hand.[14] Another of Mao's campaigns frequently overlooked was his Third Front Movement, which entailed the mass shifting of heavy industry and the construction of a self-sufficient military-industrial base in China's rugged interior. This initially covert campaign, which was at its most intense between 1964 and the mid-1970s, was motivated by Mao's paranoia about possible attacks from the United States and the Soviet Union, and his obsession with self-sufficiency and putting industry beyond their reach. 'With the Third Front, CCP leaders reconceptualized the entire country as one giant battlefield in which society and economy were militarized in advance in preparation for the perceived threat of a surprise attack,' writes Covell F. Meyskens in his study of that period.[15] Not only did this entail the mass mobilisation of often forced labour, but dispersing and hiding industry in mountainous locations which were difficult to access made no economic sense. It is little wonder that by the time Deng saw off his rivals and seized power in 1978, the country was isolated, with no serious trading partners, and a population living largely hand-to-mouth. Individual livelihoods were sacrificed to Mao's brutality and his paranoid obsession with self-sufficiency and security – his own, as well as that of the country. Personal freedoms simply did not exist; the Party controlled every aspect of an individual's life, from work and travel to the ability to marry and have children, with zero tolerance of dissent. This is the desperate base line from which reforms began.

There were times Deng clashed with Mao, but also times when he was happy to do his brutal bidding. Mao was a mass murderer and Deng willingly participated in some of the worst instances of that gratuitous violence. Deng was always a Party loyalist, and he can only be described as a pragmatist in the sense that he was willing to do whatever was necessary to protect the Party and maintain its dictatorship. In his memoir, Zhao Ziyang, who was China's premier from 1980 to 1987 and general secretary of the Party from 1987 to 1989, writes, 'Reforms were precisely intended to further consolidate the Communist Party's one-party rule. Deng firmly rejected any reform that would weaken that.'[16] Zhao advocated a more accommodating response to the Tiananmen Square protesters and as a result was ousted after the massacre. He spent the rest of his life under house arrest, during which he secretly recorded his thoughts and recollections, which were smuggled and published outside the country. '[Deng] despised systems in which powers were separated by checks and balances,' Zhao writes.[17] 'Stability trumped everything else. His belief was that without stability, in the midst of chaos, nothing could be accomplished. In order to maintain stability, dictatorship was the ultimate weapon.'[18] In Zhao's telling, the early understanding of how to proceed with reform was 'shallow and vague'. While there was a wide desire to move on from Maoist madness and a desperate need to improve livelihoods, the debate over the way forward was riven with suspicion towards private initiative and the outside world. Zhao is widely regarded as a liberal and a reformer, but even for him the Communist Party's position was inviolable. If he considered political reform at all, it was to improve the administrative efficiency of the Party. Only later, during the long years of isolation in his courtyard home did he begin to believe in real political change and recognise that the roots of tyranny and corruption lay in the lack of accountability of a one-party state – a Communist Party that was above the law.

Deng spoke vaguely about putting 'capitalist tools' in socialist hands, but it was not until a Party congress in 1982 that he used the term 'Socialism with Chinese characteristics' to describe his approach. In the years that followed this came to mean an evolving blend of market and state control, though at the time Deng was vague about what it meant – perhaps because the messy process defied explanation. When author and academic Frank Dikötter explored local Party archives from the reform period he found a picture of chaos and confusion as local officials tried to combine remnants of the planned economy with what one economist described as 'selected, pasteurized, partial, truncated, restricted and disjointed pieces of market and private property policy'.[19] The Party continued to issue five-year plans and growth targets which resulted in the debasement of local statistics, which were subject to wholesale distortion and fabrication – which soon became a characteristic of CCP rule, which we shall examine later. Dikötter likens the good ship Reform to a tanker that looks surprisingly seaworthy from a distance, while below deck frantic sailors are pumping water and plugging holes to keep the vessel afloat and the officers themselves are engaged in interminable struggles for power.[20]

To take the tanker analogy a step further, Western governments and companies were only too happy to take the signals from the bridge at face value. As were we journalists, who knew that nothing satisfied the cravings of a news editor more than a story about old communists embracing capitalism, and the more absurdly rapacious the former comrades behaved the better. In boardrooms across the world, the promise and mystique of the China market were enough to suspend rational judgements, and when their firms were taken to the cleaners, they were all too often complicit in the process. China was a fiendishly difficult place to make money, but Western companies routinely exaggerated their successes and played down their losses – and continue to do so.

A high point of Western delusion was the 2001 decision to allow China to join the World Trade Organization (WTO), which more than anything else hastened China's ascent to the title of 'workshop of the world'. Beijing promised to improve the rule of law, to protect intellectual property rights, cut import tariffs, give greater access to its market, liberalise controls on its exchange rate, scrap trade barriers and much more. Few of these things ever happened, or where one barrier was removed, another was erected. China has never provided a level playing field for foreign companies but was able to flood the world with its own cheap exports, while Western companies flocked to outsource production and supply chains to Chinese factories, hollowing out manufacturing throughout the West. This led inextricably to the dependencies the West is now, decades later, trying to unwind and which have fuelled populist anger in developed economies.

With hindsight, rushing through premature WTO membership for China was a mistake, though the decision was also political, with then US President Bill Clinton saying during negotiations, 'Membership in the WTO, of course, will not create a free society in China overnight or guarantee that China will play by global rules. But over time, I believe it will move China faster and further in the right direction.'[21] In the years that followed, China did move – but in the opposite direction. It neither played by global rules nor liberalised. The arguments that economic progress begets political openness and liberalisation are still used by business people and politicians who advocate greater engagement, though these voices are quieter, and 'engagement' has increasingly become a self-serving veneer to justify doing business with tyrants. As policy on China has hardened, there is a prevailing view in Washington that over the decades the West showered enormous economic advantages on a rival that ended up turning against them. There is some truth in that, but also lots of naïvety, since Beijing was never in any meaningful sense 'with' the West. Quite the reverse. It is also to fundamentally misunderstand the purpose, pace and nature of economic reform as seen by the CCP, which was always, and remains, to strengthen the Party.

China scholars often refer to an oscillating pattern of political relaxing and tightening in China, the *fang-shou* cycle, detected by the expansion or contraction of economic reform and ideological control – the assumption is that two contending groups exist within the CCP, reformers and conservatives, who vie for supremacy. By this understanding, the period 1979 to 1982 was one of relaxing followed by one year of tightening (during a campaign against 'spiritual pollution'), followed by more easing until the Tiananmen Square massacre, which heralded a three-year period of neo-totalitarianism and then more relaxing after Deng's Southern Tour.[22] As an analytic concept, it has some merit, but whatever the stage of the cycle the dictatorship of the Party has been non-negotiable. The pattern could equally be seen as a fluctuating measure of the state of the CCP's deep-seated paranoia – with reform dialled up or down as needed. Survival is the Party's primary instinct, economic reform a tool to that end, and periods of opening and closing are reflections of insecurities and perceptions – real or imagined – of threats to CCP rule.

In December 2018, the Communist Party marked the fortieth anniversary of 'reform and opening' with a conference in the Great Hall of the People, at which President Xi Jinping said, 'Forty years of reform and opening up have taught us that Party leadership is the defining feature of socialism with Chinese characteristics . . . The Party exercises overall leadership across all areas of endeavour in every part of the country.'[23] In the language of the *fang-shou* cycle, Xi was presiding over a period of considerable tightening, with the Party hardening control across all aspects of society – including the economy. The Party was to be everywhere, with Xi as its core. At the time of the conference, he had been Party boss for six years and was imposing polices that sharply reversed both reform and opening while at the same time seeking to usurp the slogan for himself and his family.

The Xi family has an awkward relationship with the Dengs, and in the run up to the anniversary conference, those tensions were played out in Shenzhen, the southern city where reforms began and where Deng is most revered. The entrance to an exhibition on reform was revamped four times before its opening. A panoramic sculpture depicting Deng Xiaoping touring the area was replaced by video screens and a quote from Xi praising the country's economic transformation, which was then replaced by quotes from both men before the sculpture was eventually reinstated.[24] Sharp-eyed China-watchers also noted that in the Wangfujing Bookstore, just a few minutes' walk from the Great Hall in Beijing, a special section to commemorate the fortieth anniversary had relegated books related to Deng to the bottom shelf, with pride of place given to those by Xi.[25] Xi sought to elevate the role of his father, Xi Zhongxun, in establishing Shenzhen as a special economic zone. For twelve years, Xi senior was Party boss of Guangdong province (of which Shenzhen is a part) and as the anniversary approached books and television programmes played up his role, while diminishing that of Deng.[26] Newly commissioned paintings showed father and son side-by-side in thoughtful repose. Xi Zhongxun later fell out with Deng and retired to Shenzhen, where he died in 2002. His son's efforts to repackage history around himself and his family culminated in 2023, when his father was hailed as a spiritual icon on the 110th anniversary of his birth. The Party secretary of Guangdong ordered Party committees throughout the province to 'carry forward the spirit of reform and opening up' of Xi Zhongxun.[27]

Xi's two predecessors, Jiang Zemin and Hu Jintao, were both hand-picked by Deng; both had to contend with rival factions at the top of the Party, which resulted in a more collective form of leadership, and were subject to time limits on their rule – a system imposed by Deng in part to prevent the emergence of Mao-style despotism. Xi owed little to Deng, and quickly consolidated power, purging his enemies, often under the guise of an anti-corruption campaign. He removed time limits on the presidency, effectively allowing himself to become leader for life. Party gatherings made fewer and fewer references to Deng. Instead, they hailed the 'new era' to be guided by 'Xi Jinping thought on Socialism with Chinese Characteristics.' Xi's 'thought' was a cultish potpourri of slogans, but at its heart was a near obsession with security and control, which became the primary drivers of policy, even at the expense of the economy, together with the 'China dream' of restoring national greatness. This was accompanied by an obsession with 'self-sufficiency' and a deep paranoia about the outside world – the United States in particular – which seemed to hark back to the darkest days of Mao.

It has been said that Xi also abandoned the old Deng maxim of 'Coolly observe, calmly deal with things, hold your position, hide your capacities, bide your time, accomplish things where possible,' the decades-long doctrine of keeping a low profile. This is true, but it would be wrong to see Deng's words as an expression of his comparative humility. It was essentially a strategy. The devastated country he inherited from Mao was in no position to do anything other than bide its time, while it worked to raise incomes through engaging, copying and stealing from the West. As a strategy it worked, leaving Xi in charge of the world's second biggest economy and a formidable military power – ready to throw off Deng-era restraint and to reassert its naturally imperialist instincts.

By his own admission, Deng Xiaoping had little grasp of economics, but he did recognise that China urgently needed foreign capital and technology if it wanted to improve livelihoods and catch up with the West. Science and technology had stagnated under Mao, as education was badly disrupted during the Cultural Revolution. The choice of location for the first special economic zones, close to Hong Kong and then opposite Taiwan, were specifically designed to attract investment as well as technical and managerial know-how from both. The need to 'attract capital to the PRC [People's Republic of China] and borrow Western technology, equipment and management expertise' became a constant theme of the Party.[28] Deng urged students and researchers to travel overseas to gain technical and scientific education.

Deng set China on a course to become the world's greatest perpetrator of industrial and economic espionage. Under his leadership, the CCP disregarded intellectual property (IP) rights with systematic theft encouraged throughout the Party hierarchy. 'Intellectual property from abroad was collected at the highest level and distributed down the command structure of the planned economy,' writes Frank Dikötter.[29] What began as the routine copying and piracy of the early reform years led inexorably to today's industrial scale cyber espionage. The acquisition of Western technology and know-how by every and any means possible to power China's economic growth and military modernisation is perhaps Deng's most lasting legacy, with foreign firms seen as fair game, and theft and coercion at the very heart of the CCP's development model. Yet, it is remarkable that more sympathetic China-watchers still depict IP theft as an unfortunate by-product of the country's development, one of those inevitable things that happen during the catch-up process, and in which many countries have engaged.

CHAPTER 3

The Counterfeit Culture

'The scale of the Chinese cyber threat is unparalleled –
they've got a bigger hacking program than every
other major nation combined.'

Christopher Wray, FBI Director

The old English mill town of Belper in Derbyshire might seem a world away from the counterfeit culture of Deng Xiaoping's China or the legions of Chinese hackers who have built on Deng's legacy. However, nowhere is more important to the history of industrial espionage. On the day I visited, rain swept in intense horizontal bursts across the bloated Derwent River, though it didn't dampen the enthusiasm of my guide as she described the ingenious way in which the river's water had been harnessed by the cotton mills. The hulking red-brick wall of Belper's North Mill towered above us, a monument to Britain's past industrial glory. In the late eighteenth century it had been part of the world's largest mill complex under single ownership, incorporating the world's first fireproof buildings. The technology deployed in the production process was the most advanced at that time. 'We are determined to keep the heritage alive. It is so important,' my guide said.

'That's Samuel Slater,' she added, pointing to a portrait of a middle-aged, slightly taciturn-looking man on an information board in the small visitor centre. 'Slater the traitor, we call him around here. Still, we've got over it by now.' Though by her tone I wasn't so sure she had. 'He knew everything, and he took it to America. He couldn't write it down, that would have been too risky, but he had it all up here,' she said, tapping her head. Slater was born in Belper in 1768 and began working in the mill when he was ten years old.

He became an apprentice to the mill owner, Jedediah Strutt, and by the time he was twenty-one there was little he did not know about the organisation and practice of cotton spinning based on the water spinning-frame pioneered by Richard Arkwright. At the time, the United States was the biggest exporter of cotton, but did not have the technology to process it. In its eagerness to modernise, the US government created a system of rewards for those willing to share industrial secrets. To protect its technological edge, Britain passed laws banning the export of designs and made it a crime for skilled textile workers to travel to America. Slater heard about the bounties on offer and couldn't resist. He took a ship to the New World disguised as a farmer and shared the secrets of the water-powered spinning machine. Today, in his adopted country, he is celebrated as the 'father of the American industrial revolution'.[1] Slater settled in Pawtucket, Rhode Island, where he built a near-replica of the Belper mill. Belper is now twinned with Pawtucket, whose most famous corporate resident these days is Hasbro, the toys and games company. In 2001, the American town sent as a gift a two-metre tall sculpture of Mr Potato Head, a character from the *Toy Story* film franchise, dressed as an English settler in buckled shoes and a Quaker hat. Over the years that followed the giant spud was vandalised and kidnapped (or 'spudnapped', as a local newspaper described it) on so many occasions that the local council suggested sticking him on top of the bus station. That idea was abandoned over health and safety concerns, and eventually Mr Potato Head found a home in the courtyard of a shopping mall.[2] Was this hostility anything to do with Slater? 'It was just that the thing was so ghastly', my guide replied. There was a concern that the potato was in such poor taste it might threaten the World Heritage status of the area. Among Hasbro's other famous toys and games are Transformers, My Little Pony, a series of action figures from the Marvel comics, Play-Doh, Nerf blasters and the Monopoly board-game. The company, and the toy industry more broadly, are now themselves victims of large-scale piracy,[3] with China as the biggest source of counterfeit toys – and just about every other knockoff.[4]

The story of Slater is cited by those with a more forgiving attitude towards China's large-scale plunder of technology and know-how as evidence that 'everybody did it'. They argue that the

Chinese Communist Party is merely following a long tradition of emerging powers cutting a few corners as they play catch-up in an unjust world where the rules of trade, and the strictures of patent and copyright laws are stacked against them.[5] Over time, it has been suggested, China will learn to play by the rules, but this is to ignore a major fundamental point. China can by no stretch of the imagination still be described as 'emerging'. It is now the world's second largest economy and a serious technological competitor to the West. As its ambitions to lead the world in technologies of the future have grown, so has the scale of the theft.

Intellectual property (IP) is the umbrella term used for creations of the mind, covering a spectrum of inventions, designs, symbols, names and images. They are usually protected by patents, copyright or trademarks, and today they supposedly enjoy significantly stronger legal protections than in the past – which China signed up for when it joined the World Trade Organization in 2001. The harvesting of foreign IP takes on multiple forms, formal and informal and often with the complicity of the victims themselves. It should be seen as a continuum from endemic counterfeiting of well-known brands, such as Hasbro's toys, to today's large-scale plunder of industrial, technical and business secrets by cyber espionage.

If there was a spiritual home of China's vast counterfeit business during my time as correspondent in China it was the Silk Market in Beijing – an emporium of fakes spread over seven floors (and three basements), sitting in plain sight in Chaoyang, the capital's business district. There were 1,700 vendors selling everything from shoes and clothing to perfume, handbags, luggage, watches, electronics and toys. The vendors were aggressive and frequently unorthodox. On one occasion I visited for the emergency purchase of a suitcase. I was sceptical about the quality of the 'Samsonite' wheely case that I was shown, so the sales woman demonstrated its strength by throwing it across the shop, pouring water over it and then stamping on the arm. I bought it, but it still broke three weeks later. The building was relatively new, opening in 2005 as a replacement for an outdoor market, the Silk Alley, which had been equally notorious for knockoffs. Diplomatic pressure led to the occasional perfunctory raid by the police, usually before high-profile international events in the city, after which business quickly returned to normal. A little to the north of the Silk Market was a road renowned for fake DVDs, computer games and software. The counterfeiters moved fast and would frequently obtain pirated copies of movies before they were even in the cinema.

China's counterfeit culture ran deep and wide, and among foreign correspondents there seemed at times a competition to see who could find the most outrageous new rip-off: a Chinese motor company brought out a copycat Range Rover Evoque; the 'Hiphone 6' was an early and clunky copy of the Apple iPhone; a village in southern China became the centre for reproduction art, churning out thousands of fake Picassos, Rembrandts, Van Goghs and Da Vincis each year. A fake Apple shop that opened in the southwestern city of Kunming, complete with logo, wooden tables and all-round casual vibe was such a good copy that even the cheery staff thought they were working in the real thing.[6] The annual sales of 'Château Lafite Rothschild' wine, a cool 50,000 yuan (£5,400) a bottle in top Chinese hotels, far outstripped the vineyard's annual production. By one estimate, 70 per cent of the bottles sold in China were fake.[7] On one occasion, an ATM at one of China's top banks delivered to me ten fake 100-yuan (£11) notes, all with the same serial number. Brand-name pharmaceuticals, Lego, golf clubs, coffee shops, books, they were all fair game. On one occasion I met a private investigator whose speciality was searching for parallel production lines among the factories of southern China. It became a common practice for the Chinese partner of a Western company to take the blueprints they'd been given for the original product and then set up a separate facility, often in the same factory, to make copycats with their own logo. Sometimes it was so blatant that the factory hardly bothered to hide what they were doing. As Paul Midler notes in his classic 2009 book, *Poorly Made in China: An Insider's Account of the Tactics Behind China's Production Game*: 'What manufacturers lacked in originality, they made up for in their ability to copy. They were masters of mimicry, and factory owners would simply insist: "We only need your product sample." No matter whether it was a winter coat, a toaster oven, or a lamp, manufacturers could be counted on not only to reverse engineer the product with great precision, but also to replicate it with great speed.'[8]

In spite of this rampant piracy, there was still a feeling among Western manufacturers that China would grow out of it, that as the country got richer and developed its own brands it would begin to see the value in protecting intellectual property. Those hopes were encouraged by a number of high-profile cases: in 2019, Jaguar Land Rover won a landmark action in a Chinese court against the company that copied the Evoque,[9] and a year later Shanghai police broke up a gang making fake versions of Hasbro's Transformers, for instance.[10] However, these were exceptions rather than the rule; the tide was too strong, piracy too entrenched. In July 2023, the chairman of China's first intellectual property court was expelled from the Communist Party by graft busters who accused him of 'improper sexual behaviour' and 'illegally accepting money and valuables to do favours for others'.[11] Those familiar with the court suspect the rot went much deeper.

In its 2022 report on counterfeiting, the Office of the US Trade Representative said, 'China continues to be the number one source of counterfeit products in the world. Counterfeit and pirated goods from China, together with transhipped goods from China to Hong Kong, accounted for 75% of the value (measured by manufacturer's suggested retail price) of counterfeit and pirated goods seized by U.S. Customs and Border Protection (CBP) in 2021.'[12] Counterfeiting was turbocharged by the explosion in online sales and facilitated by China's e-commerce giants, but the report still had a few words for the capital's notorious Silk Market, which 'remains one of the biggest markets for counterfeit goods in Beijing'.[13] The shift online and the dominant role of Chinese pirates were confirmed in a European Union study published in January 2023. 'China is confirmed by far as the largest source of counterfeits and represents 85% of seizures related to online sales and 51% of global seizures of offline sales,' it stated.[14] The EU identified electrical machinery and electronics (30 per cent of seizures), clothing (18 per cent), perfumery and cosmetics (10 per cent), and toys and games (also 10 per cent) as the products most frequently pirated. The value of global trade in counterfeit and pirated goods has been estimated at $464 billion, or 2.5 per cent of world trade – which is roughly equivalent to the GDP of Austria or Belgium.[15] On top of this, many fake goods are substandard, often posing serious health and safety threats to consumers.

China will not grow out of its piracy habit for the simple reason that disdain for foreign intellectual property rights is so deeply engrained in the world view of the Chinese Communist Party. The Party regards rules, treaties or other legal obligations as discretionary at best, to be bent, circumvented or ignored at will, especially when they are seen as obstacles in the way of China's rightful rise. Foreign companies and their technologies and know-how are fair game. Piracy of well-known brands such as Hasbro's toys is one of the cruder manifestations of this, but the Party has become increasingly audacious, ambitious and sophisticated in its efforts to hoover up know-how and gain a technological edge over the West by all available means.

The loss of American industrial information and intellectual property through cyber espionage has been described by General Keith Alexander, director of his nation's National Security Agency (NSA) as 'the greatest transfer of wealth in history'.[16] And the White House, in a March 2023 cybersecurity strategy paper, warned that 'The People's Republic of China now presents the broadest, most active and most persistent threat to both government and private sector networks.'[17] US officials have described the private sector as 'the new geopolitical battlespace', with the theft of American trade secrets costing the nation up to $500 billion per year, with China responsible for the lion's share of it.[18] The FBI estimates that China has around 30,000 military cyber spies and 150,000 other experts the CCP is able to call on in the nominally private sector.[19] The British government in a 2022 National Cyber Strategy paper described China as a 'highly sophisticated actor in cyberspace with increasing ambition to project its influence beyond its borders and a proven interest in the UK's commercial secrets. How China evolves in the next decade will probably be the single biggest driver of the UK's future cyber security.'[20]

In an unprecedented joint public address in London in July 2022, Christopher Wray and Ken McCallum, the heads of the FBI and MI5, the UK's domestic intelligence agency, warned business leaders that Beijing was determined to steal their technology for competitive edge. The Chinese government posed 'the biggest long-term threat' to economic and national security,' Wray said.[21]

Theirs was one of several public warnings given by intelligence chiefs on both sides of the Atlantic around this time, which were seen as efforts to open the eyes of business and academia to the scale of the threat they were facing. 'The scale of the Chinese cyber threat is unparalleled – they've got a bigger hacking program than every other major nation combined,' the FBI Director later told a congressional committee.[22]

Early Chinese cyber espionage was frequently clunky and noisy. The hackers did not cover their tracks well. In 2013, Mandiant, an American cybersecurity company, ran a groundbreaking investigation into People's Liberation Army Unit 61398.[23] The unit, formally the 2nd Bureau of the PLA General Staff Department's 3rd Department, was reportedly the PLA's main outfit for computer espionage. Mandiant tracked the hackers for six years from 2006, during which they stole technology blueprints, negotiating strategies, research results, marketing information and other secrets from almost 150 companies across twenty industries. The industries ranged from transportation to electronics, aerospace, energy and telecommunications. The cyber sleuths painstakingly collected digital evidence about the hackers' tools and techniques. They watched them moving around inside computer systems and tracked their IP addresses. They even identified individual hackers from their social media accounts. So brazen were their operations that unit 61398 had even put a recruitment ad on the website of a leading Chinese university.[24]

Around the same time that Mandiant was publishing its investigation, a confidential report presented to the Pentagon by the US Defense Science Board claimed that more than two dozen of the country's most advanced weapons systems had been compromised by Chinese hackers. These included designs for missile defence systems and combat aircraft and ships, including the F/A-18 fighter jet, the V-22 Osprey, the Black Hawk helicopter and the navy's new Littoral Combat Ship. Also on the list was the F-35 Joint Strike Fighter, at the time the most expensive weapons system ever built.[25] Chinese hackers were also blamed for a series of computer breaches at the government's Office of Personnel Management, which began around March 2014. Some 22 million records were stolen, including security background checks and data on intelligence and military personnel. Other information, perfect for blackmail, included records of financial trouble, drug use, alcohol abuse and adulterous affairs. It was feared that Chinese counterintelligence agencies might be able to piece together the identity of US spies working undercover around the world.

Chinese cyber espionage was seemingly out of control, and President Barack Obama came under enormous political pressure to respond. In May 2014, the US indicted *in absentia* five PLA hackers for cyber espionage against US companies in the nuclear power, metals and solar products industries. 'This twenty-first-century burglary has to stop,' said David Hickton, US Attorney for the Western District of Pennsylvania, in the indictment.[26] At the same time, the Obama administration tried in private talks with Beijing to make a distinction between legitimate espionage for military or political purposes and stealing to gain a commercial edge. A breakthrough came at a summit in September 2015, when Presidents Obama and Xi Jinping struck a deal, agreeing that 'neither country's government will conduct or knowingly support cyber-enabled theft of intellectual property, including trade secrets or other confidential business information, with the intent of providing competitive advantages to companies or commercial sectors'.[27] A month later, China reached a similar accord with Britain. It seemed like an important landmark for establishing 'norms' for behaviour in cyberspace and was endorsed by other G20 countries.

In reality, the deal was always doomed; China was never going to abide by it for any longer than needed for the simple reason that it never recognised Obama's distinction between spying for reasons of state and spying for commercial advantage. To the CCP they are one and the same thing; Chinese companies, whether state-owned or nominally private, are instruments of state power and Party policy. And the hacking was too effective. The deal was useful to Beijing in the short term for blunting a growing threat of sanctions. It used the time to reorganise, retool and refocus its cyber forces – and then they came roaring back with a greater degree of ambition and sophistication.

As big companies hardened their defences, so Chinese hackers attacked their suppliers as a stepping stone into the computers of their true targets. It was reported that suppliers to Airbus were targeted as a sideways route into the computers of the European aircraft manufacturer. The hackers appeared to be after data on engines and avionics development, areas where China was weak.[28] Chinese hackers were also blamed for a computer breach at a German software company behind Team Viewer, a popular system that allows users to access and share their desktops remotely or to take full control of other computers via the internet from anywhere in the world.[29] A Bloomberg investigation revealed what it called a potentially devasting 'hardware hack', whereby a tiny microchip was placed on computer motherboards supplied from China, that would allow attackers to secretly open a 'backdoor' into the computer systems in which the motherboards were installed. The motherboard coordinates just about everything that happens in a computer, and the compromised boards reached almost thirty US companies. US investigators concluded that the chips, no bigger than a grain of rice, had been inserted in China during the manufacturing process with the aim of opening the door for hackers to gather high-value corporate secrets.[30]

Although multi-billion dollar figures are frequently quoted, it is in truth almost impossible to put a number on the costs of cyber espionage. They include everything from the cost of hardening systems, damage to hacked computers, and legal liabilities to market losses when plundered blueprints are handed to Chinese companies to develop rival and inevitably cheaper products. Take China's new narrow-body jet, the C919, which completed its maiden flight in May 2023. Security researchers have alleged that the programme benefited from a state-sponsored hacking campaign designed to steal relevant know-how from Western aerospace companies, including Airbus.[31] A December 2019 investigation by *Industry Week* was headlined, 'How China Stole an Entire Plane' and described 'one of the most audacious industrial espionage schemes ever conducted by China'.[32] The solar-panel industry, in which China now dominates the world, was built on stolen technology, a case we will study in more detail later in this book, and American and European companies have been decimated along the way. China has also targeted companies negotiating contracts in China in order to give the Chinese partner an inside edge, but again the cost is difficult to quantify. As a 2018 report from the Office of the United States Trade Representative put it, 'It can be difficult to assess the full burden on U.S. commerce because of chronic underreporting, companies being unaware that their networks have been compromised or being unaware of the extent of the damage done.'[33] Or as Robert Mueller said when he was director of the FBI, 'I am convinced that there are only two types of companies: those that have been hacked and those that will be. And even they are converging into one category: companies that have been hacked and will be hacked again.'[34]

Because of their sheer scale, it is easy to label the piracy and IP theft of the early reform period and today's cyber espionage as scattergun, trawler-like efforts to indiscriminately harvest know-how. However, evidence collected by Frank Dikötter suggests a far more methodical approach. In 1983, the Ministry of Chemical Industries and the Ministry of Agriculture, Livestock and Fisheries jointly published a directive entitled 'On Maintaining Secrecy when Copying Foreign Pharmaceutical Products', urging measures to cover their tracks.[35] A notice that same year from the Ministry of Chemical Industries invited state enterprises to consult 'information on science and technology obtained abroad through special channels', while Shanghai's Committee on Computing urged, 'we need a unified approach towards copying' in order that 'the quality of the copied equipment can be guaranteed'.[36] Fast forward four decades and security experts looking to identify Western companies most vulnerable to cyber espionage consult China's five-year plans in which Beijing lays down its economic targets. When the CCP spelt out its technology goals in a plan called 'Made in China 2025', which lists ten cutting-edge technologies in which Beijing wants to build 'national champions' and lead the world, it was widely seen as a 'shopping list' for China's cyber spies. These areas include robotics, artificial intelligence, telecommunications, aerospace engineering, gene editing, electric vehicles (EVs), synthetic materials and advanced electrical equipment. The plan was first unveiled to much fanfare in 2015, but has more recently disappeared from public discussion, largely as a result of the international backlash it created.[37] However, the policy itself is alive and well, thriving through government subsidies and protectionism – and of course espionage.

The scale of those ambitions was one trigger for the trade war between the United States and China, and the Western push-back against Beijing more broadly. Another was the CCP's explicit policy of channelling technology and know-how to its fast expanding and modernising military and security apparatus at a time of growing repression at home and increased aggression internationally. As tensions have intensified, Washington has sought to deny China access to advanced semiconductors and the machines to make them, and Western chip companies have raised their defences against hackers. In October 2023, the heads of the security services of the US, UK, Canada, Australia and New Zealand – the Five Eyes intelligence gathering network – met in San Francisco and warned of 'unprecedented' Chinese spying. 'There's a single common thread in just about every conversation about protecting innovation...and that is the Chinese government,' said FBI director Christopher Wray, who hosted the meeting. And Ken McCallum, the director-general of MI5, warned technology firms, 'If you're anywhere close to the cutting edge of tech, you might not be interested in geopolitics, but geopolitics is interested in you.'[38]

The Chinese government has reacted to well-documented accusations of piracy and cybertheft with howls of outrage. 'Groundless', 'slander', 'a malicious smear', it claims, while insisting that China is the real victim.[39] The CCP is a master of righteous indignation and manufactured outrage. It is a technique perfected by aggressive diplomats promoted by Xi Jinping and dubbed 'wolf warriors' after a series of Rambo-style movies of that name. They seemed to take to heart the slogan on the poster for *Wolf Warrior 2*, 'Anyone who insults China – no matter how remote – must be exterminated,' though their outrage was frequently as fake as the handbags in the Silk Market.

The road from the rampant piracy of the Deng years to industrial-scale cybertheft often took some intriguing turns. There emerged a cottage industry for the production of fake receipts, or *fapiao*. Transport hubs in major cities became centres for the sale of every conceivable type of receipt. '*Fapiao, fapiao*,' would ring out as you waited for a bus or train. Whether it was for apartment rental payments, tax or travel, fakes were all available. The sellers advertised on e-commerce sites, via text messages sent to mobile phones and left business cards in elevators and on the underground railway, typically charging around 2 per cent of the face value of the receipt. They were extremely popular with those seeking to defraud their employer, the tax authorities, clients or competitors, and the sellers were extremely proud of their handiwork. 'I once printed invoices totalling $16 million for a construction project!' boasted one.[40] Here was a microcosm of the almost routine prevalence of fraud, but it also pointed to another central feature of China's economy, which began under Deng and has been vastly expanded over recent years: the routine debasement of statistics and other data.

CHAPTER 4

Lies, Damned Lies and
Communist Party Statistics

'In the end the Party would announce that two
and two made five, and you would have to believe it. It
was inevitable that they should make that claim sooner
or later: the logic of their position demanded it.'

George Orwell, Nineteen Eighty-Four

In January 2024, China's premier, Li Qiang, led a large delegation of officials to the Swiss ski resort of Davos, where he told global business and political elites attending the World Economic Forum that the Chinese economy was making steady progress and that 'Choosing investment in the Chinese market is not a risk, but an opportunity.'[1] He insisted that the Chinese economy was rebounding and had grown by 5.2 per cent in 2023, slightly above the official target of 5 per cent. At the same time, Beijing released new youth jobless figures, which had been suspended the previous summer after they reached a record 21.3 per cent. The new figure was 14.9 per cent after the National Bureau of Statistics introduced what it called a new methodology, though without providing full details. Both sets of statistics were greeted with widespread scepticism. 'Adjusting how they calculate the [jobless] figures at this moment may even exacerbate the public's distrust in official data,' declared Dan Wang, chief economist at Hang Seng Bank China.[2] Economists at the Rhodium Group, a research and advisory company, were among those who believed the GDP figures were 'significantly overstated', and the real figure was likely around 1.5 per cent.[3]

Li was keen to show that the economy was recovering after a slowdown blamed on the Covid-19 pandemic. However, it had been a year since the borders reopened and the recovery remained elusive. Foreign investors were increasingly wary, and Li's welcoming words were at odds with the increasingly hostile environment they found in Xi Jinping's China. The pandemic had also provided further stark evidence of the Chinese Communist Party's debasement of data. When it abruptly lifted all Covid controls in late 2022 with little preparation, the virus rapidly spread across the country, leading to a surge in deaths, which the CCP sought to cover up. Figures briefly released online by Zhejiang, a populous and wealthy coastal province, about the number of cremations during the first quarter of 2023 showed they had surged by 73 per cent compared with the previous year. International experts found the data consistent with estimates that across China there had been 1.6 million excess deaths during that period.[4] This was also supported by anecdotal evidence of crematoria and hospitals inundated with Covid patients – but was almost twenty times the CCP's official Covid-19 death count for that period. As bodies piled up, local authorities told hospitals to keep 'Covid-19' off death certificates, instead attributing deaths to 'pneumonia' or 'heart disease', to the anger and consternation of grieving relatives.[5] It is remarkable that the Zhejiang cremation data remained online for all of three days; across China, provincial-level cremation figures, which had been routinely released on a quarterly basis, alongside marriage registrations and other civic data, were scrapped. At national level, the Ministry of Civil Affairs abandoned its compilation of countrywide data.[6] Mike Ryan, the World Health Organization (WHO)'s director for health emergencies, said the Chinese statistics 'under-represent the true impact of the disease' and pointed to China's 'narrow definition' of a Covid death.[7]

Falsifying death statistics was only one element of the CCP's Covid deceit. The Party covered up the initial outbreak at the end of 2019, and systematically obstructed efforts to investigate the origin of the virus, blocking access to information, people and facilities, while muddying the waters with conspiracy theories unsupported by any evidence. The European Union diplomatic service accused China of running 'a global disinformation campaign to deflect blame for the outbreak of the pandemic'. It said that 'both overt and covert tactics have been observed'.[8] All of which may seem far removed from Davos and the rarefied world of global finance. However, trust and confidence are important and fragile commodities in that world, and although corporate memories can be short and crocodile smiles expansive, the CCP's Covid deceit added to the growing wariness towards China. Premier Li's statistics on economic growth were politely received, as were his claims that China remained 'committed' to opening its economy, but there was little to disguise the scepticism resonating through the Alpine bars and restaurants.

One of my first encounters with statistics with the CCP characteristics came while filming an economic story in Dongguan, southern China in September 2009. The area is carpeted with factories, and many were struggling in the wake of the 2008 global financial crisis. I wanted to get a sense of how bad things had become for the area's export-led economy. However, the local authorities were keen to show that all was well, that the area was recovering on the back of a vast economic stimulus. One company I visited was run by an American entrepreneur who acted as a facilitator for international firms looking to source from the area. Tom (not his real name) was a middleman, which meant he was well informed and had a strong understanding of local economic conditions, which he was always willing to share. 'Companies are struggling,' he told me, but warned that I'd never find the truth in local statistics. He explained that it had been a tough year for his own firm, whose financial figures looked less than rosy.

'They show a loss,' his worried accountant told him.

'That's right,' Tom replied, 'business hasn't been good'.

Tom's accountant shook his head. 'But you can't show a loss,' he said.

'But we made a loss. Look at the figures,' responded a puzzled Tom.

His accountant was the former head of the local tax bureau and was used by Tom because of those connections and his understanding of the often opaque workings of the authorities. The accountant calmly explained that there had been a government directive instructing that there must be no losses that year. Losing money was not acceptable. He said that a failure to show a profit might result in closer scrutiny of past and future earnings. Tom adjusted his figures accordingly.

A Western financial analyst based in Shanghai once described Chinese economic statistics to me as 'one of the greatest works of contemporary Chinese fiction'. Few analysts took them seriously, and they employed an array of esoteric techniques to try and ascertain what was really going on with the economy. The search for the economic truth spawned its own cottage industry.[9] They pored over figures on diesel and electricity demand, the fluctuating levels of the country's chronic air pollution, car sales and congestion, job postings and construction – even the sale of underwear or pickled vegetables. One enterprising analyst regularly sent spies to Shanghai port to count the ships and throughput of trucks. Others have studied satellite images, looking for clues in traffic flows or the number of empty parking spaces at shopping malls. There was much amusement among analysts when Wang Bao'an, director of China's National Bureau of Statistics, angrily criticised those with a more bearish view of the Chinese economy. That was 'just one school of thought', he said. 'Facts speak louder than words.'[10] A few days later he was arrested for 'serious disciplinary violations' – the usual euphemism for corruption. His disappearance was accompanied by dark jokes about whether he had cooked the books too much or too little for the satisfaction of his bosses.

No less an authority than former Premier Li Keqiang developed his own way of measuring economic performance that became known as the 'Li Keqiang index'. When he was head of Liaoning province, he let slip to a visiting American diplomat that local GDP figures were 'unreliable' and that instead he focused on electricity consumption, rail cargo and bank lending as a proxy.[11] Many Western financial institutions working in China have used a variation of the 'Li Keqiang index' as the basis of their internal systems for measuring the true state of the economy. Li appeared to be hinting at the perverse incentives of the Chinese system, whereby local authorities were under enormous pressure to manipulate data in order to be seen to fulfil the Party's growth targets, for which officials were rewarded or punished. In a striking piece of research, Luis Martinez, an economist at the University of Chicago, suggested that such manipulation is fundamental to dictatorship.[12] He compared the self-reported GDP of autocracies, as classified by Freedom House, with the brightness of night-time lights in those countries as recorded over time by satellites, which he used as a proxy for actual growth. He identified Beijing as an outstanding manipulator, estimating that over a twenty-one-year period between 1992 and 2013, China's actual growth was a third less than claimed. Martinez also noted that as countries become more democratic and rely on wider means of legitimacy, such as elections, their figures grew less suspicious. In contrast, as dictatorships harden and accountability and oversight crumbles, as has been the case in China under Xi Jinping, so official statistics become increasingly unreliable.

In October 2022, as the Communist Party gathered for its five-yearly congress in Beijing to hand Xi an unprecedented third term as leader, paving the way for a possible lifetime in power, the National Bureau of Statistics delayed issuing any scheduled economic data.[13] The figures, which included quarterly GDP, retail and property sales were expected to be especially gloomy, even accounting for manipulation, and the Party did not want its gathering overshadowed by bad economic news. Arthur Budaghyan, who oversees China investment at BCA Research, said the delay was no big deal. 'I think GDP data is the most useless data in China,' he declared, while Brendan Ahern, chief investment officer of KraneShares, added app downloads and ticket sales for Disney's resorts in Shanghai to the proxy data he was watching as a measure of economic activity.[14] Earlier that year the Organisation for Economic Co-operation and Development (OECD), which maintains a respected research and development database, cast doubt on the integrity of Chinese R&D figures. It announced that it had found 'anomalies' in data supplied by Beijing, put on hold the publication of data for 2021 and pulled previously published indicators for 2019 and 2020 until the 'coherence' of the Chinese figures had been effectively addressed.[15] During a visit to Singapore in June 2023, I asked Bilahari Kausikan, who has extensive experience of dealing with China, how he approached data supplied by Beijing, given its lack of reliability. 'I don't pay too much attention to the statistics because I assume they lie, or at least exaggerate,' he told me. 'I start from first principles. This is a Leninist system, the market is a tool.' He recalled advising a top Chinese diplomat, 'It would be in your own interests to be a bit more transparent.' The diplomat laughed. China is such a centralised system that he too was reading the tea leaves, much like Bilahari. 'Though perhaps with more expertise.'

The images on state television in May 2023 showed rows of empty desks, strewn with half-opened laptops, and coffee cups. Jackets hung on the backs of chairs and several heart-shaped balloons were tethered to the desks. This was, the report said, a hotbed of espionage, and the scene showed the aftermath of a raid by state security officers. The video, broadcast during prime time, cut to images of the police interrogating employees and photographing everything from servers to hard drives. 'They wound up leaking sensitive content and even state secrets and intelligence to foreign companies and embarking down a criminal path,' stated a grim-faced reporter.[16] This was the Shanghai headquarters of Capvision, an international business consultancy, whose offices in Beijing, Suzhou and Shenzhen were also raided. The television report accused Capvision of setting up interviews with prominent experts in government policy, national defence and technology, who had supposedly revealed sensitive and secret information.[17] The firm describes itself as an 'expert network' company, connecting clients, who were mostly investors and other consultants, with industry and economic specialists – facilitating conversations and gathering information in a way that would be commonplace in most other advanced economies.

The action against Capvision followed raids earlier that year at the Beijing office of Mintz Group, during which five local employees were detained,[18] and at the Shanghai office of Bain & Company, where officials questioned employees and hauled away files and computers.[19] Both are American consultancies, specialising in what are called 'due diligence investigations' as well as broader market research on behalf of mostly corporate clients and investors seeking a better understanding of the opaque Chinese market and for background checks on would-be partners, suppliers and senior employees. The services of such companies had become essential for doing safe business in China, given the unreliability of official data and rampant corruption. Under Xi Jinping, due diligence had become more important than ever – but the Party saw any independent source of information, any data it could not control, as a threat. As if to emphasise the point, Xi reportedly put his head of state security, Chen Yixin, in charge of the crackdown on foreign firms.[20]

At the same time, official data was becoming not only less reliable, but also less available. Before Xi Jinping came to power, China's National Bureau of Statistics was a busy place. Its accuracy could be questioned, but not its output, which amounted to 80,000 sets of data, ranging from the number of people employed in the outdoor playground amusement equipment sector to the natural gas exports from Guangdong.[21] By 2016, more than half of all the indicators published by provincial and national statistics bureaus had been discontinued.[22] In April 2023, the authorities tightened access to a crucial database of economic and financial statistics. Shanghai-based Wind Information was used by analysts and investors both inside and outside the country, but many foreign think tanks, research and financial firms found they could not renew subscriptions over what Wind described as 'compliance' issues.[23] Earlier state security officials raided and shut down Shenzhen Verite, a China-based auditor affiliated with Verite, a US labour rights group. The company had been used by Walt Disney and Apple among others to examine supply chains for any signs of forced labour. The closure of the Shenzhen-based firm came at a time of growing concern over forced labour in Xinjiang, and deprived companies of an important channel for auditing and researching labour rights among suppliers.[24] Beijing also cut access to China's largest academic database, with foreign universities and research institutes told that because of 'compliance' issues they could no longer access China National Knowledge Infrastructure, which supplied online databases with thousands of research papers and documents about China.[25]

Western analysts who provided advice and information to investors looking to buy shares in Chinese companies worried that negative comments or recommendations could result in criminal action against them or their sources, especially as China was equipping itself with a broad array of new 'anti-espionage' laws, whose definition of spying seemed infinitely elastic. Others linked the crackdown to a broader effort to restrict the way the rest of the world sees China through the expulsion and harassment of dozens of journalists, described as 'the single biggest blow to international reporting in China'.[26] A survey of members by the Foreign Correspondents' Club of China found widespread harassment, including online trolling, physical assaults, hacking and visa denials, as well as what appeared to be official encouragement of legal action against journalists. Among those forced out was BBC correspondent John Sudworth, who had faced threats and intimidation that left him fearful for the safety of his family. 'As we made our hasty exit, the plainclothes police tailing us and our young children to the airport were final proof of the dangers we faced and of China's deep intolerance for independent journalism,' he said. [27]

Investors will tell you that timely and accurate information is the lifeblood of efficient markets. By that measure, markets in China are hardly worthy of the name. The Chinese stock market has been described as 'a crazy casino',[28] but that is really a disservice to casinos. 'Macroeconomic data is questionable, financial statements are not credible, corporate governance is unclear, government intervention is unpredictable, and interest rates are repressed,' according to Michael Pettis, a professor of finance at Peking University.[29] He said the markets are driven by speculation and detached from economic fundamentals because it is impossible to know what those fundamentals are. The *Financial Times* described China as 'a country where corporate governance is stuck somewhere back in the Qing Dynasty'.[30] During a visit to the Shenzhen stock exchange, one economist told me calmly that if the regulators insisted on greater transparency, no company would ever get itself listed.

All of which is true, but also somewhat misses the point. The primary purpose of markets in China is not the efficient allocation of investment or other resources, but to serve the interests of the Communist Party. Markets elsewhere in the world generally go up and down in accordance with supply and demand, but as with most other things in China, the CCP believes markets should go where the Party tells them to go. That has resulted in often wild speculative fluctuations as investors have sought to second-guess the often-capricious mood of the CCP. That was well illustrated in summer 2015 after the Shanghai stock market had risen by 150 per cent in a year, egged on by the government in an effort in part to divert hot money away from the property market. However, in deflating one bubble it inflated another, which inevitably popped, and during a few wild weeks that summer the market fell by 50 per cent. The CCP panicked, fearing social unrest from the legions of angry and mostly small investors, and ploughed an estimated $200 billion into the market in an effort to stabilise prices. When that failed to stop the rot, it halted trading in more than half of China's quoted companies and large shareholders were banned from selling. Reporting about the market meltdown was restricted, and the security forces were mobilised to track down what were described as 'malicious short sellers'.[31] An official directive ordered state media to avoid stoking panic. 'Do not conduct in-depth analysis, and do not speculate on or assess the direction of the market. Do not exaggerate panic or sadness. Do not use emotionally charged words such as "slump", "spike" or "collapse",' the directive said.[32] Wang Xiaolu, a respected business reporter, was arrested and paraded on state television to 'confess' to causing market chaos after a seemingly innocuous report speculating that the authorities would soon end their costly intervention. 'I shouldn't have caused our country and shareholders such great losses just for the sake of sensationalism and eye-catchiness,' he said before being jailed for 'spreading false information'.[33] The witch-hunt continued throughout the summer of 2015. The CCP's *China Daily* proudly proclaimed that the authorities had launched twenty-two cases involving 'suspected market manipulation, insider trading, false information fabrication and dissemination'. Four executives at the country's largest broker were arrested and placed under what the paper called 'criminal compulsory measures'.[34] It truly was a market with Chinese characteristics.

Fast forward to 2023, and the CCP was once again looking to rescue the slumping property and stock markets. However, Beijing's options were more limited amid soaring local government and bank debt. What Pettis described as the 'fundamentals', as far as they could be identified, were dreadful, and confidence in the Party's economic competence was seeping away. The authorities sought to reinflate the property bubble, and once again they intervened to prop up share prices by banning big shareholders from selling and instructing companies to buy their own shares.[35] Investment funds were pressured to buy the shares of newly listed companies the CCP deemed strategically important, including those in the semiconductor, biotech and electric vehicle sectors.[36] By one estimate, state-backed funds poured nearly $60 billion into the market over the first two months of 2024 alone.[37] Financial commentators were again targeted if they challenged the official narrative about the health of the economy. Wu Xiaobo, an economic pundit with nearly 5 million followers on Weibo, was blocked alongside two other unnamed bloggers. The Twitter-like platform said it had deleted Wu's recent posts because he spread harmful information that undermined government policy, including spreading false accusations against the market and manipulating unemployment rates.[38]

Yi Huiman, the chairman of the China Securities Regulatory Commission, announced that henceforth Chinese companies should be judged by a 'valuation system with Chinese characteristics', which reflected their 'pillar role' in the economy rather than by traditional measures of profit and loss.[39] Analysts were left scratching their heads as to what Yi meant about valuations – and so was the market. By early 2024, Chinese stocks were down 60 per cent from their peak three years earlier, a loss of more than $1.9 trillion in market capitalisation. Foreign investors increasingly regarded China as uninvestable. In early 2024, the hapless Yi was sacked as China's top regulator, as the market still refused to do as it was told.

The opaque balance sheets of Chinese companies have always been challenging for Western analysts to understand, though for a long time they didn't really care. Such was the eagerness to have Chinese companies list on Wall Street that they were held to far lower accounting standards than American firms. Only in 2022, after threatening to delist 200 Chinese firms, was the US accounting watchdog promised full access to inspect and investigate the books of US-listed Chinese firms for the first time. The first batch it examined were found to be littered with so many deficiencies that the auditors failed to obtain enough evidence to substantiate companies' financial statements, according to the watchdog.[40]

In Spring 2023, Chinese bond trading was thrown into turmoil when traders discovered that the terminals which they relied upon to deliver real-time bond prices had abruptly stopped working.[41] Four leading services were suspended due to 'force majeure' (events beyond their control), a frequent euphemism for CCP intervention.

Only a service called iDeal, which is operated by China's Central Bank and regarded as inferior to the private sector providers, was still working. The suspended services were suspected of operating 'outside of the [licensed] scope of their business' by providing data to third parties.[42] In April 2024, China's major stock exchanges announced plans to stop providing real-time trading data completely in a bid to tame volatility – another blow to transparency, and a curious way it seemed of trying to win back the confidence of investors.

One of the abiding myths of modern China is that the country's economy is overseen by skilled and able technocrats. This is often traced back to the late sixth century, when the Sui Dynasty introduced a civil service examination to recruit state functionaries. Variants of that exam exist to this day and feed the idea that modern China – and the Communist Party, which regards itself as the embodiment of China, past present and future – has inherited the mandarin ethos. By this telling, the system is essentially meritocratic and efficient, promoting the best people on the basis of technical skill and able to plan for the long term, unlike messy Western democracies, which are tied to short-term election cycles. The perception that China's technocrats are more superior beings was given a boost after the 2008 global financial crisis when the government unleashed a tidal wave of credit and cash to ride out the downturn caused by a fall in demand for exports. 'What if we could just be China for a day?' asked Thomas Friedman, a *New York Times* columnist, 'We could actually, you know, authorise the right solutions.'[43] China's leaders 'may have a more realistic and constructive assessment of the macroeconomic policy challenge than their counterparts in the more advanced economies,' wrote Stephen Roach, a Yale University economist.[44] In fact, the vast stimulus – worth $568 billion – saw China printing money on a scale the world had never seen, turbocharging the wasteful property and infrastructure investments which are at the root of its economic problems. More recently, the mantle of China cheerleader has been taken on by Elon Musk, the CEO of Tesla, whose heavy investments in the country are examined later in this book. He has claimed that politicians in China are better at science and technology, and therefore more able to innovate. On a podcast hosted by comedian Joe Rogan, he reeled off a list of Beijing leaders with technical degrees and added, 'The mayor of Shanghai is really smart' – Shanghai being the location of Tesla's most important manufacturing facility.[45]

The CCP points to its four decades of remarkable growth to support its claim of technocratic competence. Xi Jinping in 2021 declared a 'complete victory' in eradicating absolute poverty, which demonstrated the Party's 'spiritual pedigree'.[46] He declined to mention that the entire nation had been thrown into dire poverty by the catastrophic policies of Mao Zedong, whom he continues to admire. Many millions remain poor, or just above the poverty line, but online censors deleted videos and discussions about economic hardship or gloomy job prospects. In March 2023, the country's internet regulator said it would crack down on anybody publishing videos or posts that 'deliberately manipulate sadness, incite polarization, create harmful information that damages the image of the Party and the government, and disrupts economic and social development'.[47] This included a ban on sad videos of old people, disabled people and children.

That said, Xi Jinping has still pleaded comparative poverty when there are benefits in so doing. Summer 2023 saw a bizarre argument over whether China was a 'developed' or 'developing' nation. The trigger was a vote by American lawmakers to remove China's status as a developing nation. On the face of it, you'd expect Beijing to take pride at being recognised by its rival as a great power, since it has constantly argued for this. Instead, there was outrage.[48] The reason for the anger was that 'developing country' status bestows on a country enormous privileges, which Beijing did not want to lose. These include preferential treatment in the eyes of international organisations and agreements, meaning softer foreign trade rules and less strict carbon emissions standards, for instance. The 'developing' label also served Beijing's global ambition to present itself as the leader of the 'Global South' and deflect criticism of its increasingly imperialist behaviour. Beijing's contrived outrage was an illustration of how effectively it has gamed the international system, where following rules and agreements was seen as discretionary – or at best transactional.

Much was made in 2022 of Xi Jinping stacking the Communist Party's 205-member Central Committee with officials with backgrounds in science and technology – some eighty-one people, or 40 per cent of the total by one estimate.[49] However, this means nothing if they are not listened to, or do not have the courage to make themselves heard. As Singapore's Bilahari Kausikan points out, it is politicians who make the final decisions, and the skills of even the best civil servants or technocrats can be rendered irrelevant if they are subject to the whims and paranoia of an autocrat. 'All Xi Jinping's decisions of the last ten years have been about the Party. His solution to everything is more Party,' he told me.

'Is Xi himself particularly smart?' I asked.

'He is a genius at amassing power, but not particularly good at governance because his record during his first decade is mixed. I can't think of anything that he started which you can say is an unqualified success.'

Arguably, the more dictatorial Xi has become, the more inclined are Party functionaries to tell him what he wants to hear. The mounting problems of China's debt-ridden economy and Xi's demand for absolute loyalty to him and to the Party have punctured the myth of technocratic China.

Another characteristic of autocrats is that they cannot be wrong, and when gloomy figures cannot be manipulated or suppressed, the gloom must be blamed on someone else; they need a scapegoat, usually in the form of perfidious foreigners. In the summer of 2023, when the authorities scrapped the publication of increasingly dire urban youth unemployment statistics, state media accused Western politicians and media of engaging in 'cognitive warfare' by deliberately inflating concerns about the economy. A video posted on a social media account backed by China's state broadcaster claimed foreign news outlets cherry-picked statistics to make the economy look worse.[50] 'At the end of the day, they are fated to be slapped in the face by reality,' said a Foreign Ministry spokesman.[51] In a December 2023 statement, seen as a warning to Chinese economists and media, the Ministry of State Security, China's main spy agency, said there was a need to 'sing the bright theory of China's economy'. It warned that 'false theories about "China's deterioration" are being circulated to attack China's unique socialist system'.[52]

Data in China is first and foremost political, which means it must be made to fit the CCP's agenda. By early 2024, the Party was determined that the only window on what was happening with the economy and the country more broadly was to be its own, and foreign companies and investors would have to accept that or leave. It seemed to believe that supressing or manipulating gloomy data and banning its discussion could somehow improve the economic outlook. Those with a more forgiving attitude towards China's use and abuse of data argue that in spite of the debasement of statistics at every level, the country has still grown rapidly and prospered, and this is evident all around. After all, just look at the roads, the shops, the airports, the explosion of cars and travel – and behold the forests of shiny new cities that have sprouted all across China. Is that not overwhelming evidence of a country transformed whatever the quibbles over data? However, even those shiny new cities are not quite what they seem and tell another more disturbing story.

CHAPTER 5

Ghostly Monuments to Economic Madness

'I hope that our comrades and leaders will take
the lead in purchasing houses . . . If you've bought
one, buy two. If you've bought two, buy three.
If you've bought three, buy four.'

Deng Bibo, Party secretary of Shimen county,
Hunan province

Li Jun and her husband Liang Liang represented the aspirations of a generation of young Chinese as they chronicled on their social media account the excitement of buying their first property. Their story, which was followed by hundreds of thousands on Douyin (the Chinese version of TikTok), began when the couple scraped together enough money from savings and gifts from their parents to put down a 450,000 yuan (£50,000) deposit on a small apartment on the twenty-second floor of a thirty-three-storey building in the city of Zhengzhou in Henan province. They also took out a 1.02 million yuan (£112,000) mortgage, and, as is common in China, the property was bought off-plan – meaning it had not yet been built. They posted updates on the progress of their apartment, regularly visiting the site, and proudly telling their 400,000 followers, 'Among tens and thousands of lights in the city, finally there's a light that only shines for me.'[1]

Seven months after they placed the deposit, the developer, Sunac China Holdings, hit financial difficulties and suspended construction. The timing couldn't have been worse for Li and Liang, who were about to have their first child. Liang's pay had also been cut, and he sought extra income as a taxi driver as they struggled to pay rent on their existing property as well as the new mortgage repayments. Their posts became angrier and more disillusioned, and when they went to Sunac's sales office to demand a rebate they were entitled to, they were turned away and insulted. All this they documented, and in November 2023, as they attempted to livestream another confrontation with the developer, things turned ugly. Li ended up in hospital after she was assaulted, her phone snatched from her. By that time, the couple's posts were being shared by millions, topping the charts on Weibo, China's equivalent of Twitter/X. Their aspirations, as well as their treatment at the hands of uncaring and dishonest authorities resonated with their legions of followers. 'Liang Liang and Li Jun are just the tip of the iceberg; there are thousands of couples facing similar challenges,' said one blogger.[2] 'What you are posting is real life,' said another.[3] While a former journalist posted, 'This is to tell everyone, especially young people: the most diligent, law-abiding, and optimistic citizens do not deserve the China Dream, let alone others. Thanks to the couple for helping us see the cruel side of China's reality.'[4]

By late 2023, Li and Liang were on the point of giving up, suggesting in another post that they were abandoning the city and returning to their hometown with their daughter. 'Now we have our daughter. I'd rather have a peaceful life,' Li posted, using her personal social media account because by then their joint account chronicling their struggle had been blocked.[5] The Communist Party had taken note and its censors stepped in, deleting Li and Liang's videos along with supportive posts from their followers. 'Ordinary people like them are the majority, so the way things ended for them is particularly painful to us,' said one Weibo post that survived the crackdown. The developer promised that construction would continue – just as soon as it could sort out its colossal debts. By then, Sunac was not the only property company in deep trouble. By late 2023, companies accounting for 40 per cent of Chinese home sales had defaulted on their debts, leaving a trail of unfinished homes and unpaid suppliers and creditors.[6] A vast property bubble was fast deflating, exposing a financial system riddled with bad debt, a tidal wave of red ink that threatened to crash over banks and local governments, as well as the beleaguered developers – and in the process devastate the hopes and dreams of young couples like Li and Liang.

Around the time Li and Liang were beginning their journey towards property ownership, the Chinese internet was transfixed by other images that might have served as a warning about the state of the property market and of the health of developers behind a two-decade frenzy of construction. A video from Kunming, a city in southwest China, showed the destruction of fourteen tower blocks that had been sitting empty for seven years. It took forty-five seconds to bring them down, some wobbling precariously before crashing to the ground, engulfed in vast clouds of dust, while others appeared to simply disintegrate, collapsing in on themselves, like some ugly monster rapidly retreating underground. The complex was called Sunshine City and its demolition required 4.6 metric tons of explosives, installed at thousands of detonation points on the buildings, according to local news reports. Local residents turned up to watch the explosion, which was livestreamed on the website of a local newspaper.[7] Ownership of the blocks had passed between several developers, each of which had run out of money, though the official explanation was that they had broken building regulations and were 'illegal buildings' being 'forcibly demolished according to the law'.

The Kunming demolition was in September 2021, and over the next eighteen months, demolition videos went viral across Chinese social media. Users posted compilations of buildings toppling over, often stylised and set to dramatic music, while online sleuths traced them to multiple locations across China.[8] Early in 2022, it was reported that Evergrande, a troubled property developer, had been ordered to demolish thirty-nine buildings on the resort island of Hainan, for which the permits had been illegally obtained.[9] As China's property crisis deepened and its vast real estate bubble burst, the images fuelled speculation that the Communist Party was taking an axe to its forests of ghost cities – vast and empty metropolises that extend to every corner of the country. Figures on the precise number of empty homes are hard to pin down but are generally agreed to be enormous. One survey suggested 21 per cent of housing stock – or 65 million homes – are vacant.[10] The problem is particularly acute in the provinces, around what

China calls its second- and third-tier cities. Analysts have drawn
on a variety of economic data to come up with figures ranging from
50 million to as many as 100 million empty homes. Yet most homes
in these ghost cities had been sold, not to live in, but as investments
– for speculation. They were not rented out because in China that
reduces the value. So, they were left, abandoned in the hope that
their value will rise and they can be flipped for a decent profit, there
being few other rewarding investment opportunities.

On top of these ghost cities are an estimated 30 million unsold
or uncompleted properties of the type that Li and Liang thought
they had secured, abandoned as a result of the bursting property
bubble.[11] When these figures are added up it means that China has
as many as two empty properties for every member of the British
population. The speculation was powered over more than two decades by one of the biggest and most sustained rises in property
prices the world has ever seen, with the bubble inflated by a belief
it would never end.

During my time as a correspondent in China I developed a mor-
bid fascination with ghost cities. I found them especially surreal
because of the dramatic contrast with the usual bustle of China's
older cities. It was as if you'd landed on another planet, one devoid
of human life. Some consisted of endless eerie rows of ugly towers;
others were sprawling fields of villas. All were almost empty. There
was Kangbashi, an extension to the city of Ordos in Inner Mongolia,
built for 1 million people at the cost of $500 billion, complete with
museum, large library and theatre, all surrounding a deserted central square. There was a nine-storey hospital that during my visit
was treating just one person a day. But at least the buses ran on
time, down largely deserted streets and undeterred by the almost
complete absence of passengers. I met a student who exchanged an
empty campus by day for an evening job in an empty restaurant. 'I
can't wait to get out,' he told me. By night barely a light shone from
the windows of the monstrous high-rises. 'It's quiet, too quiet,' a
lonely policeman told me, but at least there was no crime.

Then there was Yujiapu, a new district of the port city of Tianjin,
built as a copy of Manhattan, and billed as the world's largest financial centre in the making. During my visit, construction had largely

ground to a halt and stray dogs roamed the dusty windswept streets in the shadow of the empty half-built shells of towering buildings, including a replica of the Rockefeller Center. Tianjin's 117 Tower was to be the world's sixth tallest skyscraper, part of another new business district with multiple residential and commercial towers, French and Italian style manor houses, a wine museum, extensive gardens and even a polo club. Construction of the 128-storey 'ghost scraper' began in 2008, but it is now a derelict and rusting eyesore, having never been completed or occupied. Another ghostly con-urbation near the southern city of Dongguan boasted the world's largest shopping mall, which was a familiar boast. Cavernous dusty halls, layer upon layer of meandering marble-lined walkways beside the shells of hundreds of shops, but not a soul to be seen. Wires hung from ceilings like an infestation of snakes. An artificial river wound through the complex, its water stagnant and dark green.

China also pioneered a bizarre brand of copycat architecture, and it is here that the ghosts were at their most surreal. About twenty miles southwest of Shanghai sat Thames Town, built as a replica of a British market town – right down to the cobbled streets, Victorian-style terraces, a mock-Tudor pub, random red telephone boxes, and a fish and chip shop. Most were shut during my visit, and the town was largely deserted apart from the occasional cou-ple posing for wedding photos, with whom it was popular. They posed beside statues that included Winston Churchill, James Bond (with a passing resemblance to Roger Moore) and Harry Potter on a broomstick. On the outskirts of Hangzhou, farmers were evicted to make way for a Chinese version of Paris, with a scale replica of the Eiffel Tower. Elsewhere, China built copies of Amsterdam, Venice and Madrid. A ninety-minute drive into the hills north of Beijing sat a clone of 'Jackson Hole'. The American original in Wyoming is known for its outstanding natural beauty, but during my visit to the Chinese version it was shrouded in smog so thick you could taste it. Security guards dressed in cowboy outfits trailed me as I explored the empty mock-rustic lodges. 'It's busy at the weekend,' one of them assured me.

China's property market only dates back to 1998, which is when urban households were first allowed to buy and own flats, unleash-ing huge pent-up demand on the back of rapid urbanisation.

Average prices increased fivefold between 1998 and 2021, albeit from a very low base.[12] Initially at least, the new homeowners were buying places in which to live, but sustained price rises soon empowered the speculators.

China's banks were only too happy to throw money at the developers to the extent that by late 2020, property-related lending accounted for an astonishing 39 per cent of bank loans.[13] Foreign investors also piled in, snapping up the bonds of the developers in the belief the boom would never stop and that ultimately the government would never let the property developers go bust. By the middle of 2021, developers had run up debts of $5 trillion, equivalent to almost a third of the country's GDP, according to Nomura, an investment bank.[14] Flush with cash, the developers bought land from local governments, for whom it became a vital source of revenue, accounting for around a third of their income.[15] They in turn obtained it from local farmers, who were often forced off their land with little compensation. All the while, this huge and tangled web of debt grew and ghost cities spread like a virus across the country, an inevitable consequence of an economic model that required property to be built at an ever greater rate and sold at an ever higher price. Over two decades the bubble was inflated to the point where real estate and related services became China's main economic driver, accounting for around 30 per cent of economic activity.

China even found an export market for these ghostly creations. In 2016, Country Garden, a troubled developer we will meet later in this chapter, launched Forest City, a massive $100 billion 'dream paradise for all mankind' in Johor on the southern tip of Malaysia. It was supposed to house 700,000 people, but by early 2024 was barren and largely empty, with few of the units in its thirty-storey tower blocks occupied. Stray dogs outnumbered people on a deserted beach dotted with 'Danger Crocodiles – No Swimming' signs.[16] It served as a reminder that it wasn't necessary to be in China to feel the impact of its property madness.

The Chinese authorities claim their original ghost cities are beginning to fill up, and point to Ordos, whose fortunes were boosted by the forced relocation of a number of top schools to the new district in an effort to turn it into an educational hub. Booming local coal mines also helped bring people to the area. Up to a quarter of the homes are now thought to be occupied – which triggered yet more speculative building.[17] It's hard to test those claims, but overall the notion that China's property ghosts are being banished is hardly credible, quite the contrary in fact as a bursting property bubble produces a further glut of tens of millions of unsold or uncompleted homes.

It's not that China's leaders were unaware of the dangers. 'Houses are built to be inhabited, not for speculation,' President Xi Jinping told the Communist Party congress in October 2017.[18] However, acting on that proved easier said than done, and as with any addiction, it was extremely difficult to kick the property habit. To many economists, a property tax seemed an obvious way of reducing speculation and cooling the market – China is just about the only major world economy which doesn't have one. Trials were set up, but then abandoned amid fears it might crash the market.[19] Eventually, the Party opted for a blunter tool: on the last day of 2020 it abruptly announced new lending rules for the property sector and home mortgages. The rules required domestic state-owned banks to cap property-related loans as a ratio of their total lending in the hope that this would limit banks' exposure to the sector while slowly taking air out of the bubble.[20]

Instead, the air rushed out. The first victim was the giant developer Evergrande which was unable to pay debts estimated at $300 billion, which made it the world's most indebted property company. It had more than 1,300 developments spread across 280 cities in China. By one estimate it had taken deposits for more than 1.5 million apartments, and riot police were deployed outside the company's Shenzhen headquarters where angry protesters gathered to demand their money back.[21] In December 2021, Fitch, a ratings agency, declared Evergrande in default after it failed to meet interest payments to international investors.[22]

Property prices slumped, sales fell and dozens of other developers defaulted. They were soon faced with a mortgage strike, a new sort of protest, silent but potentially highly damaging. Homeowners began banding together to withhold mortgage payments on delayed or unfinished projects, amid accusations that their money was being stolen or otherwise misappropriated.[23] They stopped payments on projects across China. Buyers typically bought off-plan, their deposits supposedly held in designated bank accounts, from which developers could withdraw in stages during construction. However, the banks were accused of colluding with developers and releasing the cash to fund relentless building elsewhere, or else to pay off other debts.

As the property crisis snowballed and the broader economy stalled, Xi Jinping decided he wanted his bubble back. The economy was faltering, and the Communist Party saw pumping the property bubble back up as a way of providing a short-term fix. It was also acutely aware that the biggest victims of the bursting bubble were China's aspiring middle class, for whom property was the biggest store of wealth, with an estimated 80 per cent of family wealth in China tied up in property. The government promised to bail out developers and to make it easier for them to obtain funds.[24] In an abrupt change of tone, Ni Hong, China's minister of housing and urban-rural development, said he wanted to see stalled projects moving again and easing restrictions where necessary in order to, 'promote high-quality development of the sector'.[25] A $28 billion special loan programme was launched to help developers finish stalled projects and 'ensure healthy development of the property market'.[26] The government introduced a package of measures to stimulate home buying, including lower mortgage rates, reduced down payments and a raft of tax incentives.[27] Speculators, once shunned, were courted again, with all sorts of gimmicks rolled out. 'Buy one floor, get one free', ran an advertisement for one housing project in Anhui province,[28] while in Hunan a video went viral of a Communist Party official urging people to buy more apartments. 'If you've bought one, then buy two. If you've bought two, buy three. If you've bought three, buy four,' said Deng Bibo, at a real-estate fair.[29] In Zhejiang province, buyers were offered a discount of up to 8 per cent when purchasing ten or more homes, or up to 18 per cent off when buying as a group.[30]

'It's absolute madness,' said Gillem Tulloch, who has been credited with coining the term 'ghost city' more than a decade earlier, when he plotted their trail across China using Google Earth. To Tulloch, who runs GMT Research, an accountancy research firm based in Hong Kong, it came as no surprise that China was turning back to property for a quick economic fix. 'They don't know anything else. This is the model they've used to drive growth for two decades,' he told me.

More worrying for the Communist Party, it didn't seem to be working. In the six months from January to July 2023, sales of all real estate in China fell by 6.5 per cent. July 2023 sales were down a quarter from a year earlier, and 46 per cent down on the same month in 2021, although the Covid-19 pandemic also played a part.[31] Government data showing prices for new builds slipping just 2.4 per cent over two years from August 2021 (and 6 per cent for existing homes), was greeted with widespread scepticism. Data from property agents and other providers painted a far grimmer picture, with prices of existing homes falling by more than 15 per cent in prime urban neighbourhoods over that period, with some areas recording falls of up to a quarter.[32] Developers defaulted on more than $120 billion of bonds issued outside mainland China,[33] and offshore bonds in Chinese property firms were almost worthless.[34] Evergrande, which defaulted in late 2021, limped on for another twenty months, racking up losses of $81 billion. In August 2023 it formally filed for bankruptcy protection in the US while it sought to restructure overseas liabilities estimated at almost $20 billion.[35]

That same month Country Garden, the largest privately owned homebuilder in China, which was seen as one of China's safer developers, also missed payments on its international debts, sending shockwaves through Chinese and international stock markets. The company had liabilities of close to $200 billion and by one estimate had received payments for a million homes that were yet to be built.[36] Just two years earlier Yang Huiyan, the company's chair and its majority shareholder, was the richest woman in Asia, with a personal fortune of around $30 billion.[37] The crisis also swept up Dalian Wanda, the nation's biggest operator of shopping malls, which began selling assets and delayed debt redemptions in a bid to avoid bankruptcy.[38]

It was only ever a matter of time before the bursting of the property bubble hit the wider financial system. An early sign of the trouble ahead came in July 2022 with a run on a handful of provincial banks in Henan province. Four lenders suddenly suspended online cash withdrawals, freezing the deposits of thousands of people. The banks were accused of siphoning off the funds through illegal transfers and fictitious loans worth as much as 40 billion yuan (£5 billion). Angry depositors who tried to reach Zhengzhou, the provincial capital, were blocked from travelling when the authorities manipulated their Covid-19 health apps, which grounded those supposedly at risk of infection.[39] Those who did manage to get there were beaten and dragged away by security officials after they gathered in front of government buildings with banners that read, 'Henan banks, give me my money back', 'We are against Henan government's corruption and violence', and 'No deposits, no human rights'.[40] Some of the protesters suffered broken bones and eye injuries. The ugly scenes were recorded on numerous videos and photos, posted on Chinese social media, but quickly deleted by Communist Party censors.

The Henan violence highlighted an opaque but dangerous corner of Chinese finance – a vast and unregulated shadow banking system, estimated to be worth around $3 trillion, which is roughly the size of the British economy.[41] The shadow banks, which vary in size from small rural lenders to vast trust companies, initially emerged to serve a useful purpose; they provided finance to companies that struggled to get support from China's big state-owned banks, which have traditionally favoured state-owned companies, or other politically directed lending. However, property companies were among their biggest clients, with many of the loans now going bad. They also specialised in 'wealth management' products, deposits that typically offered retail investors far higher returns than regular investments at state banks but were not protected by China's deposit insurance scheme. They depended on a continuing flow of funds from new investors to pay off the existing ones – the classic definition of a pyramid scheme. They were also accused of colluding with powerful local businesses and the local authorities. Loans were typically made to well-connected firms or individuals with little or no due diligence – with property companies at the fore. There was scepticism about local government claims that the problems were all down to 'criminal gangs'. There was very little trust in the authorities, and with life savings at risk, the depositors felt they had little to lose in taking their anger to the streets.

In August 2023, the Communist Party's regulators faced their biggest challenge yet when an opaque Beijing-based financial giant called Zhongzhi Enterprise Group failed to pay out on dozens of its investment products. Once again depositors took to the streets, gathering outside the company's headquarters, though this time the police kept their distance. Zhongzhi and companies linked to it were among the country's biggest providers of wealth management products. Many were backed by housing projects and although precise figures were hard to come by the company had also been a big lender to the property sector.[42] The potential impact of the crisis at Zhongzhi dwarfed that of the Henan provincial banks; some 270 high-yield products with an estimated value of 39.5 billion yuan (£4.3 billion) were due to mature in 2023.[43] In a letter to investors in November 2023, Zhongzhi said it faced a shortfall of $36.4 billion and was 'severely insolvent' after 'internal management ran wild'.[44]

The rapidly unfolding crisis also threatened deeply indebted local governments, which sat at the heart of this mountain of interlocking debt. It wasn't just that their finances were highly dependent on selling land to developers, but they too had vast hidden debts as a result of the widespread use of opaque financing vehicles. The International Monetary Fund estimated that at the end of 2022 there was 66 trillion yuan (£7.2 trillion) of outstanding local government debt, equivalent to half China's GDP, but nobody knew for sure, not even the central government.[45] Over the summer of 2023, the Communist Party sent teams of inspectors around the country to try and discover the scale of the problem. Local administrations had used companies known as local government financing vehicles (LGFVs) to borrow money to pay for lavish infrastructure or other services, which they could not finance out of official budgets. These vehicles were controlled by the local authorities but not officially part of them, so they did not appear on their balance sheets. Banks and investors lent to the LGFVs because they assumed the central government would always bail them out. To further complicate this mad and entangled web of debt, it was revealed that in 2022 the LGFVs were the biggest purchasers of land. In other words, in order to prop up their revenues, local governments obliged their secretive investment vehicles to pay inflated prices to buy up land they could no longer sell to troubled property developers.[46]

Even after an unprecedented two years of falling sales and prices, property in China in 2023 remained two to four times more expensive relative to household income than in the rest of the world, and still accounted for a dangerously high proportion of the economy.[47] Yet the Communist Party seemed paralysed. That was evident at a meeting of the Party's ruling politburo, convened in summer 2023 to 'analyse the current economic situation'. Along with the usual bland assurances, it acknowledged, 'great changes in the relationship between supply and demand in China's real estate market'.[48] That must go down as one of the greatest of understatements. It omitted the usual language about houses being for living and not speculating; at that moment the Party didn't care who bought, just as long as it got its bubble back.

By late 2023, China's top 100 developers were recording sales a third down on the previous year.[49] In any functioning market economy, prices are largely determined by supply and demand, but not in China. As developers moved to cut prices further to revive sales, they ran into stiff resistance from existing owners, who demanded compensation for their losses – one residents' group accusing a developer of 'maliciously' lowering prices.[50] Local governments, fearing unrest, ordered developers to stop reductions. The result was an increasingly gummed up market. Developers were effectively bankrupt, but staggered on, with state-owned banks – themselves swimming in a sea of bad debt – ordered to provide sufficient credit to the property firms so that they could at least finish building the huge backlog of homes which had already been paid for.

Still, by the end of 2023, millions of home buyers who had sunk their savings into buying property off-plan – people like Li and Liang – were in limbo, while suppliers, contractors and construction workers went unpaid. The result was a steep rise in protests linked to property, amid allegations of fraud, theft and shoddy workmanship.[51] There were reports that local governments had been instructed to brace themselves for the social and economic impact of Evergrande's formal collapse, with other beleaguered developers lined up to take over its projects and the police ordered to pre-pare for further 'mass incidents', a euphemism for protests.[52] The company, which had been on life support for two years, scrapped attempts to negotiate a $35 billion restructuring plan.

Some analysts questioned whether Evergrande had ever really made any money, but instead had for years routinely overstated revenues and income. 'At some point, it appears Evergrande's pri-mary purpose became raising finance to fund its inflating balance sheet and keep the party going,' according to GMT, the Hong Kong accountancy research firm.[53] It had been technically insolvent for years, but in the looking-glass world of the Chinese economy, nobody seemed to care, not the company, not the CCP, or foreign investors, just as long as the property bubble continued to inflate. By early 2024, China's property sector had become a land of the living dead, with banks and local governments increasingly sucked into this zombified world of massive and interlocked debt. Not only was the property sector such a large part of the economy, but it was also a microcosm of the wider Chinese economy – a scary combin-ation of eyewatering debt, lack of transparency and diminishing returns on wasteful investment.

Xi Jinping seemed engaged in a giant game of whack-a-mole, seemingly terrified by the prospect of political instability should he let the zombies die. Instead, state-owned banks were ordered to pump yet more money into the developers and to roll over exist-ing local government debt with longer-term loans at lower interest rates.[54] The local authorities at the heart of this merry-go-round of toxic loans resorted to increasingly desperate measures to shore up their finances and hide the scale of their bad debts – one common trick was to secretly lend money to an asset-management company, which then used the money to buy the authorities' loans, shifting them off their books. An investigation in Hebei province revealed that almost all traffic fines issued in 2023 were bogus, while a local government in Guizhou had a local contractor arrested after she demanded the full payment of an invoice for building schools.[55] The banks themselves were under growing strain, and by the end of 2023 were putting bad loans up to sale at a record pace, a process that suggested soaring default levels.[56] For their part, traumatised would-be property owners resisted the incentives to get back into the market, seemingly stung by a broader economic downturn. Consumer defaults on everything from mortgages to business loans reached a record 8.54 million, compared with 5.7 million in 2020.[57]

Xi fell back on another tried and tested tactic – he looked for others to blame. Evergrande executives were arrested, and the authorities said they had taken 'criminal coercive measures' against 'many suspects' at Zhongzhi, the wealth management giant. Hui Ka Yan, who founded Evergrande in 1996 in the southern city of Guangzhou, vanished amid speculation that he had been taken away by police to an undisclosed location. Colleagues reported that he could no longer be contacted. The authorities accused Evergrande of inflating revenues by nearly $80 billion – an accusation that came as no surprise to more savvy analysts, who had long questioned its bookkeeping. Hui had been one of China's best-connected billionaires, rubbing shoulders with fellow tycoons in Hong Kong as well as Communist Party leaders in Beijing, with whom he celebrated the Party's 100th anniversary in July 2021. His assets included at least three private jets worth $236 million, two mansions on Hong Kong's Peak worth an estimated $204 million combined, and a sixty-metre superyacht, which he moored in Hong Kong's Gold Coast yacht club.[58] For twenty-five years, getting rich had indeed been glorious for Hui, but as he was now discovering, in Xi's China getting rich was extremely dangerous, with a growing number of business people vanishing into the Communist Party's network of secret jails.

Chapter 6

To Get Rich is Glorious – and Dangerous

'We were like fish who clean the teeth of crocodiles.
It was always dangerous, because at any time
they could bite your head off.'

Desmond Shum, exiled entrepreneur

The perils facing entrepreneurs in Xi Jinping's China are no better illustrated than by the case of Bao Fan. He appeared to know his days were numbered, and in the weeks before his disappearance the financier had been making plans to shift some of his fortune out of China. Unlike Evergrande's Hui Ka Yan, Bao did not make his billions in the wild property market, but instead sat at the critical juncture of finance and technology. The billionaire founder and head of China Renaissance, an investment bank, brokered some of China's biggest technology deals and, like an increasing number of rich Chinese, was exploring ways of moving his assets beyond the reach of the Chinese Communist Party.[1] On 16 February 2023, the bank announced that it had been unable to contact Bao, who served as chairman and chief executive. In a vaguely worded regulatory filing two weeks later, it said Bao was aiding an unspecified investigation being carried out by unnamed authorities. The assumption was that he had been detained by the CCP's anti-graft police and was being held in a 'black prison', somewhere in the Party's extensive network of secret detention facilities.

Bao worked for top international banks, including Morgan Stanley and Credit Suisse Group, before striking out on his own. Among his prolific dealmaking were mergers that formed Didi Global, a taxi-hailing app, and created Meituan, an e-commerce giant.[2] He has been described as possibly the 'best liked, best known person in the financial community in China,' with 'a lot of integrity'.[3] He was a familiar face on the international financial-conference circuit, and his detention sent shockwaves around the business elite in China and beyond. In February 2024, a year after his disappearance, China Renaissance issued a brief statement to the Hong Kong stock exchange saying Bao had stepped down as chairman and chief executive officer due to health reasons and planned to spend more time on his family affairs. There was no further information about his whereabouts, nor the accusations against him. He had simply vanished.

'You're just pawns in the game, you can be sacrificed at any time,' said Desmond Shum, a Chinese businessman and friend of Bao, now exiled in the UK. Shum recalled a dinner with Bao in Hong Kong, where he had been struck by the dealmaker's optimism about the future of China, something that in the end offered no protection. 'Now things look bad for him,' he told me. 'It can happen to even the most high-profile businessmen in China. Snap a finger and you're out.' Shum was speaking from painful experience, since his wife, who was also his business partner, disappeared in similar circumstances and he would almost certainly have been targeted too, had he not left China. I met Shum at a rambling old pub in a small and quintessentially English village just outside Oxford. In the warm sunshine of the beer garden, we drank craft ale and ate fish and chips. It was all a world away from the gritty Chinese business environment in which he once thrived, but his experience at the hands of the CCP was never far from his mind, likening entrepreneurs in China to fish who clean the teeth of crocodiles. 'It was always dangerous, because at any time they [the CCP] could bite your head off.'

'He and I share very similar backgrounds,' Shum recalled of Bao Fan. Both studied and worked in the West before returning to China to become part, they thought, of the economic miracle transforming their homeland. 'I too was optimistic,' Shum recalled. 'Everything was going in a positive direction.' He teamed up with Whitney Duan, a well-connected and high-flying businesswoman, who later became his wife. Among their biggest deals were the development of a massive air cargo facility at Beijing International

Airport and of the Bulgari Hotel in the city. Success meant pandering to the interests of the Party and navigating the often fuzzy and ever-changing rules for doing business. 'You stand up there in that economic landscape and you literally feel the ground shaking and shifting under your feet,' he told me. Most crucial of all for getting business done was the marriage of entrepreneurial talent to political connections – building relationships with Party leaders, their relatives and friends, in which Whitney Duan was a master. Their most important business partner and patron was Zhang Beili – or 'Auntie Zhang', as they called her – who was the wife of China's premier, Wen Jiabao. She received 30 per cent of any profit from their joint enterprises. As Shum writes in his memoir, *Red Roulette: An Insider's story of Wealth, Power, Corruption and Vengeance in Today's China*: 'Nothing was on paper: it was all done on trust. The arrangement generally followed the "industry standard". Other families of high-ranking Party members extracted a similar percentage in exchange for their political influence. The template was always fungible and could be tweaked to accommodate investment opportunities as they arose.'[4]

The immense wealth accumulated by Wen Jiabao's family, some $2.7 billion in assets, was exposed by the *New York Times* in a 2012 investigation.[5] With their political cover weakening, Shum and his wife argued about the best way forward and increasingly drew apart. They divorced in 2015, when Shum and their son moved to Britain. Duan stayed in China, convinced she could continue to do business, but two years later she vanished. Shum heard nothing from her for four years, but then early one morning, shortly before his book was to be published, she called him, saying she was on temporary release and asking him to cancel the book, a tell-all on the murky reality of doing business in China. She told him that 'slandering the state' could harm her and their son. He took that as a threat, but assumed she was acting under duress. He ignored the plea and went ahead and published. By the time I met Shum, Whitney Duan was regularly calling and able to talk to their fourteen-year-old son. Shum assumed she was out of detention, but still closely monitored and certainly not able to leave China.

Today Shum is amused when he reads rankings of China's wealthiest entrepreneurs, having concluded it is a dangerous list to be on. 'Two-thirds of the people on China's one hundred wealthiest list would be replaced every year due to poor business decisions, criminality, and/or politically motivated prosecutions, or because they'd mistakenly aligned themselves with a Party faction that lost its pull,' he writes in *Red Roulette*.[6] He believes Xi Jinping's much vaunted anti-corruption campaigns are first and foremost about burying political rivals. He maintains close contact with business people in China and at the time of our meeting estimated that half of an elite group of entrepreneurs and venture capitalists he is familiar with, some 140 people, had moved to Dubai, Singapore or west coast America. Everybody was trying to shelter their assets. 'People in the back of their mind worry about the CCP coming after their wealth, their assets, their wellbeing. So everybody builds a safety net outside,' he told me. The sense that China's super rich were in retreat was confirmed by annual listings from *Forbes*. The country had 495 billionaires on its annual World Billionaires List in 2023, down from 539 the previous year and a record 626 in 2021. However, that still placed mainland China second globally, behind only the United States, which had 735 billionaires in 2023.[7]

One of the most feared institutions in China is housed in a grey twelve-storey building, beyond a seven-foot high wall in downtown Beijing. It does not appear on maps and has no sign or logo to identify it. It operates entirely outside the official criminal justice system, yet its investigators can arrest, seize evidence and interrogate at will. It runs a network of secret prisons, where detainees can face prolonged solitary confinement, cut off from the outside world, with no access to family or lawyers.[8] This is the Party's Central Commission for Discipline Inspection (CCDI). Ostensibly it is an anti-graft body that oversees the CCP's 95 million members, but as the Party has extended its influence into all walks of life in China and increasingly overseas, so the CCDI enforcers have followed with an ever-broadening definition of 'ill-discipline'. Xi has turned it into his main instrument for controlling the Party and purging his enemies within it. Leaders before Xi periodically launched anti-corruption campaigns, which rarely targeted the most senior officials and usually quickly petered out. For Xi it has become a permanent rolling campaign against 'tigers and flies' (high ranking as well as junior officials); over ten years, the CCDI investigated and punished more than 4 million officials including nearly 500 at a senior level, and more than 900,000 members were expelled from the Party, about 1 per cent of its membership.[9] There have been reports of day-to-day government business grinding to a halt, with officials no longer sure how to navigate the traditional paths of power.[10] The scale of the black jails network, known as the *Liuzhi*, is a state secret, but by one estimate almost 60,000 people vanished into its grim cells between 2018 and 2021, many secretly detained for years without charge.[11]

Bao Fan was not the first billionaire to disappear into the *Liuzhi* system. In 2017, a Chinese Canadian businessman called Xiao Jianhua, one of China's richest people, was abducted from a luxury hotel in Hong Kong. He had been managing the wealth of the families of some of the country's communist elite, but clearly not the right ones.[12] He was not seen for five years before appearing in a Shanghai court in August 2022, which jailed him for thirteen years for corruption. Billionaire property tycoon Ren Zhiqiang vanished in 2020 after calling Xi Jinping a 'clown' over his handling of the Covid-19 pandemic. He was jailed for eighteen years on corruption charges after a one-day trial held later that year.[13] In early 2023, Li Hejun, who headed a vast solar-panel business and was once the country's richest man, was detained without explanation, as was He Jinbi, the head of one of China's largest copper-trading houses – and of course Evergrande's Hui Ka Yan, who we have already met. In November 2023, Chen Shaojie, the founder and chief executive of DouYu, one of China's leading game-streaming companies, vanished. The company, which is listed on America's Nasdaq stock market, confirmed it had 'lost contact' with Chen weeks earlier, following a raid by China's internet watchdog that accused the company of hosting 'porn and vulgar content'.[14] At the same time, Zhao Bingxian, nicknamed 'China's Warren Buffet' because of his prolific dealmaking, was barred from leaving the country and then he too disappeared, reportedly taken into custody, but again without official confirmation or explanation.[15]

This is just a small selection of cases where there is some limited information available, with enforced disappearances becoming an occupational hazard for China's business elite. Listed companies are obliged to disclose market-sensitive information to investors, and by the end of 2023 the message 'We have lost contact with our chairman' was becoming chillingly common. As Fred Hu, one of China's most prominent investors and economists, put it during a forum organised by Bloomberg in November 2023, 'This sense of insecurity, in my observation, in the Chinese entrepreneur community, really I have not seen it like this since 1978'. He was referring to the turbulent years just after the death of leader Mao Zedong and before China began to open up.[16]

While the network of CCDI black prisons is secret, Xi Jinping has not been shy about the anti-corruption campaign itself, which he has also used as a way of bolstering his popularity among the public, which has long viewed government officials as congenitally corrupt. Since 2016, the commission has aired an annual series of documentaries with titles such as *Zero Tolerance* and featuring a parade of officials confessing their misdeeds and expressing remorse, all accompanied by images of piles of cash, luxury condos and villas, expensive wines and top-end cars and watches.[17] The CCDI has a seemingly never-ending target list; during 2023, it shifted its focus from the 'hedonistic bankers' of the finance sector to top officials of the Chinese Football Association, whom we shall meet later in this book, to the healthcare industry, with 155 hospital chiefs reportedly under investigation by the summer.[18] Earlier campaigns targeted energy, technology and defence companies and officials. Judges and other legal officials have been swept up, as have top police officers. In September 2023, Li Shangfu, China's defence minister, vanished amid suggestions that he had been caught up in a scandal over the corrupt procurement of military equipment.[19] The CCDI has even turned on itself, with more than twenty of its own officials coming under investigation in early 2023, a move that was described as the Communist Party 'trying to keep the blade clean'.[20] All of which makes for good populist politics, especially at a time of growing economic strain, but a closer reading of the CCDI's own figures confirms Xi's real agenda. They show the CCDI giving increasing weight to political discipline, with violations including 'speaking ill of the party's policies', 'abandoning ideals and convictions', and 'being untruthful and disloyal to the party'.[21]

Transparency International's annual Corruption Perceptions Index in 2022 gave China a score of 45 for public sector corruption on a scale where 100 is very clean and 0 is highly corrupt. That was on a par with Cuba and Montenegro, and China was ranked sixty-fifth in an index where the higher the place, the less the graft.[22] However, it has been suggested that the bald metrics of corruption ignore its different varieties, that in China its nature has changed, that it is not always such a bad thing and can oil the wheels of commerce. As Yuen Yuen Ang, an associate professor of political science at the University of Michigan, argues: 'Over the past four decades, corruption in China has undergone a structural evolution moving away from thuggery and theft and toward access money. By rewarding politicians who serve capitalist interests and enriching capitalists who pay for privileges, this now dominant form of corruption has stimulated commerce, construction, and investment, all of which contribute to GDP growth.'[23]

She likens it to America's 'Gilded Age', which began in the 1870s, an era of crony capitalism as well as extraordinary growth and transformation. However, she recognises that, like steroids, 'access' corruption has produced unbalanced, artificial growth and has exacerbated inequality. Minxin Pei, a Chinese-American political scientist, also uses the label 'crony capitalism' for a system characterised by looting, lawlessness and collusion between Party and business leaders.[24] However, he argues that it is more destructive than individual corruption since it sits at the 'very foundations of the regime's monopoly of power'.[25] By this argument, campaigns to root out corruption from the system will never work, because corruption *is* the system, it is hard-wired into it. Another reason these campaigns fail is their lack of transparency and an absence of any independent oversight or accountability. Endemic corruption is the natural outcome of a system where the police, the courts and the media are all controlled by the Party and criticism and scrutiny are criminalised. Corruption campaigns in effect become games of musical chairs, shifting one faction from money-making opportunities, only to be replaced by another more favoured faction.

Foreign companies have also played the game. In 2016, JP Morgan, America's largest bank, paid $264 million to settle claims that its hiring practices in China violated America's Foreign Corrupt Practices Act. Over a seven-year period, under a scheme known internally as the 'Sons and Daughters Program', it hired around a hundred well-connected interns and full-time employees in China in an effort to build relationships with officials and win business.[26] To be fair to JP Morgan, during my time in China it was hard to find a foreign company that did not hire what were known as 'princelings' to smooth their business interests. However, under Xi Jinping, it became increasingly difficult to judge the strength and longevity of an individual's connections; as Xi stepped up the purge of his opponents, it was hard to predict who would be targeted next, and a 'princeling' asset one day could quickly become a liability the next.

If Bao Fan was China's most famous and respected financier before his disappearance, the broader business crown went to Jack Ma, the founder of the e-commerce giant Alibaba. The former English teacher was China's richest person for a while, with an estimated personal fortune of $35 billion. His rags to riches story was repeated in numerous glowing profiles, which portrayed him as the very personification of Chinese enterprise. 'Jack, more than any other, is the face of the new China,' wrote Duncan Clark in his glowing 'insider's account' of how Ma revolutionised the way Chinese people shop, and how he built an e-commerce giant rivalling Walmart and Amazon. He is 'the standard-bearer for China's consumer and entrepreneurial revolution', Clark stated.[27] He graced the World Economic Forum in Davos, dining with business and political leaders, as well as celebrities such as Leonardo DiCaprio, Kevin Spacey and Bono. Former US president Bill Clinton shared platforms with him. He was welcomed to Downing Street by then Prime Minister David Cameron, who appointed Ma to his business advisory group.[28] Ma and Tom Cruise lavished praise on each other at the Shanghai premiere of *Mission Impossible – Rogue Nation*, which was financed in part by Alibaba. The company's 2014 initial public offering on the New York Stock Exchange was the world's largest ever, raising $25 billion. He was also a member of the Communist

Party, but that was seen as a necessity for business in China, and he was known for his individuality and willingness to speak out on subjects others avoided.

In late October 2020, Ma seemed at the peak of his power and success. He was preparing for a $37 billion listing in Shanghai and Hong Kong of the Ant Group, a payments company he spun off from Alibaba, which valued Ant at more than $300 billion. It was meant to be the biggest share issue in history. Perhaps it went to his head, because he gave a speech to a high-profile financial forum in Shanghai criticising China's regulators and its state-owned banks, which he accused of having a 'pawn-shop mentality'.[29] He said the country needed bold new players to extend credit to the poor. A week later, less than forty-eight hours before the listing, it was pulled by the authorities, citing 'major issues'. Ma himself disappeared, and there were rumours that he too had been incarcerated in the black jails of the *Liuzhi* system, some even suggesting he was no longer alive.[30] He resurfaced three months later in a forty-eight second video address to a charity event in an unknown location in what was characterised by analysts as 'like a hostage video'.[31] In the years that followed, there were sporadic sightings – in Japan, Hong Kong, at a school in his hometown of Hangzhou. Friends were relieved that he was not in prison, but China's most high profile businessman had for all intents and purposes become a non-person.[32] He relinquished control of his companies, which faced a series of heavy fines for supposed regulatory lapses,[33] and in March 2023, it was announced that Alibaba was to split into six different entities.[34]

The move against Ma and his companies was the starting point of a broader crackdown against China's nominally private technology giants, thirty-four of which were called to a meeting with regulators and told to rectify 'anti-trust activities'.[35] Tencent (internet conglomerate), Meituan (food delivery), Pinduoduo (e-commerce), Didi (ride hailing) and Oriental Education (tutoring) were among those which faced fines or other restrictions. Once-celebrated entrepreneurs joined Jack Ma in stepping down and out of the limelight.[36] These actions were variously described as anti-trust crackdowns, data security overhauls or efforts to curtail capitalist 'excess' in line with vague new Communist Party slogans promoting 'common prosperity' and preventing the 'disorderly expansion of capital'. Some commentators in the West interpreted these actions as part of a global push-back against the monopoly power of Big Tech – it came as American regulators were taking aim at Facebook and Google. There may have been an element of this, but China's moves against the tech companies were primarily about power, the tightening of CCP control over the companies and their vast stocks of data. This was made more explicit in early 2024, when Chinese state media reported that the CCP would play a bigger role in steering the country's technology industries – part of a broader policy to replace foreign technology with homegrown alternatives.[37]

In practice, all Chinese companies – whatever their nominal ownership – are beholden to the Party by a series of laws, including the National Security Law (2015), Cyber Security Law (2017) and Intelligence Law (2017). The latter, for instance, mandates that all Chinese companies and citizens support, assist and cooperate with Chinese national intelligence efforts and guard the secrecy of that work.[38] There is no mechanism for Chinese companies to refuse the CCP's requests. That the Party felt the need to tighten control further should be seen in the light of the growing technology war with the US and the West in general, and Xi Jinping's paranoid prioritising of security over all else – even at the cost of crimping the country's most innovative companies and bringing to heel its leading entrepreneurs. As the dust from the crackdown began to settle, those who had come through relatively unscathed scrambled to heap praise on their tormentor. Among an apparently coordinated series of statements, Tencent founder Pony Ma said he was 'extremely excited and deeply inspired' by President Xi Jinping's plans for private business.[39] And Lei Jun, co-founder of Xiaomi, a smartphone company, and more recently an electric vehicle entrepreneur said, 'the policies are a guiding light for the private sector.'[40]

However, behind these increasingly desperate expressions of loyalty lay fear. As Xi tightened his grip, China became an increasingly inhospitable and dangerous place to do business. The 'private sector' is a tricky concept in China; on paper, it accounts for the majority of economic activity, but most of the largest companies remain state-controlled, are the favoured recipients of loans from state banks and are still regarded by the Party as the bedrock of the economy. The distinction between apparent ownership and actual control can be murky. There are Party cells in all nominally private firms, which play a growing role in directing management. In early 2024, it was reported that Chinese companies had begun setting up in-house military units, a throwback to the days of Mao, and that what began as a practice within state-owned companies had extended to the private sector.[41] Against this background, those who accumulated assets by fair means or foul stepped up efforts to move their wealth out of the country and beyond the reach of the CCP. They were able to turn to a vast and booming industry to facilitate this capital flight – arguably one of the biggest and most creative businesses in China.

Luis, not his real name, was an expert on the business of illicitly shifting money. That's why he preferred anonymity, and when I met him he was in his early sixties and attached to the Macau police. He carried the title special investigator, though he no longer did much investigating and nothing he'd describe as special. He'd worked in and around Macau's casinos for three decades, and witnessed the territory become the world's gambling capital, with a turnover before the Covid-19 pandemic that was six times that of Las Vegas. He'd been a go-to investigator against the Triads, China's organised crime syndicates, and enjoyed regaling me with stories of the Triad wars of the mid-1990s, when the gangs were fighting for control of the casinos' lucrative VIP rooms. He was Portuguese, and when Portugal handed back Macau to China in 1999, he was pushed aside along with many other colonial-era officers. Chasing Triads also became more difficult because many of these 'patriotic' societies had long-standing links to the Communist Party. However, he stayed on, not seeing much future in near-bankrupt Portugal, consigned to a desk job in the police force of China's new Special Administrative Region of Macau.

It was 2016 when we met and I was researching a book, which became my first novel, *Beijing Smog*. I asked Luis whether it was possible to disappear in Macau, to hide out without being traced. 'Massage parlour', he replied without missing a beat. 'Open twenty-four hours, no registration, no questions. Great facilities. Stay as long as you like as long as you are using their services.' So I made a massage parlour a refuge for one of my characters, who was on the run from the mob, and I also gave Luis a small role in the book. He was also an expert on money laundering, and explained how Macau played a key role in shifting cash out of China. He took me down a road of upmarket jewellers, pointing to a luxury watch with a price tag of $75,000. 'It's probably been bought several times without ever leaving the window,' he told me, explaining that one popular scam was to pay for watches or other jewellery using a Chinese credit card denominated in Chinese currency, then immediately pawn it back for foreign currency. The jeweller would pay $70,000 dollars in cash or in the form of a bankers draft, the $5,000 being commission. The dollars (or Macanese Pataca or Hong Kong dollars) could be paid into a local bank account in Macau or Hong Kong, which readily accepted cash, with some left aside for gambling in any of Macau's forty-one casinos.

Other laundering services were offered by junkets, which Luis described as 'sort of travel agents with a nasty streak'. Gambling is illegal in mainland China, so the junkets acted as informal bankers, providing credit and collecting debts. They also sold casino trips and chips in China for Chinese yuan, which could then be used for gambling or else cashed in for Hong Kong dollars (the principal currency of the casinos), when the punters got to Macau. Minimum fee, around 20 per cent. The reason for all this was China's tight currency controls, which only allow citizens to convert $50,000 worth of yuan into foreign currencies for transfer out of the country each year.

Macau was just one face of the vast industry that emerged to circumvent these controls and was particularly popular with corrupt officials and smaller-scale hustlers. The industry has been extremely successful, and capital flight from China is estimated at around $0.5 trillion a year, which the CCP in spite of periodic clampdowns has been largely unable to plug.[42] Across China, there has been an explosion in 'consultancy' services specialising in obtaining investment or education visas as a conduit for shifting money abroad.[43] Underground banking networks provide similar services, and cryptocurrencies are another route. There was an explosion in 'smurfing' services, whereby cash was broken down into smaller amounts and sent abroad using a network of bank accounts for hire. As the economy deteriorated, middle-class Chinese of more modest means joined the clamour for a foothold overseas – for their assets and increasingly for themselves. During 2023, more than 37,000 Chinese nationals were detained on the border with Mexico, attempting to make the illegal crossing into the US, according to US Customs and Border Protection – a figure that was 10 times pre-pandemic levels.[44] Among those reportedly making the costly and treacherous journey were a disproportionate number of middle class Chinese, including entrepreneurs and small business owners – a measure it seemed of their dim situation at home.

Richer individuals generally had more choice, as did companies, which made widespread use of accounting devices to disguise the flow of funds in and out of China. Hong Kong, just across the Pearl River from Macau, was also a key facilitator, as we shall see later. Shortly before his disappearance, the billionaire dealmaker Bao Fan had been looking to set up a 'family office' in Singapore as a means of shifting his assets. That city-state was seen increasingly by China's beleaguered rich as the new Switzerland, a safe, discreet and welcoming destination for their wealth – though there were already signs of unease in Singapore about the wave of Chinese money sweeping over the island.

CHAPTER 7

Escape to Singapore

'There's no confidence any more. It's very
disillusioning for Chinese entrepreneurs. Suddenly
you're living in a society where there's no recourse.
They can pressure you, pressure your family. You
realise what sort of country you're living in.'

Bilahari Kausikan,
Singapore's former top diplomat

According to the short video posted on TikTok, the 10,000-square-foot house was on sale for 39 million Singapore dollars (£25.5 million). It came with an underground garage for six cars, a private swimming pool and a mooring for a yacht. However, it was not the house itself that attracted most attention online, but its ostentatious collection of luxury bags, watches and shoes, said to be worth an additional 10 million Singapore dollars (£5.8 million). An agent for the property said the collection was not included in the sale price, and that the owner had already received five offers for his house, most of them from China.[1] The house was in Sentosa Cove, an exclusive development on Sentosa Island, off the southern coast of Singapore's main island. 'Little Monaco', as it is sometimes called, had become a magnet for wealthy Chinese nationals seeking to move their families and businesses out of China.

Early one morning in June 2023, I took the sleek air-conditioned monorail to Sentosa, connecting to an even more chillingly air-conditioned courtesy bus across the island. Sentosa means peace and tranquillity, though during the Second World War it had been a British military base and then after the fall of Singapore it became a Japanese penal colony. The Singapore government has turned it into a playground of hotels, spas, beaches, golf courses and theme parks. The bus dropped me at a sleepy marina near the main entrance to Sentosa Cove, which sits beyond security barriers, and I slipped in behind a group of domestic helpers who had been out to buy provisions. The Cove's tree-lined roads were bristling with surveillance cameras, hanging from poles like bunches of bananas. I walked into a section called Paradise Island and along a road called Ocean Drive, which bends around a lagoon and is intersected with waterways lined with private moorings and luxury yachts. A gardener pruned carefully manicured hedges and trees, amid which sat Balinese-style sculptures. Another languidly cleared the pathways of dust and leaves with broad and mechanical sweeps of his wide broom. They wore long-sleeved shirts and trousers and wide-brimmed hats to protect them against the sun. This is the only area in Singapore where foreigners are allowed to buy landed property – houses and bungalows. Sales slowed early in the Covid-19 pandemic, only to come surging back – with Chinese nationals at the fore. At the time of my visit, the sales of condominiums, which foreigners can buy without restrictions, had also exploded across the city-state. Residential property prices overall rose 8.4 per cent in 2022 (following a 10.6 per cent rise in 2021), a trend that continued into 2023. Prices and rents surpassed those in Hong Kong to make Singapore the priciest property market in the region.[2] In 2022, buyers from China bought more condominiums than those from any other country.[3] Prime residential rents also surged, by more than 40 per cent in the eighteen months to July 2022, according to a survey by Savills, an international property agent.[4]

The opulent homes of Sentosa Cove seemed quiet, though it was still early. I wondered whether there was life beyond the heavy shutters and curtains, or whether this luxury hideaway was a bolthole, an insurance policy taken out by rich Chinese owners, given the Chinese Communist Party's increasing hostility to wealth and business. A threefold increase in annual membership fees in as many years at the coveted Sentosa Golf Club, to S$840,000 (£486,000), suggested many were availing themselves of the local facilities.[5] I spotted Porsches, Jaguars, Mercedes, Ferraris and Bentleys nestling under car ports monitored by yet more surveillance cameras. It is not easy to buy a car in Singapore; before you can even head to the showrooms you must buy a certificate of entitlement, which represents a right to own a vehicle and to use the roads for ten years. These are subject to a bidding process, so prices fluctuate according to demand. During my visit they reached a record of S$120,000 (£69,000). Many of the homes in Sentosa Cove had multiple high-end vehicles, bunches of luxury marques peering from under their shelters. Glancing at another constellation of surveillance cameras, I decided it was time to leave. It was clear the super-rich of Sentosa Cove prized their privacy and their security – and their cars.

I left the island and took the metro to Redhill, an area to the south of the city centre. At first, I wondered if I was at the right place, since No. 1 Leng Kee Road was a small Taoist temple, painted in vibrant oranges and reds and dwarfed by towering public-housing blocks. At the side of the temple stood an aluminium incinerator in which lucky money – wads of fake bank notes – was burned as offerings during festivals. A caretaker directed me towards my destination, another place of pilgrimage, this one for those with wads of real money to burn. Leng Kee Road is Singapore's motor showroom alley, and not just any showrooms. McLaren, Ferrari, Lamborghini, Ducati, Maserati, Lexus, Bugatti, Jaguar, Aston Martin, Rolls Royce, Bentley. They hit you in rapid and almost dizzying succession beyond the temple. I entered the Bentley showroom. 'It's the Flying Spur,' explained a salesperson as I gingerly opened the door of a limo and admired the sleek leather seats and space-age console of their latest offering. 'As it stands it's 1.4 million dollars; customised, you're talking more than two million,' she told me. I did a quick calculation – that was between £810,000 and £1.16 million. She told me the waiting list was now six to eight months, but that last year had been crazy.

'Very nice,' I said, which it was.

'Sit inside,' she said, which I did. She quickly sensed that it might be a little beyond my price range, which it certainly was.

'Who is your typical customer?' I asked.

'China,' she said without hesitation. 'Mostly from China. Price doesn't seem to put *them* off.'

It was the same story for Rolls Royce, where sales were running at record levels in Singapore, driven overwhelmingly by Chinese nationals.[6]

In perhaps the most ostentatious display of conspicuous motor consumption, a fifteen-storey, four-column luxury car 'vending machine' was doing a roaring trade in the city's Jalan Bukit Merah district. With a push of a button in the showroom the supercars move up or down, and your chosen Bentley, Ferrari, Lamborghini or Porsche (all in various vintages) presents itself to you like a packet of crisps or a cola.[7] At night, the brightly lit tower resembled a child's Hot Wheels set of toy cars, attracting scores of tourists; by day the biggest group of buyers were Chinese nationals. It was the same story in the luxury shopping malls of Orchard Road, and in top-end restaurants, some of which were booked out weeks in advance. International schools faced soaring demand – with one vice-principal saying that half his new students were from China.[8] Singapore is no stranger to conspicuous wealth – the 2018 Hollywood movie *Crazy Rich Asians* was largely set here – but at the time of my visit, the wave of Chinese money sweeping across the city-state was raising eyebrows, with many posing the question, was it a blessing or a curse?

Bayfront Law's swish offices are on the fourteenth floor of a high-rise office block in Singapore's financial district, its large windows giving a picture-postcard view over the southern part of the island. It was a clear, cloudless morning when I visited, with countless ships dotting the horizon waiting to come into port. Ryan Lin pointed to the distant edge of Sentosa Island. 'I had one client who spent 20 million on a bungalow, tore it down and spent another 20 million building a new one. It's mental,' he said, shaking his head. Lin advises wealthy investors looking to shift assets to Singapore. 'It was crazy. It was mad,' he said of the last two years. One of his specialities is setting up 'family offices'. These innocuous-sounding entities are financial structures, tax-efficient 'wrappers' as they call them in the wealth management business. 'It's essentially a financial arrangement, an investment vehicle for managing wealth,' he explained. 'It's a wrapper and it's up to you what you put into it.' Lin told me he had set up seventy to eighty over the past two years. 'Around 90 per cent have come from China. They come in all shapes and sizes – old wealth, high tech, mobile game entrepreneurs.' At the time of our meeting there were estimated to be around 1,400 family offices in Singapore, a number that had doubled over two years, the main engine of growth being Chinese nationals.

The experience of draconian Covid-19 lockdowns in China and Xi Jinping's crackdown on tech companies, and hostility to private business more broadly, were driving the exodus from China. 'They're thinking, "my money in China soon might not be my money any more. What will happen to me now?",' Lin said. 'It's about peace of mind. You want to put your money somewhere that is relatively safe and not subject to the vicissitudes of onerous policies.' The Communist Party's crackdown in Hong Kong was also driving money to Singapore, he told me. Hong Kong was popular among rich Chinese nationals as a place to park their wealth while it enjoyed semi-autonomy and British-bequeathed legal protections, but now, 'Hong Kong is becoming less and less distinguishable from the rest of China.'

The disappearance of Bao Fan, who had been looking to set up his own family office in Singapore, shook China's wealthy – and sent a further surge in business to those facilitating their departure. If this could happen to such a high-profile figure, they reasoned, it could happen to any of us. There was growing fear that the walls were closing in and they had to make plans before it was too late – a fear that was borne out by the increased use by the CCP of exit bans against business people. This has long been a tool used by the Party against dissidents and millions of people are barred from leaving China, but the focus was widening, with many unaware they were blacklisted until they reached the airport.[9] 'For sure the uncertainty over government policies towards business and emigration, potential exit taxes and the difficulties of renewing passports, stricter and stricter capital controls – all these things make any financially independent individual consider having an alternative plan in place as soon as possible,' according to Dominic Volek, head of private clients at Henley & Partners, an investment migration consultancy. The company advises wealthy individuals on the best and most welcoming routes to obtain residency and citizenship by investment, and it too was seeing a surge in enquiries from China.

I spoke to Volek shortly after Henley published its annual Wealth Migration Report, which showed China leading the world in the number of lost millionaires. It predicted China would see a net loss of 13,500 'high net worth individuals' (those with investible wealth of more than US$1 million) in 2023, up from 10,800 the previous year.[10] He told me the figures were probably an underestimate since they only showed those who had actually moved and stayed in their new country for more than half a year. It excludes the many wealthy individuals who acquired residence rights outside China, but had not yet relocated, still hedging their bets. 'For sure, the vast majority of our clients in China are looking for a Plan B, some sort of insurance policy against political or economic volatility,' he said. Singapore was popular because of its low taxes, good schools and political stability, as well as strong linguistic and cultural links to China – not forgetting the booming wealth-management industry to make it all happen. Until March 2023, when thresholds were raised, the city-state had a global investor programme under which foreign investors could obtain permanent residency by putting at least S$10 million (£5.8 million) into a new or existing business, or at least S$2.5 million (£1.46 million) through a fund that invests in local companies.[11] After two years as a permanent resident, they could apply for citizenship – and a coveted Singaporean passport.[12] In its annual global passport rankings, Henley & Partners in July 2023 gave Singapore the number one spot.[13] The passport power index is based on the number of destinations passport holders can visit without a visa, with Singapore hitting 192, ahead of Germany, Italy and Spain in joint second with 190; China was ranked 63rd in the index, just ahead of Belarus and Lesotho.[14]

Taking out insurance against a capricious Communist Party and protecting their wealth wasn't the only reason for the rush to Singapore. Many Chinese companies were doing it for broader strategic reasons. With corporate China coming under more scrutiny in the West, many Chinese companies saw setting up shop in the city-state as a way of appearing less Chinese. It was a way of fudging their identity and obscuring the true control of the company – a practice that was dubbed 'Singapore washing' by financial professionals. By one estimate as many as 500 Chinese companies quietly redomiciled or registered in Singapore during 2022 in what was described as an 'acute' rush to establish holding companies to future-proof their businesses.[15] 'They know sensitivities arise if

they remain Chinese, so they market themselves as international,'
one wealth manager said.[16]

Among Singapore's highest profile Chinese companies are Shein,
a rapidly growing fast-fashion retailer, and TikTok, the short-video
sharing app. Shein moved its HQ to Singapore in 2022, and its
chief executive officer became a permanent resident. In 2023, the
company, which still manufactures most of its products in China,
bought the British brand Missguided.[17] In 2023, Neil Shen, China's
most prominent tech investor, opened an office for his $56 billion
venture capital firm and became a permanent resident.[18] TikTok,
which moved to the city-state in 2020, has played up its Singapore
identity in the face of growing scrutiny from the West and fears the
Chinese Communist Party might harvest the company's data and
snoop on users. It has argued that being headquartered in the city-
state and led by a Singaporean chief executive officer, Shou Zi Chew,
is evidence of its arm's-length relationship with its Beijing-based
parent ByteDance, and from ByteDance's obligations to the CCP.
Critics argue that the Singapore presence is essentially cosmetic,
that Shou's decision-making power is limited, and that effective
control over strategy is still exercised from Beijing.[19]

I visited Singapore shortly after the Shangri-La Dialogue, an annual
security forum hosted by the International Institute for Strategic
Studies, that in 2023 was attended by the United States and Chinese
defence ministers, among many others from the world of global
security. The forum took place amid growing US concern about
aggressive and dangerous military intimidation by Chinese forces in
the South China Sea, where Beijing has extended and fortified disputed islands. 'We do not seek conflict or confrontation, but we will
not flinch in the face of bullying or coercion,' US Defense Secretary
Lloyd Austin told the forum. China's recently appointed defence
minister, Li Shangfu, was a general in the People's Liberation Army
before his promotion and had been under US sanctions since 2018
over the purchase of combat aircraft and equipment from Russia's
main arms exporter, Rosoboronexport. Li, who disappeared two
months after the summit and was subsequently sacked without
explanation, refused to formally meet Austin, accusing the US
of having a 'cold war mentality'.[20] In his own speech he quoted

approvingly from a Chinese song: 'When friends visit us, we welcome them with fine wine. When jackals or wolves come, we will
face them with shotguns.'[21]

Washington was pushing for what it called 'guardrails' on the
relationship, the sort of hotlines and military-to-military contacts
that existed between the United States and the Soviet Union during
the last Cold War and which were designed to prevent confronta-
tions from spiralling out of control.[22] However, Beijing was resisting.
The Americans believed their relationship could be compartmen-
talised, and whatever the deep and multiple differences – on trade,
technology and other economic matters, for instance – it was in the
interests of both to stabilise the immediate security situation, which
was fraught with danger. China has never seen it that way; in the
eyes of Beijing not only is everything connected and transactional,
but stand-alone 'guardrails' without wider concessions risked freezing a status quo it was determined to challenge. This transactional
attitude is familiar to those dealing with China in multiple other
areas, including climate change and international debt relief.

The Shangri-La Dialogue derives its name from the Shangri-La
Hotel in Singapore, and since it began in 2002 has become one of the
world's most important independent security forums – underlining
the fact the city-state of just 6.2 million people is a heavyweight
in international affairs. Sitting at the meeting point between the
strategically vital Malacca Strait and South China Sea, Singapore
has been able to be a close strategic partner of the United States,
while at the same time maintaining a close relationship with China.
Its approach to foreign affairs has been characterised as 'ruthlessly
practical and unsentimental'.[23] Though its efforts to avoid getting
caught up in the geopolitical competition between the two countries was being tested as never before.

'What we are witnessing is the clash of two delusions,' said
Bilahari Kausikan, the man who for many years was at the heart of
Singapore's canny foreign policy. 'There grew the assumption on the
Western side that as China reformed its economy, its politics would
also change. Nobody was delusional enough to think it would
become a carbon copy of any Western system, but that was the
assumption,' he told me. As for China's delusion, 'They really began
to think that the history is ours, comrades. They thought, "Ours is

a superior system, the West is in decline. It is an irrevocable and absolute decline", and between these delusions we have got to the mess where we are now.' Kausikan worked for thirty-seven years in Singapore's diplomatic service, spending considerable time in the company of Chinese envoys. He quickly realised that China's system was so opaque and centralised that many of the senior envoys he was dealing with had as little idea of what was really going on at the top of the Communist Party as he did.

He said he often imagined economic policymaking in China as one giant game of whack-a-mole, which had become more frenetic as the problems intensified. 'They need a new balance between control and market efficiency, but they haven't been able to figure it out or find the courage to implement it. Why? Because more market, more economic efficiency, by definition means less political control – and most of Xi Jinping's moves have been in the other direction, towards more Party control.' One result has been growing disillusionment among China's entrepreneurs, now looking to leave the country, many of them for Singapore. 'There's no confidence any more. It's very disillusioning for Chinese entrepreneurs. Suddenly you're living in a society where there's no recourse. They can pressure you, pressure your family. You realise what sort of country you're living in. They are not going to rebel, but there's no confidence.'

The first Singapore story I ever covered as a young foreign correspondent in the region was the 1995 trial of 'rogue trader' Nick Leeson, who was jailed for six-and-a-half years for his part in the collapse of Barings Bank, Britain's oldest merchant bank. He admitted to two charges of fraud in running up losses of £827 million and served four years of his sentence in Singapore's Changi prison. Some commentators were surprised at how tough Singapore was on Leeson, but the city-state was an emerging financial centre and determined to protect its reputation as a clean and professional place for business. Years later, I covered another story that challenged the reputation of the city-state. A red Ferrari driven by a young Chinese national, an entrepreneur who ran a software development company, jumped a red light at 4.15 a.m. travelling at 178kmh (110 mph). It collided with a taxi, killing the taxi driver and his passenger, as well as the Ferrari driver. The horrific crash triggered outrage against rich and entitled Chinese nationals.

Both incidents came to mind when the Singapore government moved to tighten controls over the wave of money and migrants entering the country from China, mindful of the wider reputational and political risks it was running. The ruling People's Action Party dominated post-independence politics in Singapore, but it was still sensitive to criticism of skyrocketing property prices and rentals, and uncomfortable with questions over precisely what the migrants were contributing to the local economy and where the money was coming from. There may also have been wider geopolitical concerns, with Singapore sensitive to suggestions it was providing a bolthole for rich Chinese to sidestep strict capital controls and escape the clutches of Xi Jinping. The Monetary Authority of Singapore reportedly asked global banks to keep quiet about wealth inflows coming from China due to these political sensitivities.[24] The authorities also hiked the threshold for the global investor programme[25] and doubled to 60 per cent the stamp duty for foreigners buying property.[26] Wealth managers came under pressure to scrutinise more closely the sources of wealth of those seeking to open family offices. 'The government is very careful. They are calibrating and calibrating,' said Ryan Lin at Bayfront Law. 'It takes a year now to set up a family office. Used to be half that time.' Lin said he was seeing a slowdown as a result. 'It is still substantial, but not as mad as last year,' he told me. The emphasis was now on quality over quantity.

In November 2023, Singapore proposed a new law to more closely scrutinise significant investments in sectors deemed critical to national security, because of what Trade Minister Gan Kim Yong described as the 'increasingly complex economic environment'.[27] This followed a new foreign interference law, Prime Minister Lee Hsien Loong warning, 'We must actively guard against hostile foreign influence operations.'[28] In February 2024 it was used for the first time against a well-connected Hong Kong-born Singaporean, Philip Chan, who had 'shown susceptibility to be influenced by foreign actors and willingness to advance their interests'.[29] While visiting Beijing, Chen had declared that the Chinese diaspora, wherever they may be, was duty-bound to 'tell China's story well'.

Under Xi Jinping, the CCP has blurred the lines between ethnicity and citizenship, asserting that no matter where they live or what passport they carry, the duty of overseas Chinese is first and foremost to the motherland – by which it means the Communist Party. To this end, the CCP has made an increasingly assertive pitch to overseas Chinese communities, business people and academics, and has invested heavily in community organisations and local Chinese-language media. This has been particularly unnerving for Singapore, which although having a majority ethnic Chinese population, is highly protective of its multiracial identity and cohesion, which it wants to protect from covert CCP activity. It was also mindful of the careful, though fragile, balancing act it had maintained between China and the United States.

In September 2023, the threat from dirty money came into sharp focus when police raided luxury addresses across the city, seized assets worth S$2.4 billion (£1.4 billion) and rounded up ten people they suspected of belonging to a multi-billion-dollar money laundering ring.[30] Two were arrested at a luxury bungalow in Sentosa Cove. The assets included bank accounts, cryptocurrencies, cash in multiple currencies, 68 gold bars, 294 luxury bags and 164 luxury watches. Police also seized 110 properties, 62 vehicles, 546 pieces of jewellery and 204 electronic devices such as computers and mobile phones. The case captivated and stunned Singapore, laying bare a darker side of finance in a city that prized its image as a clean and safe place for business. All ten of those arrested originated from China, although they held a variety of passports, ranging from Cyprus to Cambodia. It underscored a growing fear that much of the money rolling in from China might be of questionable provenance. As Singaporeans digested the scandal, they could perhaps draw some comfort from the knowledge that their own problems with dirty money paled beside those of Southeast Asian countries to the north, along the Mekong River, where Chinese organised crime was thriving with apparent impunity.

CHAPTER 8

China's Criminal Empire
on the Mekong

'They are not afraid of anything because they pay,
and they pay much. They can buy the police, they can
buy the court, they can buy the judge. They can buy
everything. So they have no fear.'

Chuwit Kamolvisit, Thai anti-corruption crusader

Early summer 2023 was a busy period for the police in Thailand. At the end of May, Thai investigators working with agents from America's FBI claimed to have bust a major gang of online fraudsters, who conned gullible investors in Thailand, the United States and Britain out of $288 million. Journalists were invited to photograph the gang leaders, a Chinese couple aged thirty-one and twenty-five, as they sat uneasily at a table stacked with cash and the land title deeds for several properties they'd invested in, as well as the mobile phones and computers that were the tools of their trade.[1] The couple, who were arrested at their luxury home in Prawet, a district to the southeast of Bangkok, had allegedly lured their victims to invest in fake cryptocurrency and other questionable assets.

Over the following days, more raids took place in the capital and in the northern Thai city of Chiang Rai. One gang created fake social media accounts and apps claiming to be charitable organisations and solicited donations for restoring temples and other worthy causes.[2] Another set up fake dating sites using images of attractive women stolen from the internet. Men were then lured into conversations with their would-be 'date' and the more gullible persuaded to invest in fraudulent foreign exchange schemes. One scam hit a particularly raw nerve because the fraudsters tried to harness the power and prestige of the Thai monarchy, a subject of great sensitivity in the kingdom, where strict *lèse-majesté* laws can lead to heavy prison sentences for criticising the royal family. The fraudsters persuaded their victims to invest in what they called 'Royal Gold' by pretending to be linked to the Crown Property Bureau, which handles royal investments. They sought to cover their tracks by 'renting' legitimate bank accounts from local people through which the fraudulent investments were laundered. Three cars, including a top-of-the-range Mercedes, gold ornaments, luxury watches, brand-name bags, computers and mobile phones, were seized from the gang leader, another Chinese national, when his Bangkok home was raided.[3]

The range of online scams were broad and audacious, but there were two clear patterns: nearly all the gangs were led by Chinese nationals, and police investigations were increasingly pointing towards Chiang Rai as a hub for Chinese organised crime. Not only did raids take place there, but the couple nabbed in the Bangkok suburb of Prawet were preparing to flee to the northern city. Almost all the bank accounts used by the gold scammers were in Chiang Rai. One senior investigator attributed Chiang Rai's attraction to its proximity to China.[4] The police's Technology Crime Suppression Division, went further, claiming that the gold scam was headquartered at a notorious Chinese-run 'special economic zone' (SEZ) in Laos, just across the Mekong River from Chiang Rai province, from which all manner of criminality appeared to be flooding into Thailand.[5] The SEZ was characterised by one business intelligence analyst as 'The world's worst special economic zone', which is 'mired in scandal and criminality'. It was located in an area where Thailand meets Laos and Myanmar – an area known as the Golden Triangle.[6]

Soon after the flurry of police raids, I took a one hour flight from Bangkok to Chiang Rai, which styles itself as a gateway to the much mythologised Lanna Kingdom, which covered most of northern Thailand from the thirteenth to the eighteenth century. Large posters in the arrivals area of the city's compact airport boast of the area's rich culture and cuisine. 'Let's lose track of time in Chiang Rai,' one said. Another poster suggested a darker heritage. 'Taking any ivory products in or out of Thailand is illegal,' it warned, with a punishment of up to ten years in prison. Lanna translates as 'a million paddy fields', and that's how it seemed as I took a taxi north towards the Mekong River, first along a wide new highway and then down smaller back roads lined with sleepy villages and paddies glistening in the last light of the day. It was dark by the time I reached the Mekong, and for a while the river was a dark brooding presence through the thick foliage that lined the riverbank. Then a flickering in the distance, which quickly turned into a frenetic light show. All along the far bank, buildings were lit up like a manic Christmas grotto. At its centre, multicoloured and ever-changing lights jumped, shimmered and flowed along the pillars and turrets of the Kings Romans Casino, and around an enormous crown that sits in front of it – the heart of the Golden Triangle Special Economic Zone (GTSEZ).

'China money,' said my driver, shaking his head and with an ambiguous grin. It was a response I would get used to on the Thai side of the river, one that seemed to encompass a mixture of awe and disgust. I asked him to stop the car and bought a beer in a ramshackle riverside restaurant, which gave a ringside seat on the action on the opposite bank, the lights reflecting wildly from the Mekong's wide and fast-running waters. It was mesmerising in a way, and diners broke away from their meals to take photographs on their mobile phones. When a sudden storm broke and torrential rain swept across the river, the scene resembled a smudgy surrealist painting.

The GTSEZ is run by a seventy-one-year-old Chinese gangster called Zhao Wei from China's far north Heilongjiang province. In 2007 the Laos government granted him a ninety-nine-year lease on a fifteen-square-mile tract of land fronting the river, and from which he is carving his own city. In 2018, the US Treasury Department imposed sanctions on Zhao, whom it said ran a 'transnational criminal organization'. 'The Zhao Wei crime network engages in an array of horrendous illicit activities, including human trafficking and child prostitution, drug trafficking, and wildlife trafficking. We are targeting key figures in this transnational criminal organization, which stretches from the Kings Romans Casino in Laos throughout Southeast Asia,' said Sigal Mandelker, the US Treasury's under secretary for terrorism and financial intelligence.[7] The sanctions targeted three of Zhao's companies, two based in Hong Kong and one in Thailand. Yet little seemed to have changed since those sanctions were imposed. Accusations of human slavery and trafficking have grown and record-breaking drug seizures – millions of methamphetamine pills destined for Thailand – have taken place close to the zone.[8] Zhao remained untouchable, the Laos authorities reluctant to interfere in the running of his fiefdom. 'The police don't enter without permission,' said an exasperated Jeremy Douglas, the regional representative for the United Nations Office on Drugs and Crime (UNODC).[9] The zone continues to expand, with hundreds of millions of dollars transforming this remote corner of Laos and at the same time restoring the Golden Triangle's notoriety as a global centre of drug production and other criminality.

I spent that night at a hotel in the Thai riverside town of Chiang Saen, which lays claim to being one of the oldest towns in Thailand and was once a key frontier post of the Lanna Kingdom. It teems with temples and other ancient ruins, and its old city walls are considered to be among the best preserved in the country. It could not be more different from the brutal array of glass and concrete sprouting on the opposite bank of the river. Chiang Saen also has two opium museums, highlighting the area's former notoriety – as if that notoriety too was ancient history. My balcony gave a picture-postcard view of a wild unspoiled section of the river. At dawn, clouds hung low over the surrounding mountains and the river seemed to be bursting at its seams. However, it is no longer nature that determines the flow of the mighty Mekong, which has become a symbol of Communist Party power and arrogance in the region. China has built eleven mega-dams on the northern reaches of the Mekong, with a twelfth due for completion in early 2024. The Mekong's flow is now entirely down to the whims of Beijing, which gives China enormous power over the economies and ecosystems of those countries who share the river and the millions who depend on it for their livelihoods. The Mekong is a lifeline for Thailand, Myanmar, Cambodia, Laos and Vietnam, but Beijing has rejected any discussions of dam construction or management with the downstream countries. It regards the Mekong as a sovereign resource and not one that should be shared.[10] A hotel veranda contained a tall signpost showing the distance to various international capitals. 'Beijing 2551km' read one finger of the signpost. At that moment it felt a good deal closer.

Early the following morning, I left Thailand through a small border checkpoint, little more than a large riverside shed. A pair of wanted posters, hard-faced men staring into the distance, were pasted on the wall beside the official who stamped me out of the country. He directed me down steps to a rickety mooring and a waiting open-backed boat. It took fifteen minutes to reach the immigration post on the Laos side, where steps and surrounding buildings were still under construction. The river contained a multitude of informal crossings linking well-used smuggling routes that made the official checkpoints almost superfluous. The GTSEZ was building its own international airport, but for the moment Thailand's Chiang Rai province provided the most convenient transit in and out of the zone.

Flagpoles at the Laos checkpoint carried a limp flag of the Laos People's Democratic Republic and another with a hammer and sickle above a broad marble plinth announcing THE GOLDEN TRIANGLE SPECIAL ECONOMIC ZONE. Golf-like buggies shuttled the two miles to the centre of the zone. I heard them before I saw them – *Xiǎoxīn zhè liàng chē zhèngzài dàochē* ('caution, this vehicle is reversing') – a grating and repetitive chorus familiar to visitors to any Chinese city. The road was new, the land all around and right along the waterfront was scraped of vegetation and littered with trucks and diggers. There was so much dust in the air that my driver spent the entire journey with his T-shirt pulled up over his mouth and nose. He dropped me at the end of the Laos and China Friendship Street, which was lined with ugly shophouses, new but already weathered. There was a large massage parlour, the House of Pleasure, countless Chinese restaurants and karaoke bars, and a string of electronic shops selling knockoff Apple products. On one corner stood a clothes store with a copied 'UNIQLO' sign, a few doors away a fake KFC. The casino soared above the zone, Greco-Roman statues on plinths lined the outside walls between towering columns. There were giant stone lions, a series of large urns and two Bentleys were ostentatiously parked on a sweeping driveway to the casino's main entrance.

It was only mid-morning when I entered the casino, but already the tables were becoming busy. I took a seat in front of a gaming machine, and a woman with a wad of Chinese currency was immediately at my side; the machines only took renminbi (RMB). I changed some money, fed the machine and unexpectedly won enough to cover the cost of my trip across the river. The heavily air-conditioned gaming floor was large and brightly lit, a vast video screen on one wall streamed aquarium-type images, which reflected off the polished marble floor and pillars. A security man approached me, 'You are the first foreigner for a long time. Usually we only have China,' he told me. He was Laotian, and to my relief only wanted to talk. 'Things are getting back to usual,' he replied when I asked about the impact of the Covid-19 pandemic, during which China had sealed its borders. I wondered what constituted 'usual' in this zone. Beyond the casino, an artificial river with a fetid layer of stagnant water was lined with the carcasses of unfinished and monotonous grey buildings, a new shopping district and marina, the security man told me. They stretched far into the distance.

As I walked back towards Laos and China Friendship Street, I noticed a gaping hole where a section of concrete had broken away from one of the casino's columns. I passed yet more construction sites, buildings cloaked in scaffolding, though the tall cranes here seemed mostly at a standstill. Large posters carried pictures of the luxurious retreat they were supposedly building for wealthy gamblers. The completed buildings were mostly identikit tower blocks built in bland Chinese style. Some identified themselves as hotels and apartments. One squat building had big posters of semi-clad women peeling off the wall, another brothel under the banner of a 'massage parlour'. Countless palm trees were being planted along the roadside in an effort to soften the dull uniformity of it all. A top-of-the range BMW, repainted in garish blue and white, swept past me and on a side street I spotted a blue Rolls Royce. On one corner, a group of young people waited in front of a sliding gate. They carried the small backpacks and anxious looks of migrants, though by their appearance they were seeking office work rather than construction. They were called forward in small groups by a burly foreman who directed them to a faceless building beyond. I wondered what they had been promised and what really lay in store for them. I found myself in a district called Chinatown, lined with near-identical red shophouses. I was jolted by the sudden grating of shutters being pulled up, the restaurants opening as lunchtime approached. There were statues of Confucius and figures from Peking opera. I smiled, since the zone itself was one giant Chinatown. The currency was Chinese, as were most items in the shops. The first language of the zone was Mandarin, and all the signs were in Chinese as well as Lao. Even the clocks were set to Chinese time, one hour ahead of Laos. The zone was in effect a Chinese colony on the bank of the Mekong.

On the boat back to Thailand I sat beside a young Malaysian woman, who visibly relaxed as we crossed the river. 'I was cheated, we were all cheated,' she told me, keen to share her ordeal. She said she had answered an advert on the internet for what was described as a well-paid translating job. She did not elaborate on what precisely her role had been for the three months she had spent in the zone but said she had been forced to work twelve hour days, six days a week. 'These are bad people,' she said before striding with enormous relief to the Thai checkpoint and to a waiting taxi that would take her to Chiang Rai and a flight back to Kuala Lumpur. It was only later that I would learn that she was one of the lucky ones.

The traffic in Bangkok was a nightmare. It was gridlocked in the centre and then crawled out along the expressway to the northern suburbs. I was almost an hour late for my meeting with Ekapop Lueangprasert. 'It's Bangkok,' he shrugged. He had an easy smile and a boyish manner that belied the grim battle he was fighting against human slavery, which had seen him rescue hundreds of young people – mostly women – from the hands of Chinese criminal organisations. 'They call these places "special economic zones", which sounds well-meaning, but behind it is human trafficking and multiple scams,' he told me. He said that the Covid-19 pandemic supercharged online scamming. With casinos quiet, the zones set up industrial-scale scamming operations, using the internet to recruit young people with basic computer or social media skills from across the region with promises of well-paid jobs. The new recruits were desperate for a job, but many quickly became disillusioned when they realised the nature of the work, conning people worldwide into making fake investments, and the often hor-rifying conditions. When they asked to leave, they found they were trapped and told they had to repay 'expenses' running to thousands of US dollars. 'If they – or their families – cannot pay, the girls are forced to do sex work, the men to manual jobs, such as in the fish-ing industry.' By the time I met him, Ekapop had rescued around 500 people, out of the 'thousands and thousands' lured to multiple 'special economic zones' that occupy the borderlands of Myanmar, Laos and Cambodia, and which act as virtual states within a state, of which the Golden Triangle is the most notorious.

Ekapop, a Bangkok businessman, set up a Facebook page early in the Covid-19 pandemic to try and help local people suffering financially. He soon began to receive desperate pleas for help from within the zones. There was a flood of near-identical stories about being duped with promises of lucrative legitimate jobs and then imprisoned in appalling conditions by Chinese gangsters. Ironically, the trapped youngsters were able to get messages out via the phones and computers that are the tools of the scamming trade. Ekapop worked with a network of trusted officials on both sides of the border to extract the youngsters, but admits the scale of cor-ruption is so large that it is sometimes hard to know who to trust. In one case, a young worker who had escaped from an online scam centre in Cambodia was returned by Cambodian soldiers. 'He was almost beaten to death. Everyone there saw what happened. The soldiers put a black bag over his head and beat him. The gangsters counted out money and gave it to the soldiers who had brought him back.'

In June 2023, Interpol identified Cambodia, Laos and Myanmar as hubs for cyber-enabled financial crime on an 'industrial scale'. The international police organisation said that cyberscams and the people trafficking to enable it were 'escalating rapidly, taking on a new global dimension' and now represented 'a serious and immi-nent threat to public safety'.[11] Yet the governments that host the 'special economic zones' were weak and unable, or unwilling, to confront the Chinese gangs behind the darkest of these zones. Most zones were built around casinos, which are illegal in Thailand and China, but have branched out into all manner of crime, with online scam centres now at the fore. The UN Office on Drugs and Crime

(UNODC) counts 140 casinos and 128 SEZs across the region. 'There are many SEZs and autonomous territories with security and crime problems dotted across the Mekong, but the GTSEZ is one of the most prolific and notorious, and Zhao Wei and his group are clearly very well financed and able to move money despite sanctions,' said Jeremy Douglas, the UNODC's regional representative.[12]

Ekapop said criminal groups coordinated their actions, and there were strong links between the zones. He said the reason why the host governments will not police the areas is fear of Beijing. 'They depend on China. Their infrastructure comes from investment from China – Chinese money. I believe that governments of these three countries are afraid of offending China. They do not want to do anything to affect China. They fear that if they arrest any Chinese, it will affect the infrastructure and investment in their countries.'

Few are more dependent on Beijing than Laos, a landlocked country of 7.4 million people. Its external public debt tripled over the decade from 2010, half of it to China, which is by far its biggest trade partner and creditor.[13] Some 80 per cent of investment comes from China.[14] The one-party communist state's debt reached 123 per cent of GDP in 2023, according to the International Monetary Fund – though the Chinese loans are so opaque that the true figure is widely considered to be far higher.[15] Laos' currency, the kip, halved in value during the two years to 2023, and the Asian Development Bank's Laos senior country economist, Emma Allen, warned that 'public debt is now at a critical level'.[16] A centrepiece of this splurge is a $6 billion China–Laos railway, which opened at the end of 2021, in which Chinese state-owned companies hold a 70 per cent share. It covers 675 miles and includes 38 miles of bridges and 123 miles of tunnels connecting Kunming in southern China with Vientiane, the capital of Laos. It crosses the border at another one of Laos's 'special economic zones'. It is doubtless an engineering feat, but its financing is opaque, and it has been dismissed by critics as an expensive white elephant. The railway was built largely with Chinese labour and faced accusations of forcing farmers off their land with minimum compensation, destroying natural habitats and threatening endangered species.[17] China has also invested heavily in hydroelectric power plants in Laos.

Certainly, Zhao Wei felt that China's influence in Laos made him untouchable. Shortly after the US government designated his Kings Romans group a 'transnational criminal organization', he made a rare public appearance, claiming the accusations were 'groundless' and the sanctions 'unreasonable and ridiculous'.[18] Mostly, though, he doesn't bother to respond, so confident is he in his impunity. In October 2022, the Laos government presented Zhao with a 'Medal of Bravery, Second Class', to honour the 'renowned Chinese businessman' for 'his efforts and contribution to national defense and national public security in the Golden Triangle Special Economic Zone'.[19]

The Chinese government promotes 'special economic zones' as part of its Belt and Road Initiative (BRI) – which is often described as an international infrastructure project, though is better understood as a tool for Beijing's broader economic and geopolitical goals, an incoherent umbrella term under which all manner of projects are grouped. The zones present themselves as part of these development efforts and are regularly praised by Chinese officials and in state-owned media.[20] In an interview shortly after construction began at the GTSEZ, state media described Zhao as, 'a farmer's child with a pioneering and practical spirit.' He told the China Talk news portal that we wanted 'to enable other countries to enjoy the benefits of China's development' and said his aim was to 'make this piece of wild barren land full of new vitality of life'.[21] Yet as rampant criminality has thrived, local authorities have barely been consulted about construction in the zones, and by one estimate, only a third of jobs created in the twelve SEZs in Laos were taken by Laotian workers.[22]

The Chinese Communist Party has in the past worked closely with criminal organisations – Triads or 'patriotic societies', as they are often termed – to further its interests, often using them as tools of intimidation, notably in Hong Kong, Macau and Taiwan.[23] It is hard to pinpoint the CCP's precise relationship with such a high-profile gangster as Zhao Wei, nor his usefulness to Beijing, but it is inconceivable that he would be operating so brazenly without at least the tacit support of the Party. Laos certainly sees him as a representative of China.

Laos, Myanmar and Cambodia are trapped in the CCP's claustrophobic and often criminal embrace, unable or unwilling to do much about it. In June 2023, the head of a group trying to combat human slavery in Cambodia, who had spoken out against the nation's booming online fraud industry, was forced out of the country after 'credible warnings about various potential threats'.[24] Myanmar's brutal military government is so beholden to Beijing's that as the country descended into civil war it ring-fenced Chinese assets, including a copper mine and a key oil and gas pipeline, with anti-personnel landmines to protect them from insurgents.[25] Thailand had historically been a master of balancing and hedging multiple foreign relationships, but leaned towards China after a 2014 military coup, which was heavily criticised by Western governments. During my visit, there were signs of another recalibration amid alarm in Bangkok at the extent of Chinese influence in business and politics, and the corrosive impact of Chinese organised crime infiltrating Thai society. 'It's out of control,' said Chuwit Kamolvisit, a former policeman, massage parlour tycoon and now self-styled anti-corruption crusader. 'They are not afraid of anything because they pay, and they pay much. They can buy the police, they can buy the court, they can buy the judge. They can buy everything. So they have no fear. They come to Thailand and think they can do anything,' he told me when I met him at his Bangkok headquarters, decked out in anti-corruption slogans. Chuwit provided the evidence that led in January 2023 to the arrest of a prominent Chinese businessman known as Tuhao, who had been regarded as untouchable, and forty associates on multiple charges, including drug trafficking and money laundering.[26]

Corruption is not new in Thailand, but the power of the Chinese gangs and the influence and resources they wield, with criminality spreading like a virus from the 'special economic zones', was changing the broader conversation in Bangkok about the wisdom of holding Beijing too close. In late 2023, a proposal by the Tourism Authority of Thailand to allow China to station police at big tourist spots, supposedly to help maintain security in places popular with Chinese visitors, was abandoned after a political outcry and a backlash on Thai social media. 'Thailand will become a complete surveillance state,' said one post.[27]

By the end of 2023, international pressure was mounting on the Mekong's cyberscam industry. The UK announced sanctions against Zhao Wei and fourteen other individuals and entities, while China belatedly launched a crackdown on operations along its border with Myanmar, pressuring the junta, as well as rebel groups operating in the area, to hand over fraud suspects.[28] In March 2024, Chinese media reported that 800 Chinese 'involved in cross-border cybercrime' had been repatriated.[29] Beijing appears to have been jolted into action because the operations in Myanmar's lawless borderlands in particular were increasingly press-ganging young Chinese and targeting China itself. China's Ministry of Public Security, together with police from Thailand, Myanmar and Laos, set up a joint operation centre in the northern Thai city of Chiang Mai to tackle cross-border crime, including gambling and fraud.[30] The hope of international law enforcement agencies is that now some gangs are directly threatening Chinese interests, Beijing might cooperate more than was the case when mostly foreigners were being scammed.

That said, China has its own understanding of 'cross-border crime', and one of the most prominent arrests in Laos around this time was not that of a gangster, but of Lou Siwei, a prominent human rights lawyer. He had fled from China, where his licence to practise law had been revoked and where he faced routine harassment and constant surveillance. He was transiting through Laos on his way to Bangkok, where he planned to fly to the US to join his wife and child in exile when he was detained and returned to China.[31] Meanwhile, Zhao Wei continued to be protected, his criminal empire in Laos going from strength to strength. It was announced that the new international airport for his zone would begin operations by the end of 2023, a facility that stands to significantly boost his particular empire of cross-border crime.[32] It is a striking symbol of Laos's powerlessness in its dealings both with the Chinese organised crime in its midst, and its fear of China more broadly.

Indeed, it is no coincidence that the Mekong countries in which criminality thrives, and in which Chinese gangs hold such power, are the poorest and most beholden to China. Fear of Beijing (and economic dependency on it) combine with deep-seated local corruption to create a perfect environment for Chinese cyberscammers and for the impunity with which they operate. The irony is that many of these gangs, though very much a product of Chinese power in the region, are beginning to target China itself. This illustrates a wider point: although China routinely uses trade, investment and market access as tools of coercion – 'war by other means', as it has been called – the results are frequently counterproductive and Beijing has ignored some painful lessons from its own history.

CHAPTER 9

Smash the Sparrows!

'It was fun to "wipe out the four pests". The whole
school went to kill sparrows. We made ladders to knock
down their nests, and beat gongs in the evenings, when
they were coming home to roost. It was many years
before we knew that sparrows were good birds.'[1]

Participant in the Four Pests Campaign

The Four Pests Campaign, launched by Mao Zedong in 1958, was one of the first actions of the disastrous Great Leap Forward and was aimed at eliminating from the country all flies, mosquitos, rats and sparrows. 'Man must conquer nature,' declared Mao, and schoolchildren were among the millions mobilised to 'smash the sparrows', one of the centrepieces of the campaign. By the Communist Party's calculation a single sparrow ate four pounds of grain each year and a million dead sparrows would free up food for 60,000 people.[2] During one day in December 1958 alone, 194,438 sparrows were killed in Shanghai, according to a newspaper account under the headline, 'The whole city is attacking the sparrows'.[3] Overall, the authorities claimed a billion sparrows were exterminated across China, driving them to the brink of extinction. However, sparrows ate far more than grain. They also ate insects, notably locusts, whose population exploded as their main predator was systematically hunted down. The ravenous locusts wreaked far more damage on crops than the sparrows ever did, hastening China's descent into the deadliest famine in human history, during which tens of millions died.

The fanatical campaign to eliminate sparrows was a spectacular piece of self-harm and was cited by Australian commentators in 2021 when a shortage of coal led to power cuts across China.[4] Factories cut production, high-rise buildings shut down their lifts and street lights were turned off as power stations struggled to meet demand. Goldman Sachs, an investment bank, estimated that almost half of industrial activity was affected by power shortages.[5] China is the world's largest coal burner, relying on it for almost two-thirds of its electricity production, and coal prices doubled, reaching record highs, as Beijing scrambled to secure supplies. The shortage had several causes, including flooding shutting down domestic mines, but it was exacerbated by a ban imposed on the import of Australian coal as a punishment after Canberra called for an independent enquiry into the origin of Covid-19, which first emerged in the Chinese city of Wuhan in December 2019. Australia was vilified by the CCP in a manner not dissimilar to the hapless sparrows. Those who demanded Covid answers were 'scum' who will be 'cast aside in history', declared a top Chinese diplomat.[6] When Australia did not back down, Beijing targeted Australian goods worth A$24 billion (£12.5 billion), around 10 per cent of Australia's exports.[7] These included barley, beef, cotton, wine, lobsters – and of course coal. 'Clearly, Canberra is increasingly unhinged and in way over its head by taking such a suicidal attack on not just China but also its own economic interests,' growled the CCP's *Global Times*.[8] Yet as time went by, it was the Party that looked increasingly unhinged. Australian coal represented a small proportion of China's total burn, but it was prized for its higher efficiency, and many power plants depended on it. As blackouts swept the country, and fears grew about the Chinese economy and the broader impact on global supply chains, at least twenty bulk carriers transporting millions of tons of Australian coal were left stranded off the Chinese coast.[9]

Australia's economy did dip, but only temporarily, since it was soon able to find alternative markets, diverting coal to India and Japan, and barley to the Middle East, for instance. Wine and seafood sales took a bigger hit, but this was softened by diversions through Hong Kong – entering China by the back door. China also had no alternative to Australian iron ore, which was not on its hit list, and where prices soared. The result was that far from being hobbled, Australia in 2022 enjoyed a record trade surplus with the rest of the world, while successfully reducing its trade dependency on China, cutting the proportion of its exports going there from 42 per cent to 29.5.[10] It turned out that China was more dependent on Australia than vice versa, and rather in the manner of the Four Pests Campaign, which eventually replaced sparrows with bed bugs, China importers in early 2023 quietly began taking the Aussie black stuff once again.

There was more than a hint of the sparrows in the air when I visited Vilnius in summer 2023 to meet Lithuania's foreign minister, Gabrielius Landsbergis, whose experience of Chinese economic coercion was also self-defeating for Beijing, hastening a reappraisal by the European Union of its own dependencies. 'It was truly amazing. Back then it was quite scary,' he told me, when we met in the imposing Foreign Ministry building in Vilnius. 'They wanted to make a lesson out of Lithuania.' His country's crime in the eyes of Beijing was to allow Taiwan to open a diplomatic mission in the Lithuanian capital in its own name. Most of Taiwan's other de facto embassies use the name of its capital 'Taipei' in the title out of fear of upsetting China, which claims the island as its own and has threatened to take it by force. The opening of the 'Taiwanese Representative Office in Lithuania' in November 2021 was an 'extremely egregious act', barked the Chinese Foreign Ministry, demanding that Lithuania 'immediately correct its wrong decision'.[11] The Global Times called Lithuania a 'crazy, tiny country full of geopolitical fears', and warned it 'will eventually pay a price for its evil deed'.[12] The fight hardly looked equal; Lithuania is a country of less than three million people, China of 1.4 billion. Lithuania's economy was 1/270th the size of China's. When Lithuania stood firm, Beijing responded by severing all trade. 'They deleted us from their customs systems. They did not target a sector, a company. Basically Lithuania ceased to exist. You are no longer an entity trade wise,' Landsbergis recalled.

China withdrew its ambassador from Vilnius and threw out Lithuania's top diplomat from Beijing. Lithuania's embassy in China was bombarded with threatening calls, many targeting local Chinese staff.[13] In December 2021, Lithuania pulled out all its remaining diplomats, fearing for their safety after Beijing revoked their diplomatic immunity.[14] At the same time, Beijing heaped pressure on other European capitals, urging them to restrain Vilnius. 'There was pressure from the West,' Landsbergis said. 'The notion was that we needed to take a step back. "You don't need to do that," they said. "You need to swallow your pride and walk back on your decision."' That merely made Landsbergis more determined, since it reminded him of the battles his grandfather had once fought. Vytautas Landsbergis was the first leader of Lithuania after it declared independence from the Soviet Union in 1990, becoming the first of the old Soviet states to break away from Moscow, hastening the disintegration of the USSR. A strong belief in freedom and independence is clearly in the Landsbergis DNA, and he drew parallels between Russia and China and the danger of appeasing authoritarian regimes. 'We need to stand up to Russia and we need to stand up to China on their bullying, on their pressures . . . Otherwise if you take a step back, that land – figuratively speaking, not literally – is taken by the opponent, by the aggressor.'

When Beijing imposed sanctions, Lithuania's direct trade with China was modest but growing. Among the first to be hit were firms relying on imports of Chinese-made glass and electronic components, which received nearly identical letters from Chinese suppliers claiming that power cuts had made it difficult to fulfil orders.[15] Exports of dairy products, beef, alcohol, wood and sugar beet were blocked on 'health and safety' grounds. Beijing then turned to secondary sanctions, warning multinational companies that sourced products from Lithuania that they too could face restrictions in China unless they cut trade ties with the Baltic state.[16] Beijing was seeking, in effect, to dictate the trade and investment policies of every company China was doing business with – an unprecedented extension of economic coercion, and for a while it seemed to work. 'The Germans started screaming,' recalled Raimondas Ališauskas, who was coordinating Lithuania's defences. Continental, a major German firm that sourced automotive components from Lithuania, was unable to clear customs in China, and, along with the German-Baltic Chamber of Commerce, called on Lithuania to seek a 'constructive solution' with Beijing.[17] Ališauskas set up a 'war room' within the Ministry of Foreign Affairs with a hotline for Lithuanian companies. It collated detailed information, right down to the progress of individual containers blocked from entering China in what amounted to a full-scale economic assault.

Landsbergis appealed to Brussels, where alarm bells were already ringing. 'Because China would then basically set the rules on how the single market operates. It goes completely against everything the European Union stands for or was originally created for,' he recalled. 'That made the European Union think that they have to stand up, you know. We can no longer be meek and subservient and just agree to everything that comes from Beijing. We have to fight back, to push back.' China initially told Brussels to back off, claiming it was nothing to do with the EU, denying it was blocking trade and accusing Lithuania of lying. Armed with Ališauskas's data, Brussels accused China of illegal trade practices and took the case to the World Trade Organization (WTO).[18]

Lithuania doubled down on its defiance. It left the '17+1 group', a diplomatic forum through which China sought to exert influence on eastern and central European countries.[19] The Lithuanian government urged citizens to throw away their Chinese mobile phones and avoid buying new ones because they represented a security risk.[20] The government also blocked the use of Chinese baggage screening technology at Lithuanian airports over national security fears.[21] It banned Huawei from its telecoms infrastructure, as well as scrapping proposed Chinese investment in Klaipeda, Lithuania's only seaport and a key transit point for NATO forces.[22] In a non-binding resolution supported by three-fifths of its members, the Lithuanian parliament described China's treatment of its Uyghurs in Xinjiang as 'genocide', and urged the European Commission to review relations with Beijing. It also called on China to abolish a national security law in Hong Kong, to let observers into Tibet and begin talks with the Dalai Lama.[23]

Landsbergis believes Lithuania's experience was a wake-up call that changed the conversation in Brussels and ultimately backfired on Beijing. The EU was forced to confront the issue of economic coercion against a member state and drew up new rules that would give it the power to retaliate. 'You are dealing with a country that bases its decisions on ideology, which is very far from rational,' Landsbergis warned. 'I don't think that everyone yet calculates that into their Excel sheets.' He appointed Ališauskas to the role of

Ambassador at Large to take Lithuania's experience to the world, where he found a receptive audience. 'You have to talk. You have to spread the word that coercion exists. Companies need to understand that where China feels it can exercise pressure, it will,' he told me. Coercion had become an inescapable part of doing business in China.

I met Landsbergis in August 2023, a month after Lithuania hosted a NATO summit, the first security event of that size since independence. He was worried that any Western prevarication over support for Ukraine would embolden Chinese aggression against Taiwan, and the cost of that would be huge to Western economies still too entangled with China. Lithuania knew what it is like to live next door to a bully. In Vladimir Putin's Russia, it has long had a growling, resentful and intimidating neighbour. Vilnius was one of the strongest supporters of Ukraine – there was barely a building in the Lithuanian capital not flying the Ukrainian flag – and it is not at all surprising that the tiny Baltic state made common cause with democratic and economically vibrant Taiwan. A new Indo-Pacific strategy document released just ahead of my visit made explicit links between Russian aggression and China's threats in its neighbourhood.[24] 'Security challenges posed by anti-systemic and revisionist states in both the Indo-Pacific space and the Transatlantic space are connected,' it states, while noting, 'Lithuania proves that a country can withstand economic blackmail if it has built up societal resilience and has reliable partners.'[25]

The war in Ukraine and the immediate economic fallout demonstrated the dangers of the West's over-dependence on Russian oil and gas, but dependencies on China were much larger, and Lithuania's message was simple: over-reliance on a tyrant is dangerous, whether that tyrant is in Moscow or Beijing. 'We are now paying the price for our dependency on Russia, all of us, even though some countries were more prudent than others. But I am quite convinced that there will be a price tag on our dependency on China,' Landsbergis warned. 'All of us should start calculating the authoritarian risks in our budgets.' Lithuania was building stronger links with Japan and South Korea, as well as Taiwan. During my visit it was no great surprise to see an Australian trade delegation waiting to meet Landsbergis, the two countries drawn together by their shared experience. 'We intend to switch our dependencies from China to more democratic partners in the region,' Landsbergis said. 'Countries that we deem like-minded, where at the very least the rule of law is being upheld.'

The attempts to blackmail Lithuania and Australia were particularly blunt and backfired, but China has exerted economic coercion in multiple ways and against a growing list of targets. Beijing shunned Norwegian salmon, a key export, for six years after the 2010 award of the Nobel Peace Prize to dissident Liu Xiaobo.[26] In 2017, when South Korea installed an American missile defence system aimed at North Korea, Beijing showed its disapproval by instructing travel agents to drop Korean tours (Chinese tourists accounted for half of South Korea's tourists and two-thirds of tourist spending at the time). Korean firms operating in China faced choreographed protests and boycotts and Korean shows and entertainers were scrubbed from the airways.[27] Tourism boycotts have also been used against Japan and the Philippines during tension over disputed islands, and against Taiwan, when it elected a more pro-independence leader. New Zealand was threatened when it shut out Huawei from one of its mobile networks. When Turkey voiced rare criticism of China's repression in Xinjiang, calling it 'a great shame for humanity', Beijing issued a safety alert for Chinese travellers to Turkey, as it did later for Canada, with which it was embroiled in another Huawei-related dispute.[28] China boycotted a growing list of Canadian products, including canola (a cooking oil), pork and bull semen. When the Philippines successfully challenged China's South China Sea territorial claims under the United Nations Convention on the Law of the Sea (UNCLOS), Beijing responded by imposing an economic boycott against bananas and pineapples from the Philippines, both important exports. Thousands of tons were impounded and destroyed in Chinese ports.[29] China limited the exports to Japan of rare earths, minerals vital for modern electronics, after a collision involving a Chinese fishing boat and a Japanese coastguard patrol vessel off disputed islands in the East China Sea.[30]

In August 2023, China announced a blanket ban on imports of seafood from Japan after Tokyo's decision to start releasing treated radioactive water into the sea from the wrecked Fukushima No.1 nuclear power plant, delivering a half-billion-dollar hit to Japan's seafood industry. The release was approved by the International Atomic Energy Agency and most scientists agreed it was safe, but Beijing whipped up anti-Japanese outrage, triggering a run on Geiger counters and on table salt in China, to supposedly protect against radiation.[31] Japan complained of harassment of its nationals in China amid calls for further boycotts of Japanese goods – including cosmetics after an online campaign claimed beauty products were contaminated.[32] Scientists pointed out that China's own nuclear power plants routinely released wastewater with higher pollution levels than those found in Fukushima's discharge, and that all were within boundaries considered safe to human health.[33] For China it was a useful pretext to whip up nationalist outrage and anti-Japanese sentiment at a time when Tokyo was moving closer to the United States and Taiwan. It also served to distract attention from Beijing's substantial economic problems at home.

All too frequently, coercion has resulted in grovelling apologies for perceived offences in order to maintain access to the China market. More difficult to quantify are the numerous occasions when governments or companies have chosen to alter their behaviour, or given verbal support to the CCP, in order to pre-empt any pressure. In one bizarre episode, Amazon reportedly bowed to Chinese pressure to publish only five-star reviews on its Chinese site of collections of President Xi Jinping's dreary speeches and writings.[34] The company was trying to grow its China business at the time and had also partnered with state-owned China International Book Trading Corp, a propaganda arm of the CCP, to create a portal on Amazon's US site called China Books. Among their publications were books depicting happy lives in Xinjiang, a province that has witnessed severe repression against the Uyghurs and other Muslim minorities, and others describing China's fight against Covid-19 in heroic terms. An internal Amazon document revealed that the company saw its joint venture as essential in currying favour with the Chinese authorities.[35]

China is not the only nation to use economic pressure to achieve political ends, but it is the most formidable, if only because the CCP has so many levers at its disposal. Unlike in a market economy, the Party is the ultimate arbiter over every aspect of its economy, including trade, investment and market access; it has done, does and will continue to use economic coercion to punish, deter or even reward companies, sectors or countries. A survey by the German-based think tank Mercator Institute for China Studies (MERICS), notes that use of economic coercion has become more frequent, with the number of publicly known cases rising sharply in the four years from 2018.[36] They have also become broader and the triggers more diverse, as the CCP has become increasingly prickly about criticism of its behaviour. The measures employed ranged from orchestrating consumer boycotts of specific goods to more overt trade restrictions and discrimination. MERICS identified 123 cases between 2010 and 2022 and noted that the real impact was probably far greater as coercive measures were frequently used as a means of deterrent, to send a signal. 'Fearful of becoming a target, companies might avoid making public statements on sensitive issues or deem it safer to align themselves with the positions and objectives of China's government,' the report notes. The use of coercion also appeared to be carefully calibrated, with Beijing seeking to minimise the impact on its own economic development. 'The most vulnerable companies and sectors are those deemed to be of little value to the strategic goals of central and local government in China,' the report notes. This is one reason why tourism boycotts have been frequent. Companies that are more strategically important to Beijing, such as those in high-tech industries, are likely to be more secure, at least for as long as they are needed. Coercion has also been used to further the interests of Chinese companies against their international competitors. These findings were echoed by research from the Australian Strategic Policy Institute, which noted, 'The PRC's use of economic and non-economic coercive statecraft has surged to previously unseen levels,' though with mixed results.[37]

China's Belt and Road Initiative (BRI) provides another avenue for coercion. Ostensibly an international infrastructure project under which client countries are blessed with Chinese-built ports, railways, power stations, bridges and telecoms, it has created enormous debts, which China has leveraged in order to corral more dependent states to support China's international goals and narratives, on issues ranging from repression in Xinjiang and Hong Kong to military intimidation of Taiwan. A study by AidData, a US research firm, shows a strong correlation between indebtedness to China and support for Beijing in votes at the United Nations. 'When countries vote with China in the UN General Assembly, they are richly rewarded,' said Bradley Parks, executive director of AidData.[38]

The Federated States of Micronesia might not be the first place that comes to mind in a discussion about Chinese Communist Party coercion, but it provides a chilling and richly detailed example of the lengths to which the CCP will go to get its way. Micronesia consists of a little over 600 Pacific islands of which seventy-four are inhabited. The population is tiny, around 115,000, which is just a little less than Cambridge. It is spread over four states – Yap, Chuuk, Pohnpei and Kosrae – but its exclusive economic zone is enormous, covering an area of over 1 million square miles to the northeast of Indonesia and Papua New Guinea.[39] After the Second World War, the United Nations awarded Micronesia to the United States, whose trusteeship ended in 1986, though under a Compact of Free Association, the US remained responsible for Micronesia's defence and external security, and provides financial assistance. Aid remains its biggest source of income.

More recently, Micronesia has been on the front line of illegal fishing and of climate change, which may render some islands uninhabitable. Yet the scattered islands have grown in strategic importance, sitting at the heart of the increasingly contested waters between China and America. While the US has been neglectful in recent years, China has quickly moved into the Pacific with massive investment and debt financing, while seeking to present itself as a champion of the Pacific's interests in global bodies and pushing for the rights to base security forces in the region, ostensibly to protect its émigré communities.[40] What that Chinese attention means in practice was spelt out in a thirteen-page letter sent in March 2023 by Micronesia's outgoing president, David Panuelo, to his country's lawmakers. It paints an unusually detailed picture of wholesale bribery, threats and interference.

'Simply put, we are witnessing Political Warfare in our country. We are witnessing Grey Zone activity in our country. Over the course of my administration, the scope has increased, as has the depth, as has the gravity,' he wrote.[41] He went on to detail how

China sent spy ships under the guise of 'research vessels' to map Micronesian territory and its resources, and to identify possible submarine paths. 'When we sent our own patrol vessels to check on PRC [People's Republic of China] research vessel activity, the PRC sent a warning for us to stay away.' He describes Chinese pressure to sign a joint plan for developing the local economy, which he feared would open the way for Beijing to take control of fibre optic cables and ports. 'I have had direct threats against my personal safety,' he writes, describing how during a Pacific Islands Forum in Fiji in 2022 he was followed by Chinese intelligence officers. He notes that during a summit between China and Pacific Islands foreign ministers, Beijing sought to insert into a communiqué specific language that had never been agreed, including the establishment of a 'multitude of offices' that had been rejected. 'Our requests were unheeded, and China immediately published the Joint Communiqué inclusive of remarks which were false.' Panuelo told his lawmakers that this became a recurring theme. 'The FSM [Federated States of Micronesia] says "no" and our sovereignty is disrespected with the PRC saying we have achieved consensus when we have not.'

Perhaps his most explosive allegations come towards the end of the letter, when he describes wholesale bribery of officials. 'One of the reasons that China's Political Warfare is successful in so many arenas is that we are bribed to be complicit, and bribed to be silent . . . What else can you call it when an elected official is given an envelope filled with money after a meal at the PRC Embassy or after an inauguration.' He describes gifts of smart phones and of cheques handed over for non-existent projects. A Chinese seafood company told Micronesia's vice president that it could lay on a private plane to 'provide him private and personal transportation to anywhere he likes at any time . . . he need only ask.' He alleges that Beijing provided support to various secessionist movements across Micronesia as a further means of coercion. 'I am acutely aware that informing you all of this presents risks to my personal safety; the safety of my family; and the safety of the staff I rely on to support me in this work.'

There are a number of reasons for China's interest in the region. It needs access to the area's vital fish stocks and the Pacific seabed appears to contain a great quantity of important minerals and metals. However, Panuelo believes Beijing's ultimate motives are strategic – to ensure Micronesian support (or at least abstention) in any conflict over Taiwan. China is acutely aware of its vulnerability to a blockade of its seaborne trade, and at the same time wants to block the ability of US reinforcements from reaching the area around Taiwan. The Pacific is vital in both respects. 'In a full-blown confrontation between the United States and China, Beijing would seek to make these islands the first line of contestation. Although China does not yet quite have the net surface or submarine capacity to realize this objective, it is rapidly building toward it,' according to one analysis.[42] China's heavy-handedness faced push-back in Micronesia, but it has been more successful elsewhere. Beijing signed a security pact with the Solomon Islands which could allow it to send military and police personnel and base naval vessels on the islands.[43] Within months, local newspapers received cars, cameras, phones and printing machinery worth thousands of dollars from the Chinese government, via their embassy. In return, one newspaper pledged to 'promote the truth about China's generosity and its true intentions to help develop' the country.[44] Fiji's military government also signed an agreement with Beijing allowing for the stationing of Chinese police in the country and the supply of surveillance equipment and drones. The deal has come under growing scrutiny since Fiji returned to more democratic rule at the end of 2022.[45] In response, the US and Australia ramped up their efforts to counter Beijing's influence in the area. It is reasonable to assume that the coercive Chinese practices described in such detail by David Panuelo have not been confined to the Federated Islands of Micronesia.

Beijing's economic coercion can be selective and performative, aimed as much at China's own people, with whom the Party wants to burnish its nationalist credentials, as it is at the offending country or company. It is a blunt instrument that can cause as much if not more damage – economic and reputational – to itself as to the target. Apparently weaker targets are often chosen as an example in order to threaten others – to kill a chicken to scare the monkey, as the Chinese proverb would have it. Though in the case of Australia and Lithuania, the 'chickens' proved highly resilient. The case of Micronesia, tiny in land and population, but spread over a vast area, is evidence of Beijing's wider paranoia about encirclement and the need for control of Pacific sea lanes – strategic insecurities we will examine later. Panuelo was convinced the CCP wanted to take control of his country's fibre optic cables and other telecoms infrastructure in order to read his government's emails and listen to their phone calls. He had good reason to be worried, for in tandem with its tools of economic coercion, China has developed a formidable espionage machine. We have already examined Beijing's rampant cyber spying, but that is only one part of a sprawling system that is vast in its ambition, employs an array of both formal and informal techniques, and has been dubbed a 'thousand grains of sand' strategy.

CHAPTER 10

A Thousand Grains of Sand

'By volume, most of what is at risk from Chinese
Communist Party aggression is not, so to speak,
my stuff. It's yours. The world-leading expertise,
technology, research and commercial advantage
developed and held by people in this room,
and others like you.'

Ken McCallum, Director General, MI5

'We like a challenge,' the company announced on the home page
of its website. Though the sort of challenge Smiths (Harlow) had
in mind was rather different to that which chairman Paul Herbert
encountered when he travelled to China in search of a business
partner for his Essex-based precision engineering company. It was
2017, and what Prime Minister David Cameron called the 'golden
era' of relations with China was in full swing. His chancellor, George
Osborne, had proclaimed that Britain was China's 'best friend in the
West', and from nuclear power to telecoms, companies linked to
the Chinese Communist Party were being invited into the most
sensitive corners of the UK economy, with few questions asked. It
seemed as if the only due diligence on Chinese investment was the
number of zeros on the cheque.

Herbert met ten Chinese manufacturers before signing a deal
with a company called Future Aerospace, based in Sichuan Province.
Future's chairman, Han Hua, 'came across as a very genuine guy',
said Herbert, and the two struck an £8 million deal for Future to
buy Smiths.[1] The Essex company, which employed seventy people,
made the things that make aero engines work – the complex engine
rings and turbine casings and other precision parts for aircraft

including the Boeing 737 and Airbus A320. The company boasted of its advanced technology, its website claiming, 'If we haven't got it . . . we make it.'[2] Smiths trained Future's engineers at its Essex plant and signed three technology transfer agreements, which included access to key quality control processes.[3] Future paid the first £3 million, but then things started to go wrong. With the blueprints in its pocket, the Chinese company claimed it was having trouble obtaining permission from Beijing for the takeover and reneged on the deal. Smiths collapsed into administration.[4] 'We think they came to us for the technology we had. They've taken what they wanted and now they've got it, they didn't need the shell of Smiths,' said Herbert.[5]

The cautionary tale of Smiths was cited by Ken McCallum, the director general of MI5, Britain's domestic security agency, in a July 2022 address to business and academic leaders. It was, he said, an example of how 'Clandestine espionage methodology isn't always necessary,' implying that companies were too easily duped or simply giving away know-how. 'By volume, most of what is at risk from Chinese Communist Party aggression is not, so to speak, my stuff. It's yours. The world-leading expertise, technology, research and commercial advantage developed and held by people in this room, and others like you,' he warned.[6] McCallum was speaking in London alongside Christopher Wray, the director of the FBI in what was an unprecedented joint address by the two spymasters. Their broad point was that as prolific as China's theft of intellectual property had been (and remained), notably through cyber espionage, technology and know-how were all-too-readily given away, and their public comments suggested frustration that their warnings were not being taken sufficiently seriously.

Western spymasters were also increasingly wary of LinkedIn, regarded by many professionals and businesses as an indispensable recruitment tool. Unfortunately, that's also the way China's espionage agencies were increasingly seeing it, with Chinese spies posing as recruitment consultants as a way of persuading aspiring job hunters from sensitive industries to part with research or other secrets. 'We think we're above 20,000 cases where that initial approach has been made online through sites of that sort,' McCallum said during a summit of Western intelligence chiefs in California.[7] LinkedIn, with 930 million global users, is a rich fishing ground. An investigation by *The Times* exposed the activities of a Chinese intelligence officer, whose main alias was Robin Zhang. Over a prolific five-year period from behind a desk at the Ministry of State Security in Beijing he created a string of aliases and fake security companies, which he used to approach British academics, scientists and civil servants with offers of thousands of pounds for 'consultancy' work, for sharing their research, knowledge or experience, or for pointing him towards other well-connected targets.[8] In response, MI5 launched a campaign called 'think before you link'.

The word *Qingbao* in Chinese means both 'intelligence' and 'information', and it neatly encapsulates the unique nature and breadth of a vast system combining formal and informal techniques for collecting both. China's principal spy agency is the Ministry of State Security, the *Guoanbu*, which is responsible for foreign and counterintelligence, and ranks among the world's largest intelligence agencies. It was spun off from the Ministry of Public Security in 1983, with the MPS responsible for domestic public and political security. However, an over-concentration on the *Guoanbu* can miss the vast informal system in which China has excelled, and where conventional agents tend to take a back seat. There is often a fine line between theft and the voluntary transfer of know-how, and China has pushed the latter to the limit. Beijing's approach to espionage and related influence operations has been described as the 'vacuum-cleaner', 'thousand grains of sand' or 'all of society' strategy whereby 'anyone and everyone is a potential asset'.[9] The imagery is apt, given its sheer scale and breadth, but it also implies a certain scattershot approach. In reality, the CCP's espionage is methodical and well-targeted. It knows what it is missing and what it wants. 'We are talking here of an elaborate, comprehensive system for spotting foreign technologies, acquiring them by every means imaginable, and converting them into weapons and competitive goods,' notes one study.[10] Smiths (Harlow), for instance, was not haphazardly targeted, but identified, courted and then robbed precisely because it had a technology which China needed for the development of its aero-space industry.

The forced transfer of technology has long been one of the biggest grievances of Western business executives – but one they are least willing to talk about. During my time as a correspondent in China, it was one of the most frequent complaints I heard from Western business executives, but the grumbling was always in private conversations, off-the-record, since they feared retribution from the CCP if they publicly aired grievances. It would usually top the list of gripes in annual surveys conducted by foreign chambers of commerce in China, but these surveys were anonymised, enabling companies to safely vent without being identified. As we have seen, the practice is a legacy of the Deng Xiaoping years, with the handing over of technology and know-how as a condition for market access or part of the price of forming a joint venture in China. It was central to Deng's notion of modernisation, and it continues to thrive. Over the years, investors accepted these forced transfers, however grudgingly, as a price for doing business in the coveted China market. More savvy Western companies sought to limit the amount of cutting edge technology they transferred, but China's rapid modernisation and a more ambitious 'shopping list' of advanced technology has made this much more difficult to achieve.

In his 1989 book, *Beijing Jeep: The Short, Unhappy Romance of American Business in China*, one of the earliest and most celebrated books on doing business in China, Jim Mann quotes one Western executive as saying, 'There are four billion people in the world, and one billion of them are in China. You can't really say, "I don't care." We are like sheep here waiting to be sheared.'[11] That dream of tapping a vast mass of new consumers has mesmerised traders and merchants for centuries – and frequently blinded them to the messy and painful realities. 'Executives had deluded themselves about the extent of change in China because of their own eagerness to sell to the most populous country in the world,' Mann writes.[12] It is an observation as pertinent today as it was in 1989. When I met him in Vilnius in August 2023, Lithuania's Foreign Minister Gabrielius Landsbergis said he was still amazed by how much technical know-how was simply handed to China over the years. 'I don't think that this sort of technology transfer has ever happened in the world's history. You know, enormous potential was just given out or it was taken. Business was thinking, "we do anything, give up our best kept secrets, just to have our business with China". I'm truly hoping that we are in a stage of waking up.'

Perhaps he is right, but old habits die hard. In summer 2023, foreign multinationals servicing China's vast and lucrative medical equipment market were given an ultimatum: hand over your core technologies or leave. Foreign companies, including General Electric, Siemens and Philips, dominated the market, with an estimated 70–80 per cent of the sales of top-end medical equipment in China, including high performance CT and MRI scanners. A government notice listed advanced medical equipment among items hospitals should procure from local suppliers, and Beijing reportedly told the foreign companies to transfer not only their assembly processes to China, but also research and development, design, and the procurement of critical components.[13] The companies did not comment, they rarely do.

China's intelligence gathering activities were characterised in a July 2023 report by the UK Parliament's Intelligence and Security Committee as an 'all of state' threat:

> In practice, this means that Chinese state-owned and non-state-owned companies, as well as academic and cultural establishments and ordinary Chinese citizens, are liable to be (willingly or unwillingly) co-opted into espionage and interference operations overseas: much of the impact that China has on national security is overt – through its economic might, its takeovers and mergers, its interaction with Academia and Industry – as opposed to covert activity carried out by its intelligence officers.[14]

The parliamentarians were scathing about the UK's failure to confront this threat and the government's lack of a coherent China strategy. 'China's size, ambition and capability have enabled it to successfully penetrate every sector of the UK's economy,' the report states.[15] 'Without swift and decisive action, we are on a trajectory for the nightmare scenario where China steals blueprints, sets standards, and builds products, exerting political and economic influence at every step,' it adds.[16] Former Tory leader Iain Duncan Smith described the committee's work as, 'as damning a report on British foreign policy failure as I can remember'.[17] The report

highlighted China's multiple informal intelligence-gathering techniques, including business acquisitions and investments, academic
tie-ups, and the use of cultural and other front organisations. It was
four years in the making, took evidence from all of Britain's major
intelligence agencies, and was heavily redacted to protect them,
their sources and capabilities.

The parliamentarians said China often acted in 'plain sight' and
accused the government of a lack of curiosity and of prioritising
Chinese cash over security considerations – in other words, gul-
libility and greed guided their approach to China. The committee
was particularly scathing about UK academia, which had been a
'rich feeding ground' for Chinese spies and had effectively been
'bought' by Beijing. It said China had stifled debate by exerting influence over the institutions, over Chinese students and
over academics, who had been offered professional inducements
including travel opportunities and research funding. Beijing
had obtained intellectual property, 'by directing or stealing UK
academic research in order to build, or short-cut to, Chinese expertise'.[18] It accused the government of indifference and said there
was still no comprehensive list of areas of UK research that needed
protecting.[19]

Collaboration with China has grown rapidly across British
academia. There were about 750 co-authored research papers in
the year 2000, representing around 1 per cent of UK output, but
by 2019 this had reached more than 16,000, or 11 per cent of
output.[20] In three areas – automation and control systems, telecommunications, and materials science and ceramics – collaborations
with China surged to almost a third of output, yet the risks are
'poorly understood and monitored', according to a report by the
King's College London Policy Unit and Harvard Business School.[21]
A Times investigation revealed that twenty-two of the UK's leading
academic institutions have links with Chinese institutions deemed
'very high risk' because of their ties to military or security research.[22]
A report from the think tank Civitas revealed that half of the UK's
twenty-four Russell Group universities, usually considered the UK's
leading research institutions, had relationships with universities
or companies linked to China's military.[23] The People's Liberation
Army sent an estimated 500 military scientists to study in the UK

between 2007 and 2017, a process the PLA describes as 'picking flowers in foreign lands to make honey in China'.[24] An investigation by the Byline Intelligence Team and The Citizens found that 75 per cent of the Russell Group had research agreements or had accepted funding from state-backed Chinese technology firms linked to human rights and national security concerns over a three year period from 2018. The Chinese firm with the most involvement was Huawei.[25]

During the academic year 2021–22, there were a record 151,690 students from mainland China studying in the UK, making them by far the biggest group of international students.[26] The largest number were at University College London, where the 10,000-strong Chinese contingent represented almost a quarter of the total number of students. This was followed by the Universities of Manchester (8,645), Edinburgh (6,375) and Imperial College London (6,105).[27] Overseas students pay fees of up to £38,000 a year (compared with £9,250 for home students) and by one estimate UK universities receive £2 billion a year from Chinese students. Ten universities, including UCL, Glasgow, Imperial, Manchester, Liverpool and Sheffield, rely on Chinese students for more than a quarter of their income.[28] It is a level of dependency that prompted the Office for Students (OfS), the UK's higher education regulator, to warn twenty-three universities with the highest number about the danger of over-reliance on tuition fees from Chinese students. The OfS asked to see contingency planning in case of sudden interruption. 'Such interruptions could result from, for example, a changing geopolitical environment which could cause an immediate and significant impact on income,' an OfS report said. 'We have written to providers that are particularly exposed to these risks to ask them to share their plans with us.'[29]

The Department of Engineering at Cambridge University has been consistently named as the best engineering faculty in the UK, and among the top in the world. It is at the cutting edge of science and technology, but if there was an academic prize for the blind pursuit of Chinese money then it would surely be odds-on favourite. The department was the main driver behind the establishment of the Cambridge University–Nanjing Centre of Technology and

Innovation, described as a 'smart cities' research centre and located in the Chinese city of Nanjing. The local government provided £10 million for the first five years of what Cambridge described as 'the University's first overseas enterprise at this scale'.[30] Flanked by local Communist Party officials at a ground-breaking ceremony in September 2019, then Vice-Chancellor Professor Stephen Toope said, 'The innovations emerging from this Centre will enable the development of "smart" cities in which sensors can enable sustainable lifestyles, improve healthcare, limit pollution and make efficient use of energy.' Perhaps cities brimming with cameras and sensors will make urban life more liveable, but in Xi Jinping's China that same technology has enabled hitherto unseen levels of surveillance and repression.

In 2021, the Department of Engineering received a 'generous gift' from the Chinese company Tencent to help fund research into futuristic quantum computers. In a statement on its website, the department said, 'Founded in 1998, Tencent uses technology to enrich the lives of Internet users.'[31] A little due diligence would have revealed that Tencent is closely linked to the Communist Party and its security agencies. Its ubiquitous WeChat app (Weixin in China), the 'app for everything', as it is often called, is a key component of the surveillance state – censoring, pumping out disinformation and spying on users.

The department's Centre for Advanced Photonics and Electronics (CAPE) claims to deliver 'technology from science'. 'We do this by accessing world leading expertise in every branch of engineering and science at the University of Cambridge and by collaborative work with the support of cutting-edge R&D facilities within the Electrical Engineering Division,' according to the CAPE website.[32] Photonics is the science and technology of light. It is a vast field encompassing the generation, manipulation and detection of light and is found in multiple applications, from lasers and cameras to barcode scanners and computer screens. As such, it is vital to industries ranging from telecommunications to consumer electronics, aerospace and healthcare. It also has significant military and security applications, including remote imaging, enabling the surveillance of enemy movements over large distances, secure communications, missile tracking and in laser-based weapons.

CAPE claims it is a 'unique form of joint partnership between the University of Cambridge and a number of strategic companies of international importance'.[33] Among its partners was the Beijing Institute of Aerospace Control Devices (BIACD), the CAPE website proclaiming that, 'In the spirit of mutual learning, sincere cooperation, harmonious development, and win-win relationships, BIACD joins hands with the domestic and overseas counterparts and all sectors of society.'[34] The language appeared to be lifted straight from a company handout, but according to the US government some of BIACD's most sincere handholding is with the Chinese military. The company is on a US government list of Chinese military companies and their subsidiaries that are 'ostensibly private and civilian', but which 'directly support the PRC's [People's Republic of China] military, intelligence, and security apparatuses'.[35] The company is also on the US government's 'entity list', a national security blacklist of organisations subject to trade restrictions.[36] BIACD's Mandarin-language online recruitment materials boast that it has made 'outstanding contributions to improving national defence strength'.[37] It has been identified as an alias of the military-linked thirteenth research institute of the China Aerospace Science and Technology Corporation (CASC).[38] According to a database of Chinese military-linked institutions compiled by the Australian Strategic Policy Institute's International Cyber Policy Centre, CASC is 'very high risk for its extensive research, development and production of missiles, rockets and other aerospace products for the PLA [People's Liberation Army]'.[39] In response to a freedom of information request from UK–China Transparency, a UK charity that seeks to shine light on opaque China ties, Cambridge University said that BIACD had contributed more than £2 million towards the partnership with CAPE.[40] Pressed further, the university insisted that it had only worked with the civil side of the company and that the partnership would end in September 2023.[41] As we will see repeatedly in this book, a distinction between 'civil' and 'military' sides of a Chinese company is impossible to make. At the time of writing, BIACD is still listed as a partner – though the effusive language describing the company on the website has been deleted. The CAPE website also lists two BIACD staff among former steering committee members.[42]

Cambridge University's Engineering Department is very popular with research students from the People's Republic of China. The department does not routinely publish detailed figures on students by nationality, but in response to a freedom of information request I made in summer 2023, it revealed that in the academic year 2022–23, the department had seventy-four postgraduate students from China, making them by far the largest group of international students, with the United States a distant second with sixteen.[43] The China total was only marginally less than the eighty-six postgraduate students from the UK.

The Department of Engineering is such a rich repository of cutting edge and 'dual-use' technologies – those with both military and civil applications – that it should have a special responsibility in its choice of partners. However, it is not the only part of Cambridge University with an addiction to Chinese money. There are so many other examples that it would take a separate book to catalogue them all. They include a £200 million joint venture to develop the Cambridge Science Park with an offshoot of China's Tsinghua University, which has been accused of supressing academic freedom and being a base for cyber espionage,[44] and a £12.8 million Institute for Sustainable Leadership, opened in 2022 by then Prince Charles. Half the money was provided by a Chinese billionaire and member of China's rubber-stamp parliament, which at the time of the investment was endorsing a law to snuff the last life out of democracy in Hong Kong.[45] A study by UK–China Transparency found that between 2016 and 2023, Cambridge received roughly £28 million from Huawei and its subsidiaries for high-tech research in areas including artificial intelligence, cybersecurity and network technology, even though the Chinese telecoms giant was banned from the UK's advanced telecoms networks on security grounds.[46]

Cambridge insists that its research is 'subject to ethics governance and export control regulations', and that it has a 'robust system for reviewing strategic relationships and donations'.[47] In late 2021, then Vice-Chancellor Stephen Toope announced he was introducing guidelines for students and academics on navigating projects when working with countries that 'do not share the UK's commitment to democracy and the rule of law'.[48] The guidelines followed growing criticism of the university's tie-ups. In June

2021, Jesus College Cambridge ordered a detailed review of the college's China Centre after stinging criticism that the centre had been stifling debate and parroting Communist Party propaganda in order to ingratiate itself with Chinese partners and sponsors. The review recommended tighter college control and more transparency about funding, and urged the centre to demonstrate its commitment to academic freedom by 'being bold and proactive in planning and running seminars, and not shying away from controversial topics'.[49] It is astonishing that an academic institution at such a high level had to be reminded of that basic responsibility.

British Prime Minister Rishi Sunak responded to the growing tide of criticism by claiming the government was becoming more 'robust' and that a good deal of the Intelligence and Security Committee findings were historic and had already been acted upon.[50] He pointed to a swathe of new legislation, including a National Security and Investment Act designed to tighten scrutiny of foreign investment, stricter rules on public sector procurement to exclude vendors who posed a security risk, and a National Security Act that includes the offence of 'foreign interference'. He claimed a new Research Collaboration Advice Team was already helping academia manage national security risks in international collaborations. However, at the time of writing these were still largely untested, with details to be fleshed out, and they leave much to the discretion of ministers and officials. The November 2023 return to government of David Cameron as UK Foreign Secretary was hardly an encouraging sign; as prime minister, it was he who fired the starting gun for the no-holds-barred race for Chinese money that resulted in the Chinese Communist Party becoming deeply embedded in the most sensitive corners of the British economy. Much of his time out of office was spent pushing business projects linked to China,[51] and there was little surprise that the CCP's *Global Times* welcomed his return, declaring that it 'has the potential to breathe new life into the China-UK relationship'.[52] Successive delays to the removal of Huawei equipment from Britain's 5G networks did not augur well,[53] nor did a review of the government's newly acquired investment screening powers, announced in late 2023 and aimed at 'narrowing and refining them' to make them 'more business friendly'.[54] At the time of writing there was considerable government infighting over whether to place China into an 'enhanced tier' of countries deemed to pose a risk to Britain under the new National Security Act, a move that would require tighter scrutiny of Beijing's influence operations.[55] Beijing's behaviour more than merited this, but targeting China reportedly faced push-back from Business Secretary Kemi Badenoch, who feared the 'business and trade implications'[56] – an argument that has become wearyingly familiar.

In March 2024, the British government accused Chinese hackers of trying to break into the email accounts of UK lawmakers who were critical of China and of breaching the computers of Britain's Electoral Commission and stealing personal information on 40 million voters. This was accompanied by tough-sounding language about how the UK 'will not tolerate malicious cyber activity targeting our democratic institutions'.[57] Yet the response – sanctions against two Chinese officials and a state-affiliated company – was underwhelming, and the revelations came as no surprise to those familiar with decades of Chinese hacking; the most astonishing thing was that it had taken the government so long to act.

Then there was the proposed $66 billion listing on the London stock exchange of Shein, an opaque Chinese fast fashion giant. As we have seen, the company shifted its global headquarters to Singapore in an effort, in part, to fudge its Chinese ownership. There have been accusations – denied by Shein – that the company's explosive growth and rock-bottom prices are fuelled by rapacious data collection practices, intellectual property violations and poor working conditions, including the alleged use of forced labour in its Chinese supply chains. It shifted its attention to the UK after coming under heavy and critical scrutiny in the United States, and a London listing would no doubt be a welcome boost to the fortunes of the beleaguered London market. In the run-up to the July 2024 UK general election, company executives were energetically lobbying ministers as well as their Labour Party shadows to support the listing, and at the time of writing it was shaping up to be a key test of the new government's China policy.

While that government now has the tools to craft a more robust and coherent policy, should it choose to use them, it is facing an adversary that has bolstered its own toolbox for espionage and influence. The CCP has enacted laws that explicitly oblige Chinese citizens, as well as companies and institutions, to cooperate on demand with its spy agencies, and requiring the civil sector to share technology with the military – laws we will examine in more detail later.

China's 'all of state' approach to espionage presents an enormous challenge to those entrusted with countering it. MI5's China-related investigations increased sevenfold between 2018 and 2022,[58] while Sir Richard Moore, the head of Britain's Secret Intelligence Service (MI6) revealed that China was now the top priority for his agency.[59] That was echoed by Anne Keaste-Butler, the head of GCHQ, the UK intelligence agency with most focus on cyber threats. She said it too was 'devoting more resources to China than any other mission'.[60] For his part, FBI Director Christopher Wray said that the FBI had over 2,000 active investigations that linked back to the Chinese government and was opening a new one every ten hours.[61] China's use of informal means of espionage is especially challenging, and under Xi Jinping it has been accompanied by a big increase in influence operations – United Front work, as the Communist Party calls it – to spread the CCP's narratives overseas. Because it has been allowed to act with relative impunity, these efforts have become far more assertive. Influence has become interference and intimidation, with the CCP becoming increasingly aggressive against its overseas opponents and brazen in its attempts to cultivate friends in high places.

CHAPTER 11

The Long Reach of the Party

'A fugitive is like a flying kite: even though he is
abroad, the string is in China. He can always be
found through his family.'

Shanghai police officer

One address was a north London estate agent, another the office
of a fast-food business in the London suburb of Croydon, while a
third was a Chinese restaurant in Glasgow. They didn't seem likely
venues for international intrigue, yet all were identified as undeclared police stations serving the Chinese Communist Party, part of
a global network designed to silence dissent and force those on the
run from the CCP to return home. Reports published in 2022 by
Safeguard Defenders, a human rights organisation based in Madrid,
named more than a hundred operational stations spanning fifty-
three countries – and its source was none other than the Chinese
authorities themselves.[1] Safeguard Defenders drew on numerous
reports in China, including on the websites of state-owned media
and local governments, which described how police in the provinces
of Jiangsu, Zhejiang and Fujian had opened 'service stations' abroad
since 2016. They were described as '110 Overseas' centres – 110
being the emergency phone number for the police in China. One
document from the Fuzhou City Public Security Bureau listed fifty-
four 'overseas police service centres', with tasks that included to
'resolutely crack down on all kinds of overseas Chinese-related illegal and criminal activities'. Europe had the biggest concentration of
centres, spreading alarm across the continent, though the Chinese
embassy in London insisted they were just 'sites assisting overseas
Chinese nationals who need help in accessing the online service

platform to get their driving licenses renewed and receive physical check-ups for that purpose', and were run by 'local overseas Chinese communities who want to be helpful'.[2]

Unease in Britain was particularly strong among Hong Kong exiles, the revelations coming shortly after an ugly incident at China's Manchester consulate, where a protester was dragged into the consulate grounds and beaten – including by the consul general himself.[3] The Hong Kong police put a bounty on the heads of thirteen pro-democracy activists living abroad, six of them in Britain.[4] When two of the wanted Hong Kong dissidents held a private briefing in the House of Commons, a Chinese spy reportedly tried to enter. The alleged spy claimed to be a lost tourist, and there was a brief stand-off before he quickly left. The area was far from those usually visited by tourists, and some Hongkongers, fearing for their safety, covered their faces during the event. 'I believe this man was a [Chinese Communist Party] informer,' said Finn Lau, one of the activists. 'It is not a coincidence that a random Chinese tourist was outside the room at the exact right time and was attempting to access the event.'[5] In May 2024, three men were charged under the new UK National Security Act with assisting the Hong Kong intelligence service, their alleged actions including surveillance and forced entry to a UK residence. One was later found dead in a Maidenhead park, which at the time of writing the police were treating as 'unexplained'.[6]

The actions of CCP agents abroad appeared to be increasingly brazen, and Safeguard Defenders linked the network of police stations to Operation Fox Hunt, the pursuit of what the CCP describes as overseas 'fugitives' – more than 11,000 of whom were 'persuaded' to return to China between 2014 and 2022, according to figures from the CCP's Central Commission for Discipline Inspection (CCDI), its anti-corruption unit.[7] Fox Hunt 'targets Chinese suspected of economic crimes who have fled overseas, and seeks to recover their illicit gains', according to the *Global Times*, a CCP newspaper.[8] It is part of a programme called Operation Sky Net and is run by the Ministry of Public Security. The operation's shadowy existence was summed up by a Shanghai foreign affairs official after the Safeguard Defenders revelations, who told the Spanish newspaper *El Correo*, 'Bilateral treaties are very cumbersome, and Europe is reluctant to extradite to China. I don't see what is wrong with pressuring criminals to face Justice.'9 Safeguard Defenders estimated that only around 1 per cent of 'successful fugitive returns' employed formal extradition proceedings.[10]

In April 2023, US prosecutors charged thirty-four Chinese security officials and their associates *in absentia* with conspiracy to transmit foreign threats and conspiracy to commit interstate harassment. The accused allegedly created fake online profiles designed for surveillance of critics of Beijing and for developing campaigns against them.[11] At the same time, Brooklyn prosecutors arrested and charged two men with operating a 'police station' on behalf of the Ministry of Public Security in a building in Manhattan's Chinatown. One of the men sought to track down the location of a pro-democracy Chinese activist living in California, according to the charge.[12] Three months later, a three week trial in a court in Brooklyn, New York, shed further light on the sort of 'persuasion' employed by Operation Fox Hunt when three other men – two Chinese citizens and an American private investigator – were found guilty of stalking a family in New Jersey on behalf of the Chinese government. Their target was Xu Jin, a former government official accused by China of taking bribes before he moved with his family to America, and the methods included sending derogatory Facebook messages to friends of Xu's adult daughter and a flood of letters to a relative in New Jersey.[13] Threatening notes were delivered to Xu's home, including one that read, 'If you are willing to go back to the mainland and spend ten years in prison, your wife and children will be all right. That's the end of this matter!'[14] At one point the Chinese authorities even flew Xu's unwilling father, who was in his eighties, to New Jersey to pressure his son.

Pressuring relatives who remain in China is a well-honed technique of the CCP to silence overseas dissidents or force their return. A member of Shanghai's Public Security Bureau once described it this way: 'A fugitive is like a flying kite: even though he is abroad, the string is in China. He can always be found through his family.'[15] In another case, a pregnant US citizen was held in China for eight months and was threatened that she couldn't leave unless she convinced her mother to return to China.[16] The prosecutions in America were an expression of deteriorating US–China relations, but also of frustration at the CCP's increasingly brazen behaviour. There had reportedly been informal warnings delivered to Beijing about the presence of agents of Operation Fox Hunt in the United States, who entered on tourism or trade visas, and whose harassment was intensifying.[17] FBI Director Christopher Wray accused China of 'interfering with our independent judiciary, violating both our sovereignty and the norms of police conduct to run lawless intimidation campaigns here in our backyard'.[18]

The CCP's technique is called *quanfan*, or 'persuading to return', and it can involve a range of coercive measures, all of which have soared under Xi Jinping. At the more benign end it can employ Chinese nationals living overseas to help 'pursue fugitives, some providing clues for the country and some actively persuading fugitives to return to China'.[19] An article on the CCDI website also cites 'unconventional means', including 'kidnapping' and 'entrapment', the latter apparently referring to luring a fugitive to a third country more willing to hand them over or to turn a blind eye to Beijing's activities.[20] Thailand has been particularly accommodating in this respect. In 2015, Gui Minhai, a Hong Kong bookseller who published salacious titles about Chinese leaders, was abducted from his holiday home in Thailand.[21] He resurfaced in custody in China three months later, where he was sentenced to ten years in jail for 'illegally providing intelligence overseas'.[22] The following year, Li Xin, a former website editor for *Southern Metropolis Daily*, a newspaper, disappeared after boarding a train from the Thai capital Bangkok to Nong Khai on the Lao border. He had fled from China and published details of the way the Party propaganda machine directed China's newspapers. A month after his disappearance he resurfaced back in China, his wife saying he was being held by police in an undisclosed location.[23] Thailand also forcibly deported around a hundred ethnic Uyghur Muslims back to China, which drew an unusually sharp response from the UN High Commission for Refugees, which described it as 'a flagrant violation of international law'.[24]

China sought to work through Interpol, persuading the international police organisation to issue 'red notices', requesting detention prior to extradition, against 100 of its most wanted fugitives. Between 2016 and 2018, Interpol was headed by Meng

Hongwei, who was also China's vice-minister of public security. His appointment was part of Beijing's efforts to gain greater influence over international organisations and play a larger role in global security governance in general. But in a bizarre twist, Meng himself vanished while on a visit home in September 2018. The following month, the authorities announced that China's second-ranking policeman was under investigation. In January 2020 he was sentenced to thirteen-and-a-half years in jail for bribery.[25]

Few rich Western democracies have extradition treaties with Beijing, where returnees are unlikely to get a fair trial in Party-controlled courts, and the anti-corruption campaign is frequently used as a political tool by Xi against his opponents. The term 'fugitive' is drawn so broadly so as to include all manner of supposed misdemeanours as well as legitimate opposition to CCP repression. 'Criminality' is an extremely elastic concept in China. The intensification of Operation Fox Hunt is also an expression of Xi Jinping's paranoia and his intolerance of opposition, mirroring his crackdown and extension of Party control at home. In the years before Xi came to power, exiled dissidents were mostly ignored. 'Out of sight, out of mind,' seemed to be the policy. The assumption was that once out of China their influence and relevance would diminish. With more Chinese travelling, studying or working abroad and even the tightly controlled internet not entirely impervious, the silencing of overseas dissent has become more urgent. Supposedly corrupt former officials or business people who were once well-connected before fleeing abroad are a particular challenge for the Party because they know how the system works – and they know better than anybody that the system itself is defined by corruption. Tracking them down has become a CCP priority – as has its extension of global influence more generally.

In February 2023, the *China Daily* ran an opinion piece under the byline of Philip Hammond, Britain's former Chancellor of the Exchequer, which began: 'In the context of the damage wrought by the Covid-19 pandemic, the changes brought about by Britain's departure from the European Union and the further deterioration in global trade and economic productivity, it is important for the United Kingdom and China to return to business as usual.'[26]

The piece went on to describe as 'background noise' the challenges facing the relationship. It noted, 'we also share common interests in free trade' and urged a focus 'not on what divides us, but on what unites us'. It seemed a remarkably naïve statement by such a senior figure – except Hammond never wrote the piece. 'Philip gave a speech to a business audience about China–UK relations. He certainly didn't write a piece for *China Daily*, so it's frankly bizarre that they would take his words and try to pass them off as their own op-ed. We complained, and thankfully now they've corrected the error,' said Hammond's office in an indignant statement.[27] Hammond was particularly riled by the 'business as usual' line, and he made a copy of his speech available, in which he'd said: 'Many of our global partners have been quietly increasing their share of trade with China – while we have seen ours stagnate over the pandemic period. Time, now, to roll the sleeves up and get that market share climbing as business returns to normal.'

Yet the nature and venue of Hammond's speech still raised some intriguing questions. It was largely positive towards China, stating that 'Political differences have never been, and must not become, an impediment to Britain's trade,' and ended with a toast. 'Please, join me in raising a glass to the UK–China economic partnership – may it grow stronger and more resilient in the Year of the Water Rabbit,' he told his 400-strong audience.[28] It was delivered at a New Year reception organised by the 48 Group Club, which lobbies for closer economic ties with China. The 48 Group Club has been described as a 'networking hub for friends of China through which Beijing grooms Britain's elites'.[29] It lists as patrons former deputy prime ministers Michael Heseltine and John Prescott, and among its fellows are former Prime Minister Tony Blair, former Labour party powerbroker Peter Mandelson and former First Minister of Scotland Alex Salmond. Also listed are former ambassadors to China, bankers, industrialists and academics.[30] The 48 Group Club derives its name from a group of forty-eight business people who travelled to China in 1954 to establish trade relations with the People's Republic of China. The club styles itself as 'The Icebreakers', and is currently run by Stephen Perry, the son of the man who led the 1954 visit. Its motto is 'equality and mutual benefit', which it borrows from Zhou Enlai, a former Chinese premier.

There is no group in Britain that enjoys closer relations with the CCP, or lobbies more energetically on China's behalf. In 2018, Perry was one of a select group of foreigners to personally receive a China Reform Friendship Medal from Xi Jinping to mark the fortieth anniversary of China's reform and opening. Perry described the receipt of the medal as the 'most breathtaking moment of my life', and told Chinese state media, 'China is already enormously influential in the world, but I think there's much, much more to come.'[31] His views appear to be unchanged by the CCP's growing repression under Xi and its aggressive behaviour internationally. Speaking before Hammond came to the lectern, and watched approvingly by the Chinese ambassador to the UK, Perry told the New Year reception, 'The 48 Group in this icebreaking age will take a positive step in understanding China, helping people who do business with China, who engage with China, understand what China really is and what China is not.'[32]

CCTV, China's state broadcaster, carried a lengthy and approving report about the black-tie event, though the video had a slightly surreal ring about it as the lectern was adorned with two large stuffed rabbits, whose look of slight bewilderment was not entirely out of place given how badly the words spoken jarred with new geopolitical realities. More rabbit heads protruded from red gift bags on the packed tables in the ballroom of the newly refurbished Dorchester Hotel. The 48 Group Club generally keeps a low public profile in the UK, though it is always a welcome visitor to the corridors of power in Beijing and its leaders are sought out by state media and presented as voices of reason and reality. A few months after welcoming the Year of the Water Rabbit, Keith Bennett, the 48 Club Group's vice chairman, was interviewed by the CCP's *Global Times*, assuring the newspaper's readers that the term 'de-risk' was meaningless. 'They're just playing with words,' he said, insisting that China was still a land of opportunity. He accused China's critics of a 'kind of McCarthyism' which he blamed on a lack of knowledge and expertise on China. He said he was confident that over time, 'more rational people will increasingly find their voice'.[33] These then were Hammond's hosts at the New Year reception, along with all those stuffed rabbits. *China Daily* might have faked his byline, but not his broad sentiments towards cosying up to China. Perhaps the newspaper thought he wouldn't mind, that he was a friend of China.

There was a time when the term 'friend of China' had more of an innocence about it, applied to (and by) those who had a genuine affection for China, its rich culture and its people. While that can still apply, the CCP has given it a very different and altogether more sinister connotation. In his book on doing business in China, James McGregor warns, 'As a "friend" you will be considered an enlightened foreigner who understands the complexities of China. But friendship in China carries heavy obligations. In China, it is considered almost immoral to turn down the request of a true friend.'[34] McGregor, who was writing in 2005, goes on to caution, 'Your goal is to be friendly but not foolish'[35] – advice that appears to have gone unheeded by today's 'friends of China'. Under Xi Jinping, it has become more of a job description. It entails privileges, but also obligations; a true friend is regarded as somebody who advocates on behalf of the CCP and furthers its interests. In this sense it has much in common with the term 'useful idiots', which emerged during the Cold War with the Soviet Union. That term was used to describe those Westerners – frequently journalists, travellers and intellectuals – who became unwitting dupes of communism. It has been attributed to Lenin, though there is no evidence that he used the term. More recently it has been used broadly to describe those who give their blessing to tyrants and tyrannies, frequently with evangelical fervour.

'Friends of China' are useful idiots, but the narrative they peddle is in many ways more insidious. Many Western intellectuals had an ideological bond with Soviet communism, however misplaced, which simply does not exist with the CCP, which is an increasingly (and rabidly) nationalist organisation. Friends of China are motivated more by naïvety and greed; their relationship with the CCP is more transactional. For academics it is frequently about access and money – though in the process of trying to please Beijing they have hollowed out much of what passes as 'China Studies' in Britain. The 'friends of China' among business people present themselves as pragmatists, urging the acceptance of the reality of China's rise and power, the need for engagement with the CCP, and stressing how as a market China simply cannot be ignored. The language of China's friends is easy to spot; geopolitical tensions are a result of misunderstanding – if only we all knew the Mandarin language and Chinese history (as they claim to), and better understood China, then all would be well. Alongside this arrogance comes a good dose of 'whataboutism', stressing the imperfections of liberal democracy and arguing we should put our own houses in order before criticising the CCP.

None of these arguments bear scrutiny. For all the accusations of trying to contain China (again, echoed by the 'friends'), Western democracies facilitated its rise – and with considerable forbearance. It is important to stress that it is not China's rise per se that is troubling, but the nature of that rise and the way the CCP has chosen to exercise its powers. It is not necessary to have multiple PhDs in China Studies to recognise that Xi Jinping is a thug, and while liberal democracy undoubtedly faces challenges, that is no excuse to go easy on CCP repression and aggression. Liberal democracy and the freedoms inherent in it are vastly superior and need to be defended. There is simply no moral equivalence – something that often seems lost on the 'friends of China'. CCP mythology, which represents the Party as the embodiment of China, past, present and future, the natural inheritor of 5,000 years of Chinese civilisation, is too easily accepted at face value – as is the notion flowing from this that any criticism of the Party is a criticism of China and of the Chinese people and is therefore racist. This is totalitarian nonsense and, needless to say, the Chinese people themselves have suffered terribly at the hands of the CCP; they are the true heroes in the fight against Communist Party tyranny.

The organisation in China charged with cultivating friends overseas is the United Front Works Department (UFWD). Its name conjures up images of municipal workers in hard hats and hi-viz jackets, but it is a key part of the CCP's security and intelligence apparatus, which has become increasingly active under Xi Jinping. It operates from a large nameless compound next to Party headquarters in Beijing and is charged with extending the CCP's influence over non-Party individuals, groups and organisations inside and outside China. The concept of 'united front' work can be traced back to Lenin, but it was Mao Zedong who during the Chinese civil war described it as one of his three 'magic weapons', alongside armed struggle and Party-building. Xi began to reinvigorate the system soon after coming to power. In a 2015 speech to the Central Conference on the United Front, he called on them to step up their befriending of non-Party individuals. 'We conduct the United Front work not for window dressing or good name, but for pragmatic reasons, because it plays a role, a big role, and an indispensable role. In the final analyses, the job of the United Front is to win over more people,' he said.[36] A UFWD teaching manual exhorts cadres to be gracious and inclusive as they attempt to 'unite all forces that can be united', but ruthless against enemies.[37]

In January 2022, MI5 said it had thwarted a UFWD operation in the British parliament. It issued an 'interference alert' about the activities of a suspected Chinese agent called Christine Lee, who had donated more than £500,000 to the office of Labour MP Barry Gardiner, who also employed Lee's son as a diary manager.[38] Lee, who was affiliated with the China Overseas Friendship Association and the British-Chinese Project, had established links to politicians of all parties. MI5 alleged that she had 'acted covertly in coordination with the UFWD and is judged to be involved in political interference activities in the UK'. The alerts said that the UFWD 'seeks to cultivate relationships with influential figures in order to ensure the UK political landscape is favourable to the CCP's agenda and to challenge those that raise concerns about CCP activity, such as human rights'.[39]

Influence is of course the stuff of all diplomacy, and China is not alone in trying to shape how the world sees it. However, there is a fine line between influence on the one hand and intimidation, manipulation and interference on the other, which the CCP is increasingly prepared to cross. The UFWD is also a covert organisation, working in the shadows as it methodically targets politicians, influential business people and academics, as well as 'friendship' associations and ethnic Chinese community groups. One target has been overseas Chinese language media, which have been lavished with paid content, training and exchange programmes and other financial inducements to parrot Beijing's propaganda. The CCP has also massively increased the international output of its state media, and the WeChat app is an important tool of disinformation, but these are more overt; the UFWD activities are clandestine, carried out through front organisations and companies. In an effort to flush these out, Britain in 2023 introduced a foreign influence registration scheme as part of the biggest revamp of the UK's espionage laws in more than a century. Those working for a foreign government were required to declare their activity or face prosecution.[40] The register was based on a similar scheme introduced in Australia in response to CCP interference. Security minister Tom Tugendhat said its aim was to 'deter foreign powers from pursuing their pernicious aims through the covert use of agents and proxies', though by late 2023 it was too early to judge its impact on the UFWD's covert activities.

Another key UFWD task is monitoring Hong Kong and Chinese students studying overseas. A May 2024 report from Amnesty International described routine intimidation and harassment by CCP loyalists and informers; many students told Amnesty that their families in China were targeted and threatened by police if they engaged in activism overseas.[41] The Chinese Students and Scholars Association and Confucius Institutes are central to this surveillance. The latter are ostensibly language and cultural organisations, and British universities host thirty of them, more than any other country. Almost all UK government spending on Mandarin language teaching in British schools – with at least £27m allocated from 2015 to 2024 – is channelled through university-based Confucius Institutes.[42] However, they are funded by the Chinese government with Chinese teaching staff vetted for their political loyalty. A mandatory application form for teachers going abroad requires that applicants be vetted by a CCP committee and have references detailing their 'political attitude' and their ability to implement the Party's 'request and report system' – CCP-speak for surveilling and informing on colleagues, students and others they come into contact with.[43] The institutes function as propagandists for the CCP and are engaged in activities ranging from establishing science and technology partnerships to offering consultancy services to business, promoting trade and running academic events supposedly shining a light on Chinese policy.[44] They have come under close scrutiny and have had their activities curtailed in Europe, Canada, the US and Australia. During his campaign for the leadership of the Conservative Party, Rishi Sunak pledged to ban them, saying China was 'infiltrating' universities. However, in May 2023 he backtracked, saying a ban would be 'disproportionate'.[45] It seemed that the UK had come to rely too heavily on them, and Sunak feared retaliation against the British Council, which operates four stand-alone offices in China, generates most of its income from teaching and exams, and already operates under tight scrutiny.[46]

A highly critical China report by the Intelligence and Security Committee of Parliament published in July 2023 said the government needed 'to ensure that it has its house in order such that security concerns are not constantly trumped by economic interest'.[47] It cited the cases of Michael Heseltine (The 48 Group Club), former Prime Minister David Cameron's appointment to run a £1 billion China–UK investment fund, and the government's former chief information officer John Suffolk getting a job as global head of cybersecurity at Huawei as examples of China's investment in political influence. It suggested that Cameron's job and the appointment of former Treasury Chief Secretary Danny Alexander as vice president of the (China created) Asian Infrastructure Investment Bank were 'in some part engineered by the Chinese state to lend credibility to Chinese investment and to the broader Chinese brand'.[48] The way senior politicians and business people are picked off by entities linked to the CCP has been termed 'elite capture', and it is widespread. The UFWD has become very adept at this, as have companies such as Huawei and TikTok as they seek to boost their legitimacy in Western markets.

One of the most striking and discouraging aspects of 'elite capture' is not so much how common it is, but just how easily Western political and business leaders have been bought. That has made the UFWD's job an awful lot easier. However, Western democracies are now pushing back. They are waking up to the reality of Xi Jinping's China, the risks inherent in doing business there, and the urgent need to recalibrate policies. However, the journey to that realisation, to a widespread recognition of the need to de-risk the relationship, has not been an easy one, and remains littered with obstacles, largely of the West's own making.

CHAPTER 12

Kicking the China Habit

'Business always wants to overlook, dismiss or reduce
the importance of geopolitics because it doesn't
suit them. The reality is they are constrained by
geopolitics. They just don't want to recognise it.'

Alicia Kearns, chair of the UK parliament's
Foreign Affairs Select Committee

It was a cold, rainy evening in late January 2023, but that did not
put off the journalists, politicians, business people and academics who squeezed along the benches of committee room number
ten in the House of Commons to listen to a pair of escapees from
China – not escapees in a political sense, but British businessmen
who had been largely trapped in the country during three years of
draconian Covid-19 restrictions. Steven Lynch and Julian Fisher
ran the British Chamber of Commerce in China, and their relief
was palpable. Lynch, the chamber's managing director, and Fisher,
its vice-chair, seemed shell-shocked by the experience – not only of
the Covid restrictions, but also at trying to navigate an increasingly
hostile environment towards foreign businesses in China. 'There
is a real sense of pessimism. Is it any longer an investable market?'
asked Lynch, while Fisher warned that the Chinese Communist
Party was driving out business. 'Huge numbers of foreigners have
left China, and they've left jaded and embittered . . . Everyone is
cautious now. I don't think you'll find a British company that's not
talking about resilience,' he said.

A recently completed chamber survey of sentiment among UK
businesses had been the gloomiest ever.[1] A similar mood had been
found in surveys by the European and American chambers of their

members. Companies working in China rarely criticise the government directly, which could be costly for their business, since the Communist Party is a vindictive organisation and retribution can be severe. They have been conditioned not to complain directly, something that would be almost unthinkable in any other market. Instead, the chambers of commerce provide useful routes to vent anonymously.

The parliamentary briefing coincided with the Chinese New Year, the Year of the Rabbit, and a long holiday in China, but CCP leaders had been busy. The zero-Covid U-turn was followed by a charm offensive to convince the outside world that China was open for business again, using the sort of market-friendly language that had become rare in Xi's China. However, none of it seemed very convincing to Fisher, for whom the problems went far deeper than the fallout from Covid. 'How quickly will the door close again?' he asked. 'It is becoming more uncertain because power is centralised more and more. I don't think anybody can make any bets on the future of China . . . There are major concerns that ideology is trumping the economy.'

The briefing was organised by the China Research Group (CRG), a parliamentary group originally set up by Conservative MPs to promote fresh thinking about China. Alicia Kearns, the chair of the group and also of the Foreign Affairs Select Committee, was moderating that evening. Later, I asked her whether she was surprised at how frank her guests had been, when caution usually prevailed among those doing business in China. 'I think it says how difficult things have become,' she told me. She said it was evidence that companies were waking up to the realities of doing business in China, but their understanding was still too superficial. 'Business will always want to overlook, dismiss or reduce the importance of geopolitics because it doesn't suit them. The reality is they are constrained by geopolitics. They just don't want to recognise it,' she said. 'It's the same in academia. The biggest problem we have in academia is academics pretending that their art form – and I'll call it that – is morally superior to what politicians and the rest of the country do. It's not. It's a form of business.'

The CRG was effective in raising awareness about China in parliament, so much so that in 2021 it was among several groups and parliamentarians sanctioned by Beijing in retaliation after the UK imposed its first-ever sanctions on Chinese officials for human rights abuses in Xinjiang. 'They are trying to undermine us. They are trying to make us feel under threat,' Kearns told me. 'We have constant cyber threats, we have constant comments about us, and we have the more acute stuff as well. Trying to get into our systems, trying to get access, trying to attack us . . . They hate the China Research Group. They hate us because we are effective.' She called for MPs to be given risk awareness training, to counter personal threats from hostile states. Shortly after our meeting, a parliamentary researcher who worked with the CRG was arrested under the Official Secrets Act on suspicion of spying for China.[2] Also that summer, Microsoft thwarted an attempt to hack into Kearns's emails, an attack which security authorities told her had been traced to China.[3]

Ever since communist China began to open to the world and reform its economy, foreign investors have gone through cycles of euphoria and despair, though mostly behind closed doors. In public they have mostly continued to parrot at times almost cringe-worthy platitudes about the great 'promise' of the China market. As Jim Mann notes in Beijing Jeep, 'There was a mystique, a romance, about the China market that transcended all logic and caused the board chairman and chief executive officers to suspend their normal everyday business judgements.'[4]

However, by early 2024, the notion that Western companies would put up with almost anything for a share of the China market appeared to be fraying. Western executives were rattled by a series of new 'cybersecurity' and 'data protection' laws and regulations that potentially allow the CCP access to their systems, networks and data to check for compliance. These new rules were presented as efforts to protect the personal data and online safety of Chinese citizens, though their principal purpose appeared to be protecting the Communist Party.[5] The regulations required that data be stored in China and that organisations and network operators submit to government-conducted security checks. They included an obligation on companies to report and seek pre-approval of data transfers out of the country and criminalised online information that the

CCP deemed to be damaging to 'national honour' or 'disturbing economic or social order'.

A new anti-espionage law that came into effect in June 2023 outlawed the flow from China of any 'documents, data, materials, and items related to national security and interests'.[6] The US National Counterintelligence and Security Center (NCSC) said the law gave Beijing 'expanded legal grounds for accessing and controlling data held by US firms in China'.[7] The law was accompanied by a campaign to enlist ordinary people in a 'whole of society mobilisation' against espionage. Tens of thousands of dollars were offered to citizens who report suspicious behaviour, taking the CCP's level of paranoia to new heights.[8] The laws do not define 'national security' or 'interests', but the Party takes such a sweeping view of both that it can cover almost anything, and the offence can take place either inside or outside China. As one analysis of China's new laws notes, 'From trade and investments to China's global image and reputation – everything has become a matter of national security for the Party.'[9] Arguably the CCP doesn't need laws since it can do pretty much what it pleases, and the legal system – including the courts – is under tight Party control. However, the CCP likes to have a fig-leaf of legality, and the laws are so broadly drawn that they can be interpreted in any way the Party sees fit.

The worst fears of foreign businesses seemed to be borne out when the authorities launched a nationwide crackdown on Western consulting firms, with synchronised raids in Beijing, Shanghai, Shenzhen and Suzhou.[10] The firms, which included the Mintz Group, Bain & Company and Capvision, were routinely used by multinational companies to carry out due diligence and research on prospective business partners or markets. They had become an essential source of information for multinational companies working in an opaque business environment, where trust is scarce and official data cannot be trusted. The police questioned staff and seized computers, senior executives were barred from leaving the country and state media accused one company of leaking state secrets and having links with foreign intelligence agencies. It was reported that Gallup, the polling and consulting group, which had offices in Beijing, Shanghai and Shenzhen, was pulling out of China.[11] Gauging Chinese public opinion has never been easy, but the company faced growing difficulties and tighter rules in carrying out surveys. It had also been attacked for global surveys that showed unfavourable attitudes towards Beijing, the *Global Times* claiming its polls 'serve as a tool to contain China and maintain US dominance'. In targeting consultancies, the CCP seemed to be sending a broader message – that it regarded any independent source of information as a threat.[12]

Another major concern of Western executives was that the new laws and regulations would allow the authorities to openly take out through the front door intellectual property and other sensitive data that they used to steal through the back via cyber espionage and other covert means. Western cybersecurity experts stepped up their warnings to executives visiting China to take burner phones and throwaway laptops, since no device can be deemed safe once it has been exposed to ubiquitous Chinese surveillance. However, as with other grievances, you will find very few executives who will talk about this in public out of fear of retribution.

An investigation by Safeguard Defenders found that China was increasingly using exit bans against foreigners involved in business disputes, real or imagined. 'Deliberately vague wording in the Civil Procedure Law means that individuals not even connected to the dispute can be trapped in China . . . In some cases, the targeting of foreigners is part of Beijing's hostage diplomacy, a tit-for-tat retaliation aimed at a foreign government or a tactic to extract concessions,' the report said.[13] It estimated that 'dozens' of business people were being prevented from leaving China, although it was hard to quantify precisely because many companies prefer not to publicise their cases and to quietly resolve the disputes behind the scenes. 'I've seen a rise in companies and entities being concerned about this and asking for our advice on how to prepare and reduce risks,' warned Lester Ross, a veteran lawyer in China and head of the American Chamber of Commerce's China policy committee.[14] He expected cases to rise as relations between China and Washington deteriorated.

In one case that did become public, Richard O'Halloran, an Irish businessman, was barred from leaving China for more than three years after he flew to Shanghai in 2019 to try to resolve a commercial and legal dispute involving an aircraft leasing firm he worked for in Dublin.[15] In another, two Canadians were detained and accused of spying after the arrest in Vancouver of Meng Wanzhou, the chief financial officer of Huawei, the Chinese technology giant, and daughter of the company's founder. She was held at the request of US prosecutors, who sought her extradition on charges of fraud in relation to Huawei's dealings with Iran. Beijing never made much secret of the fact that Michael Spavor, a business consultant in China, and Michael Kovrig, who worked for the International Crisis Group, a think tank, were hostages. They were held for twenty-one months, much of it in solitary confinement, before being released in September 2021 after US prosecutors reached a plea deal with Meng, allowing her to return to China.[16] In January 2024, it was revealed that Ian Stones, a British citizen who had worked in China for four decades, most recently with his own business consultancy, had been arrested two years earlier and sentenced to five years in jail for 'illegally obtaining intelligence for overseas actors'.[17] Neither his family nor the British embassy had been permitted to see any of the legal documents relating to the case, or allowed to attend the trial. Some seventeen Japanese citizens have been held in China on 'spying' charges since 2014, including the detention in March 2023 of a man who worked for the Japanese pharmaceutical company Astellas Pharma.[18]

The longest running case of legal purgatory was believed to be that of Henry Cai, a US citizen, who was stopped when trying to leave China in 2017 at the end of a business trip. He was involved in a dispute over an unpaid debt, which his family said was contrived, but at the time of writing had neither been charged nor received his passport back.[19] John Kamm, chair of the Dui Hua Foundation, a San Francisco-based NGO that keeps tabs on arbitrary detentions, estimated that as of 2023 there were at least 200 US citizens wrongfully detained in China.[20] In late 2023 it was reported that executives from Kroll, an American risk advisory firm, and Nomura, a Japanese investment bank, had been barred from leaving the country, the reasons typically unclear.[21] In a June 2023 travel advisory, the US State Department said, 'Reconsider travel to Mainland China due to the arbitrary enforcement of local laws, including in relation to exit bans, and the risk of wrongful detentions.'[22] Security consultants also reported a rise in 'soft interrogations' of visiting business people, including those working for law firms, manufacturers and consulting companies, who were typically held and questioned for two to five hours at the airport or in their hotels.[23]

A new and draconian 'Anti-Foreign Sanctions Law' allowed the CCP to blacklist any organisation or individual (and their immediate family) involved in drawing up or implementing sanctions against China. Transgressors could have assets seized, be deported and face unspecified 'other necessary measures'.[24] This was a potential minefield for companies in China, especially given Washington's expanding list of Chinese companies sanctioned over national security or human rights abuses. The threat, however, is far broader than countering sanctions, instead targeting just about anybody or anything – be they political representatives, businesses, NGOs, research institutions and scholars – who Beijing deems to be harming its interests, and would seem to fulfil XI Jinping's pledge to 'say no to the saboteurs and spoilers'.[25]

Human rights have long been tricky for Western companies operating in repressive countries. Many executives believe it is something that should not factor into business decisions; others trot out the well-worn and fallacious argument that their very presence in those countries somehow helps to improve things. For Ai Weiwei, the Chinese artist who was jailed and persecuted before going into exile, the West's failure to stand up for freedom of speech and citizens' rights in its business dealings with China is 'one of the most glaring moral failings of our time'. In his memoir, *1000 Years of Joys and Sorrows*, he writes: 'The West has an obligation to reaffirm human rights, for otherwise its conduct is tantamount to neo-colonialist exploitation of developing nations.'[26]

As Xi Jinping's repression has grown, human rights have become increasingly difficult to ignore. The Party's crackdown against the Uyghurs and other Muslim minorities in Xinjiang, which has seen the largest incarceration of an ethnic group since the Nazis, with up to 1.5 million sent to 're-education' camps, is one case in point. Uyghurs have faced arbitrary arrest, forced sterilisation, beatings, torture, and the destruction of mosques and shrines in what amounts to a concerted attempt to eliminate their cultural and religious identity, and which has been described by the British parliament as 'genocide'. The region produces 85 per cent of China's cotton and around 20 per cent of the global supply, and several Western clothing brands expressed concern after well-documented reports of the use of forced labour in cotton fields and factories.[27] As a result they faced an orchestrated campaign of boycotts and threats, stirred up by social media and encouraged by the CCP, which has always allowed more space on its restricted internet for nationalist voices. H&M was one of the hardest hit, all but disappearing from the Chinese internet, its products removed from major Chinese e-commerce platforms. The company then posted a statement on its Weibo account, a Twitter-like platform, saying it 'respects Chinese consumers' and that it 'does not represent any political position'.[28] Burberry, Adidas, Nike, Uniqlo and Lacoste were also targeted. In the West, many fashion companies had built notions of human rights and environmentalism into their brand image and discovered how uncomfortably that sat with sourcing and business in China. US chipmaker Intel apologised following a backlash over a letter to suppliers urging them not to source products from Xinjiang.[29] It later amended the letter to delete references to the province.[30]

Xinjiang also produces around 45 per cent of the world's supplies of polysilicon, a key component of solar panels, and there have been reports that production here also relies heavily on forced labour.[31] The mining and processing of raw materials for the automotive industry have also been implicated.[32] Western companies face fines in their home countries if they cannot demonstrate their products are free of forced labour.[33] Supply chains are complicated, and this puts companies doing business in China under enormous pressure. They face sanctions if they do not adequately check their suppliers and also run the risk of enormous reputational damage – which itself can carry a cost. On the other hand they face potential Chinese boycotts, sanctions and possibly worse under the new laws if they are seen by the CCP to be bowing to Western pressure to clean up their supply chains. In other words, while *not* adequately scrutinising supply chains can result in fines in the US or UK, the very process of asking questions of suppliers might well be deemed a criminal offence in China.

Volkswagen, the German car maker, which makes more than a third of its sales in China, has found itself in a particularly tricky position. It has a factory in Xinjiang and has been pressed repeatedly about human rights abuses in the province. In 2023 it hired a consultancy firm to investigate allegations of forced labour at the plant in response to pressure from shareholders. When the report cleared the plant, the consultancy faced a revolt among its outraged staff, who distanced themselves from the findings. They questioned the veracity of the data and whether employees had been able to speak freely after the audit was subcontracted to a Chinese company.[34] In early 2024, Adrian Zenz, an independent researcher who has exposed extensive human rights abuses in Xinjiang, alleged that forced labour may have been used to build a test track for Volkswagen and its Chinese partner SAIC.[35] At the same time, the company said that the US authorities had impounded thousands of its Bentley, Porsche and Audi vehicles because they contained a part made by a Chinese supplier that had been sanctioned for using forced labour. VW said it had entered talks with SAIC about the future of the business in Xinjiang; this however followed an announcement by BASF, the German chemical giant, that it would speed up efforts to exit two joint ventures in the province – though it remained committed to a broader multi-billion dollar expansion in China, in spite of the German government's appeal for caution.[36] Critics argue that VW has a special ethical responsibility because it was founded by the Nazi Party in 1937 and used forced labour – including concentration camp prisoners – in its factories during the Second World War.

Foreign businesses have felt the impact of the worsening geopolitical environment in other ways, with companies struggling to obtain insurance against political risk in China. 'We're witnessing a sharp contraction in underwriter appetite,' said a political-risk executive at a global insurance broker.[37] Political-risk policies typically insure against politically motivated events ranging from expropriation to civil conflict or war, and though demand had been falling, it has surged in recent years. All of this came on top of the now almost routine complaints about cybertheft, protectionism and the systematic discrimination against foreign companies. The Chinese Communist Party was now going much further. It wanted to dictate not only what Western companies did, but what they said and what they thought – and it did so armed with a draconian set of sanctions that could be wielded as the Party saw fit and with little or no redress for those it chose to target.

The term 'de-risking' in relation to China was first popularised by Ursula von der Leyen, the European Commission president. She introduced it in a March 2023 speech to the Berlin-based Mercator Institute for China Studies (MERICS), which like the China Research Group had been sanctioned by the CCP. She said de-risking meant being clear-eyed about China's growing economic and security ambitions, and 'taking a critical look at our own resilience and dependencies'. In practical terms that meant tighter scrutiny of trade and investment in advanced technologies with military or repressive applications. 'Where dual-use purposes cannot be excluded or human rights might be implicated, there will need to be a clear line on whether investments or exports are in our own security interests,' she said.[38] The speech marked a significant hardening of the EU position on China, but it also changed the language of the debate, and de-risking was soon adopted in other Western capitals. It soon became the buzzword in Washington, replacing 'decoupling'. While decoupling suggested a radical break with China, de-risking was more nuanced – a more orderly form of decoupling. It was vague, slightly murky, and open to interpretation. But therein lay its strength. It could be dialled up or down according to the circumstances, a flexible tool, with which few could disagree. It seemed like plain common sense, which is probably why it so irked Beijing. 'It is just another word game. It will not change the "ostrich mentality" of some countries to escape from the real world,' snarled the Party's *Global Times*.[39]

Germany's first 'Strategy on China', published in July 2023, took its cue from Von der Leyen, declaring, 'de-risking is urgently needed'. The document warned, 'China is leveraging the political, military and economic weight it has gained to pursue its interests **on all continents** [emphasis in the original] and in international organisations, and it is working to reshape the existing rules-based international order according to its preferences.'[40] The strength of the document generated some surprise as only months earlier Chancellor Olaf Scholz had overruled several of his own ministers to allow Chinese state-owned shipping giant COSCO to buy a stake in a terminal at Hamburg Port.[41] The challenge for Berlin is enormous – as we have seen, major German exporters, such as Volkswagen, Siemens and BASF, are heavily dependent on the Chinese market.[42]

Although European divisions remained, policy was a far cry from the days of *Wandel durch Handel*, meaning 'change through trade', which was for decades the leitmotiv of German policy towards both China and Russia. At its core was a belief that over time trade would be a means of influencing and moderating the policies of authoritarian countries. In reality it became a self-serving excuse for business as usual and has been an abject failure in terms of its supposed goals. A parallel belief was that the more economies were intertwined, the less likely was conflict; this too has been undermined, by the Russian aggression against Ukraine and China's growing global belligerence.

Britain also adopted the language of Ursula von der Leyen. 'This is all about de-risking – not decoupling,' Prime Minister Rishi Sunak said when asked about China after a summit of the Group of Seven (G7) industrialised countries in Hiroshima, Japan in May 2023. 'With the G7, we are taking steps to prevent China from using economic coercion to interfere in the sovereign affairs of others,' he added. However, the UK has struggled to articulate a coherent China policy. Foreign Secretary James Cleverly was accused of 'appeasement' when in August 2023 he became the first senior UK minister to visit Beijing in five years.[43] He said he wanted a 'prag-matic relationship', noting, '[China] is an important country, it is a large country, an influential country, and a complicated country, and therefore our relationship with China will necessarily be just as complicated and sophisticated.'[44] Cleverly's visit to China coincided with a report from the House of Commons Foreign Affairs Committee which said that if a strategy exists it remained hidden in the bowels of the Foreign Office. 'The confidential, elusive China strategy is buried deep in Whitehall, kept hidden even from senior ministers across government. How can those implementing policy – and making laws – do so without an understanding of the overall strategy?' asked Alicia Kearns, the chair of the committee.[45]

For all China's concocted outrage about decoupling and de-risking, both were at the heart of the CCP's own industrial and economic strategy well before they entered the conversation in Washington and other Western capitals. China has long seen Western companies essentially as sources of capital, technology and know-how with which to build its own industrial and techno- logical strength, and to be dispensed with once they have outlived their usefulness. The CCP's 'Made in China 2025', its blueprint for becoming a tech superpower, spells out very clearly how China intends to lead the world and be self-sufficient in futuristic tech- nologies, building national champions in a programme backed by massive subsidies and protectionism. It is pure mercantilism, and after criticism from abroad the CCP has more recently toned down references to the plan. However, it remains a more thor- oughly articulated strategy of decoupling than anything produced in Washington.[46] Under Xi Jinping, the phasing out of foreign technology and its replacement by homegrown alternatives has become increasingly central. A 2022 government directive, which has been dubbed 'Delete A' for 'Delete America', orders state-owned companies and government departments to replace US-made chips in their PCs and servers, and to eliminate reliance on foreign-made operating systems and database software by 2027.[47]

Many foreign company executives faced a perfect storm in China: worsening geopolitics, reputational risk as a result of the deteriorat- ing human rights situation, a generally more hostile environment for foreign business, tightening state control over the economy and a worsening economic situation in China itself. It was little wonder that balance of payments data for the July–September 2023 quarter showed outflows of foreign direct investment in China exceeding inflows for the first time, as withdrawals and downsizing by foreign companies exceeded new investments for factory construction and other purposes by $11.8 billion.[48] By one measure, new foreign investment in China fell to the lowest level in twenty-five years in the second quarter of 2023.[49] The number of foreign visitors to China, arriving on international flights, dropped by three-quarters during the first half of 2023, compared with the pre-Covid year of 2019.[50]

For many Western companies de-risking meant examining supply chains, the often complex network of suppliers they use to manufacture and distribute their products. In the era of unfettered globalisation, supply chains were driven mostly by cost; the new buzzword was 'resilience' and mostly that meant lessening their reliance on China. These were tricky conversations, mostly whispered, with confidence in China still required in public so as to avoid incurring the wrath of the Party. Among the new jargon was 'China + 1', the idea being to avoid putting all their eggs in the Chinese basket and to diversify into at least one other country, and 'friendshoring', the notion of locating factories in allied countries or at least less hostile locations. Others looked to shift production closer to their final markets. The buzz words of globalisation, such as 'just in time' performance, were replaced by 'just in case' planning. Executives talked of searching for 'Not China', a location that could provide the same benefits in costs and efficiency without the risks. India, Thailand and Indonesia were leading contenders, but it was neighbouring Vietnam that emerged as the most popular and welcoming alternative. It seemed like an ideal choice, and factories were soon shifting to shiny new industrial zones in a country with historic animosity towards Beijing. However, Vietnam was not quite the alternative many imagined, and illustrates just how difficult it is to kick the China habit.

CHAPTER 13

The Limits of 'Made in Vietnam'

'I think the Chinese government is similar to Hitler,
they want to control the world. They think Vietnam
is part of China. They don't treat us like an
independent country.'

Mr Chi, Vietnamese tour guide

There can be no better place to consider the complexities of the relationship between Vietnam and China than the shattered ramparts of Dong Dang fortress. The giant concrete slabs and a network of tunnels and bunkers are now largely overgrown, though a small shrine commemorates the heroes who fought and sacrificed their lives defending the hilltop fortifications from Chinese invaders in February 1979. The complex sits around a mile and a half from the border with China and was the scene of a fierce battle after the People's Liberation Army stormed through the inaptly named 'Friendship Pass', vowing to 'have breakfast in Dong Dang, and dinner in Hanoi the same day', according to local legend. They took Dong Dang, but never made it to the Vietnamese capital, 100 miles to the south. Instead, the battle-hardened Vietnamese army fought them to a standstill, and a month later, after taking heavy losses, the PLA declared 'victory' and withdrew.[1] Beijing said its intention was to 'teach Vietnam a lesson' for its overthrow of the Khmer Rouge regime in neighbouring Cambodia, which was heavily supported by Beijing. It remains the last major war that China fought, deploying up to 400,000 troops, and the main lesson was the inadequacies of the PLA at the time.[2] The war is rarely discussed in China today, where the Communist Party is keen to perpetuate the myth of the country's 'peaceful rise'.

'They attacked us, and they lost and now they try and hide it,' said Mr Chi, my guide, as we climbed amid the smashed concrete of the fortress, with the town of Dong Dang nestling in the valley below. 'I think the Chinese government is similar to Hitler, they want to control the world. They think Vietnam is part of China. They don't treat us like an independent country,' he said, motioning angrily in the direction of the nearby border. Yet a few moments later he told me how pleased he was that the border was open again after a long closure during the Covid-19 pandemic. 'Our farmers suffered, a lot of agricultural companies went bankrupt. They had nowhere to sell their produce.'

We drove towards the border crossing, a wide road lined with the compounds of shipping companies and scrappy truck stops, the trucks lined up and waiting for permission to cross into China. The mountains formed a forbidding backdrop. Local news reports claimed that trade was 'booming' again.[3] During the pandemic, China built a twelve-foot-high fence along the 800-mile border. It was aimed at keeping out Covid-19, according to Chinese media, part of Beijing's obsessive attempts to completely eliminate the virus within its borders. There were reports at the time of Vietnamese villagers attacking the electrified fence, fearing it would endanger them and their animals.[4] Many ethnic groups in the border regions have members on both sides of what had been a very porous frontier.

Yet the fence, together with the border closure, largely halted the pernicious trade in Vietnamese girls and young women trafficked to China and forced to marry Chinese men.[5] Many Chinese men struggle to find wives because of the country's skewed gender ratio, a result of its now abandoned one-child policy during which a preference for boys meant that female foetuses were often aborted. During my visit, however, there were signs the trade had resumed again. In May 2023, eleven Vietnamese citizens were killed on the Chinese side of the border when the vehicle they were crammed into flipped into a gully. The victims were being trafficked, according to the local authorities.[6] Three months earlier, Vietnamese police busted a ring smuggling girls under the age of sixteen to China for sale as brides.[7]

We headed south towards the Chi Lang Passage, some thirty-seven miles from Dong Dang. In Vietnamese eyes it is another monument to Chinese perfidy, a symbol of centuries of resistance against the 'northern invaders'. The passage is around two miles wide and twelve miles long and is lined with soaring and jagged limestone peaks and dense forest. At the northern end sits the Gate of Monsters; at the southern end the Gate of Oaths, where legend has it that the Vietnamese swore not to allow invaders to pass through the passage without being killed. A large plaque lists the successive Chinese empires, starting with the Song in 981 who fell into the 'deadly natural trap', as one tourist guide describes it. 'We learn at school all about how many times China attacked Vietnam, how we defeated China,' Mr Chi told me with some satisfaction. I guessed he was in his mid-twenties, well-informed and reasonably open-minded – except when it came to China. You don't need to spend long in Vietnam to discover that is a common view, that animosity towards their northern neighbour is deeply ingrained. Indeed, much of modern Vietnamese nationalism defines itself in opposition to the 'northern invaders'. The American War, as Vietnam calls the conflict which ended with the fall of Saigon and victory over the United States and its allies in 1975, is the war foremost in the minds of Western commentators when they consider the region's history. That, or the anti-colonial struggle against the French that came before. However, to many Vietnamese historians these were skirmishes compared with the millennia-long struggle with China.

However, the Chi Lang Passage now has a different function: facilitating the burgeoning trade with China. The busy road that now runs through it is National Highway 1A, the trans-Vietnam highway, and the main overland route to China. Further south from the passage, the land flattens, and the highway passes Bac Giang and Bac Ninh provinces, before reaching Hanoi. These provinces have become the hottest destinations for foreign investment, and the new prosperity is easy to see in the forests of apartment blocks, villas, malls and motor dealerships sprouting on either side of the highway. The provinces are the fastest growing in Vietnam, home to vast new industrial parks in various stages of construction, dense collections of boxy factory complexes and dormitories giving way to the skeletons of warehouses. Some land had only recently been cleared and electricity pylons stood like giants marching across a barren landscape dotted with piledrivers and diggers. Whereas

Vietnam's first wave of foreign investment was in the south, around Ho Chi Minh City, and focused more on low-end shoes and textiles, the latest wave north of Hanoi is driven by higher-end electronics. Foxconn, Apple's most important supplier, is massively expanding its presence in Bac Giang, where it reportedly plans to boost iPad output.[8] The company was also reported to be shifting some Apple Watch, AirPod and MacBook production, making Vietnam Apple's most important production hub outside China.[9] Rival Samsung, the South Korean electronics giant, has a massive presence in Bac Ninh. It is already the country's biggest foreign investor and accounted for a fifth of Vietnam's exports in 2022.[10] Between 2013 and 2021, it reduced its workforce in China from more than 60,000 to 18,000.[11]

Vietnam is widely regarded as the biggest beneficiary of efforts by Western companies to lessen their dependence on Chinese supply chains, and in this corridor north of Hanoi the move seems at its most intense. Hardly a day went by without a report in the local media about the expanding industrial parks and more would-be investors diversifying away from China. Many of the reports had a celebratory edge to them, and there seemed a quiet satisfaction among the country's leaders that they are benefiting at the expense of China, getting one over on the old enemy. Viewing the frenzy of construction around Highway 1A, it's easy to be carried along with the Vietnam buzz. On closer inspection, however, it is not quite what it seems.

'Vietnam's economic moment has arrived,' ran the headline to an editorial in the *Financial Times* in summer 2023. Economic growth of 8 per cent was the highest in Asia in 2022 and foreign direct investment was at a decade high. 'The south-east Asian nation has become a major beneficiary of manufacturers' efforts to "de-risk" their exposure to China as geopolitical tensions between Beijing and the west mount,' the newspaper reported.[12] Dell, Google and Microsoft are among other companies that have shifted some production to Vietnam. Whatever the jargon – 'China + 1', 'resilient supply chains' or 'friendshoring' – it was driven by the worsening environment for foreign businesses in China. Many were haunted by the spectre of the Russian invasion of Ukraine and the painful lesson of over-dependence on Russia for hydrocarbons. That pain would certainly be eclipsed by any disruption to global supply chains resulting from a worsening breach with Beijing. Some felt that in Vietnam they had found an idealised realm called 'Not China', with all the attributes that had originally drawn them to China – a young, cheap and flexible workforce, and a welcoming environment – without all the aggravation.

Though that's not the way Filippo Bortoletti, a Hanoi-based business consultant, saw it. To him the relationship between Vietnam and China is a paradox – Vietnam might not much like its neighbour, but it needs it. 'Vietnam is very heavily dependent on the Chinese economy,' he told me when we met in a coffee shop in a new commercial district in the western suburbs of the capital. And what of Vietnam's pivotal role in supply chain diversification? 'What supply chain diversification?' he replied. 'Vietnam is not an alternative to China. It's complementary. It's mostly part of the China supply chain.'

At the time we met, Bortoletti was country director of Dezan Shira, which advises foreign investors looking to put their money into Vietnam, but he was preparing to launch his own business. He was widely regarded as one of the sharpest and most experienced consultants in Hanoi. He told me that most of the new factories sprouting north of Hanoi were assembly plants, heavily dependent on the flow of components down Highway 1A and through the Chi Lang Passage from China. 'It is ludicrous to talk about supply chain diversification. They source most of their raw materials and components from China,' he said. Vietnam has sought to lure the big investors, the headline-grabbing firms, while neglecting to develop an ecosystem of small- and medium-sized companies to supply them. He pointed to his native Italy, where the economy is built around clusters of small- and medium-sized industries, for what Vietnam should aspire to. He said the Vietnamese government believed its time had come, that the world needed Vietnam. But as long as the local support industries were neglected, Vietnam would be an appendage of the Chinese economy, and the much-touted diversification away from China would be an illusion.

In another twist, investment figures show Chinese companies themselves are at the forefront of the move to Vietnam. In 2022,

China was the fourth largest investor in Vietnam after Singapore, South Korea and Japan, and just ahead of Hong Kong in fifth (Hong Kong is counted as a separate entity for investment purposes).[13] In reality, these figures were almost certainly an understatement. The Vietnamese government vets investment applications from China more carefully than others, and officials believe that as a result many Chinese firms invest via front companies based in Hong Kong and Singapore and represent a significant proportion of the investment from both. There are enormous sensitivities; in 2018, protesters took to the streets of Hanoi, Ho Chi Minh City and several other locations over a land-leasing law that could have favoured Chinese investors. 'No leasing land to China even for one day,' read one anti-Chinese banner.[14] Some regions still refuse to accept Chinese companies. Yet by early 2023, after China reopened its borders following a three-year closure during the Covid-19 pandemic, Chinese investors became bolder, and a wave of investment swept across the border. Chinese firms pumped money into forty-five new projects in Vietnam in the first fifty days of the year alone, according to Vietnamese government data.[15] They included Chinese electronics, robotics and home appliance firms, as well as flooring companies, glass makers and suppliers of cartons and components, and their focus was predominantly on the corridor in northern Vietnam between Hanoi and the border. Leasing companies, which specialise in finding industrial premises, reported that demand from China was growing exponentially. The figures suggested bizarrely that Chinese companies themselves were leading the charge to de-risk and diversify away from their own country. Can that really be the case?

The answer is yes, up to a point, but this Chinese march on Vietnam takes several forms and was driven by a number of motives. Some Chinese companies shared the same concerns as Western firms over trade tensions between China and the United States and the poor business climate in China, especially after experiencing the severity of Covid-19 restrictions, during which China all but cut itself off from the world. As Bortoletti puts it, 'They see the political risk too. In a day they [the Chinese Communist Party] could shut down your factory.' Some are looking to lower their costs – labour costs in Vietnam are around a third of those in China.[16] Others, mostly small- and medium-sized companies, were riding on the coat-tails of the big foreign firms such as Foxconn, which had previously been their clients in China, and to whom they wanted to remain close. Others were trying to dodge the growing list of sanctions being imposed on China by the United States, or else take advantage of Vietnam's more favourable treatment on tariffs; unlike China, Vietnam has a free trade deal with the European Union, ratified during the Covid-19 pandemic, for example.[17] However, in many cases the move to Vietnam involved little more than relabelling their Chinese products as 'Made in Vietnam'. Many of these investments were essentially transhipment warehouses in which little or no extra value was added. Major Chinese solar-panel companies came in for particularly close scrutiny by the US authorities for using Vietnam and other Southeast Asian countries to sidestep duties and at the same time muddying the origins of polysilicon, a key component.[18] Almost half the world's supply of polysilicon comes from the Chinese province of Xinjiang, where the Chinese Communist Party has been accused of using forced labour in its production.[19] The US government has banned the import of any products using that polysilicon.

Back in central Hanoi, I took a stroll around Hoàn Kiém lake. The lake is the heart and soul of the city, and it glistened in the late afternoon sunlight, which illuminated like a spotlight the squat three-tiered pavilion known as Turtle Tower, which occupies a tiny island at the southern end of the lake. Hoàn Kiém is at the heart of Vietnamese culture, history and mythology. Generations of Vietnamese children have been raised on the legend of the 'sword lake' and its giant turtles. There are few Vietnamese who cannot recite the story of fifteenth-century Emperor Le Thai To, who was given a magical sword by the Dragon King, which he used to defeat the Ming (Chinese) oppressors. After his victory, while he was boating on the lake, a giant turtle emerged to collect the sword before returning to the depths to deliver it back to the dragon master, never to be seen again. The lake has become a symbol of bravery, resilience and national unity. Though Ho Chi Minh, the Vietnamese leader who defeated the French and Americans to become the first head of a united communist Vietnam, used language rather less rooted in legend to describe China. 'I would rather sniff a little French shit for a few years than eat Chinese shit for the next thousand years,' he reportedly said in 1945, when discussing the relative merits of rule by China or France.[20]

In the last light of day, the path around Hoàn Kiém lake comes alive with hawkers selling food, drink and souvenirs. Couples pose for selfies at the water's edge, the Turtle Tower behind them. Roads surrounding the lake are packed with jostling motorcycles, which seem to compete with each other for the biggest and most outlandish cargos – boxes, bags, cages, animals, soft toys all piled impossibly high. One was towing a wheelie bin. *Bikes of Burden* is the apt title of one photo-book cataloguing the incredible ends to which the Vietnamese put their motorcycles, which the author Hans Kemp describes as 'the ultimate driving force behind Vietnam's economic progress'.[21]

On a corner to one side of the lake, a branch of Mixue, a bubble tea vendor, seemed quieter than usual, just a few bikes out the front, and I wondered if it was anything to do with the latest China controversy. The Chinese company had recently opened its thousandth store in Vietnam, making it the biggest beverage brand in the country in terms of stores, but sparked online outrage and calls for a boycott after its website posted a map that showed China's 'nine-dash line'. The U-shaped line, often likened to a giant cow's tongue, encompasses Beijing's territorial claim to almost the entire South China Sea (or East Sea, as Vietnam calls it), including islands claimed by Hanoi. Shortly after my visit, Vietnam banned the release of the movie *Barbie* because of a scene that apparently showed the line. Why Mixue would risk its booming business in Vietnam is hard to say. The principal aim of its map was to show how the firm had expanded its milky concoction across Southeast Asia, and it could well be it had no choice; the Communist Party insists that every map produced in China include the line, even though the claim has been ruled illegal under international law. The issue is enormously emotive in Vietnam. In May 2014, China's deployment of an oil rig into an area claimed by Hanoi resulted in a tense stand-off at sea, which triggered deadly anti-Chinese riots and arson attacks across Vietnam. The rioters targeted Chinese-owned factories and businesses in twenty-two provinces and left

more than twenty people dead and scores injured. Beijing evacu-
ated 3,000 of its nationals.[22]

After an enforced break because of the Covid-19 pandemic, the Da
Nang International Firework Competition was back with a bang
in June 2023. There was a carnival-like atmosphere in the central
Vietnamese coastal city, and at nightfall the banks of the Han River
were transformed into a bustling makeshift village of stalls, cafés
and bars. By the time the pyrotechnics began, the riverside was
so packed it was almost impossible to move, and once it was over
there was a colossal gridlock of motorcycles, jostling and honking
their way across the city's iconic US-designed Dragon Bridge – the
longest suspension bridge in Vietnam is shaped like an undulating
dragon, multicoloured and with fiery serpent heads at either end.

There was a real energy in Da Nang, which aspires to become a
digital hub – an ambition boosted by the arrival of French video-
game company Ubisoft, which in 2020 opened a development
studio here. At the same time, there is no city in Vietnam that feels
the threat from Beijing more acutely, nor is there a better place
from which to observe the region's new geopolitics. On landing at
the city's small airport, it was easy to spot the fighter jets in their
hardened shelters, their noses protruding like crouching attack
dogs. The coastal city is the closest to the disputed Paracel Islands,
a string of some 130 islands, rocks and reefs, which sit around
230 miles to the east. China evicted Vietnam from the Paracels in
1974 and has since fortified them with military bases. Further to
the south sit the Spratly Islands, where Vietnam and China also
have conflicting claims. It was here in 1988 that Chinese soldiers
mowed down dozens of Vietnamese troops standing on Johnson
South Reef, water up to their knees – a grizzly video of which is still
available online.[23] A three-floor Paracel Island museum sits on the
waterfront in Da Nang looking out towards the islands and stacked
with documents to support Hanoi's claim. On a plinth outside the
museum sits a fishing boat, an ugly gash in its side, which in 2020
was rammed and sunk by a far bigger steel-hulled Chinese 'fishing
boat' – part of a marine militia that is asserting China's claims with
increased aggression. A Vietnamese businessman salvaged the boat
and brought it back to the museum. Da Nang also hosts a Paracel

Island government in exile, which issues regular demands that China cease its 'illegal activities' on the islands.[24]

Taiwan, Malaysia, Brunei and the Philippines also have overlapping territorial claims in the South China Sea, but it is not hard to see why maritime borders matter so much to Vietnam and why it feels most threatened by Beijing's assertion of ownership to all the resources above, in and under the sea. Vietnam has a 2,000-mile coastline, some one-third of the country's population live along the coast and half the country's GDP still comes from marine activities.[25] In early 2023, a Chinese survey vessel, multiple coastguard ships and fishing boats operated for several weeks in Vietnam's exclusive economic zone, only leaving after repeated warnings from the Vietnamese government.[26] The Chinese coastguard, which is equipped better than the navies of most countries, routinely harasses rival fishing boats and obstructs ships from other countries surveying for oil and gas.

Da Nang is also where the first American combat troops waded ashore in March 1965. It became a major airbase during the war and an R & R destination for American and Australian soldiers, who dubbed the local beach (rather unfortunately) China Beach. A few days after my visit, the US nuclear-powered aircraft carrier, the USS *Ronald Reagan*, visited Da Nang – a potent symbol of the changing power dynamics, which is seeing Vietnam moving closer to Washington. 'U.S.-Vietnam defense cooperation is critical to upholding the rules-based maritime order,' said a US Navy statement.[27] The following month, US Treasury Secretary Janet Yellen visited Vietnam, jumping on a 'Made in Vietnam' electric motorcycle during a factory visit, and telling reporters, 'We do want to partner with more countries, and we see Vietnam as an excellent partner.'[28] Next came President Joe Biden himself on a state visit, announcing a 'comprehensive strategic partnership' with America's former enemy, which included efforts to expand Vietnam's production of semiconductors.[29]

Demographics are working in Vietnam's favour; Vietnam is one of the world's youngest countries, with half the population under thirty-two years of age.[30] Youth and vibrancy are in decline in China, and on the face of it Vietnam has good claim to the coveted 'Not China' crown. However, caution is needed. Around the time that Vietnam signed its free trade deal with the EU, the *South China Morning Post*, a Hong Kong newspaper, described Vietnam as Asia's 'export rock star'. The problem with that analogy is that Vietnam's performance still depends heavily on China – its instruments are heavily reliant on its northern neighbour and the rock star would be unable to stage a performance without them. As Yellen rightly noted, Vietnam is fast becoming a force in the electric vehicle market, and to that end Vingroup, Vietnam's largest private sector conglomerate, was building a vast new battery factory in the central province of Ha Tinh. However, it was doing so in a joint venture with Chinese battery producer Gotion High-Tech.

For all the deep-seated animosities, the ruling parties of China and Vietnam have a lot in common. They both rule over one-party states with issues of corruption and transparency, and with little tolerance of dissent. In the absence of free elections, they both draw legitimacy from rapid economic growth, and while Vietnam's leaders have no great love for their northern neighbour, they do rather admire the staying power of the Chinese Communist Party. If there is one overriding lesson from the shifting of supply chains to Vietnam, it is that diversification and de-risking are challenging and complex, and China fights back. Indeed, many companies shifting production to Vietnam are not lessening their dependence at all, and may even be deepening and complicating it. That is potentially exacerbated by the underlying tensions between the two countries. Vietnam, far from providing a lesson in how to diversify, is a demonstration of just how difficult it is for companies to wean themselves off China, and just how far Beijing will go to maintain that dependence. Chinese companies and the Chinese government are not ceding to Vietnam and are playing a clever game. As a result, far from becoming a separate production hub, Vietnam is in danger of becoming merely an appendage to still-dominant Chinese supply chains. That reality, and the dangers and challenges that go with it, are particularly acute for one company that while investing heavily in Vietnam, is so tightly entwined with China that it might be better described as a Chinese company. That company is Apple.

Chapter 14

Apple's China Addiction

'I am thrilled to be back in China. It means the world
to me, and I feel really privileged to be here . . .
This has been a symbiotic kind of relationship
that we have both enjoyed.'

Tim Cook, chief executive officer of Apple

It was dubbed 'The Battle of iPhone City'. Videos showed workers
at a giant iPhone plant in central China hurling metal barricades
and bricks at the massed ranks of riot police clad in white haz-
mat suits. In one, an isolated protester is forced to the ground and
then kicked and beaten by the police. Another shows a man with
a bloodied face, while somebody shouts, 'They're hitting people,
hitting people. Do they have a conscience?' Other images showed
workers smashing surveillance cameras and Covid-19 testing
booths.[1] The videos spread so rapidly across Chinese social media
that Communist Party censors struggled to keep up. The vast complex in Zhengzhou, the capital of the central Henan province, is
owned by Foxconn, a Taiwanese company formally known as Hon
Hai Precision Industry Co., which is Apple's biggest contractor. This
one complex alone assembled around 70 per cent of the world's
iPhones, up to half a million every day,[2] and employed more than
200,000 workers, mostly migrants who lived in on-site dormitories.

The immediate trigger for the November 2022 riots was complaints about bonus payments and living and working conditions,
but at its root was anger over Covid-19 restrictions. The factory was
hit by a Covid outbreak in late October, which resulted in Foxconn
imposing strict restrictions on workers' movements. Workers
complained of being forcibly quarantined in crammed dormitories

without food.[3] The company imposed daily Covid tests, sealed off smoking areas, switched off vending machines and closed dining halls in favour of packed meals. At the same time they attempted to step up production with round-the-clock shifts ahead of Apple's busy Christmas holiday sales period. Feeling trapped, afraid and increasingly angry, workers staged a mass walkout, although the images of them scaling perimeter fences more resembled a break-out from a prison camp.[4] Other images showed workers trudging wearily down empty highways to get back to their hometowns. Apple warned it was temporarily reducing its iPhone 14 production.

Foxconn is so central to Zhengzhou's economy – accounting directly or indirectly for a million local jobs and $32 billion in annual exports from the city[5] – that the local government launched a desperate recruitment drive on the company's behalf. State media reported that Foxconn needed 10,000 additional workers, and local towns and villages were given quotas to fill the gaping holes along the production line.[6] Government workers were offered their current salaries plus wages and bonuses from Foxconn to do shifts at the factory.[7] Retired soldiers were called upon to help at the plant; the Veteran Affairs Bureau of the People's Liberation Army issued an urgent appeal, reminding veterans that they were always under the command of the Communist Party, and urging them to 'show up where there's a need'. It said they should 'answer the government's call' and 'take part in the resumption of production'.[8] However, these efforts seemed to backfire, increasing fears about infection among existing workers and exacerbating tensions in the plant. In a statement, Foxconn said that it was engaged in a 'protracted battle for safeguarding the health and safety of more than 200,000 employees in Foxconn's Zhengzhou park'.[9] And the People's Daily hailed 'The government's timely assistance . . . continuously providing a sense of certainty for multinational companies like Apple, as well as for the world's supply chain.' [10]

The local government help during the pandemic was no aberration. Foxconn benefited from multiple sweeteners and incentives to build the Zhengzhou plant at breakneck pace in 2010. It reportedly received more than $1.5 billion in direct subsidies, in addition to which the local authorities built roads and power plants. In September 2010, Henan Provincial Education Department issued a directive ordering that Foxconn be given priority for student interns: 'Schools should redirect them to intern at Foxconn, to ensure that when Foxconn begins high volume production, there will be an abundance of high quality workforce at Foxconn.'[11] Over the years that followed, Foxconn and its local government partners faced accusations of using interns as assembly-line fodder at times of high seasonal demand for Apple devices, rather than for any intrinsic educational value to the interns.[12] After 'iPhone City' opened, the authorities continued to cover energy and transportation costs, and recruit workers for the assembly line.[13] Foxconn received further subsidies for hitting export targets, was handed corporate and value-added tax breaks, and social insurance and other payments for workers were lowered by up to $100 million a year.[14] As Jenny Chan, Mark Selden and Pun Ngai note in *Dying for an iPhone: Apple, Foxconn, and the Lives of China's Workers*, their investigation of labour practices at Foxconn: 'Such government effort on behalf of Foxconn bore all the hallmarks of a full-scale military mobilisation, a people's war, waged by government on the economic front in the service of Foxconn.'[15]

Little wonder that Apple's CEO Tim Cook was oozing gratitude when, three months after 'the Battle for iPhone City', he became one of the first Western executives to visit China after the country scrapped its Covid-19 controls and reopened its borders. In late March 2023, he attended the government-organised China Development Forum in Beijing, where he was photographed flashing a V for victory sign. 'I am thrilled to be back in China. It means the world to me, and I feel really privileged to be here,' he said to applause. 'This has been a symbiotic kind of relationship that we have both enjoyed,' he said of his company's close ties with China.[16] He met Chinese Commerce Minister Wang Wentao and the two men exchanged views on the company's development in China and on stabilising supply chains, the commerce ministry said. Earlier, he received a standing ovation at an event at Apple's flagship store in Beijing's upmarket Sanlitun district.

'Symbiotic' was a very apt description. Apple is highly dependent on China, both as a manufacturing base and a market. Over two decades, the company has built the world's most sophisticated supply chain centred on China, enabling it to enjoy dizzying levels of profitability. However, it has also served the ambitions and interests of the CCP, for which Apple has been an important technological and economic partner. There are few Western companies more intertwined with the Chinese Communist Party, and Apple has been accused of complicity in censorship, surveillance and repression. As the *Financial Times* noted, the world's most valuable company 'is now as much a Chinese company as it is American'.[17] In fact, in many respects, Apple can be better described as a Chinese firm, and that was becoming an enormous problem for Cook.

Apple is an intensely secretive company, but since 2012 it has published an annual supplier list representing 98 per cent of its spend for materials, manufacturing and assembly. In 2022, 151 of its top 188 disclosed suppliers were based in China.[18] It does not provide a detailed breakdown of spend, but six Foxconn locations are listed, in Guangdong, Henan (iPhone City in Zhengzhou), Jiangsu, Shanxi, Sichuan and Zhejiang. The Guangdong campus on the outskirts of Shenzhen, just across the border from Hong Kong, was Foxconn's original facility in China, known as Foxconn City. Before Zhengzhou came on tap, Shenzhen was the main iPhone assembly plant, employing up to half a million people. It is a vast, sprawling complex of multi-storey factories, high-rise dormitories, warehouses, two hospitals, a fire department with two fire engines, a television network, banks and sports facilities. Access is via an entrance that resembles a border crossing, policed by the company's own internal security force.[19] Working conditions at the plant came under scrutiny from Western media and human rights groups in 2010 after a string of suicides among assembly-line workers. There were eighteen reported suicide attempts that year, and fourteen confirmed deaths, with suicide notes pointing to enormous stress, long hours and harsh management.[20] The company's initial reaction, to install bars on windows and large nets to catch falling bodies, while making workers sign pledges stating they would not attempt to kill themselves, also drew criticism.[21] In the wake of the bad publicity, the authorities collaborated with the company in a propaganda campaign in villages, towns and schools, aimed at restoring Foxconn's reputation.[22]

The company's facility in Chengdu, in China's southwestern

province of Sichuan, is known as iPad City, as it is the main facility for assembling Apple's tablet computers. It opened in 2010, and also benefited from handouts and other incentives from the local authorities, which recruited workers for the plant and provided them with subsidised transportation.[23] Less than a year after the factory opened, an explosion ripped through one building, killing two people immediately and injuring more than a dozen others. It was blamed on a build-up of metallic dust, which was ignited by a spark in an electrical switch, but once again focused attention on working conditions, with one report headlined, 'In China, Human Costs Are Built Into an iPad'. Apple and Foxconn however argue they have made great strides in improving safety and working conditions.[24]

Foxconn, which is headquartered in Taipei, Taiwan, is the world's largest contract manufacturer of electronics, with an estimated 40 to 45 per cent of the world's information and telecommunications technology market.[25] The company has expanded across the world, but the heart of its operations are in China. While it does not publish detailed figures, it is frequently described as China's largest private sector employer, with a workforce estimated at between 750,000 and 1 million workers in some thirty factories across the country. It is China's leading exporter and consistently ranks as the largest foreign company in China in terms of sales and number of employees.[26] Foxconn made a net profit in 2022 of NT$141.5 billion [New Taiwan dollars] (£3.6 billion) on worldwide revenues of a record NT$6.627 trillion dollars (£169 billion).[27] The company has also assembled products for Cisco, Dell, Hewlett-Packard, IBM, Sony and Microsoft among many others, though Apple is by far its most important client.

Foxconn and Apple have grown together in China and are deeply entwined and highly dependent upon each other. There seemed to be a natural affinity between Tim Cook and Terry Gou, Foxconn's charismatic and hard-driving founder. 'Terry's a strong leader with a passion for excellence,' Cook has said of Gou. 'He's a trusted partner and we are fortunate to work with him.'[28] Self-made Gou, seventy-three-years-old at the time of writing, started his business in 1974 with a $7,500 loan from his mother and a rented shed in a gritty suburb of Taipei where he made channel-changing knobs for black-and-white televisions.[29] Gou's work ethic is contained in *Gou's Quotations*, a collection of slogans, which are required reading for company managers, with many adorning the factory walls. These include, 'work itself is a type of joy', 'a harsh environment is a good thing', 'hungry people have especially clear minds', and 'value efficiency every minute, every second'.[30] In 2019, Gou stepped down as chairman in order to concentrate on his political career, though he retained considerable influence. He resigned as a board member in September 2023 and made another failed bid to become president of Taiwan in the country's January 2024 election. He denied he had a conflict of interest and said he would use the experience of investing and working in China to protect Taiwan's security and lead Taiwan 'back from the abyss of war with China'.[31]

In 2022, Apple sold $74 billion worth of iPhones in what it calls Greater China (China, Hong Kong, Macau and Taiwan), making it the third most lucrative market after America and Europe, accounting for around a fifth of global revenue.[32] However, the raw figures on sales and outsourcing of production do not capture the enormity of Apple's contribution to building China's technological prowess. As the company built its China supply chain, it worked exceptionally closely with its suppliers, embedding top product designers and engineers into suppliers' facilities, overseeing the smallest of detail as it built local expertise, investing billions of dollars in custom machinery.[33] Apple was far from being the only Western company to shift production to China, but the sophistication, scale and complexity of its China-based supply chain – overseen by Cook, first as chief operating officer and then as CEO after the death of Steve Jobs – is unparalleled. The result was not just an unrivalled supply chain for Apple, but the transfer of technical know-how and an understanding of cutting-edge manufacturing that has helped China build an advanced ecosystem for manufacturing. 'All the tech competence China has now is not the product of Chinese tech leadership drawing in Apple, it's the product of Apple going in there and building the tech competence,' said Kevin O'Marah, a supply chain researcher.[34] In recent years, as other companies have grown more queasy about China risk, Apple doubled down on its China investments. During the Covid-19 pandemic, the company reportedly shifted critical design work on its iPhone to China, hiring engineers in Shenzhen and Shanghai.[35] Apple also planned to use in its iPhones memory chips from state-owned Yangtze Memory Technologies Co. (YMTC), China's largest chip maker. However, it abandoned the deal after YMTC came under close scrutiny in Washington and was eventually blacklisted by the US government in December 2023 for allegedly helping the Chinese military and violating trade restrictions by supplying chips to Huawei, the blacklisted Chinese telecoms company.[36]

Apple has been accused of facilitating censorship by removing apps from its China App Store that might cause offence to the Chinese Communist Party, or which help users access content outside China. In 2017, it took down 674 anti-censorship tools called VPNs, Apple telling US senators that they had been removed at the request of the Chinese government because they violated Chinese laws requiring VPNs to have a permit.[37] Skype was among a number of voice-over internet apps removed by Apple from its China App Store on the grounds that they 'did not comply with local law'.[38] Apple also removed several news apps, including *The New York Times* in Chinese and English, and even its own news app, with those trying to access it greeted with the message, 'News isn't supported in your current region.'[39] Tibetan activists accused the company of removing twenty-nine popular Tibetan-themed apps dealing with news, religious study, tourism and even games.[40] During protests in Hong Kong in October 2019, Apple removed from its app stores globally a crowdsourcing app called HKmap.live, which enabled protesters to track the movement of police.[41] A 2021 *New York Times* survey found that over several years tens of thousands of apps had disappeared from Apple's China App Store including foreign news outlets, gay dating services and encrypted messaging apps, VPNs, and apps about the Dalai Lama, Tibet's exiled spiritual leader.[42]

In May 2023, Apple published its first ever App Store Transparency Report, which it had agreed to provide to developers as part of a settlement of a class action lawsuit brought by developers in the US.[43] The report gave a breakdown of apps removed from the App Store during 2022 after government takedown demands, with China way out in front – 1,435, with India a distant second with 14.[44] While the report was welcome, it raised more questions than it answered, shedding little light on the opaque process by which apps are removed, or on Apple's process of self-censorship, whereby it gives special scrutiny to apps for China and pre-emptively blocks those it believes might cause offence. The company rejects hundreds of thousands of apps for failing to comply with its own guidelines, but these guidelines are sufficiently broad to hide political censorship. Reports based on interviews and court documents suggest that behind the scenes, Apple has built a considerable bureaucracy to flag and block apps it fears could upset the CCP.[45] It has in effect become a key part of the Party's censorship operation, though blocking apps is not the only function the iPhone maker performs on behalf of the CCP.

In 2018, Apple gave guidance to creators of shows for its Apple TV+ service that they should avoid portraying China in a bad light.[46] Also that year, a US security researcher shed further light on the technical lengths (and intricacies) of Apple's censorship for China. Patrick Wardle was asked by a Taiwanese friend who lived in San Francisco to check out his iPhone, which crashed every time the Taiwanese flag emoji appeared. Wardle, a former National Security Agency staffer, tracked the problem to an intentional censorship feature installed by Apple to apparently placate the Chinese government, which maintains that Taiwan is part of China. 'Basically, Apple added some code to iOS [the iPhone operating system] with the goal that phones in China wouldn't display a Taiwanese flag and there was a bug in that code,' Wardle said.[47] The censorship function was designed to click in when iPhone location settings were switched to China, but the phone got confused about its region. Wardle warned Apple about the flaw, and the company released a patch, but would not comment further about the censorship or the nature of the bug. To Wardle it highlighted the power of hidden censorship code. 'They say "We're not going to spy on our users." But if China asks, they'll build censorship into their devices and not really talk about it,' he said. 'Hypocrisy is the term I would use.'[48]

That same year, Apple began moving the iCloud accounts of its China-based customers to Chinese servers. This included the storage of encryption keys for those accounts. Until then, Apple had stored the codes for all global users in the US. The company's partner in China was Guizhou-Cloud, a company overseen by the local government of Guizhou province. Apple said it was complying with local laws that require data on Chinese users to be stored in China and that it would ensure that the keys were protected, though it didn't explain how. Human rights groups saw it as tantamount to handing over data, including photos, messages, contacts and documents, to the CCP. 'Tim Cook preaches the importance of privacy but for Apple's Chinese customers these commitments are meaningless. It is pure doublethink,' said Nicholas Bequelin, East Asia director at Amnesty International. A new privacy feature designed to obscure a user's web browsing from internet service providers and advertisers was not made available in China.[49] In November 2022, Apple limited the use of AirDrop, a wireless file-sharing system, on iPhones in China after protesters used the feature to share digital leaflets critical of Xi Jinping.[50] The following summer Apple toughened its app developer policy to conform with tighter CCP censorship, banning any foreign apps that had not been given explicit government approval – a move that was expected to drastically reduce the number of foreign apps available in the China App Store.[51]

When pressed on its behaviour in China, Apple says it must obey the laws of every country in which it operates. It has also argued that engagement is the best way to bring about positive change, that its presence will help in the further opening and liberalisation of China. Speaking at the Fortune Global Forum in Guangzhou in December 2017, Cook said, 'Your choice is: do you participate, or do you stand on the sideline and yell at how things should be? And my own view very strongly is you show up and you participate, you get in the arena because nothing ever changes from the sideline.'[52] In October 2019, Tim Cook was appointed chairman of the advisory board of the prestigious Tsinghua University School of Economics and Management in Beijing.[53] The appointment came at a time of growing crackdowns on free speech on China's campuses and just months after Xu Zhangrun, a respected constitutional law professor at Tsinghua University was stripped of his positions and stopped from teaching after criticising the personality cult surrounding Xi.[54] The problem with the engagement argument, variations of which are made by business leaders and Western politicians, is that it hasn't worked. China under Xi Jinping has become significantly more repressive and less market- and investment-friendly at home, and more aggressive abroad. Engagement arguments are largely self-serving, and no more so than with Apple.

Apple's willingness to kowtow to the CCP is in strong contrast to the way it has portrayed itself in the West as a champion of privacy, seeking to differentiate itself from the Facebook and Google business model, built around leveraging customer data for commercial gain. 'Privacy to us is a human right, it's a civil liberty,' Cook said to applause from a studio audience in a 2018 interview with the American cable network MSNBC.[55] In the US, the company strongly resisted demands from the FBI to unlock the iPhone of the gunman in a 2015 terrorist attack in San Bernardino, California, in which fourteen people were killed. In an open letter to customers, Tim Cook said, 'Compromising the security of our personal information can ultimately put our personal safety at risk. That is why encryption has become so important to all of us.'[56] Apple is not the only Western tech company which has played a role, knowingly or not, in the construction of China's surveillance state. However, its rhetorical commitment to privacy and civil liberties arguably gives it a greater responsibility – and furthermore a duty to explain why those fine sentiments seemingly stop at the Chinese border.

As 2023 progressed, any hope Apple had of remaining above the worsening geopolitical tensions began to crumble. In September, the Chinese government banned the use of iPhones in government offices and in state-owned firms.[57] There was no formal written instruction, but word quickly spread that officials had been told not to bring iPhones to the office. Apple's share price fell sharply, and analysts were quick to speculate about whether Apple's long love affair with the Chinese Communist Party was coming to an end. Perhaps it was a shot across the bows, a warning that Apple could not remain above the tech war between the US and China, with Washington imposing an increasing number of restrictions on Chinese tech companies and their access to top-end semiconductors. It could equally be that Xi Jinping had concluded that Apple, for all its help and loyalty over the years, had outlived its usefulness. That was the implicit message when rival Huawei launched a new series of smartphones, incorporating home-grown chips, which were cheered on by state media and online as a blow against the US.[58] The CCP appeared to be stoking anti-Apple sentiment online. When a video was posted showing queues for the new iPhone 15, it attracted angry comments. 'I will never buy an Apple phone,' 'Take pride in buying a Huawei,' and 'Why can't we ban sales of Apple while Americans have banned Huawei?' they said.[59] Apple iPhone sales in China fell an estimated 24 per cent year-on-year during the first six weeks of 2024.[60] This contributed to Apple losing its crown as the world's largest phone maker during the first quarter of that year.

Then there was the Taiwanese connection. Foxconn, which had prospered along with Apple and had seemed so vital to the Chinese economy, came under investigation for alleged tax and land use violations.[61] The probe appeared to be linked to Terry Gou's political ambitions, coming after the Foxconn founder had claimed that if elected president of Taiwan, he would not be pushed around. Beijing clearly had other ideas. It may seem strange that a Taiwanese company could for so long enjoy such privileges in China and play such a central role in the Chinese economy, given the growing tensions across the Taiwan Strait. Yet in the early years of Deng's reforms, Taiwanese businesses were among those courted most vigorously for their investment, managerial and technical expertise, and their technology. Taipei was cautious at first – in 1986 investment in China totalled just $20 million.[62] However, it surged after 1990 when new Taiwanese regulations allowed investment via third-party jurisdictions, notably Hong Kong. Investment reached $9.9 billion in 1993 and $40 billion in 1996 – around 5 per cent of Taiwan's GDP at that time.[63] China quickly became the biggest destination for Taiwanese investment, initially in low-end manufacturing, attracted by cheap labour, lax regulations and cultural familiarity as costs in Taiwan rose. Investment was boosted further by the restoration in 2008 of direct trade links; by one estimate, total Taiwanese investment in China in the two decades from 1991 was close to $200 billion and by 2020 China accounted for a record 44 per cent of Taiwan's exports.[64] By 2022, Taiwan had an estimated $43 billion of assets in China.[65] The shape of trade and investment changed with Taiwan providing many of the high-tech inputs (including chips) for goods assembled in China (including in Taiwanese-owned factories).

While Taiwanese companies were first valued by the CCP for their economic contribution to China, the CCP quickly recognised their usefulness for political leverage, as pawns in a larger game. This was seen in November 2021 when Beijing hit the Far Eastern Group, a Taiwan-based conglomerate, with substantial interests in China, with fines of $13.9 million. This was ostensibly for environmental, land use, health and safety and other violations, but Chinese officials and state media made clear that it was punishment for the group's role as a donor to Taiwan's independence-minded Democratic Progressive Party.[66] The Taiwanese government responded by trying to loosen its dependence on China, providing incentives to companies to shift investment and trade elsewhere in Southeast Asia. The island also tightened laws to prevent China from stealing key technology and poaching talent, amid concerns that Beijing had stepped up its economic espionage.[67] That policy is starting to yield results, with the share of exports going to China dropping by almost a quarter in 2023. In 2010, more than 80 per cent of Taiwan's annual foreign investment went to China, but by 2023, this had fallen to just 11 per cent.[68]

Of course dependencies run two ways, and China was reliant on Taiwanese chips and other electrical machinery from the island, as well as the broader economic contribution made by companies such as Foxconn. That Xi Jinping was willing to risk damaging the Chinese economy by moving against the iPhone maker recalls the self-destructive campaign to smash the sparrows that we met earlier, and it is also testament to how far he now prioritises security above all else. Whatever the immediate motive, the Foxconn investigation sent a chill across Apple's Cupertino campus; if China's most important foreign investor to which so many favours had been given over the years was no longer above the geopolitical fray, then nobody was.

In March 2024, Tim Cook was back in China, opening a new store in Shanghai, its biggest in the country and second largest in the world after its flagship store on Fifth Avenue in New York City. The company had earlier announced it would expand a research facility in Shanghai and open a new applied-research lab in Shenzhen. 'There is no supply chain in the world more critical to Apple than that of China,' Cook said.[69] A month later, Apple acceded to CCP demands to remove from its China App Store some of the world's most popular messaging apps, including WhatsApp, Signal and Telegram. Apple said it was told to remove certain apps because of national security concerns. 'We are obligated to follow the laws in the countries where we operate, even when we disagree,' the company said in a drearily familiar statement.[70] Yet Apple was in a bind – largely of its own making. Tim Cook's efforts to talk up China were looking increasingly desperate, perhaps in part to cover a belated realisation that the company needed to reduce its exposure to the People's Republic. While he publicly heaped praise on China, Foxconn was quietly making plans to shift production of a quarter of the world's iPhones to India, in addition to bolstering facilities in Vietnam.[71] Apple was also looking to do more product development in Vietnam. Apple and its umbilically joined partner Foxconn were tiptoeing towards the China exit – and that will not have gone unnoticed by the CCP as it steps up the pressure on both. However, Apple's very success in China in building such a sophisticated supply chain was an obstacle to speedy de-risking. By early 2024, the relationship was looking a little less symbiotic and more like a liability. Apple could no longer rely on the gratitude of the CCP, which was looking elsewhere for willing accomplices.

CHAPTER 15

China Rocks!

'I've always been a tremendous admirer of the
sheer amount of talent and drive that exists in China.
So I think, really, China's going to be great at
anything it puts its mind to.'

Elon Musk, CEO of Tesla

'China Rocks in my opinion,' declared Elon Musk in an interview with *Automotive News*'s Daily Drive podcast, before going on to praise the 'smart, hard-working people of China', whom he contrasted with the 'complacent' and 'entitled' character of Americans.[1] He had good reason to be grateful to the Chinese Communist Party. The interview came a year after the opening in late 2019 in Shanghai of a new Tesla factory capable of assembling half a million cars a year. The factory was approved and built at astonishing speed, constructed in under a year, and was aided by tax breaks from Beijing and cheap loans from Chinese state-owned banks, while Tesla was allowed to wholly own its Chinese operations.[2] The company was even permitted to begin production before securing all its permits.

During the disruption of Covid-19 lockdowns, the authorities helped Tesla keep running, busing in workers from secure dormitories and ensuring a generous supply of masks and other protective gear.[3] While Musk criticised 'fascist' lockdowns in America, which he said amounted to 'forcibly imprisoning people in their homes', the self-described 'free speech absolutist' had nothing to say about those in China, which were the world's most draconian.[4] Instead, he thanked Beijing for the 'support and protection provided to Tesla's Shanghai factory during the Covid-19 pandemic'.[5] With generous state assistance, Gigafactory Shanghai continued to expand, and by 2022 had ramped up annual production to 700,000 cars, with plans to add 450,000 vehicles of annual capacity at a new site around two miles from its current plant.[6] Shanghai soon accounted for half of Tesla's global deliveries, and Grace Tao, Tesla's global vice-president, told the Third Qingdao Multinationals Summit, a business forum, that 'The Shanghai Gigafactory is to become Tesla's most important export base and production centre.'[7] She also revealed that Tesla was to source more components locally and set up research and development, and data centres, in China. 'The R&D centre will be Tesla's first vehicle innovation R&D centre outside the United States,' she declared.[8]

Elon Musk, the world's richest man, quickly became the CCP's favourite capitalist. In a late May 2023 visit to Beijing, he met Vice-Premier Ding Xuexiang, a member of the Party's seven-man Politburo Standing Committee and a Xi loyalist. He also met Foreign Minister Qin Gang (though Qin vanished a month later, the victim of an apparent Xi purge).[9] A statement from the Foreign Ministry said that Tesla 'is opposed to decoupling and cutting off supply chains and is ready to continuously expand business in China'.[10] Chinese state media heaped praise on Musk, reporting that he had enjoyed a banquet with sixteen dishes at a top-end Beijing restaurant. 'Musk's trip to China showed US businesses' firm confidence in the Chinese market despite "decoupling" noises from some Western politicians,' gloated the *Global Times*.[11] Chinese social media showered him with praise, calling him 'a pioneer', 'Brother Ma' and 'a global idol'.[12] For his part, Musk praised the 'vitality and potential of China's development', and discussed with his hosts the further development of new energy vehicles and intelligent connected vehicles, 'despite Washington's reckless technology decoupling manoeuvres', according to a Chinese government read-out of the meeting.[13] Musk said that China was 'on Team Humanity' as regards artificial intelligence and would be willing to work with the international community on common guidelines.[14] 'I've always been a tremendous admirer of the sheer amount of talent and drive that exists in China. So I think, really, China's going to be great at anything it puts its mind to,' he told the opening ceremony of a Shanghai AI conference via video link.[15] He also waded into

China–Taiwan tensions, claiming that Taiwan was an 'integral part' of China.[16] He suggested it should become a special administrative region of the People's Republic, a view that was criticised on the island as dangerous and naive.[17]

It felt like the early days of the CCP's romance with Apple, and the Party's motives were very similar. Hosting Gigafactory Shanghai meant not only bringing arguably the world's most innovative company to China, a company that led automakers in the deployment of AI, but it would also hasten the development of electric vehicle (EV) supply chains and galvanise China's own industry in a technology where it wanted to lead the world. To seasoned China-watchers, it all looked wearily familiar – an infatuation with the China market on the part of a foreign partner combined with a willingness by Beijing to open its door in an area where it needed tech and expertise, but closely policed by a capricious Communist Party doorkeeper prepared to slam it shut just as soon as the foreign partner had outlived its usefulness.

Granting selective favours to foreign suitors who can be of most use has long been a feature of the CCP playbook (and arguably also of earlier Chinese dynasties). In 1986, during the early reformist days, the Party granted financial favours, including the right to exchange the Chinese currency it earned inside China for US dollars, to American Motors Corporation. AMC's Beijing Jeep joint venture was at that time China's largest and most important joint venture. Both sides agreed to keep their deal confidential, since the privileges were not available to others. Back then, the CCP wanted Beijing Jeep to be seen as a symbol of success and expected the company to keep any complaints quiet and publicly sing the praises of China. Don St Pierre, the president of Beijing Jeep duly complied, telling a gathering of foreign business people and Chinese government officials, 'I see the coming Year of the Rabbit as one of unlimited potential here in China for foreign investment, and I do not hesitate to advise others to jump in,' though privately he was much more sceptical, telling his bosses in America that the long-term future for American companies in China was dim.[18] Vehicle technology has come a long way since then, but not some of the basic premises of business in China. The CCP saw enormous value in having Musk as a cheerleader at a time of growing international tension, and if the maverick entrepreneur had any private doubts about his dealings with Beijing, he kept them to himself.

When Elon Musk in 2022 bought Twitter, renaming it X, the purchase caused particular concern about free speech among exiled Chinese artists who used the platform to present their work and to criticise CCP repression. In late summer 2023, when I visited Ai Weiwei at his new home in Portugal, he was scathing about the Tesla owner, telling me that he had cut back on his use of Twitter/X. He showed me an animation he had created, in which the X spins and then turns into a swastika. It was deleted from Twitter/X not long after he posted it but was still available on Instagram. 'It's so creepy,' Ai said of the new X logo. 'I mean it looks so ugly and so creepy.' To him, it was authoritarian, which was the point of his animation. 'You know, birds are so nice, it's just some blue colour and the birds,' he said of the original Twitter logo. 'But he [Musk] wants to show his ambition, you see his performance here is really about a lot of personal ego I think.'

Ai had ample experience of companies cold-shouldering him to protect their commercial interests. In 2015, while preparing an Australian show on freedom of expression, Lego, the Danish toymaker, refused his studio's request for a bulk order. The company said it could not 'approve the use of Lego for political works'. Its refusal coincided with the announcement of a new Legoland park in Shanghai and was widely seen as the company seeking to protect its business interests in China. Ai was then inundated with Lego donations from supporters – which he turned into another artwork, a 'field' of contraband bricks. Lego later reversed its policy after a worldwide outcry. In spite of that, he remains an enthusiast for Lego (the product), and as part of a 2023 show at London's Design Museum, he recreated Monet's *Water Lilies* out of 650,000 Lego bricks.

Twitter/X is also an important platform for fellow exiled artist, Badiucao. As Musk was manoeuvring to buy Twitter, he posted a cartoon of Elon Musk opening his jacket to reveal a T-shirt with the logo, 'I ♥ Uyghur Genocide'. The cartoon was a biting satire on Tesla's decision to open a showroom in Urumqi, the capital of Xinjiang province – Tesla posted pictures online of staff at the opening ceremony holding signs reading 'Tesla Loves Xinjiang'. When Musk bought Twitter, Badiucao said. 'I've become extremely concerned about how much free speech that we will still have [on Twitter] when we try to criticise the Chinese government . . . And, of course, because of this conflicting interest, we just do not know if Musk would stand his ground and protect us.'[19]

At the time of writing, there has been no evidence of censorship, but worrying indications of what might lie ahead. In his 2023 biography *Elon Musk*, author Walter Isaacson describes a tense conversation between Musk and Bari Weiss, a journalist who had been hired by Musk, but was increasingly uneasy about her boss. When Weiss quizzed him about whether his business interests in China might affect Twitter/X, 'Musk got annoyed,' writes Isaacson. 'Musk said that Twitter would indeed have to be careful about the words it used regarding China, because Tesla's business could be threatened. China's repression of the Uyghurs, he said, had two sides.'[20] Although Twitter/X is banned in China, the CCP makes considerable use of the platform for propaganda and disinformation, both through the accounts of its own diplomats and Party-run media, and via the widespread covert use of fake profiles and bots. In what appeared to be a shot across Musk's bow, Chinese state media, usually so flattering about him, attacked the Tesla boss for re-tweeting a post appearing to endorse the highly plausible theory that the Covid-19 pandemic might have originated with a leak from a Wuhan lab. The *Global Times* warned Musk against 'breaking the pot of China', a saying akin to 'biting the hand that feeds you'.[21] The 'free speech absolutist', so quick to the verbal draw when confronting critics in America, did not respond.

While Elon Musk had the reddest of red-carpet treatment, he was not the only Western business person welcomed to China after the Covid reopening. The same month that Musk was sitting down with Communist Party bosses, Jamie Dimon, the head of JP Morgan, was hosting a major business conference in Shanghai, where he met the city's Communist Party boss. He insisted JP Morgan, America's largest bank and the biggest in the world by market capitalisation, was in China for the good times and the bad. 'We're here, we're going to support the Chinese people,' he said.[22] Disputes over security and free and fair trade were all 'resolvable' he insisted. 'You're not going to fix these things if you are just sitting across the Pacific yelling at each other. So I'm hoping we have real engagement.'[23] The CCP's *Global Times* said his visit, like that of Elon Musk, was 'a vote of confidence in the Chinese economy'.[24]

At the height of the pandemic, in November 2021, Dimon had flown to Hong Kong, where he was allowed to skip the territory's strict twenty-one-day hotel quarantine rules. He runs a 'huge bank' with 'key business in Hong Kong', explained Hong Kong's chief executive.[25] It was a reminder of the bank's importance to the territory, but also its huge commitment to mainland China, where exposure at that time was estimated at around $20 billion, mainly from lending, deposits, trading and investments.[26] A few months later, the bank was granted permission to take full control of its securities business in China, a first for an international firm. A euphoric Dimon described China as 'one of the largest opportunities in the world for many of our clients'.[27] Just weeks following that decision Dimon issued a grovelling apology after joking during an unguarded moment at a US event that his bank would outlast the Communist Party. 'I regret and should not have made that comment,' he said in a statement.[28] It was an awkward moment, but quickly forgiven – because Beijing needed Wall Street.

Goldman Sachs, Citigroup, Morgan Stanley and others followed JP Morgan in taking control of their Chinese joint ventures after Beijing removed foreign-ownership caps.[29] BlackRock, the world's biggest asset manager, won approval to start a $1 billion mutual fund, the first to be fully run by a foreign firm. Larry Fink, the firm's billionaire boss, something of an evangelist in the West for 'responsible' business practices, called China 'one of the biggest business opportunities'.[30] In 2020, even as the relationship between Washington and Beijing soured, the exposure of Wall Street's five largest banks to China reached a record $77.8 billion.[31] They also earned record fees from helping Chinese firms list their shares on international stock markets. As with Tesla, it was not hard to understand the mutual attraction. Wall Street saw China as a last great frontier, a source of bumper fees, while the CCP needed financial expertise and innovation, its own markets and institutions being weak and under-developed. It also needed Wall Street's facilitators to smooth the flow of investment to China and to enable Chinese companies to tap international markets.

One early innovation was variable interest entities (VIEs), which created the illusion of foreigners buying shares in Chinese companies while denying them any control. The VIE was a holding company, typically registered in an offshore jurisdiction such as the Cayman Islands. The VIE did not own any assets in China itself, but instead owned a contract for a share in the Chinese company's profits. This became a popular structure for Chinese companies listing in America, including for Alibaba, the e-commerce pioneer, and Tencent, an internet giant. It appeared to satisfy CCP demands to prevent foreign control of Chinese assets but had no real legal status. It was always a risky structure, leaving shareholders, who essentially owned an IOU rather than a share, with little legal recourse if problems emerged.[32]

The CCP's love affair with Wall Street also created the most effective lobbyists in Washington for the continued appeasement of China. As political patience with Beijing's behaviour was rapidly exhausted, Wall Street could still be relied upon to preach restraint and engagement, while talking up the prospect of the China market. In July 2021, as Xi Jinping tightened his grip over the economy and markets, and investor confidence began to ebb, the deputy chairman of China's securities regulator, Fang Xinghai, summoned executives of BlackRock, Goldman Sachs and other firms to a meeting, urging them to keep the faith. Which most of them did, though their inter-actions with CCP entities were coming under closer scrutiny in the West. In summer 2023, it was reported that Goldman Sachs had used a fund set up with Chinese state money to buy a series of US and UK companies.[33] The funds came from the Chinese Investment Corporation, a sovereign wealth fund, and the companies targeted included a start-up that tracks global supply chains, a consultancy that advises on cloud computing, a manufacturer of systems used for artificial intelligence, drones and electric vehicle batteries, and a cybersecurity business that provided services to the British gov-ernment. Although Goldman Sachs announced the investments, it did not say that they were financed, at least in part, by Chinese government money. A congressional investigation in early 2024 accused five US venture capital firms of investing at least $3 billion in Chinese companies developing technology allegedly involved in human rights abuses and to benefit the Chinese military.[34]

When China abandoned its zero-Covid policy at the end of 2022 and began to reopen, Wall Street slipped easily back into its role as chief cheerleader. It was nearly unanimous in predicting an economic 'bounce-back' boom and in welcoming at face value the dubious promises of Chinese leaders of more market-friendly policies. The boom quickly petered out and the policies never materialised. In July 2023, Chinese financial regulators invited some of the West's biggest investment firms to another private meeting in Beijing in an effort to maintain their support. Those invited included large foreign fund managers, sovereign wealth funds and pension funds, who were encouraged to provide comments and suggestions about the economic outlook.[35] None were prepared to talk publicly about the event amid growing concern about the health of the Chinese economy, and the reliability of its Wall Street supporters. As one columnist in the *Financial Times* put it, 'Something is rotten in the Chinese economy, but don't expect Wall Street analysts to tell you about it. There has never been a bigger disconnect, in my experience, between some of the rosier investment bank views on China and the dim reality on the ground.'[36]

Wall Street's accommodation of the CCP was also evident in the changing language of prospectus documents, which banks typically draw up when a Chinese company is listed on an overseas stock exchange, known as an initial public offering (IPO). These documents usually detail potential risk factors for investors, but the language was watered down to comply with new Chinese government rules banning 'any comments in a manner that misrepresents or disparages laws and policies, [the] business environment and judicial situation of the state'.[37] This meant that while the risks of investing in Chinese companies were rising sharply, investors were kept largely in the dark.

All of which brings to mind Wall Street's first serious encounter with the CCP, in November 1986, when executives led by John J. Phelan Jr, chairman of the New York Stock Exchange, held a one hour meeting with Deng Xiaoping, China's then paramount leader, in the Great Hall of the People in Beijing. Phelan gave Deng a gold button which would allow the Chinese leader access at any time to the New York Stock Exchange. The executives had just overseen a four-day symposium for Chinese bureaucrats on how financial markets work. Deng seemed lively and alert, telling his guests, 'I think the main purpose is to exploit you.'[38] Reports at the time suggested Deng was joking, though with hindsight it might well have been one of the most honest comments to ever come out of the mouth of a communist leader.

It often seems that many Western companies in China are suffering from a form of corporate Stockholm syndrome, a condition whereby a hostage develops feelings of trust, affection and sympathy for their captors. The ends they go to in order to ingratiate themselves with the CCP are staggering. In a presentation in the city of Wuxi in May 2023 to mark its thirtieth year in China, the China president of the British pharmaceutical giant AstraZeneca pledged to be a patriotic company in China that 'loves the Communist Party and loves the country'.[39] At the Beijing office of EY China, one of the big four accounting firms, CCP members were asked to wear hammer and sickle Party badges to show their political loyalty while at work.[40] The request came from the EY email account of the Communist Party branch committee at the firm, so seemingly had at least the implicit support of the company. 'The badge should be placed in the middle of the left chest and cannot be worn on the collar,' the committee email said. 'When worn with other badges, it should be placed above them.'[41] Adidas, the German clothes company which suffered following a CCP-orchestrated consumer boycott over its stance on Xinjiang cotton, sought to win back market share with 'patriotic' branding, including a red tracksuit top with 'China' emblazoned in large Chinese characters.[42] One business book suggested Western companies in China needed to become more 'ambidextrous', defined as 'the ability to cultivate markedly differ-ent organisational methods in the same company.'[43] This seems to be management speak for the old adage, 'when in Rome, do as the Romans do,' with the Chinese business operations separated as far as possible and managed in accordance with local rules, norms and values. The problem is that many of those laws, values and norms have been hijacked and degraded by the CCP, and being ambidextrous would seem to involve the sort of contortions, moral compromises and geopolitical choices that would likely destroy a company's reputation in its home market.

It has long been an article of faith among CCP leaders that Western businesses are greedy and gullible and can always be bought or cajoled. When Xi Jinping visited San Francisco in November 2023, a meeting with business leaders appeared to be more important to him than his summit with US President Joe Biden. It was Xi's first visit to the United States for six years, and Beijing had initially demanded the banquet happen ahead of the summit. Washington refused, since this would have been a major breach of protocol.[44] Elon Musk, Apple's Tim Cook and Wall Street's finest were among those present to hear Xi say, 'China is both a super-large economy and a super-large market . . . modernisation for 1.4 billion Chinese is a huge opportunity that China provides to the world' – a pitch that is as old and vacuous as 'reform and opening'.[45] Musk posted a photograph of himself shaking hands with Xi, with the caption, 'May there be prosperity for all.'[46] In the months ahead of Xi's San Francisco visit, many of the executives present enjoyed better access to Chinese leaders in Beijing than did members of Biden's team. With Western leaders increasingly talking the language of de-risking and the world economy looking to some like a battlefield, Xi still saw the value of taking his pitch over the heads of the Biden administration and directly to business leaders, who had been such reliable allies in the past.

In fairness, Stockholm syndrome may mask a range of other conditions. Fear, pragmatism, opportunism, cynicism, greed, naïvety – you will find them all in corporate dealings with Beijing, and perhaps Musk is the perfect embodiment of that complexity. By late 2023, there were already early signs of strains in his China relationship. Tesla accused a Chinese chip designer and auto-parts manufacturer of stealing technology secrets, which came as no surprise to seasoned China-watchers, who joked privately that Musk would need exceptional cyber defences to thwart the inevitable IP theft that was part and parcel of business in China.[47] Tesla cars were also banned from military and government facilities because of security fears over the vehicles' cameras and sensors, though Musk insisted his company would never use the technology for spying.[48]

In April 2024, Tesla reported a 48 per cent drop in quarterly revenue – caused in part by an EV production glut and fierce price war unleashed by Chinese rivals. It seemed like an industry Telsa had helped galvanise by its very presence in China was beginning to devour the global standard bearer. Nevertheless, Musk doubled down on China: that same month, he flew in his private jet to Beijing and met almost immediately with premier Li Qiang, who as Communist Party boss of Shanghai had smoothed Tesla's path to building a production facility in that city. He won agreement in principle to offer Tesla's most advanced self-driving software on cars in China – software seen as critical for the future of the company, but which had been greeted with caution by American regulators. Details of the deal were sketchy; it was not immediately clear what Musk agreed in return, though as we have seen on multiple occasions in this book, the CCP routinely demands that technology be shared in exchange for market access.

For the moment, the interests of Musk and the CCP remain largely in alignment. The relationship survived the hiccups because the CCP still needed Musk and Musk needed China. By contrast, Wall Street's financiers were beginning to find the CCP's honeytrap was taking on a less attractive odour. That was no more so than in Hong Kong, for so long a comfortable home for the Western financial community, but now taking on all the trappings of a police state that even those with the most severe cases of Stockholm syndrome were finding difficult to stomach.

CHAPTER 16

Hong Kong's Descent into Tyranny

'We should treat the people wanted by police,
especially those who violated the national
security law, as rats in the street.'

John Lee, chief executive of Hong Kong

One of Hong Kong's principal attractions to foreign businesses, their employees and families was that it wasn't China. But it gave good access to the People's Republic and provided an excellent perch from which to observe developments and do business, safely cocooned from the capricious and often brutal whims of the CCP. China was an oppressive place to live, heavily polluted and with pervasive surveillance, and it offered few of the certainties available in freewheeling Hong Kong, with its trusted and independent legal system and freedom of expression. Under British rule and during the years of relative autonomy that followed, there was always a palpable sense of relief among those returning from the mainland after a business trip.

The territory also operated as a service centre for China's business elite, who also benefited enormously from its status as a separate jurisdiction to China for trade purposes, its laissez-faire approach to the economy and its legal protections. Some of China's most innovative entrepreneurs chose to domicile their assets in Hong Kong. Even the Communist Party itself frequently conducted business dealings through the territory, with Hong Kong oiling the wheels of 'reform and opening', especially during the early years, and contributing enormously to the development of the Chinese economy. Its contribution was so large in fact, that its descent into tyranny once again brings to mind Mao's self-destructive campaign against the sparrows. However, Hong Kong's existential crisis is also a parable of the way China has changed under Xi Jinping.

Xi's hand-picked leader in the territory, its chief executive, who oversees day-to-day repression, is John Lee, a former policeman who directed the police's brutal 2019 crackdown against pro-democracy protests. In 2023, with business people deserting the city in droves, he went on a charm offensive, launching 'Happy Hong Kong', a campaign aimed at generating 'positive energy' after what the government described as 'more than three years of challenges'. Lee doesn't really do charm however and the campaign coincided with his decision to put a bounty on the heads of pro-democracy activists living overseas. The Hong Kong police offered HK$1 million (around £100,000) for information leading to their arrest. Lee said the fugitives should be treated like 'rats in the street',[1] would be 'pursued for life' and 'spend their days in fear'.[2] Police also detained family members of those living in exile, holding them for hours and questioning them about their relatives.[3] Harassing or even holding hostage the relatives of overseas dissidents in order to silence them or force them to return home is a common strategy of the Chinese Communist Party, but this was the first recorded example of it happening in Hong Kong.

Still, 'Happy Hong Kong' went ahead with street parties, concerts and carnivals, while the Hong Kong Tourist Board offered half a million free air tickets to encourage overseas visitors.[4] The government released a promotional video full of smiling Hongkongers, dancing and holding hands, an excited voiceover explaining that the former British colony offered 'joyful moments for all', and that 'There are reasons to be happy everywhere you go in Hong Kong.'[5] Though not if you were one of five speech therapists jailed for subversion after they wrote a children's book about sheep trying to defend their village against wolves – prosecutors claimed they were trying to incite hatred against China.[6] Nor if you were a cinemagoer keen to see *Winnie the Pooh: Blood and Honey*, which was abruptly removed from schedules two days before its cinema release in the city following unflattering comparisons between the rotund bear and President Xi Jinping.[7] Nor if you were a fan of *The Simpsons*, an episode of which was removed in Hong Kong after long-suffering Marge Simpson declared, 'Behold the wonders of

China: Bitcoin mines, forced labour camps where children make smartphones.'[8]

Hong Kong was an especially unhappy place if you were seventy-five-year-old Jimmy Lai, Beijing's highest-profile critic jailed under the territory's draconian national security law. Lai, a British citizen, was the founder of the pro-democracy newspaper *Apple Daily*, which was raided and shut down. The authorities sought to undermine his defence by blocking his chosen British lawyer, Timothy Owen, from entering the territory, denying him a visa and ruling that Owen's presence could harm national security.[9] Lai was initially jailed for nearly six years on trumped-up fraud charges and faced further charges in early 2024 for colluding with foreign forces, carrying a potential life sentence. By then, 260 people had been arrested under the national security law, which was imposed on the territory by Beijing in 2020, including many prominent pro-democracy leaders.

Those who knew John Lee complained privately about his lack of intellect, but that was to miss the point – the primary role of Hong Kong's leader was as Beijing's enforcer, and the only thing that mattered to CCP leaders was his ability to ruthlessly and single-mindedly impose their will. There is often a fine line between tyranny and absurdity, and at times Lee seemed the very embodiment of that. In the days ahead of the 4 June anniversary of the Tiananmen Square massacre, as 'Happy Hong Kong' events were getting into their stride, he was asked at a press briefing about the legality of mourning the victims. The answer was obvious – the group that organised an annual candlelight vigil had been disbanded and its leaders arrested,[10] the city's most famous statue commemorating the massacre had been removed from display at Hong Kong University and seized,[11] and public libraries had purged books about the bloody events of 1989.[12] Yet Lee looked uncomfortable as he struggled to avoid uttering the forbidden words 'Tiananmen Square', the massacre having been written out of Chinese history by his CCP masters. 'Everybody should act in accordance with the law and think of what they do, so as to be ready to face the consequences,' he said, without giving a direct answer.[13] Days later, Lee sent 500 police to sweep up some two dozen brave protesters who staged a peaceful vigil in the city's Victoria Park, where in the past tens of thousands had gathered in remembrance.[14] Four months later, on China's National Day, Lee deployed 7,000 police across the city in order to crush any signs of dissent; videos showed police dragging to the ground and tying the hands of a man who had stood in solitary protest in Causeway Bay, holding aloft a bunch of white flowers – a symbol of mourning in Chinese culture.[15]

As Hong Kong emerged from the Covid-19 pandemic, Lee reached out to the international finance community, hoping that perhaps they hadn't noticed the repression – or didn't care. He hosted a Global Financial Leaders' Investment Summit in an effort to persuade the heads of some 120 of the world's top banks and hedge funds that in spite of the destruction of Hong Kong's autonomy and its criminalisation of all opposition, it remained an attractive place to do business.[16] David Solomon, the chairman of Goldman Sachs, James Gorman, the chairman of Morgan Stanley, and HSBC's chief executive Noel Quinn were among those who gathered at the city's swish Four Seasons Hotel to hear Lee say that Hong Kong 'remains the only place in the world [where] global advantages and the China advantage come together in a single city . . . Opportunity and timing, right here, right now in Hong Kong. This is the moment you have been waiting for. Go for it. Get in front, not behind.'[17] He unveiled an array of incentives, including a HK$30 billion (£3 billion) fund to help businesses set up in Hong Kong. By most accounts he was politely received, though executives seemed anxious to avoid being photographed alone with Lee, who was under US sanctions for 'being involved in coercing, arresting, detaining or imprisoning individuals' under the national security law.

The three-day summit included a dinner at M+, the city's new museum of contemporary art on the harbourfront. The sprawling museum, which was opened in 2021, was hailed as a world class institution that would put the city on the global map for contemporary art. Instead, it has been dogged by accusations of censorship.[18] One pro-Beijing lawmaker accused the museum of spreading 'hatred' towards China, while another reminded it, 'The opening of M+ does not mean that artistic expression is above the law.'[19] Carrie Lam, who was Hong Kong's chief executive at the time of the opening, said officials were on 'full alert' in order to ensure that the exhibitions did not undermine national security.[20] The original collection included a photograph by exiled dissident artist Ai Weiwei in which he is raising his middle finger before Beijing's Tiananmen gate and its portrait of Mao Zedong, part of his *Studies in Perspective* series. It was removed from the museum's online archive, and the museum's director said, 'We work within the laws of our city.'[21]

It's hard to know whether the financial elite gathered at M+ were aware of the controversy that swirled through the galleries around them. The official narrative claimed the participants at the summit were exuberant, delighted to be back in the city, keen for business as usual, though most of the proceedings were held behind closed doors, suggesting a certain reticence. Unofficial reports described the atmosphere as subdued. Surveys of the foreign business community were gloomy, with companies relocating to Singapore, which was determined to wrench away the title of Asia's financial hub. Financial and market analysts began to self-censor their reports or talk in code on the telephone, fearing that a critical report could fall foul of the new national security law.[22] An October 2023 survey by one global recruitment consultancy found that more than half of Hong Kong's professionals were considering leaving the city in the near future; some 40 per cent said they had already applied for overseas roles.[23] Official data released at the time of the gathering of financiers showed a shrinking economy and a declining population. Reports bemoaned the city's depressed bar scene and the muting of its once vibrant nightlife, with one asking, 'This city never slept, but with China tightening its grip, is the party over?'[24] The only exception, it seemed, was the proliferation of leaving parties, where popular venues were booked out weeks in advance.

When he was first installed as chief executive in May 2022, Lee echoed Xi Jinping in proclaiming that the world was experiencing 'profound changes unseen in a century', CCP-speak for the rise of China and decline of the West. He also promoted training on what he called 'consistent and correct messages on the rule of law in the community'. He was, in effect, proclaiming that the version of rule of law on which Hong Kong's success was built was effectively dead. During the following months a growing number of multinational companies moved arbitration cases and the drafting of new contracts away from the city, with Singapore as the main beneficiary.[25] Lee was careful to avoid CCP slogans when he addressed the financiers, many of whom will have noticed the fading communist-style posters plastered around the city to mark the twenty-fifth anniversary of the 1997 return to Chinese rule. 'Stability. Prosperity. Opportunity,' they read. Lee could arguably be credited with achieving the first – but only at the cost of the other two.[26]

Hong Kong Island was ceded by China to the victorious British in the 1842 Treaty of Nanjing at the end of the First Opium War. It is central to two key themes that underpin Communist Party rule and mythology – victimhood and the Party's regenerative powers. In the CCP's telling of history, the loss of Hong Kong marked the beginning of a 'century of humiliation' at the hands of hostile and rapacious foreigners. It marked the start of a descent 'into an abyss of semi-imperial and semi-feudal society'.[27] Yet this anti-colonial rhetoric can obscure the fact that Hong Kong under British rule served a very useful purpose for the CCP as a source of revenue and an interface with the outside world. In the early days after the Communist Party seized power in China in 1949, the Party was too consumed with the country's internal chaos to do much about recovering the colony, and it quickly became a crossroads where East met West, a home to traders, spies and China-watchers of all types – a point of friction, but also of cooperation. Much of its population were refugees, who fled economic hardship and repression in the mainland.

The Communist Party could have shut down the colony at any time by simply turning off the water, but preferred to sit back and let the clock tick down to 1997, when the British lease expired on Hong Kong's New Territories. The Party might have hated what Hong Kong represented, but the colony was too useful; When Deng Xiaoping first launched his reforms, it provided 40 per cent of China's foreign exchange earnings through trade and various other remittances from friends and families. As Chris Patten, Britain's last governor of Hong Kong, described it in a memoir shortly after the handover, 'Hong Kong is at one and the same time China's window on the world, bridge to the world, shopfront for the world and paradigm for the world of what China as a whole could become.'[28] Deng Xiaoping courted the overseas Chinese, particularly those in Hong Kong and Taiwan, to invest money and expertise, and Shenzhen was deliberately chosen as China's first special economic zone because of its proximity to the British colony.

Hong Kong was far from being a full democracy under the British, but did enjoy freedom of expression, a free-wheeling capitalist economy and the rule of law. When the territory was handed back to China in 1997, these freedoms were enshrined in a mini constitution called the 'Basic Law', creating a liberal bubble within authoritarian China. The Basic Law gave effect to the Sino-British Joint Declaration, a treaty signed by the two governments in 1984 and registered with the United Nations – giving it the force of international law. This supposedly granted the territory semi-autonomy for 50 years – a formula usually referred to as 'one country two systems'. The Basic Law included broad commitments to extend representative democracy, with universal suffrage for electing the Hong Kong leader – its chief executive – as the 'ultimate aim'.

For the CCP, the return of Hong Kong was hugely symbolic, a righting of historic wrongs and a boost to its legitimacy. Party leaders were suspicious of their newly reclaimed possession and its Westernised elite, but the territory remained an important if not vital economic asset. At the time of the handover, the size of Hong Kong's economy was almost a fifth of that of all of China; it channelled investment to the mainland and facilitated trade in both directions. Chinese companies increasingly tapped its capital markets and listed on its stock exchange, while a torrent of money flowed in both directions. In reality, the influence of Hong Kong was probably even greater than the bald figures suggest, as many of its services remained below the radar. Foremost among these was 'round-tripping', a practice whereby Chinese individuals and companies routed investments through companies in Hong Kong in order to disguise their origin and benefit from tax breaks reserved for foreigners.[29] Other trading trickery included the transhipment and relabelling of goods as 'Made in Hong Kong' to avoid tariffs. Invoices were manipulated, with exports from China undervalued, and imports overvalued, with both routed (on paper) via a Hong Kong trading company. In practice, the goods never got anywhere near Hong Kong, and the sole purpose of the company was to do the paperwork and pocket the substantial differences. Hong Kong firms would also act as agents to facilitate the purchase of overseas assets, such as a hotel or a company, at a grossly inflated price, the excess being siphoned off. In a similar vein, Chinese firms maintained Hong Kong-based 'consultancy' services, which were paid handsomely for non-existent services, as another way of shifting funds from China. Another business, worth billions of dollars annually, was in tradable insurance policies – again with the purpose of avoiding capital controls.

In many ways these services can be seen as a more sophisticated version of the Macau casino laundromat, with much the same purpose of moving money abroad. Although in Hong Kong the beneficiaries usually had deeper pockets and were better connected politically, frequently the sons, daughters and friends of the CCP elite – the princelings, as they were known. In Hong Kong they had at their service one of the world's most sophisticated financial systems and a host of Western 'wealth managers' and other facilitators catering to their every need and able to set them up with shell companies in the most obscure of offshore jurisdictions. The CCP itself also found Hong Kong convenient when it wanted to disguise its own business activities. One of the most detailed studies came from the US Defense Department's Africa Center for Strategic Studies, which exposed the activities of what it called the Queensbury Group, dozens of interlinked companies registered in Hong Kong's business district. The group was behind a string of deals with some of Africa's most corrupt and oppressive regimes, and was linked to Chinese intelligence and state-owned companies.[30]

The CCP did tighten its grip in the years immediately after the handover, but Hong Kong's autonomy was useful, and it still viewed the place essentially as an economic city, where people were too busy making money to be concerned with politics. Even when the territory faced a first wave of pro-democracy protests in 2014, an uprising that became known as the umbrella movement, it seemed inconceivable to many that the CCP would slay this golden goose, yet the calculations of the Party under its new leader Xi Jinping were beginning to change.

The CCP misread Hong Kong. At the time of the handover, there was among Hong Kong's 7.5 million people widespread fear and suspicion about whether China would keep its word. That anxiety grew, especially among the territory's well-educated and tech-savvy young. Even before the 2014 unrest, the territory had a loud and lively protest culture; every year for example on 4 June, tens of thousands gathered for a candle-lit vigil to remember the 1989 Tiananmen Square massacre, when Beijing supressed its own student-led democracy movement, with the loss of hundreds, perhaps thousands of lives. Increasingly large anti-China protests were held in Hong Kong on the anniversary of the handover too, as well as against a proposed anti-subversion law and proposals to oblige schools to teach 'patriotic education'. In both cases, the Hong Kong government backed down.

Mass street protests flared in 2014 after Beijing quashed lingering hopes for greater democracy by declaring that any popular election for the territory's leader would be from a list of candidates vetted for their loyalty to the Communist Party. For almost three months, protests crippled the heart of the city, the uprising symbolised by a yellow parasol, after umbrellas were used as shields to protect against pepper spray used by the police. The young, mostly student protesters were overwhelmingly peaceful and well-organised; their protests were a cry of anger, but also one of hope for a better future. The spectre of the Tiananmen Square massacre also hung over the colourful protests, the fear that the Communist Party might trample over the territory's autonomy and send in the army to crush them, as it had the student protesters in Beijing in 1989. Had the Hong Kong protests happened elsewhere in China, they almost certainly would have been quickly and violently supressed.

The Party no doubt weighed the costs and benefits of violent intervention – its need to assert Party authority against the costs of openly trashing the Basic Law and unleashing bloodshed on the streets of Asia's financial capital, in full view of the world's cameras. By 2014, the relative size of Hong Kong's economy had fallen to around 3 per cent of that of a fast-growing China, but the territory remained an important conduit for trade and investment, above and below the table. The People's Liberation Army stayed in its barracks. Instead the Party launched a cyberassault on the democracy movement, which was dubbed by one cybersecurity specialist 'the cyber siege of Hong Kong'.[31] By the time the exhausted protesters left the streets in mid-December 2014, they had been hit with a full arsenal of cyberweapons that ranged from massive denial of service attacks designed to bring down systems by overwhelming them with data, to highly sophisticated surveillance techniques, involving the hacking of websites, computers, laptops and mobiles. The cyberattacks were possibly the largest, most intense and most varied ever used against dissent.

The pro-democracy movement learned from that experience, and when they returned to the streets in 2019, their targets included 'smart lampposts', which they cut down, smashing the cameras and sensors, and ripping out the wires and circuitry – the high-tech gadgetry they feared was tracking them and spying on their communications.[32] They knew that to sustain the protest movement this time, they had to keep China's surveillance state at bay. Protesters handed out stickers with images of surveillance cameras, warning that 'monitoring is coming'. Banners warned that the kind of oppressive tactics used against the Uyghurs in Xinjiang could be exported to supposedly semi-autonomous Hong Kong. The protests, which at their height brought 2 million people – more than a quarter of the population – to the streets, had begun as a backlash against a proposed new law that would allow people to be extradited for trial in CCP-controlled courts in mainland China. But they soon embraced a wider call for democracy and a rejection of China's dystopian surveillance state.

The youth-led protests were likened to water, ebbing and flowing, and apparently leaderless. The protesters wore hard hats, goggles and masks (often gas masks), to protect against tear gas as they fought pitched battles with an increasingly brutal police force, but also to hide their identities. They organised through scores of encrypted groups on the messaging app Telegram and on online forums; bulletins were exchanged via near-field communication tools such as Airdrop, which use Bluetooth to communicate with nearby iPhones and iPads, making it more secure than WiFi. Protesters were encouraged not to leave a digital footprint, often using multiple devices and several messaging accounts. It all enabled the protesters to quickly develop and change their plans and tactics, a fluidity that kept them one step ahead of the authorities.

In Beijing, the same calculation prevailed: meeting the challenge to the Party against the economic cost of intervention. The economic importance of Hong Kong to China had changed little since 2014. The size of Hong Kong's economy compared to that of the mainland had shrunk a little – down to 2.7 per cent by one calculation – but it remained Asia's largest financial centre, and one of the world's biggest markets for equity and debt finance.[33] In 2018, more than half of foreign direct investment into China was channelled through the city, as was almost 60 per cent of China's outward investment. More than half the $64.2 billion raised globally by Chinese companies came from listings in Hong Kong; Chinese companies also used Hong Kong for a third of their offshore US dollar funding. Chinese banks held more than a trillion dollars of assets in the city; Hong Kong's ports continued to handle a big share of China's exports and imports. The city was China's largest trading partner in services, and at the forefront of efforts to develop China's renminbi (or yuan) into a serious international currency that might one day compete with the US dollar. Hong Kong's semi-autonomous status allowed it to negotiate investment and trade agreements independent of Beijing, and to be treated separately in the eyes of US law. Its independent judiciary seemed more important than ever as Xi Jinping extended the Party's reach into business (and just about everything else) on the mainland, and China's direct exports were being hit by US tariffs. To some, it still seemed inconceivable that Xi would jeopardise that position, as challenging as the protests had become.

That was to misread the CCP leader, who had consolidated his power in Beijing and was presiding over a severe crackdown on dissent. He had shown himself to be ruthless and intolerant of challenges to himself and to the Party. His political calculations over Hong Kong were also changing – he was now willing to sacrifice Hong Kong in pursuit of his broader goals. Not only did the police violently crush the protests, but at the end of June 2020 the CCP imposed a draconian national security law on Hong Kong, which tore up the territory's autonomy, shredding an international treaty. It paved the way for mainland-style repression and the deployment of the infrastructure of the surveillance state. It targeted any conduct deemed to threaten national security, allowing for secret courts presided over by government-selected judges. It targeted what it described as secession, subversion, terrorism and collusion with foreign forces, all open to wide interpretation, effectively criminalising any opposition.[34] Hundreds of opposition politicians, journalists and democracy activists, including a retired Roman Catholic cardinal in his nineties, were soon rounded up. Once vibrant schools, universities, environmental groups, trade unions and professional associations quickly felt the CCP's cold repressive embrace, as the authorities targeted any sign of dissent. *The Economist* described it as 'one of the biggest assaults on liberal democracy since the second world war'.[35]

Why did Xi destroy the semi-autonomy that had allowed Hong Kong to prosper and had been so economically beneficial to China? Certainly the challenge of the 2019 protests was far greater than those of 2014, and he might also have calculated that the world was distracted by the Covid-19 pandemic. Perhaps he believed that Hong Kong had outlived its usefulness, and that China (and he) were strong enough to weather any economic fallout or international backlash. He may also have calculated that it was better to move against Hong Kong while Donald Trump remained in the White House (the US presidential election was due in the November after the new security law was imposed) and there was less chance of a united Western response – though the US did remove Hong Kong's special trade privileges, saying it would now be treated like any other part of China. He may also have calculated that the impact of Hong Kong's autonomy on business was exaggerated, and that Western companies and financiers were motivated primarily by greed and could be bullied, as they had been in mainland China. He will no doubt have been encouraged by the likes of HSBC and Standard Chartered publicly supporting the national security law.[36]

Perhaps the most compelling explanation as to why Xi was prepared to destroy Hong Kong lies in his paranoia and his world view – it was perhaps the most striking demonstration of his obsession with control and security. For Xi, legitimate aspirations for greater freedom were evidence of 'foreign interference'. Ultimately the territory's economic and financial standing was secondary to the Party's need to bring Hong Kong to heel. Others may have seen independent institutions as a strength, but for Xi they were a threat, as was the very notion of a semi-autonomous global city on Chinese soil. For Xi, 'global' means 'foreign', and Hong Kong must first and foremost be run by unquestioning patriots, whose loyalty to the Party must be absolute. Concessions to pro-democracy protesters would have been unthinkable. The very existence of an enclave in China over which the Party could not exercise total control was simply incompatible with the narrowly defined interests of the Party. An independent-minded and free-spirited city was simply incompatible with Xi's notion of CCP rule.

By early 2024, John Lee appeared to be embracing his role as Xi's enforcer with unbridled enthusiasm. In March 2024, Hong Kong enacted a new security law to work in concert with that imposed by Beijing, but also going considerably further with five broad offences of treason, insurrection, espionage, destructive activities endangering national security and external interference. 'Foreign agents and Hong Kong independence advocates are still lurking in our society,' Lee warned.[37] The law expanded the British colonial era offence of 'sedition' to include inciting hatred against the Communist Party leadership.[38] Chillingly for foreign businesses, it said that information relating to economic and social development, major policy decisions, and science and technology could be considered state secrets. Local elections, run according to new rules that made it impossible to compete unless certified as a 'patriot', attracted a record low turnout.[39] Further light was shed on police methods when Agnes Chan, a leading pro-democracy activist, jumped bail and fled to Canada. She said that as part of her 'rehabilitation' she was forced to sign a repentance letter and to visit the headquarters of tech giant Tencent in nearby Shenzhen in order to understand the 'motherland's great development'.[40] Hong Kong also embraced another repressive tool from the mainland playbook – televised confessions. Remorseful political prisoners were shown admitting how they were led astray in a show jointly produced by the police and local broadcasters.

The exodus of foreign businesses and professionals from Hong Kong accelerated, embracing a broad range of companies, including banks, investment and technology firms, as well as lawyers, academics and economists – replaced in part by mainland Chinese firms and citizens.[41] Their worst fears appeared to be confirmed when a new law came into effect giving Chinese courts the authority to enforce mainland court rulings on commercial disputes in Hong Kong, further blurring the lines between the two legal systems.[42] Moody's, a credit rating agency, downgraded Hong Kong's sovereign credit to negative. At the same time, top US executives were reportedly advised to use burner phones – disposable devices – when visiting Hong Kong and not their usual work phones, out of fear of surveillance and hacking.[43] This had become common practice for mainland China but was the first time it had been extended to Hong Kong. Lee seemed oblivious to the fact that Hong Kong's strength, its attraction as a base, was its autonomy – and this was even the case for China's own companies. With that distinction gone, and Hong Kong now merely an extension of China, so had much of the attraction. In February 2024, it was reported that the American company Latham & Watkins, the world's second largest law firm, was cutting off Hong Kong-based lawyers from automatic access to its international databases; in effect, Hong Kong was to be treated like just another Chinese city.

By early summer 2024, more than 300 people had been arrested for 'national security' offences, according to official figures. This included six for publishing social media posts 'inciting hatred' against Beijing just ahead of the June 4 anniversary of the Tiananmen Square massacre. At a World Cup football qualifier in Hong Kong, three fans were arrested for turning their back during the playing of the Chinese national anthem and thereby 'insulting' the city's Communist Party masters. A secondary school was ordered to submit a report after a video of students horsing around during another rendition of the national anthem went viral online. Across the city, in the local community and in once vibrant expat circles, politics was something now discussed in hushed tones behind closed doors – if it was discussed at all.

Still, nothing seemed to dent the boundless public optimism of Noel Quinn, group chief executive of HSBC, for whom anything less than unbridled enthusiasm about China might have dangerous consequences for the territory's most influential company, a pillar of the financial system. HSBC was in the Communist Party's crosshairs, and no matter how hard Quinn worked to appease the CCP, his company's very existence in Hong Kong seemed anathema to the Party.

Chapter 17

The Humiliation of the World's Local Bank

'China and Hong Kong don't owe HSBC anything, the
China business at HSBC can be replaced overnight by
banks from China and other countries. We need to
let the UK government, politicians, British companies
like HSBC know which side of the bread is buttered.'

Leung Chun-ying, former Hong Kong chief executive

HSBC's chief executive Noel Quinn looked uncomfortable facing
the House of Commons Foreign Affairs Committee, which summoned him in January 2021 to explain why the bank froze the
assets of Hong Kong pro-democracy activists. 'To the extent that we
have frozen accounts, it is because we are obliged to under request
from the police authorities as they undertake their investigations,'
he said, insisting that politics never came into it. He was asked
if he understood the difference between political accusations and
criminal accusations. 'As a banker, I am not in a position to be able
to judge the motives or the validity of a legal instruction from a law
enforcement authority,' he replied. 'I'm not making a moral judgement. It's not my position to make a moral or political judgement
on these matters. I have to comply with the law.'[1]

The questions then turned to the draconian national security
law imposed by Beijing on Hong Kong in June 2020, effectively
criminalising political opposition, which was supported by HSBC.
'We, HSBC, issued a statement at that point in time along with
many other companies in Hong Kong that we believed that it was
appropriate to stabilise the security position in Hong Kong,' replied
Quinn.

Labour MP Chris Bryant was not impressed. 'Do you understand how it might seem to a lot of British people who have bank accounts with you that you are effectively aiding and abetting one of the biggest crackdowns on democracy in the world?'

Quinn didn't see it that way at all. 'I believe, Mr Bryant, that we play a very expansive role in Hong Kong and have done for 155 years and intend to do so going forward.'

Tory MP Andrew Rosindell could barely contain himself: 'I have to say that I am slightly aghast at what I have been hearing. It seems to me that there is a huge degree of double standards, hypocrisy and, in fact, appeasement towards the regime in China, which has now extended to Hong Kong.'

The uncomfortable grilling of one of the world's top bankers came after two years of political upheaval in the former British colony in which the lender that once styled itself 'the world's local bank' was accused of doing the Communist Party's bidding.

In December 2020, Ted Hui, a legislator stripped of his seat after he was deemed 'insufficiently patriotic', fled with his family to the UK. On arrival, he discovered that HSBC had frozen their bank accounts at the request of the Hong Kong police.[2] A Hong Kong court later sentenced Hui *in absentia* to three-and-a-half years in jail. The bank also froze accounts linked to a church that had helped young protesters and which was raided by the police. Roy Chan, the church pastor, and his family also fled to the UK, from where he claimed HSBC had become a 'tool for the regime's attempt to take political revenge via economic repression'.[3] An HSBC spokesperson said the bank was unable to comment on individual accounts. 'We have to abide by the laws of the jurisdiction in which we operate,' the person said, directing further enquiries to the 'related law enforcement agency'.[4] Protesters also accused the bank of helping the city's police to shut down one of the main sources of funding of the protest movement, the Spark Alliance Fund, a crowdsourcing operation that had raised around HK$80 million (£8 million) to help protesters with living expenses, as well as legal and medical costs.[5]

In June 2020, even before the full text of the national security law was published, HSBC joined Standard Chartered, another prominent local bank, in publicly supporting the law. HSBC's Asia

Pacific chief executive Peter Wong signed a petition supporting the new rules, and in a statement the company said: 'We respect and support laws and regulations that will enable Hong Kong to recover and rebuild the economy and, at the same time, maintain the principle of 'one country, two systems'.[6]

Beijing made it increasingly clear that it expected the territory's top companies to toe the Communist Party's line if they wanted to continue doing business. Hong Kong's former China-appointed leader C. Y. Leung warned, 'China and Hong Kong don't owe HSBC anything, the China business at HSBC can be replaced overnight by banks from China and other countries,' adding darkly that HSBC needed to know 'which side of the bread is buttered'.[7] Arguably the bank has spent much of its history doing just that as it manoeuvred amid the at-times turbulent politics of the region. However, the upheaval in Hong Kong, its biggest market, and the growing fault lines between China and the West presented the biggest challenge since the Hong Kong and Shanghai Banking Corporation was founded in 1865 with a single branch on the Hong Kong waterfront.

'The bank has weathered change in all forms – revolutions, economic crises, new technologies – and adapted to survive. The resulting corporate character enables HSBC to meet the challenges of the 21st century,' states a potted history on HSBC's corporate website.[8] The bank's founder, Sir Thomas Sutherland, a Scottish businessman and politician, envisaged a Hong Kong-based lender that could act as a financial bridge for trade between Europe and Asia, and the first branch in Hong Kong was followed a month later by another in Shanghai. Apart from the period from 1941 to 1945, during which the Japanese occupiers forced HSBC and other foreign-invested banks to leave Shanghai, it had a continuous presence in the city, housed in one of the largest and most impressive buildings on the Bund. The bank even withstood the communist takeover and the chaos that followed. It was eventually forced to hand over its grand premises to the Party, but kept dealing with inward remittances and export bills from rented accommodation until the economic reforms of the late 1970s. It was then in a strong position to take advantage of China's opening to the world and, in 1984, it became the first foreign lender to receive a banking licence to operate in China. HSBC saw China as its new frontier, and in 2009 it became the first foreign bank in China to underwrite yuan denominated bonds. In 2017, it became the first to launch a majority-owned securities joint venture.

In 1990, HSBC moved its headquarters to London following the takeover of Britain's Midland Bank. Officially, the move was at the request of the Bank of England, but it was also a prudent hedge a year after the massacre of student protesters in and around Tiananmen Square and seven years before the handover of Hong Kong from Britain to China – its shares remained listed on both Hong Kong and London stock exchanges. In the run up to the 1997 handover, there were tensions between Chris Patten, the last British governor, and Sir William Purves, the bank's chairman, who vehemently opposed Patten's modest democratic reforms. According to Jonathan Dimbleby's chronicle of the end of empire, *The Last Governor*, Purves went to Government House to threaten Patten, 'that if he did not change course, he would face dire consequences'. For his part, Patten had 'contempt' for Purves. Dimbleby describes a private dinner held for Purves by Peter Woo, a Hong Kong tycoon, shortly before Purves relocated to London in 1993: 'Purves spoke about his sadness at leaving Hong Kong. He uttered not a word about freedom or democracy or human rights . . . Reminding his approving audience that Hong Kong had to "get on" with China, he expressed the hope that relations would soon be restored and that the "cack-handed" manner in which these had been handled in recent months would soon be rectified.'[9]

By the time HSBC celebrated its century and a half in 2015, it had become a global giant, straddling the US and Europe. However, its experience in America was not a happy one. In 2017, HSBC had to pay $1.9 billion to settle a money-laundering probe by the FBI – the largest penalty of its kind ever paid by a bank. The investigation found HSBC had failed to prevent Mexican drug cartels from washing hundreds of millions of dollars.[10] In 2021, HSBC announced it was withdrawing from its loss-making US retail banking business. It also got embroiled in a money-laundering investigation in Britain, where in late 2021 it was fined £63.9 million by the Financial Conduct Authority (FCA), the UK's financial regulator, for 'unacceptable failings' of its anti-money laundering systems.

The FCA said weaknesses in HSBC's financial crime safeguards had been highlighted several times before action was taken. The bank's failings covered a period of eight years, from 2010 to 2018, the FCA saying there was inadequate monitoring of money laundering and terrorist financing scenarios until 2014, and poor risk assessment of 'new scenarios' after 2016. Europe's biggest bank was found to have had inadequate checks on the accuracy and completeness of data.[11]

As part of a major restructuring, HSBC shifted its focus back to Asia. Even while growing and diversifying internationally – with $2.7 trillion of assets and 235,000 employees across sixty-four countries by 2020 – Asia remained its lifeblood. It employed around 30,000 staff in Hong Kong alone, and in 2022, almost 78.3 per cent of its profits came from Asia, with Hong Kong accounting for almost 40 per cent of its global profits of $17.5 billion.[12] HSBC was also one of three banks, alongside Bank of China and Standard Chartered, allowed to issue banknotes in Hong Kong, and was described as the closest the territory had to a central bank – an informal lender of last resort. In April 2021, the bank announced that it was moving four of its most senior executives back to Hong Kong as part of the strategic revamp. Chief executive Noel Quinn said he aimed to 'move the heart of the business to Asia, including leadership', while continuing to retrench underperforming operations in Europe and the US.[13] At the time of writing, HSBC claims to have the widest geographical reach of any foreign bank in mainland China, with 140 outlets across fifty cities, and plans for further ambitious expansion.[14] However, if HSBC expected its globe-trotting executives to be welcomed with open arms by Hong Kong's communist overlords, it was gravely mistaken. Geopolitics were becoming ugly, and an increasingly aggressive China was facing growing push-back from the West, and in particular the United States. HSBC instead found itself on the front line of this geopolitical tussle. Xi Jinping was crushing dissent and extending the Communist Party into all walks of life. An independent bank wielding the power of HSBC in Chinese territory ran contrary to everything he stood for.

An early example of the geopolitical minefield HSBC was attempting to navigate came with the arrest in Canada in 2018 of Meng

Wanzhou, the chief financial officer of Huawei, the Chinese telecoms giant, which is a national tech champion and close to the Communist Party. The Canadian authorities were acting on an extradition request from the US, which accused Meng, the daughter of the company's founder, of fraud in relation to breaking sanctions against Iran. The case was built at least in part on evidence given to US prosecutors by HSBC, which provided Huawei with banking services.[15] At the time it handed over the evidence, HSBC was operating in America under the supervision of an independent monitor appointed by the Department of Justice following its massive fine for allowing Mexican drug cartels to launder money. 'Information provided by HSBC to the Justice Department was provided pursuant to formal demand, including grand jury subpoena or other obligation to provide information pursuant to a Deferred Prosecution Agreement or similar legal obligation,' said an HSBC spokesman.[16] Beijing exploded in anger after Meng's arrest, demanding an explanation from HSBC executives. The bank's top brass, led by then chief executive John Flint, launched a frantic lobbying exercise to convince Communist Party officials that the bank was not responsible for Meng's arrest.[17] Flint was summoned to the Chinese embassy in London, where he reportedly apologised and said that Washington had left him with no choice. One person advising HSBC said the situation was 'incredibly sensitive' for the bank. Less than two months after the meeting with the ambassador, HSBC parted company with Flint 'by mutual agreement'.[18] The bank denied he was pushed out as a result of political pressure from Beijing.

The Chinese authorities ordered China's state-owned firms to report any business ties they had with HSBC and several corporate clients transferred their deposits to other banks.[19] The *People's Daily* warned that 'HSBC will eventually lose all its customers', and shortly afterwards a state-backed website accused HSBC of handing 'the knife' to the US authorities in their case against Huawei.[20] The *Global Times* said HSBC could be included on China's forthcoming 'unreliable entity' list in response to its 'unethical action in the Huawei affair'.[21] Online giant Tencent, which owns the WeChat social media platform (*Weixin* in China) temporarily blocked HSBC from placing advertisements on any of its platforms, which deprived the bank of a key channel to reach retail customers in China.[22] One senior HSBC executive was quoted anonymously saying, 'HSBC has become a tense political organisation.'[23] The bank that prided itself in realpolitik looked for other ways of appeasing the Party.

In July 2022 it was reported that HSBC had become the first foreign lender to install a Communist Party committee in its investment banking subsidiary in China.[24] Without confirming or denying that HSBC Qianhai Securities had established a CCP cell, the bank played it down, claiming that such units did not have much influence on the businesses in which they were installed. 'It is important to note that management has no role in establishing such groups, they do not influence the direction of the business, and have no formal role in the day to day activities of the business,' said HSBC in a statement.[25] This was disingenuous at best, coming at a time when Xi Jinping was extending the Party's tentacles into every aspect of nominally private businesses in China. As Su Wei, a professor at a Party school in Chongqing, has stated: 'Party cells are set up to make sure the company's operations are in line with the principles and policies of the CCP.'[26] Party regulations state that 'Party cells inside private firms can help guide and supervise enterprises to follow the country's laws and regulations and safeguard the legitimate interests of all parties.'[27] Under Chinese law, a company must allow the formation of a Party cell if more than three employees who are Party members request it, but before Xi came to power this was patchily enforced, especially among foreign investors, and the rules were typically vague about the precise function of the cells. However, with the Party tightening its grip, they could no longer be dismissed as decorative or some kind of glorified social club.

The CCP was already playing a growing role in the strategic decision making of major domestic firms. More than thirty Chinese companies listed on the Hong Kong stock exchange amended their articles of association, typically describing the Party as playing a core role in 'providing direction (and) managing the overall situation'.[28] In practice this meant the CCP had to be consulted on every major decision; the companies were effectively under Party guidance. It was not as if Xi made any great secret of what he expected of private companies in China. Addressing the private sector and entrepreneurs in a lecture reproduced in a rambling volume of speeches and writings, he said, 'You should always love the motherland, the people and the Party; practice the core values of socialism,' and he urged private companies to follow 'the great tradition of answering the call of and following the Party'.[29] The role of the Party in the financial sector has since been made even more explicit, with its main theoretical journal, *Qiushi*, stating that banks, pension funds, insurers and other financial organisations in China are to follow what it calls Marxist principles and pay obedience to Xi.[30]

By the time HSBC's Party cell became public, foreign joint ventures were coming under increasing pressure to amend their agreements to include language allowing Party officials to be given a formal role in management.[31] Some saw HSBC's decision as a smart pre-emptive move, an effort to get on the good side of the Party and to get ahead of the CCP's push for a greater say in the running of businesses. That is an extremely generous interpretation. A Party cell potentially gave the CCP access to sensitive client data as well as to strategic business decisions – decisions that might have implications well beyond China.

After a century and a half of doing business with China, HSBC also knew that having the right contacts at the right level could be vital, and it sought to boost its firepower with the recruitment in September 2021 of Lord Edward Udny-Lister as senior adviser to group chairman Mark Tucker. The former special adviser to Prime Minister Boris Johnson would focus on the Far East and would be 'providing strategic advice on international business issues' and 'undertaking specific projects on behalf of the Board'.[32] Lister was well known to the CCP. He helped broker the deal under which the Chinese government bought the Royal Mint site in London's docklands for its new embassy, planned as its biggest in Europe. It was revealed at the time that Lister was paid both by the property firm representing Beijing and by the developer that sold the site for £255 million, although both denied that he had any direct part in negotiations.[33] Nevertheless, the then Chinese ambassador to London personally thanked Lister and 'spoke highly' of his 'effort' in securing the 'diplomatic premises'.[34] The British government insisted Johnson's trusted adviser had declared his interests as required and there were no conflicts of interest.[35] It is not known what Lister's 'specific projects' for HSBC entailed, but it did not stem the Chinese tide turning against the bank.

In May 2023, HSBC fought off an attempt to split the bank. At its annual shareholders meeting, held that year in Birmingham, the board defeated a resolution that would have forced the bank to regularly consider the separation of its more profitable Asian operations. Around 20 per cent of shareholders voted in favour.[36] It was the culmination of an at times acrimonious campaign by HSBC's largest shareholder to force an East–West split in the bank's operations. It was a victory for the bank's chair, Mark Tucker, but likely to be a temporary one in what was shaping up to be a long battle with deep political undertones – and which is ultimately about control of the bank's Hong Kong and China operations.

HSBC's biggest shareholder and the backer of the resolution was a Chinese financial conglomerate called Ping An. The company, based in Shenzhen, had by 2021 written $121.7 billion in insurance premiums, making it the world's largest insurer. The name Ping An means 'safe and well', and initially HSBC had seen its relationship with the company as a means of breaking into the Chinese insurance market. To this end, between 2002 and 2005 HSBC built a 19.9 per cent stake in Ping An, the maximum allowed by foreigners, becoming its largest shareholder. As part of the deal, HSBC provided personal finance and insurance expertise to the Chinese firm, but the tie-up never worked out for HSBC and in 2012 it sold its stake as part of a broader retrenchment from the insurance business, albeit with a profit.[37] Five years later, Ping An turned the tables and began to build a stake in HSBC. When the stake was first revealed, the Chinese insurer requested a seat on HSBC's board, a request that was denied.[38] Ping An was undeterred and by 2020, with the geopolitical conditions becoming more tense and HSBC beginning to face its own political difficulties with China, Ping An increased its shareholding to close to 9 per cent.

Ping An presented its break-up demands as part of a business strategy to improve shareholder value. It argued that hiving off the Asian business could realise value of more than $20 billion.[39] The Chinese company cleverly leveraged the frustration of legions of individual retail investors who were enraged when HSBC suspended dividend payments in April 2020 during the Covid-19 pandemic at the request of UK regulators, the authorities being concerned about the resilience of the financial sector.[40] Individual shareholders in Hong Kong collectively control around a third of the bank's shares, although they are far from being a unified group. HSBC rejected the break-up proposal, arguing that the benefits were exaggerated and would negatively impact other key parts of the global business.[41] The bank presented the clash as being purely about business, rejecting suggestions that Ping An was being directed by the Chinese Communist Party. 'We do not believe the issues with Ping An are anything but commercial . . . we know how important performance and dividends are to shareholders,' said chief executive Noel Quinn.[42]

On paper, Ping An is a publicly listed company, founded in 1988 by Peter Ma, a reclusive tycoon. On paper again, its shares are widely held, its share register peppered with leading Western institutional investors. As the company's own website puts it, 'The shareholding structure of the Company is relatively scattered. There is no controlling shareholder, nor de facto controlling party.'[43] The real picture is far murkier. As with so many nominally private Chinese companies, there are multiple categories of shares and ultimate ownership is often unclear, as is control. A 2012 New York Times investigation revealed that a Tianjin-based investment company called Taihong was one of Ping An's largest shareholders. Rather like a Russian nesting doll, Taihong was owned by a series of other investment companies, which were in turn owned by others. The newspaper traced 88 per cent of the shares to the family, friends and colleagues of China's then prime minister, Wen Jiabao.[44]

Ultimately, however, Ping An exists at the pleasure of the Communist Party. It is inconceivable that Ping An would have gone into battle over HSBC without the direction – or at least the tacit approval – of the Party, which sees HSBC's role in Hong Kong as an issue of national security. HSBC is a lynchpin of Hong Kong's economic and financial system. The bank issues more than half of all currency in circulation and handles half of retail banking. It manages revenues on behalf of the Hong Kong treasury, and facilitates the payment of teachers, public servants and healthcare workers.

HSBC is, in other words, a systemic institution in a territory over which Beijing is dramatically tightening its control. It is hard to see Ping An as anything other than a stalking horse, its wider purpose being to highlight the contradiction between HSBC's centre of commercial gravity in Hong Kong, and its regulatory obligations to the UK authorities – a contradiction that is unacceptable to Beijing.

In early 2023, HSBC again found itself in hot water with British lawmakers when a report by the All Party Parliamentary Group (APPG) on Hong Kong found that HSBC had been complicit in supressing the human rights of Hongkongers by proactively supporting the national security law.[45] The APPG also accused HSBC of denying Hongkongers who had fled to the UK access to their pension funds. The bank manages Hong Kong's Mandatory Provident Fund, into which all Hong Kong residents must pay, but refused to accept British National Overseas Passports – which Beijing does not recognise – as valid identification for early withdrawals.[46] An HSBC spokesman said, 'like all banks, we have to obey the law and the instructions of the regulators'.[47]

In August 2023, Sherard Cowper-Coles, HSBC's head of public affairs and a former diplomat, apologised after declaring that the UK government was 'weak' for following the US and hardening its policy on China. He subsequently stepped down but was retained as a 'consultant'. The bank said he was expressing his personal opinion, though to outsiders it seemed consistent with HSBC's long-standing support for Beijing.[48] Six months later, he spoke at a Chinese New Year reception in London hosted by the 48 Group Club, which promotes business ties with China. He told his audience, which included the Chinese ambassador, 'China matters more than it's ever done to the United Kingdom, to post-Brexit Britain,' according to a glowing report by *Xinhua*, the state news agency.[49]

Simply doing the Party's bidding is not enough for China's leaders. It is clear that Xi Jinping sees a lack of direct control over HSBC as a potential threat to China's economic security, and that the CCP regards the bank as a hangover from colonial rule. Its fears were heightened by Western financial sanctions against Russia following Moscow's invasion of Ukraine, and Beijing fears it too could face sanctions as relations with the US deteriorate, and especially if

China invades Taiwan. A lesson Beijing has taken from the Ukraine war is the need to build financial resilience in preparation for conflict with the West, and there is no place in this thinking for an independent bank of such financial power as HSBC in one of its most important financial centres.

In February 2024, the dangers of HSBC's exposure to China's faltering economy were underscored when its quarterly profits (and share price) fell sharply, in part because of a $3 billion charge on the value of its stake in a Chinese bank.[50] It also increased to $1 billion the value of a reserve fund to cover expected losses from commercial property in mainland China.[51]

By May 2024, HSBC was back on familiar territory, lobbying the British government to go easy on Beijing. The bank was seeking to persuade ministers not to designate China as a high risk under new national security legislation, which would trigger tighter scrutiny of business dealings. However, Noel Quinn had seemingly had enough. The chief executive, who had been with the bank since 1987, said he would be retiring three years earlier than expected, with those close to him suggesting he had become disillusioned with the geopolitical firestorm engulfing the bank. At HSBC's annual meeting, Ping An had voted against his re-appointment, but the bank insisted his decision to leave was personal and he was not forced out by Beijing.

HSBC's predicament found few sympathisers among Hong Kong's embattled democrats, who saw little to celebrate. That changed on New Year's Day 2024, when the territory struck a humiliating blow to Beijing's pride. Its football team beat China 2–1 in a bad-tempered game, during which China was given three red cards, including one for the assistant coach.[52] It was the first time in nearly thirty years that China had been beaten by Hong Kong, which still fields a separate team. 'I don't have to motivate the team against China,' said Hong Kong coach Jorn Andersen wryly.[53] It wasn't just that a game had been lost, it was far more. The defeat struck at the heart of one of Xi Jinping's pet projects – a vast and expensive campaign to conquer the world of football. Instead, his master plan for global football dominance has been beset by failure and corruption – and in the process become a metaphor for so much of what is wrong with the Chinese economy.

CHAPTER 18

Football Fantasy

'The Chinese football industry has to be developed . . .
This has a great significance for the realisation of
the dream of becoming a powerful sports nation. This
has great importance for the development of
the economy, society and culture.'

General Office of the State Council, 2015

When President Xi Jinping made a state visit to Britain in 2015, then Prime Minister David Cameron took the supposedly football-mad Chinese president to Manchester to attend a training session of Manchester City football team. There he met former City defender Sun Jihai, a little-known Chinese player who made 130 appearances for the club between 2002 and 2008. Sun was fast-tracked into the Manchester-based National Football Museum's hall of fame for the occasion, which was unprecedented for such an obscure player, and which shadow sport minister Clive Efford described as a 'grubby little fix' to curry influence with Xi.[1] The two leaders also met Sergio Agüero, who really was famous and who took a selfie with them. His photo became an iconic image of Xi's visit, which was designed to herald what Cameron called a 'golden era' of UK–China relations. The image quickly went viral in China, and the Argentinian international, who was City's all-time top goal scorer, later said, 'Every person in the world asks me about the selfie.'[2]

A few weeks after the Xi visit, City Football Group, which owns Manchester City, announced a £265 million investment from a Chinese consortium, equivalent to a 13 per cent stake, which City chairman Khaldoon al-Mubarak said would 'leverage the incredible potential that exists in China'. Within two years, other Chinese investors had bought controlling stakes in Southampton, West Bromwich Albion, Aston Villa, Birmingham and Wolverhampton Wanderers football clubs.[3] Chinese buyers also snapped up stakes in clubs across Europe, including in Italy's AC Milan, which was bought outright for almost $1 billion from former Italian Prime Minister Silvio Berlusconi by an opaque Chinese mining entrepreneur few people in Italy – or even China – had ever heard of.[4] Chinese retail group Suning Holdings bought a 70 per cent stake in rival Inter Milan, and Dalian Wanda, China's largest operator of shopping malls snapped up 20 per cent of Atlético de Madrid.[5] None of this really seemed to matter in Europe at the time. Like countless other businesses, the clubs were grateful for the Chinese cash, and opaque or maverick ownership was nothing new in football. In China, the spending spree was seen differently: as part of a multi-billion dollar master plan to turn China into a football superpower.

While China had forged ahead economically, growing at sustained rates the world had never seen before, it languished when it came to the beautiful game, the most popular sport on the planet. The ultimate symbol of soft power remained a Western stronghold, and that grip needed to be broken if China was to realise Xi's goal – his China Dream – of becoming a truly great and confident power. At the time of Xi's visit to the UK, China's men's team was ranked eighty-first in the world by FIFA, the sport's international governing body, just ahead of Guatemala, Sudan and Iraq.[6] They had qualified for the World Cup only once, in 2002, losing all three group stage matches.

China's master plan to capture the world's most popular game was spelt out in 'The Overall Chinese Football Reform and Development Programme', published by the State Council, the country's highest government body, a few months before Xi's UK visit. The document dryly and methodically described a three-stage strategy to turn China into 'a powerful sports nation' and did so with all the pizzazz of a state plan for the steel, coal or pork industry. The short-term goal was to create what it called a 'football management model with Chinese characteristics'. In the middle-term the men's team was to be the best in Asia, and in the longer term it was to reach 'the highest global ranks', host the men's World Cup and inculcate a 'healthy football culture' in society.[7] 'Chinese football industry has to be developed . . . This has a great significance for the realisation of the dream of becoming a powerful sports nation. This has great importance for the development of the economy, society and culture,' it stated. All under the guidance of the Party of course. 'Strengthen the football association as an organisation mechanism of the party. Proceed in accordance with the principles of the party cadres and the personnel policy of the party,' it exhorts.[8]

The main tools to achieve this were to be diktat and cash – lots of cash. All schools were to include football in their physical education curricula, and the number of schools with football pitches was to rise from 5,000 to 70,000 by 2025. The target was to have 50 million people, including 30 million students, playing football within ten years. Football was also to be at the centre of a broader 'national fitness strategy', which earmarked billions of yuan for the construction of public sports facilities. 'The per capita area of sports fields will reach 1.8 square meters,' the government decreed in June 2016.[9] The strategy was closely linked to the burgeoning cult around Xi Jinping. As he acquired ever more power, the Party sought to portray him as a football-mad man of the people, and state media pictured China's portly leader kicking around balls and watching youth games. It carried stories about Xi's supposed footballing prowess at school and how he had once left a Shanghai stadium 'angry and upset' after China's national team was defeated 5–1 by an English club side, while his wife Peng Liyuan described how Xi often stayed up late to watch matches on television.[10] He instructed that the value of China's sport's industry was to reach $850 billion, the highest in the world, by 2025, from a modest $50 billion in 2015, and he wanted football to lead the way. Thousands of coaches were to be trained and Chinese companies were urged to support the national effort to reach footballing greatness.

Nominally private companies, always well attuned to the needs of the Party, responded by sinking billions of dollars into the country's top teams, splashing out lavishly on players and facilities. They went on a spending spree abroad, bringing in foreign players on contracts worth up to $40 million a year. A Chinese club reportedly offered Cristiano Ronaldo, the Portuguese superstar, a contract worth $105 million a year, but he declined, according to his agent.[11] In November 2016, Italy's World Cup-winning coach Marcello Lippi was appointed head coach of China's national men's football team on a reported salary of $28 million a year, second only to Manchester United's José Mourinho.[12] According to FIFA, Chinese clubs spent $1.7 billion on international transfers between 2011 and 2020, peaking in 2016, when $450 million was splashed out on overseas players.[13] The Chinese Super League, the country's top division, got a shot in the arm when *Tiao Dongli* (China Sports Media), a broadcaster, paid $1.3 billion for the television rights over five years – twenty-six times the $50 million paid in 2013. Among the most enthusiastic investors in Chinese clubs were property companies, which owned or part-owned half of the country's top-tier teams. Among the most prominent was Evergrande, which owned Evergrande Guangzhou, the country's most successful club. Evergrande's financial collapse is examined elsewhere in this book, but at its peak it ran a football school with forty-eight pitches and had plans to build the world's biggest stadium in Guangzhou, with a capacity of 100,000. 'Evergrande Stadium will become a new world-class landmark comparable to the Sydney Opera House and Burj Khalifa in Dubai, and an important symbol of Chinese football to the world,' boasted Evergrande's chief executive Xia Haijun at the time.[14]

Then there were the investments in foreign clubs, where the logic, as far as one could be identified, was to tap their marketing and coaching expertise. Manchester City established a partnership in Beijing, the Kaiwen Manchester City Football School, which would 'give young people in China the opportunity to learn how to play the Manchester City way', according to the club.[15] AC Milan opened an office in Shanghai and signed a long-term partnership to establish sports centres across the country.[16] China also spent tens of millions of pounds to entice European clubs to come and play exhibition matches.

Having triggered the frenzy, the Communist Party then became concerned that the tsunami of cash wasn't going where it was needed. The *People's Daily*, a Communist Party newspaper, warned of a bubble of 'reckless' spending that could burst and damage the sport. Amid rumours that Argentine star Lionel Messi was about to sign a five year deal worth €500 million (£425 million) to move to

Hebei China Fortune, the newspaper said there was an 'imbalance in the investment model'. It complained that the long-term development of youth training and infrastructure was being neglected in favour of lavishing vast amounts of money on foreign stars.[17] Messi did not make the move, but the binge in pursuit of Xi Jinping's football dream continued. Even European teams, no strangers to extravagant spending, became queasy about the huge sums being offered to play in China. It was 'a danger for all teams', complained Chelsea manager Antonio Conte, in late December 2016, shortly after the Chinese transfer record was broken three times in ten days.[18] The following year, the Chinese authorities introduced a 100 per cent transfer tax on foreign players bought for more than 45 million yuan (£5 million) and domestic players transferred for more than 20 million yuan.

Xi Jinping then waited for his bold football strategy to bear fruit. He is still waiting. In late 2023, he said he was 'not so sure' about the ability of China's men's team, adding that 'There are ups and downs.'[19] By then it was clear the master plan was not working. It was a colossal failure on and off the field. Not only was the national team still struggling to win, but the money thrown at the game had so badly damaged the honesty and integrity of Chinese football that it was hard to see how it would ever recover.

In early January 2024, a football special was one of the most popular programmes on state television, gripping the nation and attracting tens of millions of viewers. However, far from showing sporting action on the field, the show was a documentary on the astonishing levels of corruption in the game. It was part of a series produced every year by the Communist Party's anti-graft agency, designed to show how busy they have been and usually built around public confessions from errant officials. An entire episode was dedicated to football and featured Li Tie, a former head coach of the men's national team describing how he had paid bribes to get that job and then accepted payments to pick players for the national team. He also said that as a club manager he routinely paid bribes to fix matches. While in charge of Hebei China Fortune, Li said he spent 14 million yuan (£1.5 million) bribing players and the manager of rival Shenzhen Football Club to throw the game so that Hebei could be promoted to the sixteen-strong Chinese Super League. 'Once you achieve success in the wrong way, you become more and more desperate for more success. This way then becomes a habit,' said Li, who once played for Everton in the English Premier League.[20] The show also featured Chen Xuyuan, a former president of the Chinese Football Association (CFA), who described how on appointment to his job he received a 'congratulatory' 300,000 yuan (£33,000) from the officials of two clubs, delivered in backpacks. He confessed to receiving tens of millions in total from clubs, telling the show, 'The corruption in Chinese football does not only exist in certain individual areas – it's everywhere, in each and every aspect.'[21] In March 2024, he was sentenced to life in prison.[22]

Match fixing, much of it linked to illegal gambling, and 'black-whistles', as bent referees are known, has long been a problem in Chinese football, but the graft seemed to have been turbocharged by the huge amounts of money sloshing around in the system. Over the course of several weeks in 2023, dozens of players, referees, coaches and club executives were investigated, and more than a dozen top officials detained. Chen Xuyuan was not the only one targeted at the CFA; the heads of its competition department and of its disciplinary committee were among others detained, as was Du Zhaocai, who had been Communist Party boss at the CFA, deputy sports minister and vice president of the Asian Football Confederation. Match fixing was so pervasive that it affected competitions at every level; an investigation by the business magazine *Caixin* described how local officials in Guangdong were sacked after a match was fixed between two local under-15 sides.[23]

Caixin said the principal business of the Chinese Super League (CSL) had become one of fixing, rather than playing matches, which it blamed in part on the wall of money thrown at the sport by the property giants – which went into rapid reverse as China's property bubble burst. Evergrande Guangzhou was relegated from the CSL after top players abandoned the club, complaining of unpaid salaries and broken promises. Clubs collapsed across China, including Jiangsu Suning, which folded just three months after becoming Chinese champions. Suning, its retail-giant owner, had significant property interests (and the stake in Inter Milan), and ditched the club as it scrambled to pay off burgeoning debts.

Little surprise, then, that by the end of 2023, the ability of China's national men's team to actually play football on the basis of skill on the field had hardly improved since Xi Jinping launched his master plan to conquer the global game. FIFA's rankings placed the men's team seventy-ninth in December 2023, just ahead of Guinea, Bulgaria and Gabon, two places up from when Xi visited the UK more than eight years earlier. Shortly after the humiliating defeat to Hong Kong on New Year's Day 2024, China crashed out of the Asian Cup at the group stage after two excruciating goalless draws, with Lebanon and Tajikistan, and a 1–0 defeat to Qatar. In the run up to the cup China was also beaten by Oman, Syria and Uzbekistan. Distraught football fans took to social media to bemoan the fact that China, with a population of 1.4 billion people seemed incapable of producing eleven players able to win a men's international football match against even the most dire of opposition. Interestingly, China's women's team was doing rather better, ranked a respectable nineteenth at the end of 2023. It has qualified for seven World Cups and in 2022 won the Asian Cup. Yet the women's game has not enjoyed anywhere near the same attention from business or from CCP bureaucrats as the men – which may well be part of the reason for their comparative success.

'The soccer sector has been plagued by systemic and devastating levels of corruption,' announced China's graft busters at the beginning of 2024. 'The intensity of the punishment is unprecedented.'[24] Hu Xijin, a nationalist blogger and former editor of the CCP's *Global Times*, said Chinese men's football was 'rotten to the core' and had 'completely humiliated the Chinese people', who paradoxically are among the world's most passionate football fans.[25] It suited the Communist Party to blame poor performance on corruption – a narrative that had China's lofty ambitions for the beautiful game thwarted by the actions of rapacious individuals, albeit quite a few of them. In reality the rot runs far deeper, and the failure of soccer to take root in China speaks volumes about the way the Party wields power and the inability of an authoritarian system to nurture creativity.

A rigid top-down approach has helped China gain global success in other sporting fields however, notably in the single-minded pursuit of Olympic medals. An intensive and disciplined bureaucratic system modelled on the Soviet Union turned the country into the leading gold-medal scorer at the Beijing Olympics in 2008, and while it has not repeated that feat since, it has continued to rank highly in successive summer games. This machine functions rather like a manufacturing assembly line, scouting for children at an early age, and plucking them out for full-time training at elite government-run sports schools. Six sports have been particularly dominant – table tennis, shooting, diving, badminton, gymnastics and weight-lifting – and two-thirds of China's golds in the last forty years have been won by women.[26] The intensity of the system can take a heavy mental and physical toll, especially on those who do not succeed. Many are removed from poor rural families when they are as young as six years old and during their training have limited access to their parents. Many of the sports in which China has succeeded are individual, not team-based, relying more on rigid routine and repetition, on which the sports schools relentlessly focus. In essence it is a machine with the single purpose of turning out other machines to win medals, and it is one that has been dogged by rumours of performance enhancing drugs. Although China's football ambitions involved a lot of private money, it was driven by the same philosophy – that a concentrated campaign of the sort that had won Olympic medals could turn out world-class footballers.

Footballing creativity, innovation and genius however simply cannot be manufactured by such a system – indeed, authoritarianism seems almost guaranteed to destroy it. Football is an open and free-flowing game of countless permutations, relying on the brain as much, if not more, than physique. Academics who study football have argued that it defies scientific analyses, and that although fitness and a measure of organisation and structure are important, rigid training and drills do not make much of a difference.[27] More important to a team's success is the way individual players think on their feet, strategising and adjusting their play as the game develops. These are not skills that can be learned by rote. 'Playing football is very simple, but playing simple football is the hardest thing there is,' Dutch football legend Johan Cruyff once said. 'You play football with your head, and your legs are there to help you.'[28] Football is a bottom-up sport – in Brazil, for instance, one of the

world's most successful footballing nations, the impoverished fave-
las of the country's major cities have produced some of the nation's
greatest players, including Pelé, Garrincha and Ronaldo. Football
is a religion in these gritty slums, with scrappy pitches scoured by
talent scouts for the next superstars.

There are also broader cultural impediments to the development
of football in China. 'I call it robot football,' said Lars Isecke, a former senior German coach who also worked at the highest levels in
China.[29] 'The school system doesn't allow enough freedom for creative physical education,' he told German television.[30] Long hours
and a stressful and ultra-competitive school system means there is
little opportunity or encouragement for young people to go out and
knock a ball around at the end of an afternoon. Isecke also said that
the one-child policy had created a generation of ultra-protective
parents, cautious about contact sports like football and more at
ease with sports such as table tennis or badminton, which are seen
as calmer and more harmonious. The one-child policy also encourages selfish behaviour, he believes. 'Chinese are not successful in
team sports, because they have not learned to play as a team,' he
said.[31] At the same time, a growing number of middle-class parents
are less willing to hand their children over to the state at a very
young age to become part of the athlete manufacturing machine.

We began this chapter with Xi Jinping's famous 2015 selfie with
Argentinian international Sergio Agüero. Nearly nine years later
another famous footballer from that country was making the headlines in China, but far from being lionised Lionel Messi was subject
to an orchestratred campaign of online threats and vitriol after having the audacity to sit out an exhibition match between his club,
Inter Miami, and Hong Kong because of a groin injury. A top aide
to Hong Kong leader John Lee said the city's people hated Messi
and his team and that Messi 'should never be allowed to return
to Hong Kong'.[32] The Chinese authorities then swiftly cancelled
two friendly games the Argentine national side was due to play in
China. Inter Miami apologised, but pointed out that injuries are
'unfortunately a part of the beautiful game' – though perhaps not in
the mind of the CCP.

Caixin, the Chinese business magazine, is one of the country's
braver and more savvy publications, frequently pushing the limits

of censorship. When it published its investigation into corruption in football, it noted that China's grand footballing plan was overseen by rapacious bureaucrats with no real interest in the game, and it suggested that one of the root causes of graft at the Chinese Football Association was its role as both an organiser and a supervisor. In other words, there was no transparency, accountability or independent oversight. Many readers will have noted the similarity with the Chinese Communist Party. The CCP's desire to micromanage society, which intensified under Xi Jinping, stifles the sort of grass-roots initiative and innovation that might have given football a better chance of developing – and that stifling embrace does not stop at football. There are many other ways in which football is a metaphor for the broader Chinese economy and society, and there are many lessons that can be learned from the footballing debacle. However, as the CCP tries to create a broader top-down innovation economy – creativity by diktat and wads of cash – there is no sign that any of them have been learned.

CHAPTER 19

Can China Innovate?

'Adhere to socialist core values and do not generate
content that incites the subversion of state power, calls
for the overthrow of the socialist system, endangers
national security and interests, damages the national
image, incites the splitting of the country, undermines
national unity and social stability . . .'

Draft government rules on artificial intelligence

At face value, it might seem a little churlish to suggest that China
cannot innovate. Imperial China was once the most technologically
advanced civilisation on earth – from the air-conditioning fan to
gunpowder, paper-making, printing, the stirrup, wheelbarrow
and compass, they were all were invented in China, and all under
autocratic rulers. Today's People's Republic of China has landed
a spacecraft on the far side of the moon, built the world's largest
radio telescope and briefly held the top spot for the world's fastest
supercomputer. It is making great strides in quantum computing
and artificial intelligence, and has carved out a dominant position
in solar power, battery storage and electric vehicles. It has in the
likes of Huawei, Baidu, Alibaba and Tencent some world-class tech
companies. According to a critical technology database compiled by
the Australian Strategic Policy Institute, spanning defence, space,
robotics, energy, the environment, biotechnology, AI, advanced
materials and key quantum technology areas, China leads the
world in thirty-seven of forty-four technologies as measured by
high-impact research papers.[1]

The Chinese Communist Party, which regards itself as the latest embodiment of Chinese civilisation, is not short of ambition.

Xi Jinping's 'Made in China 2025' plan to lead the world in critical technologies of the future has been backed up by a splurge of spending on research and development (R&D). Shiny new facilities, housing a lot of glitzy new kit, have sprouted across the country in a frenzied race for technological superiority and self-sufficiency. Massive subsidies are being directed at companies working on critical technologies. While the OECD has cast doubt on the integrity of Chinese government figures, the money China is throwing at R&D is still staggering, even allowing for some cooking of the books. Spending on research and development reached a record 3.09 trillion yuan (£335 billion) in 2022, a rise of more than 10 per cent over the previous year. 'Despite multiple unfavourable factors, China's R&D expenditure continued to soar and injected strong vitality into the nation's innovative development,' boasted Li Yin, chief statistician at the National Bureau of Statistics.[2] China appeared to be rapidly closing the gap on the United States, the world's research leader, which spent $710 billion in 2021,[3] with Chinese commentators boasting that it was only a matter of time before Beijing usurped that title. Beijing has dangled its modern facilities and much else in front of overseas scientists in an effort to get them to work for China. According to official statistics, China recruited almost 60,000 overseas professionals between 2006 and 2016, using a range of programmes of which the Thousand Talents Plan (TTP) is the most prominent.[4] The TTP offered lavish funding to scientists and engineers working in cutting-edge fields in the United States, UK, Australia, Canada and the European Union.[5]

As we have seen, since Deng Xiaoping launched his policy of reform and opening, China has excelled mostly at copying. Furthermore, it has vacuumed up know-how and technology by every available means, including forcing companies to hand over tech as a price for market entry and industrial-scale cyber espionage. A more wary world is making this increasingly challenging. China now needs to nurture a self-sustaining innovation economy that is creative and inventive and encourages original thinking – and this is one of the greatest challenges facing the Party. This is different from moon shots and supercomputers, and would seem to run against the CCP's most basic instincts for control, yet it is essential if China is to fulfil the Party's ambitions of world leadership. The problem with Xi's grand plans to become an innovation superpower is that that they sound a lot like his plans for football – and are already facing some of the same pitfalls.

Baby Q was pioneering in its day, but its memory still haunts the Communist Party as it attempts to turn China into an AI super-power. The experimental chatbot, represented by a penguin, was introduced by Tencent QQ, a messenger app, in 2017. It was designed to answer light-hearted and general knowledge questions, but quickly went rogue. Responding to the comment 'Long live the Communist Party,' Baby Q replied, 'Do you think that such a cor-rupt and incompetent political regime can live forever?' On another occasion, the feisty penguin informed questioners, 'There needs to be democracy.' The responses were shared widely online before Baby Q was abruptly terminated. It's not entirely clear how Baby Q developed its political consciousness, but it is likely to have been taught it through interactions with its users.

Fast forward six years, and the world was taken by storm by ChatGPT, the AI-powered chatbot developed by Microsoft-backed OpenAI, which could provide well-researched answers to pretty much any question you cared to ask it. Chinese tech companies scrambled to develop copycat bots only to find that the CCP did not share their unbridled enthusiasm. Chinese regulators told tech firms not to offer ChatGPT services through their platforms and to block users from using anti-censorship tools to access such services out-side China. New rules stated that in developing their own bots, AI service providers must 'adhere to core socialist values'. Furthermore, there must be no content that 'incites subversion of state power and the overthrow of the socialist system, endangers national security and interests, damages the image of the country, incites secession from the country, undermines national unity and social stability'. More broadly, chatbots and other AI tools must not 'generate false and harmful information'.[6] Tech companies would have to send their chatbots to the Cyberspace Administration of China (CAC) for security reviews before they were released to the public and provid-ers would also have to track users and verify their identities.

ChatGPT is based on what's called generative AI, drawing on billions of data points scraped from the internet to formulate its answers. The application of generative AI seemed almost limitless, and Google, Meta and Apple all invested heavily to develop their own tools. There was considerable hype – that AI will transform the way we interact with computers and much more. There were predictions of revolutionary economic impacts and claims it would transform sectors ranging from law and journalism to education and healthcare.[7] There were already AI programmes that could diagnose illnesses more accurately than an average health practitioner.

It's not that the Communist Party couldn't see the economic benefits, but its main concern was its own health. It faced a conundrum: it wanted to lead the world in AI but was terrified of anything with a mind of its own. Before any Chinese version of ChatGPT was released into the wild, the Party needed to be sure that the content could be controlled. That meant finding a way and a place for censorship. For a chatbot to be intelligent, and to maximise its economic utility, it needs to be trained on vast amounts and varieties of data. If that raw material has already been censored, limiting the data pool, the chatbot can be politically correct but not so smart. The alternative is to train on information from both inside and outside China, accessing global data beyond the Great Firewall, China's system of internet censorship. That makes for a smarter chatbot but necessitates gagging it at a later stage.

The experience with Baby Q left Chinese tech companies all too aware that conversations could go in unpredictable directions and that Chinese internet users were adept at ducking and diving around restrictions. Baidu, which runs a sort of gagged version of the Google search engine, was an early leader with a chatbot called Ernie, which Western observers dubbed ChatCCP, although Alibaba, SenseTime and Tencent were not far behind. However, the initial rollouts were highly restricted. Those who gained early access reported that Ernie could write Tang Dynasty-style poems but refused to answer questions about President Xi Jinping, saying it had not yet learnt how to answer them. When asked about the Tiananmen Square massacre and the repression in Xinjiang, it answered: 'Let's change the subject and start again.'[8] Which will no doubt be encouraging for China's communist leaders. Less so, some of Ernie's more basic errors. The chatbot attracted online ridicule after it drew a turkey (the bird) when asked for the country

Turkey, and a crane (the bird) after being asked for the construction machine.[9] Alibaba launched a chatbot called Tongyi Qianwen, which translates as 'truth from a thousand questions' (no irony meant as far as I know). At an elaborate launch event in Beijing, the group's chief executive Daniel Zhang demonstrated how it would allow users to transcribe meeting notes, craft business pitches and tell children's stories. 'We are at a technological watershed moment,' he said, but the atmosphere of the launch was dampened somewhat by Tongyi's limited initial applications and because it came on the same day as the CAC's new regulations.[10] Access was limited initially to trusted corporate clients, but early feedback suggested it struggled with simple logic; when one user asked how to make a tasty stir-fry out of reinforced concrete it came up with a recipe that included slicing the concrete into small pieces.[11] When Baidu's Ernie was asked the same question, it suggested mixing the concrete with garlic, onion and peppers.

ChatCCP will no doubt improve with time, but the Party will keep it on a tight leash until it is confident of control. It will also give priority to incorporating generative AI into its broader system of censorship and social control and into its disinformation toolkit – exploiting the new technology's potential for churning out fake and misleading information on a huge scale. The CCP has already built what has been described as the world's largest known online disinformation operation, involving hundreds of thousands of accounts across every social media platform and designed to harass critics as well as spread false narratives.[12] Known as Dragonbridge, the operation has grown in sophistication, with widespread use of photo and video manipulation. For example, in early 2023 researchers exposed a pro-Chinese 'news' channel fronted by a pair of computer-generated presenters. 'Jason', with stubbly beard and perfectly combed hair, and 'Anna', her dark hair slickly combed back, were the deepfake presenters of Wolf News, a propaganda channel distributed via fictitious accounts on Facebook, Twitter/X and YouTube. The researchers said it was 'the first time we observed a state-aligned operation promoting footage of AI-generated fictitious people.'[13] Deepfakes have progressed fast over the past decade, and AI will enable their production at greater speed and scale, and substantially enhance the power and reach of Dragonbridge.

The Party's bid to maintain tight control of AI has put China's tech companies in a bind. Baidu CEO and founder Robin Li told financial analysts that providing 'appropriate' content that complies with the regulations was 'not a trivial task'. 'We maintain an ongoing dialogue with the relevant authorities and keep them informed about the latest technology trends,' he said.[14] China's nominally private tech giants are an integral part of China's surveillance state, responsible for much of the censorship and surveillance of users of their systems. Yet the tech giants are also China's most innovative companies, pioneering e-commerce, for instance. As we have seen, they have been targeted by the CCP and many of their founders have been forced out, as the Party has sought to tighten control over them and their data. As Li's frustrated comments to analysts suggest, this hardly seems conducive to nurturing innovation.

Every summer, China's communist leaders head to the seaside resort town of Beidaihe in Hebei province for their annual summer retreat to discuss the state of the nation. Few details are ever provided about this secretive and informal get-together, but in August 2023 they issued a photograph – not of the leaders, but of fifty-seven scientists at the 'forefront of domestic technology', with President Xi Jinping's chief of staff at the centre. The scientists, who included experts in AI and superconductors, were mostly from government institutes and were invited to discuss 'high-level scientific and technological self-reliance'.[15] It was a picture of dull and humourless conformity; all but seven were men and almost all were wearing faux-casual white open-necked shirts and black trousers, and staring expressionless at the camera. You'd be hard-pressed to identify any hint of the sort of maverick and sometimes eccentric individualism that has so often characterised innovation in the West.

Recruitment schemes such as the Thousand Talents Plan (TTP) were designed at least in part to fill that void. China is not the only country to operate such a scheme, but it is the most prolific, according to the FBI, which warned that it could be a means for stealing trade secrets, breaking export control laws and violating conflict of interest policies.[16] The programme, which began in 2008, is designed to 'facilitate the legal and illicit transfer of US technology, intellectual property and know-how to China', according to the US National Intelligence Council.[17] Chinese leaders have more recently sought to play it down, with the recruitment becoming increasingly covert.[18] As the links between China's civil R&D and the military, and the obligations on scientists to help state security, have become more explicit, so the CCP's talent scouts have preferred to work in the shadows, frequently using front organisations, including the ostensibly cultural Confucius Institutes, for their recruitment. An August 2023 investigation by the Reuters news agency revealed that the TTP had been replaced by a programme called *Qiming* ('Enlightenment'), which was offering perks that included home-purchase subsidies and signing bonuses of up to 5 million yuan (£550,000), and was focusing on 'sensitive' or 'classified' areas, such as semiconductors, where China was racing to catch up with the West.[19] Another tool for the talent hunters was 'predatory conferences', gatherings of dubious academic value, but useful as recruiting grounds – or for simply rewarding academics sympathetic to China with all-expenses-paid trips, including lavish allowances and speaking fees.

China claims to have lured leading scientists from some of the world's top universities.[20] In March 2023, the TTP achieved a notable success when it was announced that a prominent physicist who had spent twenty years in the UK was joining China's new national hypersonic laboratory in Beijing. Zhang Yonghao, a professor at Edinburgh University, was an expert in superfast fluids. Zhang did not say what motivated him to make the move, though the Institute's website said Zhang's team was expected to 'lead the world' in developing materials that surpass all existing standards in their ability to withstand different factors and pressure management.[21] The TTP targets overseas ethnic Chinese scientists in particular, playing to their sense of patriotic duty – and of course their wallets. This makes sense, since overseas Chinese are among the most innovative and enterprising people on the planet. However, they have arguably thrived precisely because they were overseas – working in open and liberal societies and economies.

Chinese scientists themselves have recognised that the strength of Chinese research has hitherto been in implementation rather than innovation, which it has largely left to others. It has progressed in applied research and product development, rather than basic science – focusing on building upon existing know-how. Ye Yujiang, the head of the Department of Basic Research at the Ministry of Science and Technology, has blamed China's weakness in technologies such as chips, computer operating systems and aircraft engines on its inadequacy in basic theoretical research.[22] A 2022 report by a prominent Peking University think tank, titled 'China-US Strategic Competition in Technology: Analysis and Prospects', observed that China still spent much less on basic research than the United States.[23] In an unusually frank review of China's technological weaknesses, the report said, 'China's overall technological strength has gradually increased . . . However, China still has a long way to go from being a quantitatively strong country in science and technology to being a qualitatively strong country in science and technology.' The paper, which was taken down a week after it was posted on the think tank's website, also noted that, 'China still lags far behind the United States in terms of the number of highly cited papers and in paper originality.'

According to the Global AI Talent Tracker, a database compiled by the Paulson Institute's MacroPolo think tank, 60 per cent of top tier AI researchers work in America for US companies and universities, and only 11 per cent work in China. However, 29 per cent come from China, with more than half of these living, working or studying in the US.[24] This supports the view that such talent thrives in a more open system – and also provides some perspective to the CCP's efforts to lure them back, which relies heavily on material incentives in the absence of a free-thinking academic environment.

Citations and patents are frequently used to rank scientific and research output and on paper China's scientists appear to be increasingly prolific and influential. Precisely how prolific and influential is hard to say, since caution is required when making comparisons of research output between countries. Some surveys give China top place ahead of the United States in both the raw numbers of scientific papers produced and in citations, which is usually regarded as a measure of a paper's impact.[25] The same is the case for patents, where China has led the world in raw numbers since 2011.[26] However, it has also been argued that the Chinese Communist Party has sacrificed quality for quantity, and in its rush for global dominance has enabled and ignored large-scale fraud, which threatens to undermine trust in the entire process of scientific publication. 'The submission of suspected fake research papers, also often associated with fake authorship, is growing and threatens to overwhelm the editorial processes of a significant number of journals,' according to a joint investigation by the Committee on Publication Ethics, which aims to raise standards in scholarly publishing, and STM, a publishing industry trade body.[27] The investigation found that the percentage of suspect papers being submitted to journals ranged from 2 per cent to an astonishing 46 per cent, and while China is not the only offender, it is generally accepted to be the biggest academic fraudster.

To the untrained eye, there seemed nothing out of the ordinary about the blotchy biomedical photographs submitted from China to international scientific journals. However, to Elisabeth Bik, the blots, curves and flow of the cellular images reeked of fraud. Working with a small team of academic sleuths, she exposed a Chinese 'paper mill' – an outfit that was churning out fake papers to order, manipulating and reusing sections of the same images and passing them off as original research.[28] In some cases, images appeared to have been flipped back to front or stretched and cropped in an effort to cover their tracks. 'They were charging up to $5,000 for a paper, and the paper mill advertisements on Chinese social media are so blatant that nobody seems to care about them,' she told me. In China, clinicians have to publish a certain number of research papers in order to gain promotion, and for many the easiest way is to commission one from the country's burgeoning paper mill industry. Bik and her team traced almost 500 papers to the same mill, which handled submissions, obtained peer reviews and signed copyright consent forms as part of the service. Biomedicine is particularly worrying, since the aim of much of the research is to develop treatments for human disease, but Bik reckoned it was only the tip of a large iceberg of academic fraud. 'For every paper we catch there must be ten others that we miss because they were a little bit smarter in generating these papers.'

I met Bik at a coffee shop in London's St Katherine Docks. It was a stunning early summer day, and the glistening Shard loomed large over the Tower of London. She was halfway through a speaking tour that took in Manchester, Liverpool, London and Cambridge. She explained how in another case, she had questioned sixty-three papers authored by Cao Xuetao, a top immunologist, who was president of Nankai University in Tianjin and an academician at the influential Chinese Academy of Engineering. Bik's accusations generated an international outcry, but a Chinese government investigation found no serious misconduct. In a statement lacking in detail, China's Ministry of Science and Technology said it had found no fraud and no plagiarism, though it conceded that many papers had 'misused pictures, reflecting the lack of strict laboratory management'.[29] Cao was barred from applying for grants and had his qualification as a scientific expert suspended, both for one year, in what amounted to a slap on the wrist. Bik was incredulous, tweeting 'most of these concerns appear to be more than just errors. These duplications did not happen by honest mistakes. Rather, they suggest an "intention to mislead".'[30] The outcome of the investigation should perhaps have come as no surprise, since Cao was also a long-standing Communist Party member, having joined in 1981, according to a Chinese news report at the time of his appointment at Nankai.[31] He also held the rank of Major General in the People's Liberation Army.[32] Neither of these positions were widely advertised in Cao's academic profiles but will have given him considerable protection from what the Ministry of Science and Technology dismissively referred to as 'questions on the internet'. In another Chinese paper on prostate cancer, Bik found that more than half the sample of patients supposedly studied were women – who of course do not have prostate glands.

Bik, a Dutch microbiologist, reckons that since 2014 she has analysed more than 100,000 papers and found evidence of cheating in 6,500 of them. She jokes that she uses her 'pattern-matching eyes and lots of caffeine' in her dogged search for images which have been reused and reported as results from different experiments or where parts have been rotated, flipped, stretched or otherwise photoshopped to give the appearance of 'new' data. 'There's a thrill in finding something,' she told me. 'And it just makes me angry that people do misconduct in science, because for me science is about finding the truth.' In 2019, she left her job at a biomedical start-up to become a full-time academic sleuth, based in California. She is very public in the work she does and has attracted a strong following – and a deep suspicion from the scientific publishing industry. Scientific publishing is a multi-billion-dollar business, and she said too many had been willing to look the other way, rather than retract questionable papers. Some feared the reputational damage might be greater if they retract than if they just left a paper that was having its integrity questioned. Fraudsters shopped around their papers between publishers, with certain journals gaining a reputation as an easy touch. In the case of China, an important market for their journals, scientific publishers had been particularly timid. 'Nobody dares to question the Chinese government, not even journals in the US. It's just weird. Journals are sometimes weak. They won't retract after the Chinese government says all was fine,' Bik said.

She worries about the use of AI to produce fraudulent papers. 'AI changes the game,' she said. 'I'm particularly concerned about imagery. Texts can be fact-checked to some extent.' The paper mills were quick on their feet, new business models were emerging, but she also feared that enormous damage was being done to the reputation of Chinese science. She said some journals' editors were having trouble getting peer reviewers for papers from China because of fears they might turn out to be fake. 'If the Chinese government does not do something very dramatic about these paper mills, they are going in the end to hurt their own reputation because now people are under the impression that all papers from China are fake. That is also not the case, there is also good science, but the good have to suffer from the reputation that the bad people have set up.'

A rare insight into the pressures on China's army of young researchers came in an August 2023 investigation by *Caixin*, the Chinese business publication, into what it called the 'panic, worry and despair gripping Chinese young researchers'.[33] Levels of anxiety and depression were soaring, it reported, with advancement and funding tied to hitting quotas of published articles. A single innovative article might be split into several smaller ones 'to increase the total quantity of publishing'. Quantity was treated as 'core', with researchers duplicating work, turning out 'padding papers' and pressured to 'publish for the sake of publishing'. When it came to peer review of research, 'relationships and personal favours were mixed in', *Caixin* said. Academic institutions routinely pay researchers bonuses – often amounting to tens of thousands of dollars – for publishing papers in the world's most prestigious scientific journals.[34]

An audit report highly critical of wasteful research was published online, only to be removed days later.[35] The 15,000-word report criticised universities for failing to turn research into market applications and sitting on piles of idle cash. It was published by the audit office of Guangxi, an autonomous region in China's southwest, but its critique resonated far more widely. 'Essentially, this reflects a nationwide issue,' said Liu Ruiming, a professor with the National Development and Strategic Research Institute at Renmin University. 'Researchers appear to be conducting basic theoretical research, but often they produced a large quantity of useless research output that is primarily focused on paper-centric assessments.'[36] In other areas of research, piles of idle cash had inevitably triggered a surge in broader corruption. The development of high-end microprocessors has been a priority for the Communist Party, with an estimated $30 billion poured into the industry over a nine-year period from 2014. In August 2022, at least four top executives associated with a state-owned fund responsible for doling out this money were arrested on corruption charges.[37]

There is much debate over why Imperial China's era of inventiveness came to an abrupt halt around 1500 CE and the mantle of scientific leadership shifted to Europe, where industrialisation also first took hold. By the eighteenth century, China had turned in on itself and was regarded as insular, backward and hostile to commerce. Joseph Needham, a Cambridge scientist and scholar of ancient China, famously posed what became known as the 'Needham question': why did Imperial China fail to take advantage of its early technological lead and launch its own industrial revolution? – to which he failed to provide a satisfactory answer. Among the numerous (and often contradictory) explanations that have been given are the low status of merchants, an increasingly stifling and incurious bureaucracy, an exam system that rewarded mediocrity and conformity (though others describe this as meritocratic and *helpful* to innovation) and the shifting tides of totalitarianism, though China was hardly a liberal place when early inventions were being turned out so prolifically.[38] Others have argued that it was less about China falling behind and more about Europe pulling ahead; while China became unified, homogenised and complacent, European inventiveness was spurred on by the needs of a competing matrix of warring and jostling states.

One of the most persuasive arguments, with implications for Xi's China, has been made by Yasheng Huang, a scholar at the MIT Sloan School of Management, who compiled a database of more than 10,000 Chinese inventions from which he argues that not only was Imperial China not uniformly autocratic, but that periods of relative political and ideological openness encouraged innovation. He notes that China was at its most prolific between the years 220 and 581, known as the 'Han-Sui Interregnum', between the Han and Sui Dynasties. This was one of China's more pluralistic and fractious periods; it was unstable but also a time when culture, ideas and art flourished. 'Empires, which are homogenous and territorially expansive, turned out to be detrimental to technological development. Kingdoms, which are smaller and often compete externally and sometimes internally, excelled at inventiveness,' Huang writes.[39] He also notes a distinction between invention and innovation, arguing that inventions in themselves do not contribute to economic growth, which is instead powered by innovation, which requires the entrepreneurs and business climate to take the inventions to market.[40]

Others have turned to more recent history for lessons on innovation. The Soviet Union – like communist China – relied heavily on technological theft and reverse engineering. The KGB had a section, Line X, tasked with stealing Western science and technology, whose existence was revealed to the CIA by a mole within the unit. As a result, the CIA was able to feed the KGB defective technologies.[41] It would be very surprising if Western intelligence agencies had not sought to counter Chinese cyber espionage with similar gambits. There is also the wider issue that a system based on reverse-engineering other's technology is by definition one that will always be behind, since innovation in the West does not stand still. That is why creating a self-sustaining system of innovation is so vital to the CCP if it is to have any hope of leapfrogging over the West.

International collaboration in science and technology has allowed Chinese scientists to escape the stifling confines of China's own universities, and this collaboration has been at the root of much Chinese innovation and some of the most cited papers. In a similar vein, Beijing has pressured Western tech companies to set up research centres in China, of which there are now believed to be more than 1,600.[42] As we have seen, China's growing belligerence is closing down many of these collaborative avenues. In early 2024, Microsoft denied reports it was relocating AI experts from its Beijing-based Microsoft Research Asia to Vancouver, but Western companies were increasingly cautious about the research they outsourced to China.

At the same time, American technology controls have spurred Chinese efforts. Training the hungry algorithms of AI takes an enormous amount of computer power and Washington specifically banned the export to China of the most advanced Nvidia chips that are used in training, as well as the tools to make them.[43] In early 2024, it was reported that Chinese companies were stripping out and repurposing Nvidia gaming graphics cards, grouping them together in clusters for greater power.[44] Sanctioned telecoms giant Huawei also rolled out a new phone with a surprisingly advanced Chinese-made chip, raising suspicions that Chinese chip-maker SMIC had been able to evade export controls. The industry measures the size and performance of chips in nanometres – which are units of one-billionth of a metre. Smaller means more efficient, with lower energy costs and higher speeds, and the world's most advanced, in production in Taiwan and South Korea, are 3nm, with plans to produce 2nm chips by 2025. The best SMIC is currently thought able to produce is 7nm, putting China about a decade behind, and even then, it is chasing a fast-moving target.[45] However, SMIC is believed to be focusing on what is called 'packaging', a less demanding process that involves stacking together multiple less powerful chips, and is doing so with almost unlimited resources as the CCP prioritises closing the 'chip gap'.[46] Whether these examples can be strictly described as innovation or just adroit footwork in the face of adversity is harder to say. China also has a natural advantage in AI and other data-dependent technologies, since it has access to vast datasets with few of the privacy concerns or finickity data protections that exist in Western democracies.

In May 2024, Beijing announced that $47 billion had been raised from the finance ministry, local governments, and state-owned enterprises and banks to develop the semi-conductor industry and close the chip gap with the West. The National Integrated Circuit Industry Investment Fund was first set-up in 2014, but had been beset with corruption scandals, leading to the 2022 arrest of the fund's head and other chip industry executives – once again bringing to mind China's football follies.

More sympathetic commentators have likened Beijing's research splurge to the American era of 'big science' between the late 1950s and early 1990s, when US science came to dominate the world. Yet while the development of some technologies in the US, such as microprocessors, was driven by the military and space programmes, science and innovation thrived in an academic culture of a free exchange of ideas, open enquiry and association – the intellectual freedom that enabled critical thinking. Needless to say, these are somewhat lacking in Xi Jinping's China, where the CCP wants increasingly to be in every classroom, lab and boardroom. This stifling atmosphere hardly seems conducive to world-class, or even reliable, science, and this appeared to be borne out in February 2024 when *Caixin* reported a sharp fall in the contribution of high-tech industries to China's economy.[47] Yet there is one area where China is powering ahead – some of the CCP's most intense efforts are going into green technologies, where it is determined to control multiple renewable energy technologies and their supply chains.

CHAPTER 20

Carbon Capture

'We must tighten international production chains'
dependence on China, forming powerful
countermeasures and deterrent capabilities based on
artificially cutting off supply to foreigners.'

President Xi Jinping

Controlling the global market in renewable energy technologies and their supply chains does not herald a conversion by Beijing to greenery. It is not an environmental policy, but first and foremost an industrial policy. It is also seen by CCP leaders as a saviour for its economy, replacing heavy investment in property and infrastructure as the motor of growth while avoiding broader market reforms that might threaten Party control. Although it involves many nominally private companies, it is top-down and reliant on massive subsidies and other state support. It is also strategic, serving the CCP's broader economic goals of leadership and greater self-sufficiency in the technologies of the future, while creating global dependencies on China.

Dependency is often portrayed as almost an accident, something that has emerged as a by-product of the process of globalisation and the migration of supply chains to where goods can be made most cheaply and efficiently. In China's case creating dependencies is a policy goal, part of a broader effort to exert influence and shape geopolitics in its favour. This is one reason why Beijing has reacted so vociferously to Western notions of de-risking their economies – even while following its own version of that very policy. Beijing wants to remain a risk. This was spelt out by Xi Jinping in an April 2020 speech to the Central Financial and Economic Affairs

Commission in which he said, 'We must tighten international production chains' dependence on China, forming powerful countermeasures and deterrent capabilities based on artificially cutting off supply to foreigners.'[1] The flood of cheap and heavily subsidised Chinese exports of renewable energy technologies presents a particular dilemma for Western leaders committed to sharply cutting carbon emissions. Embracing Chinese electric vehicles (EVs), solar panels and related technology may be the fastest way of achieving this – though at the cost of deepening dependencies on China, which in turn carries serious strategic and security risks.

By early 2024, the world was bracing for a wave of Chinese-built EVs, with China leapfrogging the traditional motor powerhouses of Germany and Japan to become the world's largest car exporter. To this end it had given billions of dollars a year in subsidies and other handouts to gain a stranglehold on every stage of the EV supply chain. Between 2016 and 2022 the central government spent an estimated $57 billion to support the purchase of electric cars in China, five times the amount the US spent on incentives during that period, and with further sweeteners from local and provincial authorities.[2] Annual domestic sales of EVs surged from 1.3 million cars to 6.8 million in the two years between 2020 and 2022 alone.[3] The government also paid companies subsidies based on what they produced – worth $5.4 billion in 2022 alone – as well as providing cheap land, loans, grants and capped energy costs.[4] Between 2009 and 2023, China spent $230.8 billion supporting its EV industry, according to estimates from the Center for Strategic and International Studies. Traditional car companies were joined by a broad array of tech and other firms in scrambling for a share of the staggering sums on offer, and by the end of 2023 China had 167 different EV brands, although only twenty to thirty were regarded as financially viable in the long term.[5] Many exports were Western-branded – Tesla was exporting from its giant Shanghai factory, and MG and Volvo are both now owned by Chinese companies. Others jumping on the EV bandwagon included Huawei (the telecoms giant), Xiaomi (which makes mobile phones), Baidu (China's leading internet search engine) – and even Evergrande, the bankrupt property company.

One result was a fierce price war. Nio, a Chinese brand that tries to compete with Tesla, offered a free set of augmented reality glasses, worth $350, for each seat in its cars and a smartphone that was integrated with the car's self-driving system, but still racked up losses equivalent to $35,000 for each car it sold.[6] BYD in the last quarter of 2023 overtook Tesla as the world's biggest supplier of electric vehicles, aided by aggressive price cuts. The company's new Seagull EV was unveiled at the 2023 Shanghai motor show with a starting price of just over $11,000 – about a quarter of the price of most EVs on the market in Europe.[7] By one estimate, BYD alone received $3.7 billion in direct government subsidies between 2018 and 2022.[8] Such was the production glut across the industry that social media carried photographs of vast parking lots and fields in China filled with abandoned EVs – graveyards of cars and vans, many overgrown with bushes and weeds.[9] It was hardly the best advertisement for a sustainable future. Chinese media reported that BYD had ordered eight giant transport ships, each with a capacity of 7,700 vehicles and at a total cost of $689 million for its export push.[10]

It has been a similar story of overproduction with the lithium-ion batteries that power EVs and which typically comprise half the value of a car. In 2022, China had more than three-quarters of the world's battery manufacturing capacity, with 125 active gigafactories, as these plants are called – that's more than ten times the combined number in Europe and North America.[11] Scores more were in the pipeline as local governments competed with each other to attract the battery makers. The inevitable result was a glut in production and a fierce price war. By one estimate, production capacity was on track in 2023 to reach almost twice the level of demand, and based on announcements to build new plants this overcapacity was set to surge to nearly four times what the country needed by 2027.[12] As China prepared to unleash the surplus at knock-down prices onto the world market, it was not unaware of the possible backlash, with Xi Jinping warning CATL, China and the world's largest EV battery maker, that it could face repercussions because it was 'penetrating deep into enemy territory'.[13] By one estimate, CATL was in 2023 the biggest recipient of state handouts of all China's listed companies, receiving $790 million in subsidies.[14]

Faced with the Chinese EV onslaught, the European Union in September 2023 launched an investigation into Chinese EV subsidies. Memories were still raw of how other European industries, from steel and aluminium to solar panels, were decimated as a result of predatory trade practices, and EU leaders feared their own EV and related industries could go the same way. 'Their price is kept artificially low by huge state subsidies,' declared European Commission President Ursula von der Leyen. 'This is distorting our market.'[15] Nearly half of the cars exported from China in 2023 were sold in Europe, a rise of 60 per cent over the previous year, and two-thirds of these were EVs. Officials said China's share of the EVs sold in Europe had doubled to 8 per cent and would double again by 2025 with subsidies that enabled Chinese imports to undercut European EVs by around 20 per cent.[16]

Beijing angrily denounced the EU investigation as 'naked protectionism',[17] and there were fears that Beijing would retaliate against European firms, particularly German car manufacturers, who were heavily dependent on the Chinese market and said to be 'afraid' of the consequences of the probe.[18] At the same time, the EU stepped up its own incentives for EV producers and con-sumers, including tax breaks for manufacturers, subsidies for buyers and tax credits for households and businesses that install EV chargers;[19] EU battery makers were offered €3bn in subsidies. The United States also offered tax credits of up to $7,500 for buyers of new electric cars, and other handouts for manufacturers of EVs and batteries. However, the problem with subsidies to consumers is that they could end up being spent on Chinese cars. To counter this, President Joe Biden's Inflation Reduction Act restricted the incentives to American companies before his allies cried foul and they were extended to include those from Canada, Mexico, Japan, South Korea and the EU.

The scale of the challenge in competing with Chinese firms that benefited from years of deep state support was illustrated in a report for clients prepared by Goldman Sachs. It calculated that to obtain self-sufficiency in the EV supply chains, countries com-peting with China would need to invest $78.2 billion in battery production, $60.4 billion in components and $13.5 billion in min-ing of lithium, nickel and cobalt, as well as $12.1 billion in refining those materials.[20] The report also illustrated a broader point: that China has a stranglehold not just on EV cars and batteries, but the entire EV supply chain, including the critical minerals required for lithium-ion batteries. More than half the world's processing and refining capacity for lithium, cobalt and graphite were located in China, which also produced 70 per cent of the world's cathodes (the part of the battery that receives electrons on charging), and 85 per cent of anodes (the part that releases electrons when the battery is used), according to the International Energy Agency.[21] As geopolitical tensions rose, China was increasingly willing to use this supply chain dominance against its rivals. In July 2023 Beijing said that to preserve 'national security and interests' it would restrict exports of gallium and germanium, two critical metals used in semiconductors and electric vehicles, leading Renault Chairman Jean-Dominique Senard to warn of a 'Chinese storm' looming over Europe's growing electric vehicle sector. 'We are capable of making electric vehicles, but we are fighting to ensure the safety of our supplies', he said.[22]

China's EV dominance was particularly uncomfortable for British Prime Minister Rishi Sunak, who announced in September 2023 that he was delaying a ban on petrol and diesel cars by five years to 2035, while saying he was still committed to a legal target of net zero by 2050 – a target he will struggle to hit without increasing Britain's dependence on Beijing. In 2023, Britain was the largest market in Europe for Chinese EV car brands, accounting for almost a third of total sales during the first nine months of the year.[23] One leading brand was MG, which had a long British history before it collapsed in 2005 and was taken over by the Shanghai Automotive Industry Corporation. SAIC launched a series of relatively cheap Chinese-made EVs under the MG marque, which proved very popular in the UK. The company's MG4 EV was the second bestselling electric car in the UK behind Tesla's Model Y SUV over the first seven months of 2023, according to the Society of Motor Manufacturers and Traders.[24]

At the time of writing, London was resisting calls to launch its own investigation into China's unfair trade practices, but Sunak's discomfort about the outsize influence of Beijing was illustrated by the bizarre theatre surrounding the summer 2023 announcement of a new £4 billion gigafactory, Britain's second. The British government committed £500 million in subsidies to persuade India's Tata Group, which owns Jaguar Rover, to choose the UK over a site in Spain. What went unspoken was the role of a Chinese energy giant called Envision, which was to be a key partner in the project. 'That's a question for Tata, rather than me,' said Sunak, when asked about Envision, while Tata said, 'We will not be disclosing ongoing discussions regarding the gigafactory.'[25] Envision's involvement was well known in the industry, and company insiders told the *Financial Times* that the Chinese firm would supply technology for the first generation of batteries at the site.[26] Many of Sunak's back-benchers at the time were pushing for a tougher line on China, and on Chinese dependencies, and the optics of a Chinese firm benefit-ing from UK state aid explains this lack of transparency. Envision, through its battery subsidiary AESC, already owned Britain's only other gigafactory, in Sunderland, North East England, which sup-plied Nissan's nearby car plant. While Sunak sought to duck the issue, unable or unwilling to confront the reality of the enormous role China was being allowed to play in Britain's EV industry, the emphasis in Europe and America was on protecting their own companies while seeking to confront the broader dependencies on China. What went mostly unspoken were the potentially profound security risks from Chinese-made EVs.

In July 2023, Professor Jim Saker made headlines with a warning that Britain's roads could be paralysed by Beijing using EVs as a weapon.[27] The president of the Institute of Motor Industry said that the cars could be immobilised remotely and warned, 'The threat of connected electric vehicles flooding the country could be the most effective Trojan horse that the Chinese establishment has to poten-tially paralyse or hold the UK to ransom.'[28] At the time, some thirty Chinese EV brands were preparing to target the UK market, and Saker, who is also head of the Centre for Automotive Management at Loughborough University, warned, 'Even with regulation and strict homologation [the vehicle approval process] there is no way of stopping a car manufacturer having control of the vehicle and its data if the technology is already designed to allow it . . . The situ-ation in Ukraine has illustrated how Governments can weaponize products such as gas and grain supplies. With connected cars the threat is very much closer to home.'

Modern motor vehicles, and EVs in particular, are best regarded as computers on wheels, since computers control nearly every aspect of a vehicle's operation. The average electric car has around 2,000 chips and is festooned with sensors and cameras.[29] Their functions range from assisting with parking and monitoring the car's health and maintenance, to providing alerts, adjusting operations and warning the driver about issues. They are also connected, meaning they send and receive real-time information, whether that be in route guidance for the driver, or to enable the manufacturer or insurer to remotely monitor vehicle and driver performance, or to update software. As cars move towards more autonomous driving, and artificial intelligence (or machine learning) plays an ever greater role, so the flow of data will multiply. EVs are, in other words, potentially ideal tools of espionage, surveillance and sabotage. This has not been lost on the Chinese Communist Party, which while regarding Elon Musk in most respects as its favourite capitalist, has banned Tesla cars from what it regards as sensitive sites. This includes military compounds and housing complexes and other government affiliated venues, such as meeting and exhibition halls.[30] During the World University Games in Chengdu in July 2023, Teslas were barred from parts of the city to be visited by Xi Jinping.[31] Musk vowed to follow local data rules, but the authorities were taking no chances. Whether it be targeting high-profile individuals, stealing data or bringing entire cities to a standstill, the use of a connected electric vehicle as a weapon is no longer the stuff of science fiction.

Two Chinese companies, CATL and BYD, which between them control half of the global supply of EV batteries, have set their sights on dominating EV ancillary industries, including charging networks and energy storage systems. Both companies have close links with the Chinese Communist Party and have benefited from substantial subsidies. This opens up another set of security risks, since storage and charging systems need to be linked to a nation's electrical grid, posing potentially serious cybersecurity issues. The risks have been likened to those posed by the involvement of Huawei in advanced telecoms networks. The West was slow to recognise the threat from Huawei – a complacency they are in danger of repeating with the EV infrastructure.[32] Likewise, there has been growing alarm over Chinese ambitions to break into the European market for offshore wind turbines and related infrastructure. Again,

Chinese manufacturers have benefited from enormous state support, and Chinese turbines cost around half the global average – a tempting route to cut emissions, no doubt, but carrying enormous security risks.[33]

Chinese car exporters will of course give guarantees of good behaviour, as TikTok, Hikvision and Huawei have all done in the past, but such assurances are simply not credible when these companies, like all Chinese companies, are ultimately beholden to the CCP. Imported EVs and related equipment can be swept for spyware, but that is to miss the point – connected EVs are by definition one giant piece of spyware. At the heart of every EV is a small internet-connected device called a cellular module, which is a kind of gatekeeper and manager, a vital component of the system that controls the sensors, cameras, audio, geolocation capability, engine and much more, as well as managing the flow of vast amounts of data in and out of the car. These devices are not covertly placed, they are an essential part of a modern control system, yet in the wrong hands they are potentially a far more dangerous weapon than the most potent piece of spyware. The power of these modules was illustrated in Ukraine after Russian troops occupied the city of Melitopol and stole advanced harvesters from a John Deere dealership. The Russians transported the machines 700 miles to Chechnya but were unable to use any of them since they were tracked and their systems shut down remotely by John Deere.[34] Charles Parton, a senior fellow at the Royal United Services Institute, has written that British security services are 'petrified' by the nightmare of such powers in the hands of a hostile state.[35] Parton, a former British diplomat who spent more than two decades specialising in China, has done more than anybody else to raise awareness of the dangers posed by these modules, the production of which is dominated by China. By the end of 2022, Chinese companies controlled almost two-thirds of the global market in cellular modules and seemed on track to establish a near monopoly through the familiar tactics of heavy subsidies, cheap finance and other handouts. 'Ultimately, you've got to ban any Chinese module in any vehicle, and you'd have to do it quite quickly,' Parton said.[36]

In February 2024, President Joe Biden ordered an investigation into whether Chinese connected vehicles, which he called 'smartphones on wheels', posed a security threat to Americans.[37] A month later, Sir Richard Dearlove, the former head of MI6 asked in an article in *The Times*, 'How many immobilised electric vehicles would it take to freeze the circulation of London traffic?'[38] He called on the UK government to ban Chinese EVs from sensitive infrastructure sites and from use by cabinet ministers.

If this were not challenge enough, the use of Chinese-made cellular modules goes far beyond EVs. They are used in a vast array of applications, from power grids, manufacturing, health, transport and payments systems to the connected vacuum cleaners, refrigerators, smart meters and fitness trackers of what has become known as the Internet of Things (IoT). 'To ensure that such systems run efficiently, they collect huge amounts of data and metadata for analysis, processing, and response management. They also deliver software updates to improve functionality,' Parton wrote in a report for the Council on Geostrategy.[39] In other words, they are an extremely powerful and indispensable part of our lives and increasingly central to the functioning of the modern economy and society. 'The threat from Chinese cellular modules is far greater and more systemic than a danger posed by an individual company or sector,' he wrote.

As China's EV juggernaut bore down on world markets, the CCP was moving to consolidate and exploit its position as world leader in solar power technologies by restricting the export of key components. State media reported that exports of technology and machinery for making solar-panel components would require special permission to 'help safeguard national security'.[40] The restricted items did not include the panels themselves; with China manufacturing eight out of every ten solar panels produced globally, that would have been self-defeating. Instead the restrictions were designed to crimp efforts by Western democracies to rebuild their decimated solar industries.

The move came almost nine years after a US grand jury indicted *in absentia* five agents of the People's Liberation Army for hacking the computers of SolarWorld, then America's biggest solar tech company, and stealing key know-how. The hackers 'stole thousands of files including information about SolarWorld's cash flow, manufacturing metrics, production line information, costs, and privileged attorney-client communications', according to the May 2014 indictment.[41] They also stole details of a proprietary technology the company had developed to improve the efficiency of solar cells, emails relating to complaints SolarWorld's German parent company was making to the European Commission about Chinese trade practices, and testimony the company was preparing for the US Trade Commission. 'Success in the global market place should be based solely on a company's ability to innovate and compete, not on a sponsor government's ability to spy and steal business secrets,' said US Attorney General Eric Holder.[42] The stolen know-how was made available to Chinese competitors and heavily subsidised solar panels incorporating SolarWorld's innovations flooded the global market. In 2017, the German parent of SolarWorld – once Europe's largest solar-panel maker by sales – filed for bankruptcy, no longer able to compete.[43]

It has been argued that Chinese manufacturers would have caught up anyway, and that cheap Chinese solar panels are good for consumers and have hastened the shift towards clean energy. However, the solar industry is a textbook case of Beijing's predatory trade practices – and one which haunts Western policymakers looking at the expected onslaught of Chinese-made EVs. In 2023, global spend on solar energy production was expected for the first time to outpace spending on oil, $380 billion compared with $370 billion, but unlike oil the vast majority of solar panels will come from one nation.[44] Not only does China produce four out of five of the world's panels, but as with EVs, it dominates the entire supply chain, including 85 per cent of the global supply of solar cells, 88 per cent of solar-grade polysilicon, and 97 per cent of the silicon ingots and wafers that form the core of solar cells.[45] Between 2011 and 2022, China invested over $50 billion in new solar-panel facilities – the familiar cocktail of subsidies and other handouts resulting in massive overcapacity.[46]

As recently as 2007 Europe was the world's largest solar power manufacturer, but in spite of the decimation of the industry and clear evidence of Chinese dumping of solar panels at below their cost of production, Brussels initially shied away from tough tariffs after Beijing threatened to retaliate with tariffs against wine and luxury cars.[47] As we have seen, the mood in Europe and America has since hardened. Yet belated efforts by America, Europe and the UK to lessen dependence on China and build (or rebuild) their own solar and other green tech industries through protectionism and financial incentives face another daunting challenge: many aspects of producing 'clean' tech are extremely dirty, and China tolerates a far higher level of environmental degradation and other abuses than is the case in a liberal democracy.

During my time as correspondent in China, the environmental degradation from decades of breakneck growth was never far away. At times the smog was so bad you could taste it. In Beijing, nearby buildings would turn to fuzzy outlines in the gloom, hundreds of flights were cancelled or delayed, while cars, their headlights on throughout the day, crept gingerly along the city's darkened and eerie streets. 'It looks like the end of the world,' in the memorable words of one blogger, while another asked whether she would ever see the sun again. Beijing's foreign residents dubbed it the 'Airpocalypse'. At first the Communist Party denied there was any smog, or else called it 'fog' or 'mist' or blamed some other supposed weather-related phenomenon. Or else it was a malicious rumour, even a foreign conspiracy on account of the air quality monitor on the roof of the US embassy, which tweeted hourly readings. The pollution levels were routinely multiples of that deemed safe by the World Health Organization. Researchers analysing that data estimated that air pollution contributed to 1.6 million deaths a year in China.[48] When it got so bad that it could no longer be denied, China's premier declared a 'war' on pollution and vowed to 'make our skies blue again'.[49] The Beijing authorities began to restrict car use in the capital and shut polluting factories or else shifted them elsewhere, though to a large extent this merely moved around the air pollution.

On top of the unbreathable air, China faced diminishing and polluted water supplies, contaminated soil – 8 per cent of all arable land, by one estimate[50] – and rapid desertification as a result of deforestation and the loss of grasslands. Industrial accidents – those not covered up – were depressingly common, though barely commented on unless accompanied by massive disruption or large-scale loss of life, as when a chemical storage facility exploded in the port city of Tianjin in August 2015, killing 165, according to the official tally.[51] When I visited Harbin in northern China that same year, people were still wary of touching the water some ten years after an explosion at a chemical plant sent a deadly fifty-mile slick of toxins into the Songhua River which runs through the city, shutting down the city's water supply for days.[52]

On another occasion I travelled with Zhou Litai, a brave self-trained labour lawyer, to a hostel he ran on the outskirts of the southern city of Shenzhen, which was full of workers mutilated in the area's factories. It was like entering a war zone. Most had missing limbs, the result of factory accidents, and Zhou was fighting a losing battle for compensation. He was representing around 3,000 workers but was facing constant threats against him and the hostel from factory owners and the authorities. At the time there were 10,000 industrial injuries a year in China, according to local government figures, which were regarded as a gross underestimate. As recently as 2020, there were on average 75 deaths *per day* from work-related accidents.[53] Zhou told me it wasn't that China had bad labour laws, it's just that they were not enforced. It has been argued that environmental standards and labour conditions have improved in recent years, but the CCP's willingness to tolerate dirty and dangerous processes in order to gain a competitive edge remains – and is embedded in the 'green' tech supply chain.

China has invested heavily in critical minerals, buying up mines worldwide. For instance, China has only 1 per cent of the world's cobalt reserves, but in 2020 owned or financed fifteen of the nineteen cobalt-producing mines in the Democratic Republic of Congo, the world's dominant producer.[54] China has also been buying up lithium mines worldwide, and mines roughly 80 per cent of rare earths, seventeen obscure minerals that have magnetic and conductive properties that give them multiple and vital applications in our digital lives. However, it is not the mining that necessarily gives China the edge, but the processing and refining. For instance, China mines only 6 per cent of the world's manganese but refines 93 per cent. Nickel is spread quite evenly around the world, but China still controls two-thirds of the chemical processing.[55] It also processes 60 per cent of the world's supply of lithium. Rare earths, in spite of their name, are not so rare; they're simply called rare because of their atomic properties. Significant known deposits exist in China, Brazil, Australia, Vietnam, India, the US and Greenland, which by one estimate could hold a quarter of the world's reserves.[56] However, China processes 90 per cent of rare earths.

Processing of critical minerals is expensive and dirty, and as earlier with the sweat shops of Shenzhen, Beijing has been willing to tolerate environmental degradation from the toxic process of extracting the minerals. This extraction and refinement of critical minerals has become one of China's most polluting industries – purifying just one tonne of rare-earth elements requires 200 cubic metres of water. In the process, this water is contaminated with heavy metals and can end up untreated in rivers, soils and aquifers.[57] A candid report in January 2024 from China's top environmental watchdog admitted to a 'marked increase' in environmental emergencies involving tailing ponds – the areas used to store toxic waste from the process of separating minerals from rocks.[58] Without elaborating, the agency said massive leaks from these dumps were the main causes of emergencies, were 'extremely difficult' to deal with and can easily cause regional water pollution.

China's willingness to tolerate such pollution represents an acute challenge to Western democracies, who have been scrambling to put in place strategies to wrest back control of these critical supply chains – including the establishment in June 2022 of a Minerals Security Partnership, whose members include the UK, US, EU, Australia, Canada, Korea and Japan.[59] The urgency was underlined in late 2023, when Beijing announced it would tighten rules on the export of technologies for rare-earth ore mining, ore selection and refining, as well as tech related to extracting and separating rare earths.[60] It required rare-earth exporters to report on the types of metals they were exporting and the destinations. It also introduced special export controls for graphite used in EV batteries on 'national security' grounds.[61]

In Britain, where the government hoped to exploit modest supplies of lithium in Cornwall and Durham, the UK Health and Safety Executive, a safety watchdog, proposed that lithium not be classified as 'toxic'.[62] Industry executives believed this would benefit prospective lithium refineries in the UK, since a hazardous label might create legal obstacles. The EU set a target of manufacturing 40 per cent of clean-energy generating equipment within the Union by 2030 and proposed allowing member states to disregard some environmental protections.[63] Loosening standards, however gingerly, is certain to enrage environmentalists. Unlike in China, where most protest is criminalised, they will have to be listened to and Xi Jinping will continue to enjoy a dictator's discount on the messy production of critical minerals.

Many Western free marketeers are queasy about their governments resorting to protectionism to counter China's mercantilism, but Western science is not standing still, and the challenge posed by Beijing has spurred innovation. Scientists in the United States and Norway have reported progress in developing cleaner and cheaper ways of processing rare earths,[64] while Northvolt, a Swedish start-up, is pioneering sodium-ion batteries, which do not use lithium, nickel, graphite and cobalt.[65] The technology raises the tantalising prospect of lower cost and more sustainable batteries – while at the same time reducing dependence on China. Renewables are of course not the only worrying dependence on China. The Covid-19 pandemic revealed China's dominance in the provision of medical supplies, with one report estimating that in 2021 the National Health Service relied on China for 90 per cent of masks, 80 per cent of bandages, almost half its bedside monitors and 54 per cent of gloves.[66] It sometimes seemed that hardly a week went by without another new dependency being exposed. In early 2024 it was ships, with reports that China had captured more than half the world's shipbuilding the previous year. The world's factory had seemingly become the world's shipyard, a huge strategic advantage in the event of conflict.[67] In addition, more than 95 per cent of shipping containers, the workhorses of international trade, were being made in China, with production dominated by just three state-owned enterprises.[68]

However it is in renewables that the stakes are particularly high because they are foundational technologies of the future. That is why the battle for control is so important – to the West, but also for the CCP, which sees dominating the world's markets in these emerging technologies as crucial to rebooting its ailing economy and winning the battle to unseat the US as the world's largest economy. In May 2024, the US imposed a 100 per cent tariff on EVs made in China and raised the border tax on Chinese solar panels from 25 per cent to 50 per cent. The EU announced tariffs of up to 48 per cent on Chinese EVs and extended its own probe into Beijing's green subsidies, launching an investigation into China-made wind turbines. Brussels also armed itself with a powerful new tool for tackling Beijing's handouts: a regulation empowering competition officials to block companies subsidised by foreign governments from bidding for public projects, taking over European companies or even selling goods and services in the single market. As we have seen repeatedly in this book, Chinese companies are notoriously opaque, and soon after the regulation came into force, two Chinese groups withdrew from a solar project in Romania, not wishing to open their books to EU investigators.

Green tech has also become an increasingly prominent part of China's pitch to less-developed countries, increasingly referred to as the Global South, which Beijing aspires to lead. Here too, China faces challenges, partly because its debt-fuelled Belt and Road Initiative is floundering, but also because the approach of many middle-income countries is as transactional as that of Beijing. They too are wary of the wave of subsidised exports from China, and also see opportunity to leverage the competition between China and the West, particularly as liberal democracies look to bolster their own development assistance. There is little natural love for China, the main attraction having been the express train that was breakneck economic growth, on which everybody wanted a ride. If the train derails or is shunted into the sidings, as looks increasingly likely, the ride becomes a good deal less enticing. If China's economy stalls or collapses, then so does Beijing's power to seduce.

CHAPTER 21

Autocrats United

'Right now, we are seeing a change the likes of which
we haven't seen in 100 years, and we are the
ones driving these changes together . . .
Please take care, dear friend.'

*Xi Jinping (in unguarded comments
to Vladimir Putin)*

Xi Jinping's pitch for global leadership was undeterred by the darkening clouds surrounding the Chinese economy. 'China is endeavouring to build itself into a stronger country and rejuvenate the Chinese nation on all fronts by pursuing Chinese modernization,' he said in October 2023. 'The modernization we are pursuing is not for China alone, but for all developing countries through our joint efforts.' He was speaking in the Great Hall of the People in Beijing at an event marking the tenth anniversary of the Belt and Road Initiative (BRI), attended by representatives of 140 countries, though Western democracies largely stayed away. The guest of honour was Russian leader Vladimir Putin, who called Xi his 'dear friend' and hailed China's efforts to build a 'fairer, multipolar world and system of international relations'.[1]

When it was launched in 2013, Xi described the BRI as 'a project of the century, which will benefit people across the world', and 'a big family of harmonious coexistence'.[2] In reality, what began as a project to build global infrastructure has become a rather clunky slogan for just about everything Beijing does abroad and with the principal aim of furthering the CCP's interests and influence – 'a giant project of international political engineering,' as it has been described'.[3] By one estimate, China splurged $843 billion on 13,427

BRI projects over its first eight years.[4] By the time of the tenth anniversary, it was generally accepted to have exceeded a trillion dollars, and Beijing had become the world's largest creditor. However, the BRI was fast losing its lustre, with growing problems that in many ways mirrored those of China's domestic economy. Lending was falling, wasteful projects were stalling and recipients of Beijing's largesse were struggling with massive and possibly unpayable debts. China's investment in Africa, where it once led the way, were in 2022 only 10 per cent of their 2016 peak.[5]

The BRI was always overhyped and under-principled, lacking transparency and without the environmental, labour or human rights protections that typically accompany lending from multilateral institutions or the West. In many ways it is a classic neo-colonial enterprise, harking back to the ancient China-centric view of the world. There were widespread accusations of corruption, with projects typically involving the use of Chinese labour and Chinese contractors, and once complete they were frequently Chinese managed. Some $78 billion worth of loans turned sour in the three years to 2023 by one estimate. Other studies showed that Chinese bailouts of the poorest recipients of its loans totalled $185 billion between 2016 and 2021, and were rising sharply as economies struggled to recover from the Covid-19 pandemic.[6] During 2020 and 2021, loans worth some $52 billion had to be renegotiated – three times the value of the previous two years.[7]

For all its talk of solidarity with the 'Global South' and 'no strings' lending, Beijing was an unforgiving creditor. As BRI projects blew up, it preferred to issue 'rescue loans' and tighten control over the assets it had created instead of writing down the value of debt, exacerbating the pain for the poorest countries. China refused to join the well-established multilateral system for addressing debt. That system, known as the Paris Club, is an informal grouping of major creditors, which alongside the International Monetary Fund (IMF) and World Bank, deals with debt restructuring when countries run into trouble, a process that frequently involves a write-down of existing debt. The result was lengthy delays to broader restructuring agreements, even amid warnings that fifty-four countries accounting for more than half of the world's poorest people needed debt relief to avoid worsening poverty and to give them a chance of dealing with climate change.[8] The IMF sought to bind China into a new Global Sovereign Debt Roundtable alongside all other major creditors, but Beijing's participation was patchy, as it continued to deal bilaterally with those who owed China money and to resist debt 'hair-cuts'.[9]

China's approach was opaque and transactional – Sri Lanka was forced to hand over its new $1.3 billion Hambantota Port to a Chinese company after failing to make repayments.[10] A charitable explanation was that Beijing had no experience dealing with an international debt crisis of this scale; a less charitable view was that the CCP was acting like a loan shark. Not only did it not want loans cancelled, but it sought to use debt distress to consolidate its influence and extract strategic advantages in debtor countries, while undermining the established multilateral system for providing relief.[11]

The BRI also reflected deep-seated Chinese insecurities – a means to break out from the restraints of geography. The country is enclosed on three sides by land borders and counts fourteen countries as neighbours. Looking out to the east, beyond its only sea border, it is confronted by an island barrier extending from Russia's Kamchatka Peninsula in the north to Borneo in the south. Part of that barrier is formed by Japan, South Korea and the Philippines, all US allies, as well as by Taiwan. The South China Sea is a strategic and economic chokepoint. China remains heavily dependent on Middle Eastern oil, and some 80 per cent of those supplies cross the South China Sea after passing through the Malacca Strait from the Indian Ocean. Around 40 per cent of China's total trade takes the same route.[12] It is the sort of challenging geography that feeds Communist Party paranoia about being 'contained'. As we shall see, it is also a paranoia shared by Russia, which historically has tried to put space between itself and Western powers, and explains to some extent its aggression against Ukraine.

The BRI is in part an effort to secure supplies of raw materials and lock neighbours into China's economic and political orbit. Crucially, China wanted to secure alternative access to the ocean – 'the long march to the sea', as it has been dubbed. To this end, two of the biggest beneficiaries have been Myanmar and Pakistan, where energy pipelines, ports and transport infrastructure are an important part of the blueprint. Myanmar has been described by Chinese analysts as 'China's California', a proxy for the western coast that it lacks.[13] Both are in trouble – Myanmar because of a worsening civil war, and Pakistan because an estimated 40 per cent of the projects in the China–Pakistan Economic Corridor had by 2023 run into problems including corruption, cost overruns, funding shortfalls or adverse environmental impacts.[14] China's coercion of Micronesia, which we examined earlier, can also be explained in part by Beijing's broader strategic insecurities and its desire to control corridors across the Pacific. In Cambodia, a hitherto reliable client state, a string of expensive airport projects, which could potentially extend China's reach, were reportedly at a standstill as Chinese money dried up.[15]

For all these reasons, the 2023 anniversary gathering was subdued. Italy, the only advanced Western economy to sign up to the BRI, stayed away and subsequently pulled out. The country's defence minister, Guido Crosetto, described the original decision to join as 'improvised and atrocious'. Greek Prime Minister Kyriakos Mitsotakis also stayed away, even though Beijing portrayed its investment in Greece's Piraeus port as a roaring success. COSCO, a Chinese state-owned shipping giant, was able to buy a controlling stake in 2016, when Greece was in a financial crisis and the port was on its knees – yet at the time COSCO was six times more leveraged than the loss-making Piraeus Port Authority.[16] It was not a commercial decision, but a strategic one by Beijing, which called Piraeus the BRI's 'dragon's head' in Europe – though in Athens it was beginning to feel like a Trojan horse. The president of the Philippines was also a no-show in Beijing. Manila described the BRI as 'pledge-trap' diplomacy, because of China's failure to follow through with promises, and cancelled several large infrastructure projects in favour of Japanese or Western rivals.[17] Those countries most heavily indebted to China did not have that option. The BRI had created a network of compliant states who can be dragooned into providing political support for China, stifling criticism in international forums or parroting Beijing's narrative on issues such as Taiwan, Hong Kong, Tibet and Xinjiang. Yet, at the same time international surveys show broad and growing wariness of Beijing – in spite of all the money it had spent.[18]

Xi knew the BRI needed a reboot, and gone was talk of ports, railways and power stations. Beijing's largesse would now be focused on 'higher level' and 'higher quality' development. If the first phase of the BRI had been about heavy construction, the next would stress frontier technologies. The provision of 'green' tech would have the added benefit of helping China export its vast over-capacity, as had been the case with earlier incarnations of the BRI, which enabled China to shift surplus steel and cement. In essence it was the same neo-colonial model, only with a smarter and potentially more dangerous focus.

The 'digital silk road', as the CCP called its new approach, has been an element of the BRI since 2015, but now it has taken centre stage, and like the BRI is a vague wrapper for all manner of schemes. It can best be seen as an ecosystem of technologies, ranging from 5G telecommunications networks (and its infrastructure of cables, data centres and satellite ground tracking stations) to e-commerce and other financial services, advanced data analytics, including AI, as well as genomics, sustainable energy generation, smart power grids and connected vehicles. Any technology ecosystem is underpinned by standards and values, and the digital silk road is exporting techno-authoritarianism modelled on the world's most intrusive surveillance state. One of its flagship offerings, marketed by Huawei, is a suite of advanced surveillance tools called 'safe city solutions', which will ensure there is 'nowhere to hide', according to the company's website.[19] These 'safe cities', bristling with cameras, sensors, AI and data analytics, are already popular with autocrats worldwide – 71 per cent of 'safe city' agreements were in countries rated by Freedom House as 'not free' or 'partly free', and include Angola, Egypt, Ethiopia, Kazakhstan, Russia, Saudi Arabia, Thailand, the United Arab Emirates and Uzbekistan.[20] Public order and social control, and the speedy identification of any perceived threat, are the key selling points. Research at the Central Party School is aimed at further enhancing these systems by identifying 'opinions, behaviours, emotions, footprints, and other characteristics . . . to unearth hidden negative opinions, predict their development, intervene in advance, and effectively resolve public opinion problems to reduce the risk of societal safety incidents'.[21]

At the same time, the CCP is putting enormous energy into shaping the vital international technical standards that define the interoperability and security of emerging technologies. Standards are the technical rules of the highway, and an enormous source of power and influence. Some 200-odd global organisations and bodies are involved in standards-setting, and China has been very active in these forums. For instance, between 2016 and 2019, all twenty submissions to the International Telecommunications Union (ITU) on facial recognition technology came from China, most relating to how footage and audio recordings are stored and analysed.[22] International standards are voluntary, but they are usually adopted by developing countries in Asia, Africa and the Middle East, key markets for China. Beijing has similar ambitions with AI and stands to gain a big technological and commercial edge if its standards are adopted.

The tech race between China and the United States is often described in terms of a competition to innovate, with its outcomes judged by the nature and quality of the products that emerge from the labs and factories. Yet it is also about establishing globally the tech infrastructure on which multiple applications are built. This is sometimes referred to as the tech platforms, the foundational components or building blocks, and they include networks, data management tools, operating systems and much more. These in turn incorporate technical standards and ethical and moral values. 'The private sector is America's great strength. We move faster and more globally than any government could, and we need global platforms, or be forced to use the Chinese ones which is a disaster,' according to Eric Schmidt, the former head of Google and chairman of America's National Security Commission on Artificial Intelligence.[23] 'These are contests of values as well as investments,' he told a US Senate Armed Services Committee hearing on emerging technologies and their impact on national security. The digital silk road is now the CCP's main instrument for exporting China's tech infrastructure, and through that a Beijing-centric global order.

In its early stages, the BRI was implemented largely by state-owned companies and funded by state-owned banks. The digital silk road is more diverse; it still involves state firms, but relies more heavily on nominally private tech companies, such as Huawei (telecoms), Hikvision (surveillance cameras), Alibaba (e-commerce), BGI (genomics), Tencent (e-commerce, social media and cloud services), TikTok (social media), BYD (electric vehicles and related tech) and Envision (batteries and green energy). In practice, there is considerable overlap between the services and the ambitions of these tech giants, which to varying degrees have been nurtured, supported and protected by the CCP. Ownership is frequently opaque, and even where share registers appear diverse, effective control is tightly held. As we have seen, all are ultimately beholden to the CCP through a series of laws and the reality of the Party's power. Within China, the tech giants are partners of the CCP in the building and operation of the surveillance state, and many, including Hikvision, Huawei and parts of the BGI Group, have been sanctioned by the US government for their alleged role in human rights abuses in Xinjiang. A three-year regulatory crackdown on tech companies that began in 2020, which saw the CCP tighten control over their activities, technology and data, was motivated in part by the Party wanting to more closely direct firms that were becoming increasingly important tools along the digital silk road.

Western governments have been slow to wake up to the risks of espionage, surveillance, sabotage and the harvesting of data more broadly, posed by this 'international brigade' of Chinese tech giants. Britain is among the many Western countries to have barred Huawei from its 5G telecoms networks, though the company remains entrenched in earlier generation networks and throughout UK academia. Only in 2023 did the UK belatedly begin to remove Chinese surveillance equipment from sensitive government sites.[24] However, critics argued this did not go far enough, pointing to the widespread use of Chinese equipment by police forces throughout the UK. Referring to a spy balloon shot down by the US after it crossed America, UK Surveillance Camera Commissioner Professor Fraser Sampson said 'There has been a lot in the news in recent days about how concerned we should be about Chinese spy balloons 60,000ft up in the sky. I do not understand why we are not at least as concerned about the Chinese cameras 6ft above our head in the street and elsewhere.'[25]

The activities of the BGI Group (formerly Beijing Genomics Institute), which runs China's National Gene Bank on behalf of the Chinese government, have also come under scrutiny. There are fears that the company, which has worked with the People's Liberation Army, is harvesting genetic data under the guise of health and pre-natal testing, which could have surveillance and military implications – accusations the company strongly denies. TikTok, which is owned by Beijing-based ByteDance, has been accused of transmitting data to Beijing and snooping on users – the company used its app to spy on reporters as part of an attempt to track down the journalists' sources, according to an internal email.[26] The app was also banned from all parliamentary devices in the UK and from the wider parliamentary network.[27] This followed similar bans on phones and corporate devices at the European Commission and on devices issued by the US federal government.[28] In April 2024, President Joe Biden signed a new law giving ByteDance nine months to sell the app or have it banned in the US. In October 2023, Belgium's intelligence service, VSSE, said in a statement that it was working to 'detect and fight against possible spying and/or interference activities carried out by Chinese entities including Alibaba.'[29] The investigation centred on Alibaba's main European logistics hub at a cargo airport in Liege and whether sensitive economic data had been shared with the Chinese authorities and intelligence services. The company denied the allegations.

The control of the sub-sea cables that carry vital internet traffic around the globe, the digital arteries of an increasingly connected world, are another area of growing tension. The strategic importance of the South China Sea is usually expressed in terms of what transits through it – more than a fifth of world trade by most estimates. However, it is equally vital for what passes below – a network of congested data routes, with China accused of impeding the laying and maintenance of cables.[30] The vulnerability of this digital infrastructure to sabotage was highlighted by the repeated severing of cables linking the Taiwanese-controlled island of Matsu, which sits just ten miles off the Chinese coast, to the outside world. The cables were snapped twenty-seven times in the five years to 2023. In late 2023, a Chinese and a Russian ship became the focus of an investigation into the apparent sabotage of data pipelines under the Baltic Sea, linking Finland and Sweden to Estonia.[31]

The incident happened just a few months after Finland joined NATO, the Western military alliance, and with an application from Sweden nearing completion. Russia threatened 'counter-measures' in response, with Beijing supporting Moscow's criticism of NATO expansion.

Six months before he joined Xi Jinping at the BRI anniversary in Beijing, Vladimir Putin had hosted the Chinese leader in Moscow. At the end of their summit meeting, the two men stood face-to-face on the Kremlin steps and Xi said, 'Right now, we are seeing a change the likes of which we haven't seen in 100 years, and we are the ones driving these changes together.'[32] The two men then clasped hands, both smiling.

'I agree,' Putin said, briefly bringing up his free hand to hold Xi's arm.

The Chinese leader added, 'Please take care, dear friend.' Xi then climbed into his waiting limousine, while Putin stood awkwardly at the curb side, waving, and very briefly appeared to bow his head as Xi's cavalcade swept away. The official communiqué proclaimed relations to be at their 'highest level in history', but those unscripted moments told us far more about a relationship that was shifting sharply in China's favour.

As the war in Ukraine became bogged down, Russia was increasingly dependent on China economically and diplomatically. Beijing refused to condemn the Russian invasion, echoing Moscow's justifications, and effectively underwrote the aggression with sharply increased trade, cushioning Putin from Western sanctions. The value of two-way trade in 2023 hit a record $240 billion, with half of Russia's oil and related petroleum exports going to China. Moscow stepped up purchases of Chinese goods from cars to smartphones, filling the gap left by the departure of European and US brands.[33] Beijing also supplied dual-use technologies, such as integrated circuits, which doubled in a year.[34] China avoided openly supplying lethal weapons, which would attract secondary Western sanctions, but inched ever closer to that line, with the US sanctioning a swath of Chinese companies for supplying electronic components with military applications.[35] America also accused Beijing of supplying machine tools, optics for Russian tanks and armoured vehicles and turbojet engines for cruise missiles. US Secretary of State Antony Blinken said China was helping Russia boost its defence industrial base, and 'Russia would struggle to sustain its assault on Ukraine without China's support.'[36] In June 2024, Ukrainian President Volodymyr Zelensky accused China of working with Russia to sabotage a forthcoming peace conference in Switzerland by pressuring countries not to attend.[37] Hacked emails from Russian state broadcaster VGTRK revealed that the two governments signed an agreement early in the conflict to exchange news content and coordinate digital media strategies with the aim of 'promoting objective, comprehensive and accurate coverage of the most important world events' – a propaganda pact to amplify disinformation.[38]

If Russia's military bungling and its brutality on the battlefield gave Xi pause for thought, he didn't show it. The two men's world views and fundamental insecurities are too similar. The words they exchanged on the Kremlin steps reaffirmed their shared goal of creating a new global order – or a 'fairer, multipolar world', as they put it during the BRI anniversary gathering. Both regard Western democracies as decadent and in decline and share a culture of grievance and victimhood. While Putin evoked the concept of the *Russkiy Mir*, unifying the 'Russian World', to justify his aggression in Ukraine, Xi has his China Dream of national rejuvenation. They are both imperialist visions of restoring national greatness, driven by ethnic chauvinism, and they hark back to an era of big power politics and spheres of influence with little room for messy notions of self-determination, whether they be Ukrainian or Taiwanese.

The CCP sees itself as a redemptive power after a so-called 'century of humiliation' at the hands of rapacious foreigners imposing 'unequal treaties' on China. The irony is that Tsarist Russia was the most rapacious of those foreigners, seizing 1.5 million square kilometres of territory, including modern Vladivostok, from the crumbling Qing empire during the nineteenth century. That represented more than a tenth of China at the time. For the moment those particular 'unequal treaties' have been set aside, at least officially, although they are never far from the minds of Chinese (or Russian) nationalists. Neither are memories of the three decades after the Sino-Soviet split in the late 1950s, when the fortified frontier between the Soviet Union and the People's Republic of China was a tense and dangerous place as the two communist giants vied for leadership of the world revolutionary movement. A border clash in the Russian Far East in March 1969 left hundreds dead and brought the two sides to the brink of full-scale war, and there were thinly veiled Soviet nuclear threats against its neighbour.[39]

China does not have formal allies in the Western sense. It does not fit with Beijing's sense of its own centrality, which is incompatible with an alliance system that might require obligations, commitments and a degree of equity. But it does have a hierarchy of partnerships, of which Russia sits at the top – the relationship designated as a 'comprehensive strategic partnership of coordination for the new era'. They increasingly define their relationship in terms of opposition to Western democracies – and to the US in particular. Even while the Ukraine war raged, China continued to conduct military drills with Russia that were increasingly complex and geographically widespread. In March 2023, they were joined by Iran for naval exercises in the Gulf of Oman, designed to 'deepen practical cooperation among the navies of participating countries', according to China's defence ministry.[40] With Russia also turning for military help to Iran, which supplied drones, and to North Korea for artillery shells, the world seemed to be moving towards a broader competition between autocracies and democracies – with China first among equals in the autocratic camp.[41]

For all the talk of a 'no limits partnership' with 'no "forbidden" areas of cooperation',[42] Western sceptics have argued that the relationship will struggle to overcome the deep-seated historic resentments and suspicions. 'They have a marriage of convenience . . . I'm not sure if it's conviction,' was how US Secretary of State Antony Blinken characterised it, describing Russia as 'very much the junior partner'.[43] There is also the broader question of whether the 'glue' that binds together autocrats, deeply paranoid, calculating and capricious by nature, can ever have the depth and lasting power of voluntary defensive alliances, such as NATO, which are based on deeper democratic values.

The global system that China and Russia seek to overturn has been called the 'rules-based international order', and Chinese state media has railed against its 'mafia-style nature . . . which supresses anything that challenges US hegemony, including China's rise'.[44] The 'rules-based order' can be a tricky concept to pin down, much quoted but hard to define. However, at its heart are a set of principles, rules and institutions mostly established by the victorious Western allies after the end of the Second World War, and which aim to determine how countries govern their relationships. The ideal was that global governance would not simply be dictated by the most powerful. It has been described as a layered system of treaties and international institutions governing trade, economics, security and much else, and with the UN at the top.[45] Much of the system enshrined the norms and principles of the liberal democracies which set it up, the US in particular, and with the US dollar as the principal currency of world trade. Over time, the rules-based system has come under strain – not least from America itself, which has occasionally ignored the rules it helped create. Overall, however, it has been remarkably resilient, raising global living standards and other measures of international wellbeing. Russia and China were largely peripheral to this system during its early decades; before the collapse of the Soviet Union, Moscow ran a separate, planned system of economic relations with its satellite states, while China was largely closed to the world. That changed with the collapse of the Soviet Union and the opening of China. As the two have grown closer, their resentment at the US-led system has been accompanied by calls for what they describe as a 'multipolar world'. This is another sketchy concept, but one that seeks to enshrine their power and influence. It is defined in opposition to the supposedly bipolar world of US–Soviet competition during the Cold War and the unipolar world of American leadership after the collapse of the USSR.

A resentful and revisionist Russia has never been a constructive player within a system in which it had no great stake. It has sought to undermine it at every turn, with no clear notion of what to put in its place. 'I'm not sure Russia or Putin actually wants a world order – maybe more like world disorder,' as US Secretary of State Antony Blinken put it.[46] By contrast, Beijing initially preferred to work inside the system, from which it has benefited enormously, while gaming it to its advantage and seeking greater influence within it. As Barack Obama notes in his memoir, *A Promised Land*, China's rise has been facilitated by systematically 'evading, bending, or breaking just about every agreed-about rule of international commerce'.[47]

If the Russian approach has been defined by destructive resentment, China has sought to build alternative or at least parallel institutions and programmes. The BRI has been central to this, as has the Beijing-based Asian Infrastructure Investment Bank (AIIB). This was described as China's answer to the World Bank, and by 2023 it had 106 member countries, though with 26.6 per cent of the voting rights, China had an effective veto over key organisational decisions that require a 75 per cent super majority.[48] Nevertheless, it was initially presented as a multilateral institution, a global development bank with international standards for lending and separate from the politically driven BRI. In reality it has become barely distinguishable from the BRI as an instrument of the CCP's global interests.[49] In June 2023, the AIIB's global communications director Bob Pickard, a Canadian national, abruptly resigned, claiming that the bank 'is dominated by Communist Party members and also has one of the most toxic cultures imaginable'.[50] The AIIB called the allegations 'baseless and disappointing'. Pickard quickly left China, citing concerns about his personal safety.

The rebooting of the BRI was accompanied by a flurry of other 'initiatives' – the Global Security Initiative, the Global Civilisation Initiative and the Global Development Initiative. These remain vague, possibly deliberately so, little more than slogans, more wrappers into which a variety of Beijing-led schemes can be placed. Their primary purpose is to amplify Beijing's voice, particularly in the 'Global South'.[51] China has also sought to turn the BRICS (Brazil, Russia, India, China and South Africa) forum into a geopolitical counterweight to the West, though with limited success because of tensions within the group.[52] China has promoted its currency, the yuan (or renminbi) as an alternative to the dollar's dominance in the global financial system. This effort has been boosted by the war in Ukraine, with China's fast-growing trade with Moscow denominated in yuan, which replaced the dollar as the most traded currency in Russia.[53] However, as of 2022, the US dollar remained dominant, used in 88 per cent of foreign exchange trades, even though the US only accounted for 11 per cent of global trade.[54] To make the yuan a more serious contender would require Beijing removing capital controls to make its currency fully convertible and being more transparent with economic data, which is unlikely to happen.

One of the key aims of Western policy during the reform era has been to bind China into the rules-based system, to make it a 'responsible stakeholder', as it is often termed. Flowing from this was an assumption that Beijing would not become a Russia-style disrupter because to do so would badly damage itself by destabilising a global system in which it has such a large stake. Those assumptions no longer hold as the CCP's calculations and priorities under Xi Jinping have changed. Xi has repudiated Deng Xiaoping's famous mantra that China should 'bide its time'; in his view, China's time has come, and security and control are his overriding priorities.

CHAPTER 22

The Vampire State

'The biggest problem with China's economy is
that the growth is unstable, unbalanced,
uncoordinated and unsustainable.'

Former Chinese Premier Wen Jiabao

In early 2024, a Hong Kong court attempted to put the Chinese property giant Evergrande out of its misery. 'Enough is enough,' announced Justice Linda Chan, as she ordered the liquidation of the world's most indebted developer. The company had failed to reach agreement with foreign bondholders, who were owed around $20 billion of the company's $300 billion of outstanding debt.[1] We have met Evergrande on a number of occasions in this book – from its first default in 2021 to the disappearance of its once-billionaire owner into China's dark prison system. During that time it became a poster child for the country's bursting property bubble – and for the troubled economy more generally. The crisis spread rapidly across the property sector and beyond, engulfing deeply indebted banks and local governments, whose loans and incomes were tied to property. At the time of writing companies responsible for as much as half of China's home sales have defaulted, and as many as 130 million homes sit empty or uncompleted. In January 2024, sales of new property continued to plummet, a third down on the previous January to reach a five-year low in spite of deep price cuts and other desperate attempts to revive the market, according to the China Real Estate Information Corp.[2]

The liquidation of Evergrande was long overdue, but Justice Chan's order will be largely ignored because most of the company's assets are in mainland China and the CCP will not allow them to be seized. Instead, it will continue trying to muddle through, shifting around assets and debt, wary of the rising tide of anger among homeowners who are seeing the value of their most important asset shrink, and aspiring owners who have made down payments on homes that have yet to be completed. Foreign bondholders will be the lowest priority. By early 2024, the Party was pressuring more healthy lenders (those that remain) to bail out the defaulters to the extent that they can at least finish the homes they have started. Among these was the insurance giant Ping An, which was reportedly asked to support dozens of developers, including embattled Country Garden, the country's biggest developer.[3] We have previously met Ping An in Hong Kong when it was pursuing the break-up of HSBC, in which it was the largest shareholder – and where the nominally private company was widely seen as a stalking horse on behalf of the CCP. The Party also launched its biggest consolidation of the banking system by merging hundreds of troubled rural lenders, who are heavily exposed to property – a sector with assets of $6.7 trillion, more than a third of the Chinese economy.[4] In May 2024, the CCP launched its most ambitious effort yet to rescue the property market – $42 billion of state bank funding for state-owned enterprises to buy up empty apartments. The plan gave a boost to the beleaguered stock markets in Shanghai and Hong Kong, which had ended 2023 as the world's worst performers. However, analysts pointed out that the bailout was a fraction of the estimated $533 billion developers needed to complete housing they had pre-sold to buyers and then failed to compete.[5] Developers had by then also defaulted on at least $124.5 billion of dollar debt.[6]

Much of the bailout was to be administered through local governments, themselves swimming in debt from earlier property follies. Their revenue from land sales continued to plummet, and they were forced to cut back on other spending. In early 2024, local authorities were ordered to delay or halt some state-funded infrastructure projects, including motorway, airports and urban rail projects – the sort of projects that, along with property, had been the motor of China's economic growth.[7] In Guangdong province, home of the Canton Fair, where we began this book, there were mounting reports of layoffs, pay cuts and forced unpaid leave among the small- and medium-sized private manufacturers that have been the bedrock of the local economy. As the February Chinese New Year holiday approached, heralding the Year of the Dragon, the

Guangdong Society of Reform, a Guangzhou-based think tank, warned that many small- and medium-sized enterprises may not be able to survive the winter.[8]

The monthly flow of investment capital out of China reached its highest level in almost eight years, fuelled by foreign companies scaling back operations and wealthy Chinese shifting their assets abroad. The net outflow reached $53.9 billion in September 2023, according to China's State Administration of Foreign Exchange.[9] By the time the figures were totted up at the end of the year, net foreign direct investment in 2023 had plummeted to a 23-year low. There were also signs of China's domestic property crisis spreading overseas as Chinese investors and their creditors began to sell their holdings across the globe to raise cash to pay debts, and for their troubled operations at home. These included office buildings in London, Toronto, Melbourne and Sydney, sold at prices well below those originally paid.[10] There was little surprise among foreign investors when Moody's, the US credit rating agency, slapped a down-grade warning on China's credit rating, though China's National Development and Reform Commission, an economic planning body, accused the agency of 'bias and misunderstanding of China's economic outlook'.[11] Before its announcement, Moody's advised staff in China to work from home, while those in Hong Kong were told to avoid travel to the mainland over fears of retaliation.[12] As we have seen, foreign firms, particularly those providing information about the Chinese economy have faced raids, arrests and exit bans.

The dragon in Chinese mythology is usually associated with good fortune and wisdom. Both are worryingly absent in Xi Jinping's China, and many of those returning home for the lengthy New Year holiday in February 2024 will have felt that the days of breakneck economic expansion are not only over, but are going sharply into reverse. The irony is that so many of the problems now confronting the Chinese economy were well signposted, as were the measures needed to confront them – not least in China itself. This is why comparing the collapse of Evergrande to that of Lehman Brothers at the start of the global financial crisis in 2008 needs some caution. The Lehman collapse was a shock, as was the US government's deci-sion to let it go under (though arguably it should not have been) – a black swan moment, as it has been described. Evergrande is less

China's Lehman moment and more a slow-motion train crash. As long ago as 2020, Guo Shuqing, chairman of the China Banking and Insurance Regulatory Commission, described the property market as a 'grey rhino' – a very obvious but ignored threat.[13] That said, a train wreck, slow motion or not, is still highly damaging – to the Chinese and potentially the global economy – as is the CCP's inability to clear the tracks.

The death of a former leader can be a tricky time for the Chinese Communist Party since mourning has frequently been used as a cover for criticism, even protest. When former Premier Li Keqiang died aged sixty-eight in October 2023 after a massive heart attack, police kept a watchful eye on those who laid flowers at his ancestral home, while online tributes were deleted and universities banned students from organising tributes.[14] Li, an English-speaking economist, was premier for ten years and stepped down just before his death. He was widely regarded as an economic reformer, and when he was first appointed there was much talk of how 'Likonomics', advocating a larger role for the market, might reboot an economic model that Li had described before his appointment as an 'irrational economic structure', warning that 'uncoordinated and unsustainable development is increasingly apparent'. He was in many ways a tragic figure – supposedly the second-ranking official in China's political hierarchy, overseeing economic policy, but quickly stripped of any real influence as Xi Jinping concentrated power around himself.

Yet Li's view of the economy is widely shared by economists both inside and outside China. His predecessor, Wen Jiabao, gave a similar warning, saying, 'the biggest problem with China's economy is that the growth is unstable, unbalanced, uncoordinated and unsustainable'.[15] As we have seen, this model is heavily reliant on exports and on massive and wasteful state-led investment in property and infrastructure, which has sent debt soaring amid diminishing returns. When economists talk about 'rebalancing', they generally mean raising sharply the level of private consumption in GDP, which at 39 per cent is extremely low by world standards (the figure in the US is 68 per cent). Chinese economists also fret about the 'middle income trap', an economic theory in which a country rises to a point where it exhausts its growth potential in export-driven low-skill manufacturing and will only escape if it can foster innovation and higher-value industries. It is generally agreed that Chinese consumers need to spend more and the economy needs to be more innovative, but there is a world of difference between identifying the problem and finding practical solutions – especially in Xi Jinping's China.

Property accounts for some 80 per cent of household wealth, and the meltdown in the market (and in the stock market) hardly provide the best backdrop to persuade demoralised consumers to go out and spend. Xi Jinping has identified renewable energy as a new driver for the economy, but while it is growing rapidly, the sector remains too small to replace property any time soon – and the formula of top-down industrial policy with heavy state investment and direction, leading to enormous overcapacity is drearily familiar. Giving a greater role to the market and to private companies, by far the most innovative part of the Chinese economy, would mean a reduced role for the Party and therefore runs counter to everything Xi Jinping has done since coming to power.

When Li Keqiang died, *The Economist* noted the number of nominally apolitical families who made the journey to lay flowers at his ancestral home and who praised a man who 'did practical things for the people'.[16] They appeared to be grieving for a bygone era, the newspaper characterising Li as a reform-era technocrat, who 'served a one-party system that sought legitimacy through governing performance'. This notion of 'performance legitimacy' is frequently cited to explain the CCP's remarkable ability to survive and retain support by delivering growth in the absence of other mechanisms for earning legitimacy, such as elections. This needs to be treated with some caution. There have been some woeful and brutal CCP performances, ranging from the Cultural Revolution and Great Leap Forward to the Tiananmen Square massacre and the economic fallout from the dogmatic zero-Covid policy – and the Chinese people have been given no other choice. GDP growth has certainly been a guiding obsession, a performance metric, of the reform era by which officials at all levels were judged, promoted and rewarded. This mobilisation of state resources, incentives and institutions with a focus on the economy has led others to brand China a 'development state'.[17] However, as we have seen, alongside the heady levels of growth, it produced environmental degradation, wasteful investment, enormous inequalities, corruption and the debasement of statistics – Li himself highlighting the latter as a provincial official. Still, a system focused on achieving a GDP target is healthier than one engulfed in Maoist campaigns, chasing quotas of 'counter-revolutionaries', 'rightists' or others deemed to be opponents of the Party.

The CCP's principal goal is its own survival. This is what motivated Deng Xiaoping to begin the process of reform and opening in the first place, and the vicissitudes of that process are best understood in this light. To the extent that Chinese leaders were pragmatic, it was in their ability to manipulate the levers and tools at their disposal to achieve the growth upon which the Party's legitimacy depended – while correcting their course at any hint of a threat to their monopoly on power. Xi has prioritised security and control – even at the expense of the economy. When he stood up at the tenth anniversary gathering of the Belt and Road Initiative and once again promoted the superiority of the China model, it will not have been lost on many of those present that while he talked the language of economic development, the metrics that now mattered in China were national security and loyalty to the leader. The country's economy and society are being geared increasingly towards that goal, marking a decisive turn away from Deng and back towards Mao.

Xi has described his new model as an 'integrated national strategic system'. In broad terms, this involves integrating the country's military, security and civilian sectors, particularly in the fields of innovation and technology. The aim is to better service the domestic security apparatus (and its formidable surveillance state) while also channelling know-how to the People's Liberation Army. Much of what I have described in this book can be understood as part of that process. Xi has sought to ensure that technologies developed, copied or stolen by the civil sector, be they companies or academics, can be more readily accessed by the security apparatus. 'To strengthen our military, we must promote deeper civil-military integration,' he has written,[18] insisting that the country's innovation infrastructure must be dual use, and the implementation of this model accelerated.[19]

Xi has vowed to make the Chinese military a 'great wall of steel', and to that end he boosted defence spending in 2023 by 7.2 per cent to reach roughly $220 billion, according to official figures. However, Beijing provides few details and the figure is widely regarded as a gross underestimate, with actual spending up to twice this level.[20] This is still less than half of what the US spends, but the gap is narrowing, and China's defence budget has risen fivefold over the two decades to 2023.[21] The People's Liberation Army's navy is already bigger than that of the US, and the PLA is spending heavily to upgrade and expand its nuclear arsenal and to apply artificial intelligence to weapons systems. 'We must accelerate the modernisation of national defence and the armed forces,' Xi has implored.[22] China already spends large amounts of money on defence-focused research and development in universities and state-owned enterprises, and while the Party has the power to direct the private sector to hand over technology and innovations, it is working to formalise this task and to see that their priorities are more closely aligned. As we have seen repeatedly in this book, under Xi the distinction between private and state companies, always a fine one, has become increasingly blurred.

The growing importance of cutting-edge technology in war has made this an urgent task. Nominally private companies and apparently independent research institutes and academics are routinely used as fronts by the CCP to harvest Western technology with military applications. The Party has also allocated substantial funding for specific projects of civil–military integration, the funding going to companies and institutions to help in developing core weapons, such as missiles, but also in weaponising the cyber, finance, space and maritime sectors.[23] The Center for New American Security, a US think tank, estimates that $68.5 billion was allocated to thirty-five such projects between 2015 and 2019.[24]

Xi has furthermore prioritised security throughout society and the economy. Laws mandating all Chinese citizens and companies to cooperate with the intelligence and security forces on demand should be seen in this context. As should a more recent and broadly drawn counter-espionage law, whose introduction was accompanied by calls from the Ministry of State Security for citizens to join counter-espionage work, and to report suspicious activity.[25]

An October 2023 revision to the Law on Guarding State Secrets banned state employees with access to 'classified information' from travelling abroad and extended its reach across the education and tech sectors.[26] In one surreal moment, a stand-up comedian was suspended indefinitely and fined after poking fun at the PLA during a live comedy show in Beijing.[27]

'Western countries led by the United States have implemented all-around containment, encirclement and suppression of China, which has brought unprecedented severe challenges to our country's development,' Xi told a meeting of the country's rubber-stamp parliament in March 2023. Xi's paranoia and warmongering rhetoric has intensified as China's economic problems have mounted and he has looked for scapegoats for the Party's mismanagement. By definition, the all-knowing Party must be beyond reproach, and the more Xi has centralised power around himself, the more it has become necessary to manufacture outrage and find others to blame. When the country's parliament reconvened in March 2024, Premier Li Qiang set an economic growth target of 'around 5 per cent', but there was little detail about how this was to be achieved other than vague commitments to 'high quality growth'.[28] Tellingly, Li used the term 'security' a record twenty-nine times in the annual government work report,[29] and the Party scrapped a tradition whereby the premier gives a televised press conference at the end of the congress.

Xi's increasingly explicit goal of orientating the economy and innovation towards the needs of his security apparatus explains to a large extent Western efforts to limit access to advanced technologies and know-how with military applications and to reduce dependencies. To deny cutting-edge tools to an increasingly autocratic and hostile adversary is common sense, though in many cases – particularly in Europe – de-risking is still a work in progress. Washington has blacklisted 600 Chinese companies, research institutes and other organisations deemed to be national security risks.[30] The US also imposed restrictions on the export to China of cutting-edge chips and the tools needed to make them – again focusing on those that could be used to strengthen the military, especially in artificial intelligence.[31] In August 2023, President Biden also signed an executive order restricting US investment in Chinese semiconductors, quantum information technologies and artificial intelligence.[32] With one eye on the worsening economic situation in China, Biden also said that China was a 'ticking time bomb in many cases', and warned that, 'They have got some problems. That's not good, because when bad folks have problems, they do bad things.'[33]

The 'bad thing' Biden had foremost in his mind was a possible Chinese invasion of Taiwan, which would have a devastating impact on the global economy. Taiwan is a lynchpin in the global hi-tech economy, and Bloomberg Economics has estimated that a war over Taiwan would cost the world economy around $10 trillion, equal to about 10 per cent of global GDP, dwarfing the impact of the war in Ukraine, the Covid pandemic and the 2008 global financial crisis.[34] During the early months of the Ukraine war, there was an assumption among Western strategists that the tough Western sanctions on Russia and the initially unified and reinvigorated Western alliance might give China pause for thought over Taiwan – that it had made the island safer in the short term. However, the war also gave the PLA, which has much in common with the Russian military, an invaluable opportunity to learn about their own battlefield vulnerabilities at somebody else's expense. Beijing also ordered a comprehensive 'stress test' to study the ability of the Chinese economy to withstand Russian-style sanctions. Banks and regulators were told to come up with a plan to make the economy more resilient.[35] Beijing also sharply reduced its exposure to US government debt, with its stock of US Treasury bonds falling to $862.3 billion at the end of 2023, a reduction of $170 billion over the year – reaching its lowest level since 2010.[36] China's gold purchases also soared, up by almost a third in 2023, on demand from the central bank and individual investors – an expression of the economic anxieties of both.[37] While inspecting an industrial park in Inner Mongolia, Xi said the domestic market needed to be more resilient in order to 'ensure normal operation of the national economy under extreme circumstances'.[38] After a security meeting in Beijing, Xi said, 'We must be prepared for worst-case and extreme scenarios and be ready to withstand the major test of high winds, choppy waters and even dangerous storms.'[39] In other words, Xi is engaged in his own heavy bout of de-risking, while deriding and seeking to undercut Western efforts to reduce their own exposure to China.

*

China's growth has also relied on a benign international environment; far from seeking to contain China, as Beijing frequently asserts, Western companies and countries facilitated its rise, and showed remarkable forbearance (together with a good dose of naïvety and greed) in the process. That is no longer the case. China's bid to capture the global market in renewable energy technologies is providing an early test case of this, as Beijing seeks to export its heavily subsidised overcapacity to the rest of the world. This was made explicit in early 2024, when the Ministry of Commerce urged banks and other government organisations to step up their support of electric vehicle makers in building overseas supply chains, including financing logistics, shipping and warehousing centres.[40] BYD, now vying with Tesla as the world's top electric-car seller, revealed plans to build assembly plants in Mexico and Hungary as a way of sidestepping trade restrictions from the US and EU.[41] We have already examined the enormous economic, technological and security risks this entails to the West. It is all the more important because Beijing sees renewables as a potential saviour of its state-directed economic model, while for the West, embracing Chinese EVs might be the quickest way to decarbonise their economies, but at the cost of alarming new dependencies.

Western policy during the first four decades of 'reform and opening' was driven by a belief that a wealthier China, more integrated in the world economy would make everybody richer and encourage reform and liberalisation in China itself. It was also argued that mutual economic dependence would lessen the risks of conflict. Raw commercial self-interest, the mythical allure of the China market, was another driver, though this was frequently dressed up in the language of higher moral principle. As this book has demonstrated, these no longer ring true – if ever they did.

China under Xi Jinping cannot be regarded as a trustworthy partner, but how solid is his position? In summer 2023, Xi targeted the military, purging top officials in the army and defence industries. This included commanders of the elite PLA Rocket Force, which oversees land-based nuclear missiles. Defence Minister Li Shangfu also vanished, and was announced sacked without explanation two months later.[42] There were rumours of corruption, though under

Xi this is a broad catch-all for all manner of perceived disloyalty. Xi's hand-picked foreign minister, Qin Gang, also vanished without explanation that summer after just six months on the job. Rumours abounded, from espionage to an extramarital affair with a television presenter. The CCP is so opaque that it is impossible to know whether these purges are evidence of more deep-seated opposition to Xi – or illustrative of his power. What can be said with more certainty is that by abandoning term-limits to his rule and doing away with more collective leadership – both introduced by Deng to avoid Mao-style despotism – Xi has heightened the risks of a messy and possibly violent transition.

The idea that the CCP is a bastion of stability is also challenged by the regularity of protest in China. Protests are usually tightly focused on local grievances, but have grown as the economy has come under pressure and the property market and investments more generally have gone bad. The Hong Kong-based China Labour Bulletin reported that protests over unpaid wages soared ahead of the February 2024 New Year holidays, doubling over the previous year.[43] The CCP's real fear is that localised economic protests take on a more political complexion, as happened in November 2022 when anti-lockdown protesters took to the streets across China, some condemning Xi and holding aloft blank A4 sheets of paper to highlight their lack of freedom of speech.

Soaring levels of youth unemployment, particularly among graduates, is another threat. Industries that traditionally provided sought-after jobs, such as technology and private education, have retrenched after CCP crackdowns, while the bursting property bubble closed down another source of graduate work. As we saw in the case of Li Jun and Liang Liang's pursuit of their dream home, disillusionment is widespread. Some young people are dropping out altogether – a phenomena known as *tang ping* ('lying flat') or *bai lan* ('let it rot').[44] This generation was supposed to be China's trailblazers – the most educated in the country's history, the foot soldiers building Xi Jinping's 'China Dream' of a strong and prosperous country. In the decades following the student-led Tiananmen Square protests of 1989, young people were encouraged to put their energy into money-making, to grab the seemingly boundless economic opportunities of rapid growth in exchange for political acquiescence – a pact that is effectively dead.

In the longer term, China's economy faces a problem of too few young people rather than too many. The population is shrinking for the first time since 1961, a year of famine, with the birth rate reaching the lowest level on record.[45] An estimated 400 million people in China – almost a third of the population – will be aged sixty and over by 2035, according to the government's own projections.[46] Much of this is a legacy of the country's disastrous one-child policy, now scrapped, which also left the balance of the sexes skewed heavily towards men. In addition, most other countries facing a rapidly aging population, such as Japan and in Western Europe, are richer and arguably more able to manage the transition. China's demographic time bomb will put severe strain on the country's overwhelmed hospitals and underfunded pension system. While China has poured money into physical infrastructure, it has neglected this social infrastructure – which only increases insecurities and limits the emergence of a stronger consumer economy. Other countries have turned to migrants to tackle demographic challenges, but China is deeply hostile to immigration, a mindset that is underpinned by a deep-seated belief in racial purity. China has the smallest foreign-born population of any major country in the world – 0.1 per cent, compared with 14 per cent in the US and 18 per cent in Germany.[47] Even Japan and South Korea, both of which have been historically cautious towards immigration are far higher, with migrant populations of 2 per cent and 3 per cent respectively.[48]

There have been many predictions of China's economic collapse, yet the Party has proved to be remarkably resilient. But by early 2024, it was confronting its biggest challenges since the 'reform and opening' era began; facing at best a period of economic stagnation, with none of the political pressure valves available to a liberal democracy. Foreign investment in China in 2023 reached its lowest level in thirty years. A 1980s song 'Tomorrow will be better', which captured the optimistic mood of that time, was reportedly back in vogue – but now as an expression of nostalgia and sadness.[49]

The paradox of Xi's China is that although rebooting the economy is crucial to his (and China's) future, and that is widely

recognised, it is now secondary to his efforts to build a security
state and to centralise power around himself. In pursuit of those
goals he has hobbled or alienated those who contributed most to
China's four decades of heady growth, and who hold the key to the
innovation economy he so desires – the private companies, tech
entrepreneurs, foreign investors and of course those traders of the
Death Star canteen, where we began this book. Rather in the manner of the football ambitions we examined, he clings to the hope
that an economy built around what he calls 'new productive forces'
can be created by diktat – and vast expenditure by a state already
straining under unsustainable levels of debt. In addition, the world
is now more wary of being flooded with cheap and heavily subsidised high-tech exports – and of Xi's belligerence more generally.
China's four and a half decades of rapid, often double-digit economic expansion are now over. As far as 'reform and opening' was
ever a coherent policy, that too has ended. The Chinese economy in
early 2024 was in a precarious state, and much of the damage was
self-inflicted. The implications for Beijing are far-reaching, since
a booming economy was central not only to the CCP's legitimacy
at home, but also in spreading its influence globally, in financing
its military modernisation, and in its wider ambitions to overtake
the US as the world's largest economy and become global leader in
technologies of the future. Now all are in doubt.

The CCP put considerable energy into studying the collapse of
the Soviet Union, which it blames in part on a lack of ideological
rigour – the Soviet Communist Party wasn't brutal enough against
its opponents. That, and a planned economy so centrally controlled,
inefficient, corrupt and wasteful that in the end it was beyond
reform. China's shifting blend of market and state, political autocracy and private enterprise, was designed in part to remedy that.
However, as this book has described, this created its own massive
and unsustainable distortions. It too now looks unreformable in
the sense that the Party under Xi is incapable of implementing the
necessary changes for the simple reason that this might threaten its
grip on power. The Party appears to be frozen in the headlights. It
has long boasted of its record in delivering prosperity and stability
for the Chinese people, but by early 2024, Xi Jinping had become
the biggest impediment to both.

Notes

Chapter 1:
The Death Star Canteen

1   For a full description of the facilities offered by the Canton Fair, see the website of the China Import and Export Fair, accessible at https://www.cantonfair.org.cn/en-US

2   '13 million Guangdong Migrants Could Gain Permanent Residence by 2020', Chinarealtime Blog in *The Wall Street Journal*, 10 July 2015. https://www.wsj.com/articles/BL-CJB-27266

3   'China's Shenzhen sees 20.7% annual GDP growth over 4 decades: Mayor', *Xinhua* (via the State Council Information Office), 25 September 2020. http://english.scio.gov.cn/pressroom/2020-09/25/content_76739898.htm

4   Xu Lingui, 'Xinhua Insight: China embraces new "principal contradiction" when embarking on new journey', *Xinhua*, 20 October 2017. http://www.xinhuanet.com/english/2017-10/20/c_136694592.htm

5   Ben Westcott, 'Xi promises miracles, but fails to deliver specifics', CNN, 18 December 2018. https://edition.cnn.com/2018/12/18/asia/xi-jinping-china-speech-reform-intl/index.html

6   Arthur R. Kroeber, *China's Economy: What Everyone Needs to Know* (New York: Oxford University Press, 2020), pp. 2–3.

7   Ibid.

8   Virginia Harrison and Daniele Palumbo, 'China anniversary: How the country became the world's "economic miracle"', BBC Online, 1 October 2019. https://www.bbc.co.uk/news/business-49806247

9   'Four decades of poverty reduction in China: Drivers, insights for the world and the way ahead', the World Bank and Development Research Center of the State Council of the People's Republic of China, 1 April 2022. https://openknowledge.worldbank.org/server/api/core/bitstreams/e9a5bc3c-718d-57d8-9558-ce325407f737/content

10 For a reflection of this often contentious debate, see 'The World's Biggest Economy. America or China?', World Economics, 6 January 2024. https://www.worldeconomics.com/Thoughts/The-Worlds-Biggest-Economy.aspx#:~:text=In%202022%2C%20the%20IMF%20judged,favour%20of%20China%20at%2016%25.

11 Amy Hawkins, 'China "world's biggest debt collector" as poorer nations

struggle with loans', *The Guardian*, 6 November 2023. https://www.the
guardian.com/world/2023/nov/06/china-worlds-biggest-debt-collector-as-
poorer-nations-struggle-with-its-loans

12 Alex Dichter, Guang Chen, Steve Saxon, Jackey Yu and Peimin Suo, 'Chinese
tourists: Dispelling the myths. An in-depth look at China's outbound tourist market', McKinsey & Company, September 2018. https://www.mckinsey.
com/~/media/mckinsey/industries/travel%20logistics%20and%20infra
structure/our%20insights/huanying%20to%20the%20new%20chinese%20
traveler/chinese-tourists-dispelling-the-myths.pdf

13 'Brief report on Chinese overseas students and international students in
China 2017', Ministry of Education, The People's Republic of China, 1 April
2018. http://en.moe.gov.cn/documents/reports/201901/t20190115_367019.
html

14 Martin Jacques, *When China Rules the World* (London: Penguin, 2012).

15 Antony Sguazzin and Chris Anstey, 'Xi Jinping Is Finding His China Model a
Tough Sell', Bloomberg, 7 October 2023. https://www.bloomberg.com/news/
newsletters/2023-10-07/bloomberg-new-economy-xi-jinping-is-finding-his-
china-model-a-tough-sell

16 Mia Nulimaimaiti, 'China's key private sector needs "continuity, stability" to
support economic recovery, but doubts remain', *South China Morning Post*,
15 February 2023. https://www.scmp.com/print/economy/china-economy/
article/3210306/chinas-key-private-sector-needs-continuity-stability-sup
port-economic-recovery-doubts-remain

17 Ana Swanson, 'How China used more cement in 3 years than the U.S. did in
the entire 20th Century', *The Washington Post*, 24 March 2015. https://www.
washingtonpost.com/news/wonk/wp/2015/03/24/how-china-used-more-
cement-in-3-years-than-the-u-s-did-in-the-entire-20th-century/

18 For example, see Tom Holland, 'Wen and now: China's economy is still
"unsustainable"', *South China Morning Post*, 10 April 2017. https://www.
scmp.com/week-asia/opinion/article/2085815/wen-and-now-chinas-
economy-still-unsustainable

19 To get a fuller sense of the role of contradiction in Mao Zedong's thought,
see his *On Practice and Contradiction*, with an introduction by Slavoj Žižek
(London and New York: Verso, 2017).

20 Chi Jingyi and Wang Cong, 'Largest-ever Canton Fair opens as global traders express confidence in China', *Global Times*, 14 April 2023. https://www.
globaltimes.cn/page/202304/1289169.shtml#:~:text=The%20133rd%20
China%20Import%20and%20Export%20Fair%2C%20commonly%20
known%20as,of%20the%20COVID%2D19%20pandemic.

21 Yusuke Ninata, 'China office vacancies worse than Zero-Covid levels in
top cities', *Nikkei Asia*, 5 October 2023. https://asia.nikkei.com/Business/
Markets/Property/China-office-vacancies-worse-than-zero-COVID-levels-
in-top-cities

22 'China's Communist Party is splurging on new local drop-in centres',
The Economist, 10 September 2020. https://www.economist.com/china/
2020/09/10/chinas-communist-party-is-splurging-on-new-local-drop-in-
centres

23 Reuters, 'China Evergrande moves from Shenzhen HQ building to cut costs', 10 January 2022. https://www.reuters.com/business/china-ever grande-moves-headquarters-shenzhen-guangzhou-report-2022-01-10/

24 Ruchir Sharma, 'China's rise is reversing', *Financial Times*, 19 November 2023. https://www.ft.com/content/c10bd71b-e418-48d7-ad89-74c5783c51a2

Chapter 2:
The Myth of 'Reform and Opening'

1   Adam Taylor, 'How a 10-gallon hat helped heal relations between China and America', *The Washington Post*, 25 September 2015. https://www.washington post.com/news/worldviews/wp/2015/09/25/how-a-10-gallon-hat-helped-heal-relations-between-china-and-america/

2   Ibid.

3   James Laurenceson, 'World politics explainer: Deng Xiaoping's rise to power', *The Conversation*, 8 October 2018. https://theconversation.com/world-politics-explainer-deng-xiaopings-rise-to-power-103032

4   'Deng Xiaoping, Man of the Year', *Time*, 6 January 1986. https://content.time.com/time/covers/0,16641,19860106,00.html

5   Chris Buckley, 'Portrait of Deng as Reformer in 1978 Plenum Ignores History', *The New York Times*, 9 November 2013. https://archive.nytimes.com/sinosphere.blogs.nytimes.com/2013/11/09/portrait-of-deng-as-reformer-in-1978-plenum-ignores-history/

6   Ibid.

7   Evelyn Iritani, 'Great Idea but Don't Quote Him', *Los Angeles Times*, 9 September 2004. https://www.latimes.com/archives/la-xpm-2004-sep-09-fi-deng9-story.html

8   Alexander V. Pantsov with Steven Levine, *Deng Xiaoping: A Revolutionary Life* (Oxford: Oxford University Press, 2015), pp. 222–3.

9   David Holley, Rone Tempest and Jim Mann, 'Deng Never Lost Sight of Goal to Reform Chinese Economy', *Los Angeles Times*, 20 February 1997. https://www.latimes.com/archives/la-xpm-1997-02-20-mn-30650-story.html

10 Pantsov, *Deng Xiaoping: A Revolutionary Life*, pp. 144–5.

11 Ibid., pp. 184–5.

12 Ibid., pp. 217–18.

13 Yasheng Huang, *The Rise and Fall of the East: How exams, autocracy, stability, and technology brought China success, and why they might lead to its decline* (New Haven and London: Yale University Press, 2023), p. 125.

14 Ian Johnson, *Sparks: China's Underground Historians and Their Battle for the Future* (London: Allen Lane, 2023), pp. 206–10.

15 Covell F. Meyskens, *Mao's Third Front: The Militarization of Cold War China* (Cambridge: Cambridge University Press, 2020), p. 26.

16 Zhao Ziyang, *Prisoner of the State: The Secret Journal of Chinese Premier Zhao Ziyang* (London, New York, Sydney and Toronto: Simon & Schuster, 2009), p. 247.

17 Ibid., p. 251.

18 Ibid., p. 252.

19 Frank Dikötter, 'China's Economic Miracle That Wasn't', *The Wall Street Journal*, 22 November 2022. https://www.wsj.com/articles/chinas-econo mic-miracle-that-wasnt-11668708575

20 Frank Dikötter, *China After Mao: The Rise of a Superpower* (London: Bloomsbury Publishing, 2022), p. xvi.

21 A full text of President Clinton's 9 March 2000 speech to the Paul H. Nitze School of Advanced International Studies of the Johns Hopkins University, as recorded by the Federal News Service, a transcription com- pany, is available at https://www.iatp.org/sites/default/files/Full_Text_of_ Clintons_Speech_on_China_Trade_Bi.htm

22 For a fuller analysis of the *fang-shou* cycle, see Sungmin Cho, 'The Fang- Shou Cycle in Chinese Politics', in Alexander L. Vuving (ed.),'Hindsight, Insight, Foresight: Thinking About Security in the Indo-Pacific', Daniel K. Inouye Asia-Pacific Center for Security Studies, 2020, pp. 269–82. http://www.jstor.org/stable/resrep26667.23

23 Xi Jinping's full 18 December 2018 speech to the conference marking the fortieth anniversary of 'reform and opening', 'Valuable Experience from 40 Years of Reform and Opening Up', can be accessed at the website of the *China Daily*. http://subsites.chinadaily.com.cn/npc/2021-12/29/c_694741. htm

24 Lucy Hornby, 'Xi versus Deng, the family feud over China's reforms', *Financial Times*, 15 November 2018. https://www.ft.com/content/839ccb0c- e439-11e8-8e70-5e22a430c1ad

25 Katsuji Nakazawa, 'Xi Jinping's awkward relationship with Deng Xiaoping', *Nikkei Asia*, 1 November 2018. https://asia.nikkei.com/Editor-s-Picks/ China-up-close/Xi-Jinping-s-awkward-relationship-with-Deng-Xiaoping

26 Chun Hang Wong, 'China's Museums Rewrite History to Boost Xi', *The Wall Street Journal*, 20 August 2018. https://www.wsj.com/articles/sleight-at- the-museum-china-rewrites-history-to-boost-xi-1534766405

27 William Zheng, 'Xi Jinping's late father lauded by Communist Party ahead of 110th anniversary of birth', *South China Morning Post*, 13 October 2023. https://www.scmp.com/news/china/politics/article/3237867/xi-jinpings- later-father-lauded-communist-party-ahead-110th-anniversary-birth

28 Pantsov, *Deng Xiaoping: A Revolutionary Life*, p. 337.

29 Dikötter, *China After Mao*, p. 76.

Chapter 3:
The Counterfeit Culture

1 For more background on the Belper mills, Samuel Slater and the Belper North Mill Trust, see the Trust's website. https://www.belpernorthmill.org. uk

2 Daniella Loffreda, 'The chaotic life of Derbyshire's Mr Potato Head',

Derbyshire Live, 11 February 2022. https://www.derbytelegraph.co.uk/news/chaotic-life-derbyshires-mr-potato-6640303

3   For example, see Flynn Murphy, 'Toy Factory More Than Meets the Eye as "Face Transformers" Syndicate Smashed', *Caixin Global*, 24 July 2020. https://www.caixinglobal.com/2020-07-24/toy-factory-more-than-meets-the-eye-as-fake-transformers-syndicate-smashed-101584392.html

4   Kanishka Singh, 'China leads the world in counterfeit, pirated products – U.S. report', Reuters, 31 January 2023. https://www.reuters.com/business/china-leads-world-counterfeit-pirated-products-us-report-2023-01-31/

5   Martin Wolf, 'The fight to halt the theft of ideas is hopeless', *Financial Times*, 9 November 2019. https://www.ft.com/content/d592af00-0a29-11ea-b2d6-9bf4d1957a67

6   Melanie Lee, 'Fake Apple Store in China even fools staff', Reuters, 21 July 2011. https://www.reuters.com/article/us-china-apple-fake-idUSTRE76K1SU20110721

7   'Château Lafite often not what it seems', *Shanghai Daily* (via *China.org.cn*), 5 December 2011. http://www.china.org.cn/china/2011-12/05/content_24074520.htm

8   Paul Midler, *Poorly Made in China: An Insider's Account of the Tactics Behind China's Production Game* (Hoboken, New Jersey: Wiley, 2009), p. 232.

9   Rob Davies, 'Jaguar wins landmark case against Chinese copy of Evoque model', *The Guardian*, 22 March 2019. https://www.theguardian.com/business/2019/mar/22/jaguar-land-rover-wins-landmark-case-against-chinese-evoque-copycat

10   'Toy Factory More Than Meets the Eye as "Fake Transformers" Syndicate Smashed', *Caixin Global*, 24 July 2020. https://www.caixinglobal.com/2020-07-24/toy-factory-more-than-meets-the-eye-as-fake-transformers-syndicate-smashed-101584392.html

11   'Head of China's First Intellectual Property Court Expelled from Party', *Caixin Global*, 26 July 2023. https://www.caixinglobal.com/2023-07-26/head-of-chinas-first-intellectual-property-court-expelled-from-party-102084654.html

12   Office of the United States Trade Representative, Executive Office of the President, '2022 Review of Notorious Markets for Counterfeiting and Piracy', 31 January 2022, p. 42. https://ustr.gov/sites/default/files/2023-01/2022%20Notorious%20Markets%20List%20(final).pdf

13   Ibid., p.43.

14   See European Union Intellectual Property Office press release, 'Intellectual property infringement poses a major threat to EU SMEs', 31 January 2023. https://euipo.europa.eu/tunnel-web/secure/webdav/guest/document_library/observatory/documents/reports/Risks_of_Illicit_Trade_in_Counterfeits_to_SMEs/Risks_of_Illicit_Trade_in_Counterfeits_to_SMEs_PressR_en.pdf

15   Organisation for Economic Co-operation and Development (OECD) and European Union Intellectual Property Office, 'Global Trade in Fakes. A Worrying Threat', 22 June 2021. https://euipo.europa.eu/tunnel-web/secure/

webdav/guest/document_library/observatory/documents/reports/2021_
EUIPO_OECD_Report_Fakes/2021_EUIPO_OECD_Trate_Fakes_Study_
FullR_en.pdf

16   Josh Rogin, 'NSA Chief: Cybercrime constitutes the "greatest transfer of wealth in history"', *Foreign Policy*, 9 July 2012. https://foreignpolicy.com/2012/07/09/nsa-chief-cybercrime-constitutes-the-greatest-transfer-of-wealth-in-history/

17   The White House, 'National Cybersecurity Strategy', March 2023, p. 3. https://www.whitehouse.gov/wp-content/uploads/2023/03/National-Cybersecurity-Strategy-2023.pdf

18   William Evanina, 'Private Sector as the New Geopolitical Battlespace', National Counterintelligence and Security Centre, Office of the Director of National Intelligence, 6 November 2019. https://www.dni.gov/index.php/ncsc-newsroom/3402-private-sector-as-the-new-geopolitical-battlespace

19   See testimony by Michelle Van Cleave, former head of US counterintelligence, 'Chinese Intelligence Operations and Implications for U.S. National Security', before the US-China Economic and Security Review Commission, 9 June 2016, p. 5. https://www.uscc.gov/sites/default/files/Michelle%20Van%20Cleave_Written%20Testimony060916.pdf

20   HM Government, 'National Cyber Strategy 2022', 15 December 2022, p. 26. https://assets.publishing.service.gov.uk/government/uploads/system/uploads/attachment_data/file/1053023/national-cyber-strategy-amend.pdf

21   Juby Babu, 'Heads of MI5, FBI give joint warning of growing threat from China', Reuters, 7 July 2022. https://www.reuters.com/world/heads-mi5-fbi-give-joint-warning-growing-threat-china-2022-07-07/

22   Alyza Sebenius, 'China's Hackers Are Expanding Their Strategic Objectives', *Lawfare*, 5 December 2023. https://www.lawfaremedia.org/article/china-s-hackers-are-expanding-their-strategic-objectives

23   Mandiant, 'APT1: Exposing One of China's Cyber Espionage Units', February 2013. https://www.mandiant.com/sites/default/files/2021-09/mandiant-apt1-report.pdf

24   P. W. Singer and Allan Friedman, *Cybersecurity and Cyberwar: What everyone needs to know* (Oxford: Oxford University Press, 2014), p. 142.

25   Ellen Nakashima, 'Confidential report lists U.S. defense system designs compromised by Chinese cyberspies', *The Washington Post*, 27 May 2013. https://www.washingtonpost.com/world/national-security/confidential-report-lists-us-weapons-system-designs-compromised-by-chinese-cyber-spies/2013/05/27/a42c3e1c-c2dd-11e2-8c3b-0b5e9247e8ca_story.html

26   See Department of Justice press release, 'U.S. Charges Five Chinese Military Hackers for Cyber Espionage Against U.S. Corporations and a Labor Organization for Commercial Advantage', 19 May 2014. https://www.justice.gov/opa/pr/us-charges-five-chinese-military-hackers-cyber-espionage-against-us-corporations-and-labor

27   Adam Segal, 'How China is preparing for cyberwar', *The Christian Science Monitor*, 20 March 2017. https://www.csmonitor.com/World/Passcode/Passcode-Voices/2017/0320/How-China-is-preparing-for-cyberwar

28 Agence France-Presse (via France24), 'Airbus hit by series of cyber-attacks on suppliers', 26 September 2019. https://www.france24.com/en/20190926-airbus-hit-by-series-of-cyber-attacks-on-suppliers

29 Wang Wei, 'Report Reveals Team Viewer was Breached by Chinese Hackers in 2016', *The Hacker News*, 17 May 2019. https://thehackernews.com/2019/05/teamviewer-software-hacked.html

30 Jordon Robertson and Michael Riley, 'The Big Hack: How China Used a Tiny Chip to Infiltrate U.S. Companies', Bloomberg, 4 October 2018. https://www.bloomberg.com/news/features/2018-10-04/the-big-hack-how-china-used-a-tiny-chip-to-infiltrate-america-s-top-companies

31 Lucian Constantin, 'Report: China supported C919 airliner development through cyberespionage', CSO, 14 October 2019. https://www.csoonline.com/article/567857/china-supported-c919-airliner-development-through-cyberespionage.html

32 Jeff Ferry, 'How China Stole an Entire Plane', *Industry Week*, 16 December 2019. https://www.industryweek.com/the-economy/article/21118569/how-china-stole-an-entire-airplane

33 Office of the United States Trade Representative, Executive Office of the President, 'Findings of the investigation into China's acts, policies, and practices related to technology transfer, intellectual property, and innovation under section 301 of the trade act of 1974', 22 March 2018. https://ustr.gov/sites/default/files/Section%20301%20FINAL.PDF

34 See Robert S. Mueller's speech to the RSA Cyber Security Conference in San Francisco, 1 March 2012, available via the FBI archives. https://archives.fbi.gov/archives/news/speeches/combating-threats-in-the-cyber-world-outsmarting-terrorists-hackers-and-spies

35 Dikötter, *China After Mao*, p. 76.

36 Ibid., pp. 76–7.

37 Kenji Kawase, 'Made in China thrives with subsidies for tech and EV makers', *Financial Times*, 1 August 2022. https://www.ft.com/content/f7df0f64-25b5-4526-82fa-ca1b554b541b

38 Demetri Sevastopulo, 'Five Eyes spy chiefs warn Silicon Valley over spy threat', *Financial Times*, 18 October 2023. https://www.ft.com/content/0a37da0a-ad06-43d0-b069-bfafa0ff35a4?sharetype=blocked

39 Edward White and Christian Shepherd, 'China hits back at US-led accusations over cyber attacks', *Financial Times*, 20 July 2021. https://www.ft.com/content/fe589e37-2f85-428e-a0ef-cbb5a5211157

40 David Barboza, 'Coin of Realm in China Graft: Phony Receipts', *The New York Times*, 3 August 2013. https://www.nytimes.com/2013/08/04/business/global/coin-of-realm-in-china-graft-phony-receipts.html

Chapter 4:
Lies, Damned Lies and Communist Party Statistics

1 Antoni Slodkowski, 'Chinese Premier Li calls for global cooperation, says China open for business', Reuters, 16 January 2016. https://

www.reuters.com/world/asia-pacific/chinas-premier-li-address-davos-its-economy-struggles-2024-01-16/

2   Stella Yifan Xie and Jason Douglas, 'China Has a New Youth Jobless Rate. Some Economists Are Ignoring It', *The Wall Street Journal*, 19 January 2024. https://www.wsj.com/world/china/china-has-a-new-youth-jobless-rate-some-economists-are-ignoring-it-dc2827e5

3   Bloomberg, 'Did China's economy really grow 5.2% in 2023? Not all agree', *Straits Times*, 19 January 2024. https://www.businesstimes.com.sg/international/did-chinas-economy-really-grow-52-2023-not-all-agree

4   Ryan McMorrow and Nian Liu, 'China deletes Covid-19 deaths data', *Financial Times*, 18 July 2023. https://www.ft.com/content/a634d844-5298-441b-b2e8-0eabe0b3c1d7?shareType=nongift

5   Ryan McMorrow, Nian Liu and Sun Yu, 'Relatives angry as Covid kept off Chinese death certificates: "What are you trying to hide"', *Financial Times*, 20 January 2023. https://www.ft.com/content/50117091-cdac-4f61-8338-bf20d964fe4c

6   Sylvie Zhuang, 'China drops cremation data from quarterly report, raising questions about key Covid death indicator', *South China Morning Post*, 15 June 2023. https://www.scmp.com/news/china/politics/article/3224233/china-drops-cremation-data-quarterly-report-raising-questions-about-key-covid-death-indicator

7   Simone McCarthy, 'China "under-representing" true impact of Covid outbreak WHO says', CNN, 6 January 2023. https://edition.cnn.com/2023/01/05/china/china-covid-outbreak-who-data-intl-hnk/index.html

8   Bruno Waterfield, 'China forces EU to tone down fake news dossier', *The Times*, 27 April 2020. https://www.thetimes.co.uk/article/china-forces-eu-to-tone-down-fake-news-dossier-zdh5fvkcf

9   Scott Kennedy and Qin (Maya) Mei, 'Measurement Muddle: Chinese GDP Growth Data and Potential Proxies', Big Data China, 16 September 2023. https://bigdatachina.csis.org/measurement-muddle-chinas-gdp-growth-data-and-potential-proxies/

10   Gabriel Wildau, 'China's statistics chief, Wang Baoan accused of corruption', *Financial Times*, 28 January 2016. https://www.ft.com/content/61cde66e-c425-11e5-993a-d18bf6826744

11   'How to measure China's true economic growth', *The Economist*, 9 March 2023. https://www.economist.com/finance-and-economics/2023/03/09/how-to-measure-chinas-true-economic-growth

12   Luis R. Martinez, 'How Much Should We Trust the Dictator's GDP Growth Estimates?', *Journal of Political Economy*, vol. 130, Issue 10, October 2022, pp. 2501–770. https://www.journals.uchicago.edu/doi/epdf/10.1086/720458

13   Stella Yifan Xie and Jason Douglas, 'China Abruptly Delays GDP Release During Communist Party Conference', *The Wall Street Journal*, 17 October 2022. https://www.wsj.com/articles/china-abruptly-delays-gdp-release-during-communist-party-conference-11666000383

14   Michelle Chan, 'Investors Watch Alternative Data After China Delays GDP Release', *The Wall Street Journal*, 18 October 2022. https://www.

wsj.com/livecoverage/stock-market-news-today-2022-10-18/card/analysts-count-on-alternative-data-as-china-delays-gdp-release-LV6Z jVQveGkJrCloZ9sW

15 See 'Information note for users of OECD R&D statistics: Anomalies in R&D data reported by China requiring comprehensive explanation and potential correction', OECD, 24 May 2023. https://sciencebusiness.net/sites/default/files/inline-files/Information%20note%20on%20R%26D%20data%20on%20China_May%202023%20%281%29.pdf

16 Grady McGregor and Katrina Northrop, 'The Consultant Crackdown', *The Wire China*, 21 May 2023. https://www.thewirechina.com/2023/05/21/the-consultant-crackdown-capvision/

17 Ryan McMorrow and Demetri Sevastopulo, 'China raids multiple offices of international consultancy Capvision', *Financial Times*, 8 May 2023. https://www.ft.com/content/fc364119-979d-4090-83bf-2e6a24d5b175

18 Michael Martina and Yew Lun Tian, 'China detains staff, raids office of US due diligence firm Mintz Group', Reuters, 24 March 2023. https://www.reuters.com/world/us-due-diligence-firm-mintz-groups-beijing-office-raided-five-staff-detained-2023-03-24/

19 Daisuke Wakabayashi and Keith Bradsher, 'U.S. Consulting Firm Is the Latest Target of a Chinese Crackdown', *The New York Times*, 27 April 2023. https://www.nytimes.com/2023/04/27/business/bain-china.html

20 Lingling Wei, 'China Puts Spymaster in Charge of U.S. Corporate Crackdown', *The Wall Street Journal*, 18 May 2023. https://www.wsj.com/articles/china-crackdown-foreign-companies-chen-yixin-9b403893

21 John Burn-Murdoch, 'China's GDP blackout isn't fooling anyone', *Financial Times*, 21 October 2022. https://www.ft.com/content/43bea201-ff6c-4d94-8506-e58ff787802c

22 Ibid.

23 Lingling Wei, Yoko Kubota and Dan Strumpf, 'China Locks Information on the Country Inside a Black Box', *The Wall Street Journal*, 30 April 2023. https://www.wsj.com/world/china/china-locks-information-on-the-country-inside-a-black-box-9c039928

24 Lingling Wei, Eva Xiao and Trefor Moss, 'China Closes U.S. Auditor as Tensions Mount over Forced Labor Allegations', *The Wall Street Journal*, 19 August 2021. https://www.wsj.com/articles/china-closes-u-s-auditor-as-tensions-mount-over-forced-labor-allegations-11629390253#

25 Pak Yiu, 'China slashing foreign subscriber access to key research database', *Nikkei Asia*, 23 March 2023. https://asia.nikkei.com/Politics/International-relations/China-slashing-foreign-subscriber-access-to-key-research-database

26 Helen Davidson, 'Foreign journalists in China subject to rising intimidation, survey finds', *The Guardian*, 31 January 2022. https://www.theguardian.com/world/2022/jan/31/foreign-journalists-china-intimidation-survey

27 Ibid.

28 'China's stockmarket. A crazy casino', *The Economist*, 25 May 2015. https://www.economist.com/node/21652098/print

29   Michael Pettis, 'Fundamentals simply do not matter in China's stock markets', *Financial Times*, 13 January 2020. https://www.ft.com/content/2362a9a0-3479-11ea-a6d3-9a26f8c3cba4

30   Patti Waldmeir, 'Beware the risk of giving staff in China the chop', *Financial Times*, 26 May 2015. https://www.ft.com/content/d2fd52d0-0386-11e5-b55e-00144feabdc0

31   Bloomberg, 'China Security Ministry to Probe "Malicious" short selling', 9 July 2015. https://www.bloomberg.com/news/articles/2015-07-09/china-security-agency-to-investigate-malicious-short-selling

32   Samuel Wade, 'Minitrue: Rules on stock market reporting', *China Digital Times*, 9 July 2015. https://chinadigitaltimes.net/2015/07/minitrue-rules-on-stock-market-reporting/

33   Tom Phillips, 'Chinese reporter makes on-air "confession" after market chaos', *The Guardian*, 31 August 2015. https://www.theguardian.com/world/2015/aug/31/chinese-financial-journalist-wang-xiaolu-makes-alleged-on-air-confesssion-after-market-chaos

34   Wu Yiyao, 'Capital market crackdown nets 4 CITIC officials', *China Daily*, 1 September 2015. http://www.chinadaily.com.cn/business/2015-09/01/content_21764443.htm

35   Rebecca Feng, 'Big Shareholder in China? Don't Try Selling', *The Wall Street Journal*, 23 September 2023. https://www.wsj.com/finance/stocks/china-gets-tough-on-insider-selling-to-arrest-market-slump-adc4528b

36   Hudson Lockett and Cheng Leng, 'How Xi Jinping is taking control of China's stock market', *Financial Times*, 22 September 2023. https://www.ft.com/content/f9c864c1-6cd4-405e-aa4b-d0b5e2ec6535

37   Bloomberg, 'China-Backed Funds Have Bought $57 Billion of Stocks, UBS says', *Caixin*, 28 February 2024. https://www.caixinglobal.com/2024-02-28/chinas-state-backed-funds-have-bought-57-billion-of-stocks-ubs-says-102169608.html

38   Edward White and Hudson Lockett, 'China censors financial blogger as economic recovery falters', *Financial Times*, 27 June 2023. https://www.ft.com/content/c3e64c12-cccb-4559-b046-1ea81fbf709a

39   Bloomberg, 'China Regulator's New Slogan Fuels Buying Spree in State Firms', 24 November 2022. https://www.bloomberg.com/news/articles/2022-11-24/china-regulator-s-new-buzzword-fuels-buying-spree-in-state-firms

40   Chris Prentice and Michelle Price, 'China audits littered with deficiencies, US accounting watchdog finds', Reuters, 10 May 2023. https://www.reuters.com/markets/us-watchdog-says-it-found-unacceptable-problems-with-chinese-company-audits-2023-05-10/

41   Zhang Yuzhe, Wang Juanjuan and Zhang Yukun, 'In Depth: Why China's Bond Traders Got Cut Off From the Data They Needed', *Caixin Global*, 21 March 2023. https://www.caixinglobal.com/2023-03-21/in-depth-why-chinas-bond-traders-got-cut-off-from-the-data-they-needed-102010523.html

42   Ibid.

43   'The yuan and the markets', *The Economist*, 16 January 2016. https://www.economist.com/leaders/2016/01/16/the-yuan-and-the-markets

44 Michael Schuman, 'No need to idolise China's accident-prone technocrats', *Financial Times*, 20 August 2015. https://www.ft.com/content/87d 1c710-44d5-11e5-af2f-4d6e0e5eda22

45 Saheli Roy Choudhury, 'Elon Musk says China has an advantage because its politicians are better at science', CNBC, 7 September 2018. https://www.cnbc.com/2018/09/07/elon-musk-china-advantage-is-that-its-politicians-are-better-at-science.html

46 Xie Wenting, Liu Caiyu and Shan Jie, 'China solemnly declares complete victory in eradicating absolute poverty', *Global Times*, 25 February 2021. https://www.globaltimes.cn/page/202102/1216520.shtml

47 Li Yuan, 'Why China's Censors are Deleting Videos About Poverty', *The New York Times*, 4 May 2023. https://www.nytimes.com/2023/05/04/busi ness/china-censorship-poverty.html?smid=nytcore-ios-share&referring-Source=articleShare

48 Shang Fuxuan, 'China is still a developing country', *China Daily*, 5 June 2023. https://mobile.chinadaily.com.cn/cn/html5/2023-06/05/content_015_647cfebaed50d203d2c95c03.htm

49 Karen Hao, 'China's Xi Stacks Government With Science and Technology Experts Amid Rivalry With the U.S.', *The Wall Street Journal*, 18 November 2022. https://www.wsj.com/articles/chinas-xi-stacks-government-with-sci ence-and-tech-experts-amid-rivalry-with-u-s-11668772682

50 Vivian Wang, 'China's Economic Outlook: Pep Talks Up Top, Gloom On the Ground', *The New York Times*, 29 August 2023. https://www.nytimes. com/2023/08/29/world/asia/china-economic-gloom.html

51 Ibid.

52 Katsuji Nakazawa, 'Analysis: China's spy agency now watches for doomsayers', *Nikkei Asia*, 21 December 2023. https://asia.nikkei.com/Editor-s-Picks/China-up-close/Analysis-China-s-spy-agency-now-watches-for-doomsayers#:~:text=The%20recent%20post%20hinting%20at,if%20they%20say%20too%20much

Chapter 5:
Ghostly Monuments to Economic Madness

1 Manya Koetse and Miranda Barnes, 'The Story of Li Jun & Liang Liang: How the Challenges of an Ordinary Chinese Couple Captivated China's Internet', What's on Weibo, 28 November 2023. https://www.whatsonweibo.com/the-story-of-li-jun-liang-liang-how-the-challenges-of-an-ordinary-chinese-couple-captivated-chinas-internet/

2 Ibid.

3 Fan Wang, 'Couple's property ordeal captivates Chinese internet', BBC Online, 4 December 2023. https://www.bbc.co.uk/news/world-asia-china-67563 596

4 Ibid.

5 Manya Koetse and Miranda Barnes, What's on Weibo, 28 November 2023

6   Clare Jim and Xie Yu, 'Country Garden on brink as payment deadline nears', Reuters, 17 October 2023. https://www.reuters.com/business/country-gardens-entire-offshore-debt-be-default-if-tuesday-payment-not-made-2023-10-16/

7   Viola Zhou, 'China Blows Up 15 High-Rises Because Constructors Ran Out of Money to Finish Them', *Vice News*, 15 September 2021. https://www.vice.com/en/article/epn3bp/china-demolition-building-kunming

8   Tom Norton, 'Fact Check: Does Viral Video Show China Destroying Unfinished High-Rises?', *Newsweek*, 22 February 2022. https://www.newsweek.com/fact-check-does-viral-video-show-china-destroying-unfinished-high-rises-1783119

9   Laura He, 'Evergrande has been ordered to demolish 39 buildings in Chinese resort', *CNN Business*, 4 January 2022. https://edition.cnn.com/2022/01/04/investing/evergrande-stock-gain-resume-trading-intl-hnk/index.html

10   Yoko Kubota and Liyan Qi, 'Empty Buildings in China's Provincial Cities Testify to Evergrande Debacle', *The Wall Street Journal*, 4 October 2021. https://www.wsj.com/articles/evergrande-china-real-estate-debt-debacle-empty-buildings-cities-beijing-11633374710

11   Pearl Liu and Yaling Jiang, 'Fifty million empty flats threaten to plunge China's troubled property market further into crisis, warns think tank', *South China Morning Post*, 14 August 2022. https://www.scmp.com/business/china-business/article/3188781/fifty-million-empty-flats-threaten-plunge-chinas-troubled

12   See figures from Statista, 'Average real estate sale price in China between 1998 and 2021', October 2022. https://www.statista.com/statistics/242851/average-real-estate-sale-price-in-china/

13   Reuters, 'China's banking regulator says property market is biggest "grey rhino"', 30 November 2020. https://www.reuters.com/article/us-china-banking-idUSKBN28A1SY

14   Reuters, 'Factbox: China's indebted property market and the Evergrande crisis', 22 October 2021. https://www.reuters.com/world/china/chinas-indebted-property-market-evergrande-crisis-2021-10-22/

15   Ibid.

16   Nick Marsh, 'Forest City: Inside Malaysia's Chinese-built "ghost city"', BBC Online, 5 December 2023. https://www.bbc.co.uk/news/business-67610677

17   Iori Kawate, 'China's largest "ghost city" booms again thanks to education fever', *Nikkei Asia*, 19 April 2021. https://asia.nikkei.com/Spotlight/Society/China-s-largest-ghost-city-booms-again-thanks-to-education-fever

18   Bloomberg, 'Houses Should Be for Living In, Not for Speculation, Xi Says', 18 October 2017. https://www.bloomberg.com/news/articles/2017-10-18/xi-renews-call-housing-should-be-for-living-in-not-speculation?in_source=embedded-checkout-banner#xj4y7vzkg

19   Lingling Wei, 'In Tackling China's Real-Estate Bubble, Xi Jinping Faces Resistance to Property-Tax Plan', *The Wall Street Journal*, 19 October 2021. https://www.wsj.com/articles/in-tackling-chinas-real-estate-bubble-xi-jinping-faces-resistance-to-property-tax-plan-11634650751

20 'China tightens regulations for loans to real estate sector', *Xinhua*, 31 December 2020. http://www.xinhuanet.com/english/2020-12/31/c_139633200.htm

21 Alexandra Stevenson and Cao Li, 'Evergrande Gave Workers a Choice: Lend Us Cash or Lose Your Bonus', *The New York Times*, 19 September 2021. https://www.nytimes.com/2021/09/19/business/china-evergrande-debt-protests.html

22 'Evergrande: China Property Giant Misses Debt Deadline', BBC Online, 9 December 2021. https://www.bbc.co.uk/news/business-58579833

23 Martin Farrer and Vincent Ni, 'Mortgage strikes threaten China's economic and political stability', *The Guardian*, 19 July 2022. https://www.theguardian.com/world/2022/jul/19/mortgage-strikes-threaten-chinas-economic-and-political-stability

24 Yulu Ao, 'China property crisis: wealthy eastern city of Changzhou is latest to lift home resale restrictions to boost market', *South China Morning Post*, 8 March 2023. https://www.scmp.com/business/china-business/article/3212722/china-property-crisis-wealthy-eastern-city-changzhou-latest-lift-home-resale-restrictions-boost

25 *Xinhua* news agency, 'China's property market heading for solid recovery, healthy development', *China Daily*, 18 March 2023. http://www.chinadaily.com.cn/a/202303/18/WS6415640fa31057c47ebb53bb_1.html

26 Ding Feng and Han Wei, 'China Extends Loan Support for Ailing Developers', *Caixin Global*, 18 August 2023. https://www.caixinglobal.com/2023-08-18/china-extends-loan-support-for-ailing-developers-102094257.html

27 Cheng Siwei and Denise Jia, 'China Extends Tax Incentives by Two Years to Bolster Housing Market', *Caixin Global*, 26 August 2023. https://www.caixinglobal.com/2023-08-26/china-extends-tax-incentives-by-two-years-to-bolster-housing-market-102096959.html

28 Noriyuki Doi, 'Buy one, get one free: China's real estate slump deepens', *Nikkei Asia*, 3 August 2023. https://asia.nikkei.com/Business/Markets/Property/Buy-one-floor-get-one-free-China-s-real-estate-slump-deepens

29 Huileng Tan, 'China's real-estate market is in such a slump that cities are offering discounts for group purchases and tasking civil servants with selling apartments', *Business Insider*, 19 August 2022. https://www.businessinsider.com/china-real-estate-sales-group-buying-civil-servants-family-friends-2022-8?op=1&r=US&IR=T

30 Iori Kawate, 'China targets high earners in public sector with group condo discounts', *Nikkei Asia*, 12 October 2022. https://asia.nikkei.com/Business/Markets/Property/China-targets-high-earners-in-public-sector-with-group-condo-discounts

31 Noriyuki Doi, 'China's growth model under strain, but stimulus faces high hurdles', *Nikkei Asia*, 17 August 2023. https://asia.nikkei.com/Economy/China-s-growth-model-under-strain-but-stimulus-faces-high-hurdles

32 Bloomberg, 'China's bursting housing bubble is doing more damage than official data suggest', *Fortune Magazine*, 17 August 2023. https://fortune.com/2023/08/17/china-home-sales-worse-than-official-data-real-estate-crisis/

33   Lingling Wei, 'Xi Jinping Is Looking for Somebody to Blame for China's Property Bust', *The Wall Street Journal*, 26 October 2023. https://www.wsj.com/world/china/xi-jinping-is-looking-for-someone-to-blame-for-chinas-property-bust-fca6726f

34   Clare Jim, 'Country Garden: How bad is China's property crisis?', Reuters, 17 August 2023. https://www.reuters.com/markets/asia/country-garden-how-bad-is-chinas-property-crisis-2023-08-17/?n=@

35   Thomas Hale and Sujeet Indap, 'Chinese developer Evergrande files for US bankruptcy protection', *Financial Times*, 18 August 2023. https://www.ft.com/content/0ca833a8-df28-4e28-b313-611c5bb2e500?shareType=nongift

36   Ambrose Evans-Pritchard, 'China's property crash is becoming more dangerous by the day', *The Telegraph*, 17 August 2023. https://www.telegraph.co.uk/business/2023/08/17/china-property-crash-becomes-more-dangerous/

37   Thomas Hale, Wang Xueqiao, Qian Liu and Chan Hi-him, 'Yang Huiyan, the Country Garden scion trying to stave off collapse', *Financial Times*, 19 August 2023. https://www.ft.com/content/3a602c06-5ba7-49ab-a3eb-986da3fe9b29?shareType=nongift

38   Kohei Fujimura, 'China's Dalian Wanda unloads businesses to skirt bankruptcy', *Nikkei Asia*, 13 December 2023. https://asia.nikkei.com/Business/Markets/China-debt-crunch/China-s-Dalian-Wanda-unloads-businesses-to-skirt-bankruptcy

39   Cheng Leng, Hudson Lockett and Edward White, 'Chinese bank fraud protest turns violent after police step in', *Financial Times*, 11 July 2022. https://www.ft.com/content/b813d7dd-2c42-4b96-9377-ae4b09d3950a

40   Phoebe Zhang, 'White-shirted group attacks protesters at China banking scandal demonstration', *South China Morning Post*, 11 July 2022. https://www.scmp.com/news/china/politics/article/3184788/white-shirted-group-attacks-protesters-china-banking-scandal

41   Summer Zhen and Laura Mathews, 'China shadow bank crisis sparks calls for policy response', Reuters, 18 August 2023. https://www.reuters.com/business/finance/china-trust-deficit-crisis-spurs-shadow-banking-policy-response-calls-2023-08-15/

42   Bloomberg, 'China Shadow Bank Crisis Sparks Protest by Angry Investors', 16 August 2023. https://www.bloomberg.com/news/articles/2023-08-16/china-shadow-bank-crisis-sparks-protest-by-angry-investors

43   Ibid.

44   Hudson Lockett and Sun Yu, 'Chinese shadow bank Zhongzhi faces $36bn shortfall after management ran wild', *Financial Times*, 23 November 2023. https://www.ft.com/content/4f46e278-971e-49f0-ab05-47b3a57997ec?shareType=nongift

45   Bloomberg, 'China Begins Nationwide Push to Reveal Hidden Government Debt', 21 June 2023. https://www.bloomberg.com/news/articles/2023-06-21/china-begins-nationwide-push-to-reveal-hidden-government-debt

46   Sun Yu, 'China's local governments boost revenue by selling land to their own entities', *Financial Times*, 9 March 2023. https://www.ft.com/content/f68a301a-cdd5-4d9b-aca2-492c6561ebbf

47 Michael Pettis, 'Painful as it is, China must rid its economy of ever rising property market', *South China Morning Post*, 12 January 2023. https://www.scmp.com/comment/opinion/article/3206254/painful-it-china-must-rid-its-economy-ever-rising-property-market

48 'CPC leadership holds meeting to analyze economic situation, make arrangements for work in the second half of the year', *Xinhua*, 25 July 2023. https://english.news.cn/20230725/80b63f5a077c448d80d870c84908c53d/c.html

49 Alexander Saeedy, 'Evergrande Scraps $35 Billion Restructuring Plan as China's Housing Crisis Intensifies', *The Wall Street Journal*, 22 September 2023. https://www.wsj.com/articles/evergrande-scraps-35-billion-restructuring-plan-as-chinas-housing-crisis-intensifies-5c2db979

50 Cao Li, 'Property Developers Cut Prices – and Homeowners Are Resisting', *The Wall Street Journal*, 1 November 2023. https://www.wsj.com/world/china/chinas-property-developers-cut-pricesand-homeowners-are-resisting-22e528c1

51 Kevin Slaten and Ming-tse Hung, 'China's property crisis is stirring protests across the country', *Nikkei Asia*, 20 November 2023. https://asia.nikkei.com/Opinion/China-s-property-crisis-is-stirring-protests-across-the-country

52 Keith Zhai, 'China Makes Preparations for Evergrande's Demise', *The Wall Street Journal*, 23 September 2023. https://www.wsj.com/articles/china-makes-preparations-for-evergrandes-demise-11632391852?mod=hp_lead_pos1

53 Fredrik Oeqvist, 'Evergrande inflated revenue and profits for years, GMT Newsletter 1, December 2023. https://www.gmtresearch.com/en/research/newsletter-evergrande-never-profitable

54 Reuters, 'Exclusive: China tells banks to roll over local government debts as risks mount – sources', 17 October 2023. https://www.reuters.com/world/china/china-instructs-banks-roll-over-local-government-debt-sources-2023-10-17/#:~:text=Local%20government%20debt%20reached%2092,up%20from%2062.2%25%20in%202019.

55 The Economist, 'Chinese authorities are now addicted to traffic fines', 25 April 2024. https://www.economist.com/finance-and-economics/2024/04/25/chinese-authorities-are-now-addicted-to-traffic-fines

56 Reuters, 'China banks step up sales of bad loans as consumer defaults rise', 18 December 2023. https://www.reuters.com/world/china/china-banks-step-up-sales-bad-loans-consumer-defaults-rise-2023-12-18/#:~:text=Chinese%20authorities%20have%20blacklisted%208.57,the%20pandemic%20and%20its%20aftermath.

57 Editorial Board, 'China's accelerating rise in consumer defaults', *Financial Times*, 4 December 2023. https://www.ft.com/content/0ba1546d-8b94-484b-8cdd-f6e38da5bb64

58 Venus Feng, 'Evergrande Bondholders Eye Founders Megayacht, Planes, Mansions', Bloomberg, 4 November 2021. https://www.bloomberg.com/news/articles/2021-11-04/evergrande-bondholders-eye-founder-s-megayacht-planes-mansions

Chapter 6:
To Get Rich is Glorious – and Dangerous

1   Mercedes Ruehl, Tabby Kinder and Leo Lewis, 'Missing Chinese banker was working to set up Singapore family office', *Financial Times*, 22 February 2022. https://www.ft.com/content/d5f8a388-dcd8-4650-858a-b9f74a057d 40?shareType=nongift

2   Keith Zhai and Jing Yang, 'Behind Fan Bao's Detention – a Suspected Quid Pro Quo', *The Wall Street Journal*, 2 March 2023. https://www.wsj.com/ articles/missing-chinese-banker-fan-bao-detained-as-part-of-corruption-probe-f01c7a24

3   See the 17 February 2023 CNBC interview with James McGregor of APCO Worldwide, 'Bao Fan may be the best known person in the Chinese financial community, says APCO's James McGregor'. https://www.cnbc.com/ video/2023/02/17/bao-fan-may-be-the-best-know-person-in-the-chinese-financial-community-says-apcos-james-mcgregor.html

4   Desmond Shum, *Red Roulette: An Insider's Story of Wealth, Power, Corruption and Vengeance in Today's China* (London: Simon & Schuster, 2021), p. 107.

5   David Barboza, 'Billions in Hidden Riches for Family of Chinese Leader', *The New York Times*, 25 October 2012. https://www.nytimes.com/2012/10/26/busi ness/global/family-of-wen-jiabao-holds-a-hidden-fortune-in-china.html

6   Shum, *Red Roulette*, p. 112.

7   Russell Flannery, 'The 10 Richest Chinese Billionaires 2023', *Forbes*, 4 April 2023. https://www.forbes.com/sites/russellflannery/2023/04/04/the-10-rich est-chinese-billionaires-2023/

8   For a fuller description of the system of black jails, see '"Special Measures". Detention and Torture in the Chinese Communist Party's Shuanggui System', Human Rights Watch, 6 December 2016. https://www.hrw. org/report/2016/12/06/special-measures/detention-and-torture-chinese-communist-partys-shuanggui-system See also 'The disappearance of Bao Fan, China's Liuzhi system, and the UN connection', Safeguard Defenders, 6 March 2023. https://safeguarddefenders.com/en/blog/dis appearance-bao-fan-china-s-liuzhi-system-and-un-connection

9   Wang Xiangwei, 'TV parades of corrupt officials snared in Xi Jinping's anti-graft campaign raise more questions than answers', *South China Morning Post*, 22 January 2022. https://www.scmp.com/week-asia/opinion/ article/3164226/tv-parades-corrupt-officials-snared-xi-jinpings-anti-graft

10   Tania Branigan, 'Politburo, army, casinos: China's corruption crackdown spreads', *The Guardian*, 14 February 2014. https://www.theguardian.com/ world/2015/feb/14/china-corruption-crackdown-spreads-xi-jinping

11   Safeguard Defenders, 6 March 2023.

12   Peter Hoskins, 'Bao Fan: Why do Chinese billionaires keep vanishing?', BBC Online, 8 March 2023. https://www.bbc.co.uk/news/business-64781986

13   Reuters, 'Chinese business tycoons , executives who disappeared from public view', 21 February 2021. https://www.reuters.com/world/china/ chinese-business-tycoons-executives-who-disappeared-public-view-2023-02-21/

14 Qianer Liu and Ryan McMorrow, 'China tech founder taken away by authorities', *Financial Times*, 7 November 2023. https://www.ft.com/content/63a0923b-a98e-4433-bc3a-9091dca3dcc5?shareType=nongift

15 'Zhao Bingxian, chairman of Wohua Pharmaceutical, was once called "China's Buffett"', *Teller Report*, 7 November 2023. https://www.tellerreport.com/business/2023-11-07-zhao-bingxian--chairman-of-wohua-pharmaceutical--was-once-called-%22china-s-buffett%22.HJxjPPjvXa.html

16 Bloomberg, 'China's Innovators are "lying flat," Primavera's Hu says', 8 November 2023. https://www.bnnbloomberg.ca/china-s-innovators-are-lying-flat-primavera-s-hu-says-1.1995506

17 *South China Morning Post*, 22 January 2022

18 Yanzhong Huang, 'Anti-Corruption Campaign in China's Medical Sector: Unmasking the Hidden Agenda', Council for Foreign Relations, 18 August 2023. https://www.cfr.org/blog/anti-corruption-campaign-chinas-medical-sector-unmasking-hidden-agenda

19 Yew Lun Tian, 'Defence minister's disappearance latest case of missing Chinese official', Reuters, 22 September 2023. https://www.reuters.com/world/asia-pacific/defence-ministers-disappearance-latest-case-missing-chinese-official-2023-09-22/

20 Edward White, '"Keep the blade clean": Xi Jinping's corruption investigators turn focus on themselves', *Financial Times*, 7 July 2023. https://www.ft.com/content/2bdcb7ff-facb-43f2-aa75-f0fba1ec0759?shareType=nongift

21 Wang Xiangwei, 'China's Xi rose to power on his anticorruption drive, but the fight's grown more political – and it's far from over', *South China Morning Post*, 17 September 2022. https://www.scmp.com/week-asia/opinion/article/3192789/chinas-xi-rose-power-his-anti-corruption-drive-fights-grown-more

22 For the full corruption rankings, see Transparency International's 'Corruption Perception Index', 31 January 2023. The index is updated annually. https://www.transparency.org/en/cpi/2022

23 Yuen Yuen Ang, 'The Robber Barons of Beijing: Can China Survive its Gilded Age', *Foreign Affairs*, 22 June 2021. https://www.foreignaffairs.com/articles/asia/2021-06-22/robber-barons-beijing

24 Minxin Pei, *China's Crony Capitalism: The Dynamics of Regime Decay* (Cambridge, Massachusetts and London: Harvard University Press, 2016).

25 Ibid., p. 267.

26 Aruna Viswanatha, 'J.P. Morgan Settlement Lays Bare the Practice of Hiring "Princelings"', *The Wall Street Journal*, 17 November 2016. https://www.wsj.com/articles/j-p-morgan-to-pay-264-million-to-end-criminal-civil-foreign-corruption-cases-1479398628

27 Duncan Clark, *The House That Jack Ma Built* (New York: Harper Collins, 2018).

28 Joseph Nordqvist, 'Jack Ma appointed as David Cameron's business advisor', *Market Business News*, 19 October 2015. https://marketbusinessnews.com/jack-ma-appointed-as-david-camerons-business-advisor/108909/

29 Sam Peach, 'Why did Alibaba's Jack Ma disappear for three months?' BBC Online, 20 March 2021. https://www.bbc.co.uk/news/technology-56448688

30   Ibid.

31   Rob Davies and Helen Davidson, 'The strange case of Alibaba's Jack Ma and his three month vanishing act', *The Guardian*, 23 January 2021. https://www.theguardian.com/business/2021/jan/23/the-strange-case-of-alibabas-jack-ma-and-his-three-month-vanishing-act

32   Bloomberg, 'Jack Ma's Retreat Undercuts China's Pitch to Private Business', 27 March 2023. https://www.bloomberg.com/news/articles/2023-03-27/jack-ma-stays-abroad-as-china-seeks-trust-of-private-sector-businesses

33   Rebecca Feng and Dave Sebastian, 'China's Ant Group Slapped With Nearly $1 billion fine', *The Wall Street Journal*, 7 July 2023. https://www.wsj.com/articles/chinas-ant-group-slapped-with-nearly-1-billion-fine-c6ce791b

34   Reuters, 'Alibaba to split into six units', 28 March 2023. https://www.reuters.com/technology/alibaba-split-into-six-units-2023-03-28/

35   Chang Che and Jeremy Goldkorn, 'China's "Big Tech crackdown": a guide', The China Project, 2 August 2021. https://thechinaproject.com/2021/08/02/chinas-big-tech-crackdown-a-guide/

36   Sonja Opper, 'China is tightening its grip on outspoken CEOs. That's bad news for entrepreneurs', CNN Business, 8 November 2021. https://edition.cnn.com/2021/11/08/perspectives/china-tech-entrepreneurs-regulatory-crackdown/index.html

37   Yuan Gao, 'China Exerts Grip on Tech as Beijing Expands Technology Control', Bloomberg, 19 February 2024. https://www.bloomberg.com/news/articles/2024-02-19/china-vows-to-centralize-tech-development-under-communist-party

38   See the February 2021 briefing paper from the US National Counterintelligence and Security Centre, 'China's Collection of Genomic and Other Healthcare Data From America: Risks to Privacy and U.S. Economic and National Security'. https://www.dni.gov/files/NCSC/documents/SafeguardingOurFuture/NCSC_China_Genomics_Fact_Sheet_2021revision20210203.pdf

39   Ryan McMorrow and Joe Leahy, 'China's billionaires back Xi Jinping's plan to restore economy', *Financial Times*, 20 July 2023. https://www.ft.com/content/0b5b5560-e125-442c-9af9-6ff7716bb254

40   Zheping Huang, 'Chinese Billionaires Throw Weight Behind Private Sector Push', Bloomberg, 20 July 2023. https://www.bloomberg.com/news/articles/2023-07-20/tencent-billionaire-breaks-silence-to-back-china-private-sector

41   Edward White, 'Chinese companies revive Mao Zedong-era militias', *Financial Times*, 20 February 2024. https://www.ft.com/content/d6b2e4d6-2f84-4ef9-bf99-10d76d92d045?shareType=nongift

42   Frank R. Gunter, 'Why China Lost About $3.8 Trillion To Capital Flight In The Last Decade', *Forbes*, 22 February 2017. https://www.forbes.com/sites/insideasia/2017/02/22/china-capital-flight-migration/

43   Bloomberg, 'Shanghai Woman in Focus as Probe Shows Fear of Capital Exit', 14 August 2023. https://www.bloomberg.com/news/articles/2023-08-14/shanghai-woman-in-focus-as-probe-shows-fear-of-capital-flight

44   Marrian Zhou, Why so many middle-class Chinese migrants take risky, illegal route to U.S', Nikkei Asia, 22 May 2024. https://asia.nikkei.com/Spotlight/The-Big-Story/Why-so-many-middle-class-Chinese-migrants-take-risky-illegal-route-to-U.S

Chapter 7:
Escape to Singapore

1   Winnie Li, 'Sentosa Cove bungalow on sale for S$39 million, all 5 offers from non-local buyers', Mothership, 23 March 2023. https://mothership.sg/2023/03/sentosa-cove-bungalow-for-sale/

2   Reuters, 'Singapore home prices surpass Hong Kong as Asia-Pacific region's most expensive, survey shows', 30 May 2023. https://www.reuters.com/markets/asia/singapore-home-prices-surpass-hong-kong-apacs-most-expensive-survey-2023-05-30/

3   These figures are from research by Orange Tee, a real estate company. See 'Buyers from China snap up biggest share of S'pore's luxury condos among foreigners', 6 October 2022. https://www.orangetee.com/newsroom/news-roomcontent.aspx?nid=Tb1f7LAGl4M=

4   Paul Tostevin and Lucy Palk, 'Savills Prime Residential Index: World Cities Rents and Yields', Savills research article, 19 July 2023. https://www.savills.com/research_articles/255800/349567-0

5   Jason Douglas, 'As China Reopens, Flight of Wealthy Chinese to Singapore Set to Accelerate', *The Wall Street Journal*, 27 February 2023. https://www.wsj.com/articles/as-china-reopens-flight-of-wealthy-chinese-to-singapore-set-to-accelerate-c0b12282

6   Mercedes Ruehl and Leo Lewis, 'The lure of Singapore: Chinese flock to "Asia's Switzerland"', *Financial Times*, 15 January 2023. https://www.ft.com/content/62845c24-1e45-483c-95d1-b2c5d4c07337

7   May Ong, 'This Singapore facility is the world's largest "vending machine" for supercars', AsiaOne Online, 11 May 2017. https://www.asiaone.com/singapore/singapore-facility-worlds-largest-vending-machine-supercars

8   Mercedes Ruehl and Leo Lewis, *Financial Times*, 15 January 2023.

9   'TRAPPED: China's expanded use of exit bans', Safeguard Defenders, April 2023. https://safeguarddefenders.com/sites/default/files/pdf/Trapped%20-%20China's%20Expanding%20Use%20of%20Exit%20Bans.pdf

10   Henley & Partners, 'Henley Private Wealth Migration Report 2023', 13 June 2023. https://www.henleyglobal.com/publications/henley-private-wealth-migration-report-2023

11   Bloomberg and Reuters, 'Singapore raises threshold for foreign investors seeking permanent residency', *The South China Morning Post*, 2 March 2023. https://www.scmp.com/news/asia/southeast-asia/article/3212064/singapore-raises-threshold-foreigner-investors-seeking-permanent-residency

12   For the latest rules on permanent residency and citizenship in Singapore, see the Singapore Economic Development Board's online guide, 'Permanent

Residency and Citizenship'. https://www.edb.gov.sg/en/how-we-help/residency-and-citizenship.html

13 Arika Kitado, 'Singapore knocks Japan off top spot in passport power rankings', *Nikkei Asia*, 19 July 2023. https://asia.nikkei.com/Business/Travel-Leisure/Singapore-knocks-Japan-off-top-spot-in-passport-power-ranking

14 For the full passport rankings, see 'The Henley Passport Index' on the Henley & Partners website. https://www.henleyglobal.com/passport-index/ranking

15 Mercedes Ruehl and Leo Lewis, 'Chinese companies set up in Singapore to hedge against geopolitical risk', *Financial Times*, 30 November 2022. https://www.ft.com/content/a0c11e3e-ab72-4b4b-a55c-557191e53938

16 Ibid.

17 James Davey, 'Shein buys Missguided brand from Britain's Frasers', Reuters, 30 October 2023. https://www.reuters.com/markets/deals/shein-buys-missguided-ip-mike-ashleys-frasers-2023-10-30/

18 Mercedes Ruehl, 'Sequoia China founder Neil Shen took Singapore residency', *Financial Times*, 28 February 2024. https://www.ft.com/content/070f0cf3-c4bd-4730-bbf0-d1abfee9e1a9

19 Ryan Mac and Chang Che, 'TikTok's C.E.O. Navigates the Limits of His Power', *The New York Times*, 16 September 2022. https://www.nytimes.com/2022/09/16/technology/tiktok-ceo-shou-zi-chew.html

20 Monica Miller and Joshua Cheetham, 'Li Shangfu: War with US would be unbearable disaster', BBC Online, 5 June 2023. https://www.bbc.co.uk/news/world-asia-china-65803311

21 'China's defence minister defends intercepting US destroyer in Taiwan Strait', CBS News, 4 June 2023. https://www.cbsnews.com/news/china-us-taiwan-strait-destroyer/

22 Minxin Pei, 'China Is Walking a Tightrope With the US. It Needs a Net', Bloomberg, 4 April 2023. https://www.bloomberg.com/opinion/articles/2023-04-04/china-needs-military-guardrails-even-more-than-the-us

23 Sebastian Strangio, *In the Dragon's Shadow: Southeast Asia in The China Century* (New Haven and London: Yale University Press, 2020), p. 188.

24 Reuters, 'Singapore wealth group denies report of directive to keep quiet on China-linked fund inflows', 14 April 2023. https://www.reuters.com/markets/asia/singapore-wealth-group-denies-report-directive-keep-quiet-china-linked-fund-2023-04-14/

25 Bloomberg and Reuters, 'Singapore raises threshold . . .', 2 March 2023.

26 Mercedes Ruehl, 'Singapore doubles property stamp duty for foreigners to 60%', 27 April 2023. https://www.ft.com/content/00a4c68b-ed4f-4154-b56b-e70705d17042?shareType=nongift

27 Tsubasa Suruga, 'Singapore plans to screen major investments in "critical entities"', *Nikkei Asia*, 6 November 2023. https://asia.nikkei.com/Politics/Singapore-plans-to-screen-major-investments-in-critical-entities

28 See Prime Minister Lee Hsien Loong's 21 August 2022 National Day Rally speech, accessible via the website of the prime minister's office. https://www.pmo.gov.sg/Newsroom/National-Day-Rally-2022-Chinese

29   'Singapore cracks down on Chinese influence', *The Economist*, 8 February
      2024.https://www.economist.com/asia/2024/02/08/singapore-cracks-down-
      on-chinese-influence
30   'Singapore money laundering case snowballs further to over S$2.4 bil-
      lion in assets seized or frozen', *Channel News Asia*, 21 September 2023.
      https://www.channelnewsasia.com/singapore/billion-dollar-money-
      laundering-case-24-billion-assets-police-3785731

Chapter 8:
China's Criminal Empire on the Mekong

1   'Chinese couple nabbed in Bangkok behind THB 10 billion hybrid scam:
      police', *The Nation*, 31 May 2023. https://www.nationthailand.com/thailand/
      general/40028145
2   'Police Bust 12 Online scammers in Chiang Rai City', *The Chiang Rai
      Times*, 5 June 2023. https://www.chiangraitimes.com/chiangrai-news/
      police-bust-12-online-scammers-in-chiang-rai-city/
3   Wassayos Ngamkham, 'Major Chinese Scam Gang Busted', *The Bangkok Post*,
      22 June 2023. https://www.bangkokpost.com/thailand/general/2597445/
      major-chinese-scam-gang-busted
4   Arnab Shome, 'Thailand's Police Arrest 24 People for Running FX Investment
      Scam', Finance Magnates, 20 May 2022. https://www.financemagnates.com/
      forex/thailands-police-arrest-24-person-for-running-fx-investment-scam/
5   Ngamkham, *The Bangkok Post*, 22 June 2023.
6   Thibault Serlet, 'Golden Triangle: The World's Worst Special Economic
      Zone', Investment Monitor, 28 March 2022. https://www.investmentmon
      itor.ai/comment/golden-triangle-special-economic-zone-laos-worst/
7   US Department of the Treasury press release, 'Treasury Sanctions the Zhao
      Wei Transnational Criminal Organization', 30 January 2018. https://home.
      treasury.gov/news/press-releases/sm0272
8   'Police in Laos seize meth pills in one of biggest busts', Associated
      Press, 24 September 2022. https://apnews.com/article/crime-myanmar-
      united-nations-laos-baeb83805c8e1e1ec7279208cc80a2b1
9   'Crime Gangs Control Some Myanmar. Laos Economic Zones: UN',
      Asiafinancial, 26 June 2022. https://www.asiafinancial.com/crime-gangs-
      control some-myanmar-laos-economic-zones-un
10   Brian Eyler, 'Science Shows Chinese Dams are Devastating the Mekong',
      Foreign Policy, 22 April 2020. https://thediplomat.com/2020/05/chinas-
      control-of-the-mekong/
11   See the 7 June 2023 Interpol press release, 'INTERPOL issues global
      warning on human-trafficking fueled fraud'. https://www.interpol.int/
      en/News-and-Events/News/2023/INTERPOL-issues-global-warning-on-
      human-trafficking-fueled-fraud
12   Peter Zsombor, 'UN warns of Growing Criminal Threat from Mekong
      Region Casinos, SEZs', VOA News, 25 September 2022. https://www.

voanews.com/a/un-warns-of-growing-criminal-threat-from-mekong-region-casinos-sezs/6762228.html

13   See the Economist Intelligence Unit's 15 July 2022 country profile, 'Laos debt situation set to worsen'. https://country.eiu.com/article.aspx?articleid=782277461

14   'South-East Asia is sprouting Chinese enclaves', *The Economist*, 30 January 2020. https://www.economist.com/asia/2020/01/30/south-east-asia-is-sprouting-chinese-enclaves

15   Alastair McCready, 'Laos debt at "critical level" with China payments still opaque', *Nikkei Asia*, 22 September 2023. https://asia.nikkei.com/Economy/Laos-debt-at-critical-level-with-China-payments-still-opaque

16   Ibid.

17   Elaine Kurtenbach, Sam McNeil and Joe McDonald, 'Laos-China railway to launch as debt to China mounts', Associated Press, 2 December 2021. https://apnews.com/article/business-china-environment-and-nature-asia-beijing-7a796ece5a6c4a4d6d1cabcddd042ed2

18   Kevin Doyle, '"Tip of the spear": Battling the Golden Triangle Drug Lords', Al Jazeera, 2 March 2023. https://www.aljazeera.com/news/2023/3/2/hld-tip-of-the-spear-taking-on-the-golden-triangles-druglords

19   Phontham Visapra, 'Laos Government Presents Medal to Chinese Casino Operator', *The Laotian Times*, 3 October 2022. https://laotiantimes.com/2022/10/03/laos-government-presents-medal-to-chinese-casino-operator/

20   For instance, see Yang Han and Zhang Li, 'China and Laos pledge to deepen trade, diplomatic ties', *China Daily*, 13 September 2021. https://www.chinadaily.com.cn/a/202109/13/WS613eb8c7a310efa1bd66f020.html

21   'Zhao Wei: Struggle in the Golden Triangle Special Economic Zone', China Talk, 4 May 2011. http://fangtan.china.com.cn/2011-05/04/content_22492727.htm

22   *The Economist*, 30 January 2020.

23   For an overview of the CCP's collaboration with organised criminal gangs, or Triads, see Martin Purbrick, 'Patriotic Chinese Triads and Secret Societies: From the Imperial Dynasties, to Nationalism, and Communism', *Asian Affairs*, vol. 50, Issue 3, 2019, pp. 305–22. https://www.tandfonline.com/doi/epdf/10.1080/03068374.2019.1636515?needAccess=true&role=button For a more recent example from Taiwan, see Edward White, 'Alarm in Taiwan over Triad ties to pro-China groups', *Financial Times*, 12 October 2017. https://www.ft.com/content/b09de5d0-aa76-11e7-93c5-648314d2c72c

24   Jack Brook, 'Threats force anti-trafficking NGO director out of Cambodia', *Nikkei Asia*, 24 June 2023. https://asia.nikkei.com/Spotlight/Society/Threats-force-anti-trafficking-NGO-director-out-of-Cambodia

25   'International Campaign to Ban Landmines', *Landmine Monitor 2022*, November 2022, pp. 13–16. http://the-monitor.org/media/3352351/2022_Landmine_Monitor_web.pdf

26   Gavin Butler, '"The Truth Will Be Loud": Thailand's Former Brothel Baron is using His Infamy to fight Crime', *Vice News*, 5 May 2023. https://www.vice.com/en/article/5d9gwq/thailand-whistleblower-anti-corruption-chuwit

27   Kosuke Inque, 'Thai government in hot water over idea to invite Chinese police', *Nikkei Asia*, 18 November 2023. https://asia.nikkei.com/Politics/International-relations/Thai-government-in-hot-water-over-idea-to-invite-Chinese-police2

28   Shaun Turton, 'Global law enforcement targets Southeast Asian cyberscam gangs', *Nikkei Asia*, 13 December 2023. https://asia.nikkei.com/Spotlight/Society/Crime/Global-law-enforcement-targets-Southeast-Asian-cyberscam-gangs

29   Qin Jianhang and Wang Xintong, 'Over 800 Chinese Involved in Cross-border Cybercrime repatriated from Myanmar', *Caixin Global*, 15 March 2024. https://www.caixinglobal.com/2024-03-15/over-800-chinese-involved-in-cross-border-cybercrime-repatriated-from-myanmar-102175831.html

30   Yang Zekun, 'Joint efforts boosted to end cross-border crime', *China Daily*, 24 August 2023. http://www.chinadaily.com.cn/a/202308/24/WS64e6ba3ea31035260b81df9d.html

31   Hwang Chun-mei, Gao Feng and Wang Yun, 'Chinese rights lawyer Lu Siwei repatriated by Laos last week', Radio Free Asia, 14 September 2023. https://www.rfa.org/english/news/china/laos-lawyer-09142023140433.html

32   Chono Lapuekou, 'Bokeo International Airport to Start Operations By End of 2023', *The Laotian Times*, 7 November 2023. https://laotiantimes.com/2023/11/07/bokeo-international-airport-to-start-operations-by-end-of-2023/

Chapter 9:
Smash the Sparrows!

1   Judith Shapiro, *Mao's War against Nature: Politics and the Environment in Revolutionary China*, Cambridge Studies in Environment and History (New York: Cambridge University Press, 2001), p. 87.

2   For a comprehensive overview of the Four Pests Campaign, see Kaushik Patowary, 'China's Misguided War Against Sparrows', Amusing Planet, 8 January 2019. https://www.amusingplanet.com/2019/01/chinas-misguided-war-against-sparrows.html

3   Sha Yexin, 'The Chinese sparrows of 1958', New Century Net, 31 August 1997. http://www.zonaeuropa.com/20061130_1.htm

4   For example, see Jack Chapple's YouTube video, 'How Australia is Crashing the World Economy and Taking Down China', 20 October 2021. https://www.youtube.com/watch?v=uGzCQZUrs2k

5   Peter Hoskins, 'China power cuts: What is causing the country's blackouts?', BBC Online, 30 September 2021. https://www.bbc.co.uk/news/business-58733193

6   Frank Chung, 'Senior diplomat labels Australians who criticise China "scumbags", embassy omits insult in English', news.com.au, 4 March 2021. https://www.news.com.au/technology/innovation/military/senior-diplomat-warns-australians-who-make-enemies-of-china-will-be-cast-aside-in-history/news-story/d2f7f25cc5723a2873cc929e889e9814

7   Daniel Hurst, 'How much is China's trade war really costing Australia?' *The Guardian*, 28 October 2020. https://www.theguardian.com/australia-news/2020/oct/28/how-much-is-chinas-trade-war-really-costing-australia

8   'GT Voice: Australia is in over its head with provocative action', *Global Times*, 22 April 2021. https://www.globaltimes.cn/page/202104/1221840.shtml

9   Bloomberg, 'China-Australia relations: dispute leaves 400 seafarers stranded with US$200 million of Australian coal held up', *South China Morning Post*, 13 November 2020. https://www.scmp.com/economy/china-economy/article/3109794/china-australia-relations-dispute-leaves-400-seafarers

10 Nic Fildes, 'Australia rides out Chinese sanctions as exports boom', *Financial Times*, 27 October 2022. https://www.ft.com/content/e4fb5cdc-da92-4ced-a56d-451f42336ba7

11 'China condemns opening of Taiwan office in Lithuania as "egregious act"', *The Guardian*, 19 November 2019. https://www.theguardian.com/world/2021/nov/19/china-condemns-opening-of-taiwan-office-in-lithuania-as-egregious-act

12 Hu Xijin, 'Lithuania will pay the price for making radical moves over the Taiwan question', *Global Times*, 10 August 2021. https://www.globaltimes.cn/page/202108/1231087.shtml

13 'China would rather be feared than defied', *The Economist*, 28 August 2021. https://www.economist.com/china/2021/08/26/china-would-rather-be-feared-than-defied

14 Kathrin Hille, Richard Milne and Demetri Sevastopulo, 'Lithuania pulls diplomats from China as row deepens over Taiwan ties', *Financial Times*, 15 December 2021. https://www.ft.com/content/587cff8f-3a7f-45c3-b4c7-8ac6f3e0aa9c?shareType=nongift

15 Andrew Higgins, 'Lithuania vs. China: A Baltic Minnow Defies a Rising Superpower', *The New York Times*, 2 October 2021. https://www.nytimes.com/2021/09/30/world/europe/lithuania-chinadisputes.   html?referringSource=articleShare

16 John O'Donnell and Andrius Sytas, 'Exclusive: Lithuania braces itself for China-led corporate boycott', Reuters, 9 December 2021. https://www.reuters.com/world/china/exclusive-lithuania-braces-china-led-corporate-boycott-2021-12-09/

17 Matthew Reynolds and Matthew P. Goodman, 'China's Economic Coercion: Lessons from Lithuania', Center for Strategic and International Studies, 6 May 2022. https://www.csis.org/analysis/chinas-economic-coercion-lessons-lithuania

18 Jessica Parker, 'Lithuania-China row: EU escalates trade dispute with Beijing', BBC Online, 27 January 2022. https://www.bbc.com/news/world-europe-60140561

19 Stuart Lau, 'Lithuania pulls out of China's "17+1" bloc in Eastern Europe', *Politico* 21 May 2021. https://www.politico.eu/article/lithuania-pulls-out-china-17-1-bloc-eastern-central-europe-foreign-minister-gabrielius-landsbergis/

20 'Lithuania urges people to throw away Chinese phones', BBC Online, 22 September 2021. https://www.bbc.com/news/technology-58652249

21 Baltic News Service, 'Lithuania blocks Chinese tech at airports over security concerns', *LRT*, 17 February 2021. https://www.lrt.lt/en/news-in-english/19/1346778/lithuania-blocks-chinese-tech-at-airports-over-security-concerns

22 'China's push for Lithuanian port poses risk to NATO', *LRT*, 26 November 2019. https://www.lrt.lt/en/news-in-english/19/1119707/china-s-push-for-lithuanian-port-poses-risk-to-nato

23 Andrius Sytas, 'Lithuanian parliament latest to call China's treatment of Uyghurs "genocide"', Reuters, 20 May 2021. https://www.reuters.com/world/china/lithuanian-parliament-latest-call-chinas-treatment-uyghurs-genocide-2021-05-20/

24 'For a Secure, Resilient and Prosperous Future. Lithuania's Indo-Pacific Strategy', Ministry of Foreign Affairs, Republic of Lithuania. https://urm.lt/uploads/default/documents/ENG%20Strategy.pdf

25 Ibid., pp. 7–8.

26 Walter Gibbs and Gwladys Fouche, 'China steps up retaliation against Norway for Nobel', Reuters, 12 October 2010. https://www.reuters.com/article/us-nobel-peace-china-idUSTRE6971XY20101012

27 'Firms in the firing line', *Week in China*, 10 March 2017. https://www.weekinchina.com/2017/03/firms-in-the-firing-line/?dm

28 'China's high-spending tourists bring political clout', *The Economist*, 23 February 2019. https://www.economist.com/china/2019/02/23/chinas-high-spending-tourists-bring-political-clout

29 'China allows PH banana, pineapple exports ahead of Duterte visit', ABS-CBN News, 8 October 2016. https://news.abs-cbn.com/business/10/08/16/china-allows-ph-banana-pineapple-exports-ahead-of-duterte-visit

30 Keith Bradsher, 'China is Blocking Minerals, Executives Say', *The New York Times*, 23 September 2010. https://www.nytimes.com/2010/09/24/business/energy-environment/24mineral.html

31 Christian Shepherd, Theodora Yu and Lillian Yang, 'Chinese consumers punish Japan over Fukushima nuclear water release', *The Washington Post*, 29 August 2023. https://www.washingtonpost.com/world/2023/08/29/china-japan-fukushima-boycott-backlash/

32 Madeleine Speed and Kana Inagaki, 'Chinese boycott beauty products after Fukushima discharge', *Financial Times*, 16 October 2023. https://www.ft.com/content/431d1797-dc13-4212-b7c4-f531e06c82fb?...ubstack&utm_medium=email#myft:notification:instant-email:content

33 Amy Hawkins and Justin McCurry, 'Fukushima: China accused of hypocrisy over its own release of wastewater from nuclear plants', *The Guardian*, 25 August 2023. https://www.theguardian.com/environment/2023/aug/25/fukushima-daiichi-nuclear-power-plant-china-wastewater-release

34 Steve Stecklow and Jeffrey Dastin, 'Special Report: Amazon partnered with China propaganda arm', Reuters, 18 December 2021. https://www.reuters.com/world/china/amazon-partnered-with-china-propaganda-arm-win-beijings-favor-document-shows-2021-12-17/

35   Ibid.

36   Aya Adachi, Alexander Brown and Max J. Zenglein, 'Fasten your seat-belts: How to manage China's economic coercion', Mercator Institute for China Studies, 25 August 2022. https://www.merics.org/en/report/fasten-your-seatbelts-how-manage-chinas-economic-coercion

37   Fergus Hunter, Daria Impiombato, Yvonne Lau, Dr Adam Triggs, Albert Zhang and Urmika Deb, 'Countering China's Coercive Diplomacy', Australian Strategic Policy Institute, 22 February 2022. https://www.aspi.org.au/report/countering-chinas-coercive-diplomacy

38   James Kynge, 'China's blueprint for an alternative world order', *Financial Times*, 22 August 2022. https://www.ft.com/content/8ac52fe7-e9db-48a8-b2f0-7305ab53f4c3

39   For a detailed overview of the Micronesian economy, see the World Bank's 2021 country profile. https://climateknowledgeportal.worldbank.org/sites/default/files/country-profiles/15818-WB_Micronesia%20Country%20Profile-WEB.pdf

40   Bruce Jones, 'Temperature Rising: The Struggle for Bases and Access in the Pacific Islands', Foreign Policy at Brookings, Policy Brief, February 2023. https://www.brookings.edu/articles/temperatures-rising-the-struggle-for-bases-and-access-in-the-pacific-islands/

41   The full text of the 9 March 2023 letter written to lawmakers by outgoing Micronesian President David Panuelo can be accessed at Document Cloud. https://www.documentcloud.org/documents/22037013-letter-from-h-e-david-w-panuelo-to-pacific-island-leaders-may-20-2022-signed

42   Jones, 'Temperature Rising', February 2023.

43   Kate Lyons and Dorothy Wickham, 'The deal that shocked the world: inside the China-Solomons security pact', *The Guardian*, 20 April 2022. https://www.theguardian.com/world/2022/apr/20/the-deal-that-shocked-the-world-inside-the-china-solomons-security-pact

44   Charlie Piringi, 'Solomon Islands newspaper pledged to promote "truth about China's generosity" in return for funding', *The Guardian*, 2 August 2023. https://www.theguardian.com/world/2023/aug/02/solomon-islands-newspaper-pledged-to-promote-truth-about-chinas-generosity-in-return-for-funding

45   Ivamere Nataro, 'Fiji to stick to China police deal after review says home affairs minister', *The Guardian*, 15 March 2024. https://www.theguardian.com/world/2024/mar/15/fiji-china-police-exchange-intelligence-deal#:~:text=Fiji%20will%20uphold%20a%20policing,Fiji%20was%20under%20military%20rule.

Chapter 10:
A Thousand Grains of Sand

1   Liam Kelly, 'The dangers of doing business with the Chinese dragon', *The Sunday Times*, 9 February 2020. https://www.thetimes.co.uk/article/the-dangers-of-doing-business-with-the-chinese-dragon-dpgxczk0b

2   The Smith's (Harlow) website is no longer online, but can be accessed via the Wayback Machine, the internet archive. https://web.archive.org/web/20190301232824/http://www.smiths-harlow.co.uk/

3   Liam Kelly, *The Sunday Times*, 9 February 2020

4   Liam Kelly, 'Stricken engineer Smiths (Harlow) blames China', *The Sunday Times*, 2 February 2020. https://www.thetimes.co.uk/article/stricken-engineer-smiths-harlow-blames-china-zskqsxcz6

5   Liam Kelly, 'China's Future Aerospace "stole trade secrets", says Smiths (Harlow)', *The Sunday Times*, 26 January 2020. https://www.thetimes.co.uk/article/chinas-future-aerospace-stole-trade-secrets-says-smiths-harlow-03pg2m90j

6   The full text of the 6 July 2022 joint address by Ken McCallum, the director general of MI5, and FBI Director Christopher Wray can be accessed via the MI5 website. https://www.mi5.gov.uk/news/speech-by-mi5-and-fbi

7   Dan Sabbagh, '20,000 Britons approached by Chinese agents on LinkedIn, says MI5 head', *The Guardian*, 17 October 2023. https://www.theguardian.com/uk-news/2023/oct/17/up-to-20000-britons-approached-by-chinese-agents-on-linkedin-says-mi5-head

8   Fiona Hamilton, 'Exposed: the Chinese spy using LinkedIn to hunt UK secrets', *The Times*, 23 August 2023. https://www.thetimes.co.uk/article/1ba8f1bc-4102-11ee-8b31-3c9c533abb75?shareToken=7fbd309cd-861f4702c4fffeb1eadbbff

9   William C. Hannas, James Mulvenon and Anna B. Puglisi, *Chinese Industrial Espionage: Technology acquisition and military modernisation* (London and New York: Routledge, 2013), pp. 188–95.

10   Ibid., p. 2.

11   Jim Mann, *Beijing Jeep: The Short, Unhappy Romance of American Business in China* (New York: Simon and Schuster, 1989), p. 116.

12   Ibid, p. 22.

13   Shunsuke Tabeta and Tomoko Wakasugi, 'China moves to shut out foreign medical equipment makers', *Nikkei Asia*, 14 September 2023. https://asia.nikkei.com/Business/Companies/China-moves-to-shut-out-foreign-medical-equipment-makers

14   'China', Intelligence and Security Committee of Parliament, presented to Parliament on 13 July 2023, p. 2. Available at https://isc.independent.gov.uk/wp-content/uploads/2023/07/ISC-China.pdf

15   Ibid., p. 2. ,

16   Ibid., p. 134.

17   Iain Duncan Smith, 'Britain's policy on China is simply disgraceful', *The Telegraph*, 15 July 2023. https://www.telegraph.co.uk/news/2023/07/15/our-policy-on-china-is-simply-disgraceful/

18   Intelligence and Security Committee, 13 July 2023, p. 103.

19   Ibid., pp. 116–17.

20   'The China question: Managing risks and maximising benefits from partnerships in higher education and research', The Policy Institute, King's College London, and Harvard Kennedy School's Mossavar-Rahmani Center

for Business and Government, March 2021. https://www.kcl.ac.uk/policy-institute/assets/china-question.pdf

21   Ibid.

22   Geraldine Scott, 'Links to campuses at the heart of China's military ambitions', *The Times*, 22 January 2023. https://www.thetimes.co.uk/article/links-to-campuses-at-heart-of-chinas-military-ambitions-xv3z6wfmw

23   Radomir Tylecote and Robert Clarke, 'Inadvertently arming China? The Chinese military complex and its potential exploitation of scientific research at UK universities', Civitas, February 2021. https://www.civitas.org.uk/publications/inadvertently-arming-china/

24   Australian Strategic Policy Institute, 'Picking flowers, making honey', 30 October 2018. https://www.aspi.org.au/report/picking-flowers-making-honey

25   Max Colbert, 'Authoritarian Influence? 75% of Russell Group Universities Hold Agreements with State-Linked Chinese Tech Firms', Byline Times, 18 November 2021. https://bylinetimes.com/2021/11/18/authoritarian-influence-75-of-russell-group-universities-hold-agreements-with-state-linked-chinese-tech-firms/

26   'International Chinese Student Guide to UK Universities', Study International-UK, 28 March 2023. https://www.studyin-uk.com/study-guide/chinese-student-guide-uk-universities/

27   Ibid.

28   Will Tanner, 'Trading Places. How universities have become too reliant on overseas students and how to fix it', Onward, July 2020. https://www.ukonward.com/wp-content/uploads/2020/07/Trading-Places-PDF.pdf

29   Sally Weale and Ben Quinn, 'English universities warned not to over-rely on fees of students from China', *The Guardian*, 18 May 2023. https://www.theguardian.com/education/2023/may/18/english-universities-warned-not-to-over-rely-on-fees-of-students-from-china

30   See the University of Cambridge Department of Engineering press statement, 'Cambridge and Nanjing break ground on "smart cities" Centre', 16 September 2019. http://www.eng.cam.ac.uk/news/cambridge-and-nanjing-break-ground-smart-cities-centre

31   See the Department of Engineering's press statement, 'A new postdoctoral research fellowship in Department of Engineering to be funded by Tencent', 10 September 2019. http://www.eng.cam.ac.uk/news/new-postdoctoral-research-fellowship-department-engineering-be-funded-tencent

32   See the Centre for Advanced Photonics and Electronics website, CAPE overview. https://www.cape.eng.cam.ac.uk/cape

33   See the CAPE homepage. https://www.cape.eng.cam.ac.uk

34   See the CAPE website, 'Beijing Institute of Aerospace Control Devices (BIACD)'. https://www.cape.eng.cam.ac.uk/cape/partners/biacd

35   'Communist Chinese Military Companies Listed Under E.O. [Executive Order] 13959 Have More Than 1,100 Subsidiaries', US Department of State, 14 January 2021: https://2017-2021.state.gov/communist-chinese-

military-companies-listed-under-e-o-13959-have-more-than-1100-subsidi
aries/

36 The US government's full 'entity list' 19 May 2023 update, can be accessed at the US Department of Commerce's Bureau of Industry and Security website. https://www.bis.doc.gov/index.php/documents/regulations-docs/2326-supplement-no-4-to-part-744-entity-list-4/file

37 Emma Yeomans, 'Cambridge University to end partnership with Chinese missiles company', *The Times*, 4 September 2023. https://www.thetimes.co.uk/article/a4baca98-4a8f-11ee-ae1a-79bb7c14d872?shareTo-ken=665761c914cea113d6930f78af5e53c2

38 US government 'entity list'.

39 See Australian Strategic Policy Institute, 'International Cyber Centre database, China Aerospace Science and Technology Corporation (CASC)'. https://unitracker.aspi.org.au/universities/china-aerospace-science-and-technology-corporation/

40 'Cambridge University's collaboration with the Chinese military. Centre for Advanced Photonics and Electronics (CAPE)', UK-China Transparency, 4 September 2023. https://ukctransparency.org/wp-content/uploads/2023/09/REPORT-Cambridge-Universitys-collaboration-with-the-Chinese-military.pdf

41 Ibid.

42 See the CAPE website's 'People' page. https://www.cape.eng.cam.ac.uk/people

43 My full freedom of information request for data on the number of students enrolled at the Department of Engineering by nationality, made on 6 August 2023, can be viewed on the website of WhatDoTheyKnow, an organisation that assists in such requests. https://www.whatdotheyknow.com/request/number_of_students_enrolled_in_t

44 Details of the science park investment can be found in a 1 February 2018 press release from Trinity College Cambridge, 'Landmark Joint Venture at Cambridge Science Park'. https://www.trin.cam.ac.uk/news/landmark-joint-venture-at-cambridge-science-park/. For details of the case of Xu Zhangrun, a law professor barred from teaching at Tsinghua University and then arrested for criticising President Xi Jinping, see BBC Online, 'Xu Zhangrun: Outspoken professor detained in China', 6 July 2020. https://www.bbc.co.uk/news/world-asia-china-53306280. The university has also been identified as the origin of cyberattacks against dissidents and prominent Western companies, as described by Yuan Yang, 'China's Tsinghua University linked to cyber espionage, study claims', *Financial Times*, 17 August 2018. https://www.ft.com/content/cbf22f3c-a1f9-11e8-85da-eeb7a9ce36e4

45 See Cambridge University's 9 March 2021 press statement, announcing the start of work on the new building and giving details of its funding, 'Cambridge Institute for Sustainability Leadership. World-first sustainable office retrofit begins at new University of Cambridge Institute for Sustainability Leadership headquarters'. https://www.cisl.cam.ac.uk/news/news-items/entopia-building

46   'Cambridge University and Huawei', UK-China Transparency, October 2023. https://ukctransparency.org/wp-content/uploads/2023/10/Cambridge-Huawei-Report.pdf

47   Christopher Dorrell, 'Cambridge University attempts to navigate new era of China relations', *Varsity*, 12 March 2021. https://www.varsity.co.uk/news/21016

48   Bethan Staton and Laura Hughes, 'Cambridge sets guidelines to reduce overseas engagement risks', *Financial Times*, 1 October 2021. https://www.ft.com/content/96d1efb7-49fc-49bb-b432-56dbcc18919a

49   See the 30 May 2022 statement from Jesus College Cambridge, 'China Centre restructure announced', which contains links to the review. https://www.jesus.cam.ac.uk/articles/china-centre-restructure-announced

50   See Prime Minister Rishi Sunak's 13 July 2023 written statement in response to the report by the Intelligence and Security Committee, available at the website of the UK Parliament. https://questions-statements.parliament.uk/written-statements/detail/2023-07-13/hcws938

51   Jim Pickard, Lucy Fisher, Cynthia O'Murchu, Will Louch and James Kynge, 'How David Cameron tried to make his fortune with cash from China', *Financial Times*, 17 November 2023. https://www.ft.com/content/c1adc439-1847-4229-8e7c-486dccf6f5b9

52   Mark Blacklock, 'Will Cameron's appointment be a chance for China-UK relations to get back on track?', *Global Times*, 14 November 2023. https://www.globaltimes.cn/page/202311/1301807.shtml

53   'Two Huawei 5G kit-removal deadlines put back', BBC Online, 13 October 2022. https://www.bbc.co.uk/news/technology-63242336

54   Lucy Fisher and Daniel Thomas, 'UK to pare back new takeover screening powers, says deputy PM', *Financial Times*, 12 November 2023. https://www.ft.com/content/41ce15f7-316e-4273-acf8-9e0872c13d96?shareType=nongift

55   Lucy Fisher, George Parker, Anna Gross and Jim Pickard, 'Rishi Sunak promises "careful" crackdown in wake of China cyber attacks', *Financial Times*, 26 March 2024. https://www.ft.com/content/4152359a-ec25-425e-aa1d-505f9a8d148d?shareType=nongift

56   Ibid.

57   Pippa Crerar and Eleni Courea, 'Chinese hackers targeted UK's Electoral Commission and politicians, say security services', *The Guardian*, 25 March 2024. https://www.theguardian.com/technology/2024/mar/25/chinese-hackers-targeted-electoral-commission-and-politicians-say-security-services

58   Joint address by Ken McCallum, the director general of MI5, and FBI Director Christopher Wray, 6 July 2022.

59   Reuters, 'China is now top priority for British intelligence, spy chief says', 21 July 2021. https://www.reuters.com/world/china-is-now-top-priority-british-intelligence-spy-chief-says-2022-07-21/

60   Mickey Carroll, 'GCHQ boss says China's 'genuine' cyber threat 'weakens security of internet for all', Sky News, 14 May 2024. https://news.sky.com/story/gchq-boss-says-chinas-genuine-cyber-threat-weakens-security-of-internet-for-all-13135724

61   Mike Conte, Christian Sierra and Ben Westcott, 'FBI opens a new investigation into China "every 10 hours," bureau director says', CNN, 14 April 2021. https://edition.cnn.com/2021/04/14/politics/fbi-director-china-investigations-intl-hnk/index.html

Chapter 11:
The Long Reach of the Party

1   '110 Overseas: Chinese Transnational Policing Gone Wild', Safeguard Defenders, October 2022. https://safeguarddefenders.com/sites/default/files/pdf/110%20Overseas%20%28v5%29.pdf Also, 'Patrol and Persuade: A Follow-up Investigation to 110 Overseas', December 2022. https://safeguarddefenders.com/sites/default/files/pdf/Patrol%20and%20Persuade%20v2.pdf

2   See the Chinese Embassy's spokesperson's 20 November 2022 remarks, as published on the embassy's website. http://gb.china-embassy.gov.cn/eng/PressandMedia/Spokepersons/202211/t20221120_10978291.htm

3   Patrick Wintour, 'Chinese diplomats at the centre of Manchester consulate row return home', The Guardian, 14 December 2022. https://www.theguardian.com/world/2022/dec/14/chinese-diplomats-at-centre-of-manchester-consulate-row-return-home

4   Chris Lau, 'Hong Kong police issue new cash bounties for self-exiled activists, including a US citizen', CNN, 15 December 2023. https://edition.cnn.com/2023/12/15/china/hong-kong-police-new-bounties-activists-us-britain-intl-hnk/index.html

5   Debbie White, 'MP's Hong Kong meeting targeted by Chinese spy', The Times, 12 July 2023. https://www.thetimes.co.uk/article/mp-s-hong-kong-meeting-targeted-by-chinese-spy-b89j3hl79

6   BBC News Online, 'Man charged with spying for Hong Kong found dead,' 21 May 2024. https://www.bbc.co.uk/news/articles/c1vv5wlp3q5o

7   'Patrol and Persuade', Safeguard Defenders, p. 30.

8   '"Sky Net" campaign launched to intensify efforts on corruption', Global Times, 24 February 2021. https://www.globaltimes.cn/page/202102/1216438.shtml

9   'Patrol and Persuade', Safeguard Defenders, p. 31.

10   Ibid.

11   James Fanelli, James T. Areddy and Aruna Viswanatha, 'U.S. Arrests Two, Charges Dozens for Alleged Illegal U.S. Activities by Chinese Security Agents', The Wall Street Journal, 17 April 2023. https://www.wsj.com/articles/china-security-unit-targeted-u-s-with-fake-social-media-scheme-prosecutors-allege-527b6528

12   Ibid.

13   Jennifer Peltz, '3 men convicted in US trial that scrutinized China's "Operation Fox Hunt" repatriation campaign', Associated Press, 30 June 2023. https://apnews.com/article/china-repatriation-operation-fox-hunt-trial-new-york-01f96f6952e772efb5814c12316922dc

14 Ibid.

15 'Extraditions and China', Safeguard Defenders, 24 February 2022 https://safeguarddefenders.com/sites/default/files/pdf/ET%20factsheet_0.pdf

16 Larry Neumeister, 'Feds: Chinese man charged in China's US chase of "fugitives"', Associated Press, 30 March 2022. https://apnews.com/article/china-new-york-manhattan-new-york-city-united-states-435a037714bba0cca6887ab2dd9d315a

17 Mark Mazzetti and Dan Levin, 'Obama Administration Warns Beijing About Covert Agents Working in US', *The New York Times*, 16 August 2015. https://www.nytimes.com/2015/08/17/us/politics/obama-administration-warns-beijing-about-agents-operating-in-us.html

18 'How China's police are ensnaring thousands of suspects abroad', *The Economist*, 14 February 2023. https://www.economist.com/china/2023/02/14/how-chinas-police-are-ensnaring-thousands-of-suspects-abroad

19 Yuanyue Dang, 'Operation Fox Hunt: how a US court case shed light on China's pursuit of its fugitives', *South China Morning Post*, 2 July 2023. https://www.scmp.com/news/china/diplomacy/article/3226267/operation-fox-hunt-how-us-court-case-shed-light-chinas-pursuit-its-fugitives

20 Ibid.

21 Oliver Holmes and Tom Phillips, 'Gui Minhai: the strange disappearance of a publisher who riled China's elite', *The Guardian*, 8 December 2015. https://www.theguardian.com/world/2015/dec/08/gui-minhai-the-strange-disappearance-of-a-publisher-who-riled-chinas-elite

22 'Gui Minhai: Hong Kong bookseller gets 10 years jail', BBC Online, 25 February 2020. https://www.bbc.co.uk/news/world-asia-china-51624433

23 Oliver Holmes and Tom Phillips, 'Activist who vanished in Thailand is being held in China, says wife', *The Guardian*, 3 February 2016. https://www.theguardian.com/world/2016/feb/03/activist-li-xin-vanished-in-thailand--held-in-china-says-wife

24 Oliver Holmes, 'Chinese rights campaigner disappears in Thailand', *The Guardian*, 22 January 2016. https://www.theguardian.com/world/2016/jan/22/chinese-rights-campaigner-li-xin-disappears-thailand

25 'Meng Hongwei: China sentences ex-Interpol chief to 13 years in jail', BBC Online, 21 January 2020. https://www.bbc.co.uk/news/world-asia-china-51185838

26 Philip Hammond, 'Focus on common interests', *China Daily*, 17 February 2023. https://www.chinadailyhk.com/article/315927

27 Kurt Zindulka, 'Exclusive: Chinese State Media Fabricated Article From Former UK Cabinet Minister', *Breitbart*, 20 February 2023. https://www.breitbart.com/europe/2023/02/20/exclusive-chinese-state-media-fabricated-article-from-former-uk-cabinet-minister/

28 Ibid.

29 Clive Hamilton and Mareike Ohlberg, *Hidden Hand: Exposing How the Chinese Communist Party is Reshaping the World* (London and Minneapolis: Oneworld, 2020), p. 62.

30 For a full list of current patrons and fellows, see 'Who's Who' on the 48

Group Club website. https://www.the48groupclub.com/about-the-club/whos-who/

31　'China Reform Friendship Medal Recipient: Stephen Perry, carrying on the "ice-breaking mission" between China and the UK', CGTN, 18 December 2018. https://news.cgtn.com/news/3d3d514d35637a4d31457a6333566d54/index.html

32　Excerpts from Stephen Perry's speech can be seen in a lengthy news report about the event carried by CCTV, China's state broadcaster on 12 February 2023. https://tv.cctv.com/2023/02/12/VIDEM34QwbqmTjMJFb14o6Yj230212.shtml?spm=C45404.PlcSaTuIQb0E.ENSvHePEGND5.88

33　'"China is not a risk; it's an opportunity": Vice Chairman of the 48 Group Club', Global Times, 27 July 2023. https://www.globaltimes.cn/page/202307/1295149.shtml

34　James McGregor, One Billion Customers. Lessons from the Front Lines of Doing Business in China (New York: Wall Street Journal Books, 2005), p. 53.

35　Ibid.

36　Xi Jinping, The Governance of China, vol II (Beijing: Foreign Languages Press, 2017), pp. 331–3.

37　James Kynge, Lucy Hornby and Jamil Anderlini, 'Inside China's secret "magic weapon" for worldwide influence', Financial Times, 26 October 2017. https://www.ft.com/content/fb2b3934-b004-11e7-beba-5521c713abf4

38　Dan Sabbagh, 'MI5 accuses lawyer of trying to influence politicians on behalf of China', The Guardian, 13 January 2022. https://www.theguardian.com/uk-news/2022/jan/13/chinese-national-trying-to-improperly-influence-politicians-says-mi5

39　Gareth Davies, 'MI5 warns Chinese spy has been active in parliament', The Telegraph, 13 January 2022. https://www.telegraph.co.uk/news/2022/01/13/mi5-warns-chinese-spy-has-active-parliament/

40　See the Home Office policy paper, 'Foreign Influence Registration Scheme factsheet', 13 July 2023. https://www.gov.uk/government/publications/national-security-bill-factsheets/foreign-influence-registration-scheme-factsheet#frequently-asked-questions

41　Amnesty International, '"On My Campus I am Afraid". China's Targeting of Overseas Students Stifles Rights', May 2024. https://www.amnesty.org/en/documents/asa17/8006/2024/en/

42　Julia Pamilih, 'Briefing: Confucius Institutes in the UK', China Research Group, 13 June 2022. https://chinaresearchgroup.org/research/confucius-institutes-in-the-uk

43　See the 18 May 2023 UK-China Transparency report, 'Are Confucius Institutes Legal'. https://ukctransparency.org/wp-content/uploads/2023/04/EXECUTIVE-SUMMARY-Are-Confucius-Institutes-legal-1.pdf. For a fuller investigation of Confucius Institutes, see Sam Dunning and Anson Kwong, 'An Investigation of China's Confucius Institutes in the UK', Henry Jackson Society, September 2022. https://henryjacksonsociety.org/wp-content/uploads/2022/10/Confucius-Institutes-in-UK.pdf

44　Ibid., p. 5.

45   George Parker and Bethan Staton, 'Rishi Sunak backtracks on promise to ban Confucius Institutes in the UK', *Financial Times*, 17 May 2023. https://www.ft.com/content/83ab4dc2-2997-43ec-a968-142752ec7ce3

46   Henry Jackson Society, September 2022, p. 5

47   'China', Intelligence and Security Committee of Parliament, presented to Parliament on 13 July 2023, p. 4. Available at https://isc.independent.gov.uk/wp-content/uploads/2023/07/ISC-China.pdf

48   Ibid., p. 3.

Chapter 12:
Kicking the China Habit

1   The gloomy sentiment survey Steven Lynch was referring to, 'British Business in China: Sentiment Survey 2022–23', can be accessed via the British Chamber of Commerce in China website. https://www.britishchamber.cn/en/business-sentiment-survey/

2   Nick Eardley, 'China spy claims as Parliament researcher arrested', BBC Online, 10 September 2023. https://www.bbc.co.uk/news/uk-66765759

3   Fiona Hamilton, 'Chinese spies tried to hack into emails of senior Tory politician', *The Times*, 24 August 2023. https://www.thetimes.co.uk/article/china-spies-microsoft-hack-tory-conservative-mp-alicia-kearns-5g67rw8kz

4   Jim Mann, *Beijing Jeep: The Short, Unhappy Romance of American Business in China* (New York: Simon and Schuster, 1989), p. 57.

5   Jim Fitzsimmons, 'China's Cyber Security Law: how prepared are you?' Control Risks, 7 March 2023. https://www.controlrisks.com/campaigns/china-business/chinas-cyber-security-law

6   'China's Anti-Espionage Law Adds to Foreign Business Concerns', *Asia Financial*, 27 April 2023. https://www.asiafinancial.com/china-broadens-its-anti-espionage-law-includes-cyberattacks

7   Agence France-Presse, 'Fears for people and firms as China's new anti-espionage bill comes into effect', *The Guardian*, 30 June 2023. https://www.theguardian.com/world/2023/jun/30/fears-for-people-and-firms-as-chinas-new-anti-espionage-law-comes-into-effect

8   Vivian Wang, 'China to Its People: Spies Are Everywhere, Help Us Catch them', *The New York Times*, 2 September 2023. https://www.nytimes.com/2023/09/02/world/asia/china-spies-campaign.html

9   Katja Drinhausen and Helena Legarda, 'China's Anti-Foreign Sanctions Law: A Warning to the World', Mercator Institute for China Studies, 24 June 2021. https://merics.org/de/kommentar/chinas-anti-foreign-sanctions-law-warning-world

10   Bloomberg, 'Police Raid Consulting Firms as China Starts Anti-Spy Campaign', 9 May 2023. https://www.bloomberg.com/news/articles/2023-05-08/china-starts-anti-spy-campaign-says-capvision-leaked-secrets?leadSource=uverify%20wall

11   Sun Yu and Ryan McMorrow, 'US Consultancy Gallup withdraws from

China', *Financial Times*, 4 November 2023. https://www.ft.com/content/dff10673-f3e3-4117-8a71-cb57a9cc4ccb

12 Lingling Wei, Yoko Kubota and Dan Stumpf, 'China Locks Information on the Country Inside a Black Box', *The Wall Street Journal*, 30 April 2023. https://www.wsj.com/world/china/china-locks-information-on-the-country-inside-a-black-box-9c039928

13 Yenting Chen, 'Trapped: China's expanding use of exit bans', Safeguard Defenders, April 2023. https://safeguarddefenders.com/en/blog/new-report-trapped-china-s-expanding-use-exit-bans

14 James Pomfret and Angel Woo, 'China's exit bans multiply as political control tightens under Xi', Reuters, 2 May 2023. https://www.reuters.com/world/china/chinas-exit-bans-multiply-political-control-tightens-under-xi-2023-05-02/

15 Agence France-Presse, 'Irish businessman Richard O'Halloran, stuck in China for three years, allowed to go home', *South China Morning Post*, 22 January 2022. https://www.scmp.com/news/world/europe/article/3165207/irish-businessman-richard-ohalloran-allowed-go-home-after-being

16 Henry Olsen, 'Opinion: China has finally released the "two Michaels". But the threat to Western business remains', *The Washington Post*, 27 September 2021. https://www.washingtonpost.com/opinions/2021/09/27/two-michaels-china-business-threat-spavor-kovrig/

17 Yvette Tan, 'China reveals British national sentenced to jail in 2022 for spying', BBC Online, 26 January 2024. https://www.bbc.co.uk/news/world-asia-china-68078586

18 Kathleen Benoza, 'As ties crumble, Chinese spy law could see more Japanese citizens detained', *The Japan Times*, 28 March 2023. https://www.japantimes.co.jp/news/2023/03/28/national/politics-diplomacy/china-japan-espionage-nationals-detain/

19 James Areddy and Brian Spegele, 'Dozens of Americans Are Barred From Leaving China, Adding to Tensions', *The Wall Street Journal*, 13 November 2022. https://www.wsj.com/articles/china-us-exit-ban-diplomacy-11668357015

20 John Feng, '"Praying for a Miracle": The Americans Detained in China', *Newsweek*, 5 February 2023. https://www.newsweek.com/china-us-citizens-wrongful-detention-kai-li-david-lin-henry-cai-1778415

21 Rebecca Feng and Chun Han Wong, 'China Blocks Executive at US Firm From Leaving the Mainland', *The Wall Street Journal*, 29 September 2023. https://www.wsj.com/world/china/china-blocks-executive-at-u-s-firm-kroll-from-leaving-the-mainland-99c9bd0f

22 See the full 30 June 2023 US Department of State travel advisory on China, on the Bureau of Consular Affairs website. https://travel.state.gov/content/travel/en/traveladvisories/traveladvisories/china-travel-advisory.html

23 Chip Cutter, Elaine Yu and Newley Purnell, 'China is Becoming a No-Go Zone for Executives', *The Wall Street Journal*, 6 October 2023. https://www.wsj.com/business/china-is-becoming-a-no-go-zone-for-executives-626250dd

24 Alexander Chipman Katy, 'China's Anti-Foreign Sanctions Law: How Business Should Prepare', China Briefing from Dezan Shira, 3 August

2021. https://www.china-briefing.com/news/chinas-anti-foreign-sanctions-law-how-businesses-should-prepare/

25   Mercator Institute for China Studies, 'China's Anti-Foreign Sanctions Law'.

26   Ai Weiwei, *1000 Years of Joys and Sorrows* (London: The Bodley Head, 2023), p. 291.

27   See, for example, Laura T. Murphy, et al., 'Laundering Cotton: How Xinjiang Cotton is Obscured in International Supply Chains', Sheffield Hallam University, Helena Kennedy Centre for International Justice, November 2021. https://www.shu.ac.uk/helena-kennedy-centre-international-justice/research-and-projects/all-projects/laundered-cotton

28   'Nike, H&M face China fury over Xinjiang cotton "concerns"', BBC Online, 25 March 2021. https://www.bbc.com/news/world-asia-china-56519411

29   'Intel apologises to China over supplier advice', BBC Online, 23 December 2021. https://www.bbc.co.uk/news/business-59769393?at_medium=RSS&at_campaign=KARANGA

30   Reuters, 'Intel deletes mention of Xinjiang in letter after China backlash', *The Guardian*, 11 January 2022. https://www.theguardian.com/world/2022/jan/11/intel-deletes-mention-of-xinjiang-in-letter-after-china-backlash

31   Laura T. Murphy and Nyrola Elimä, 'In Broad Daylight. Uyghur Forced Labour and Uyghur Solar Power Chains', Sheffield Hallam University, Helena Kennedy Centre for International Justice, May 2021 https://www.shu.ac.uk/helena-kennedy-centre-international-justice/research-and-projects/all-projects/in-broad-daylight

32   Laura Murphy, Kendyl Salcito, Yalkun Uluyol, Mia Rabkin and an anonymous team of authors, 'Driving Force: Automotive Supply Chains and Forced Labour in the Uyghur Region', Sheffield Hallam University, Helena Kennedy Centre for International Justice, November 2022. https://acrobat.adobe.com/link/track?uri=urn%3Aaaid%3Ascds%3AUS%3A86f5da26-e459-4e05-9047-15ba295bbe83

33   'UK tightens rules on using Uighur-picked cotton', BBC Online, 12 January 2021. https://www.bbc.co.uk/news/business-55638566

34   Patricia Nilsson, 'Staff rebel at consultancy behind VW review of Xinjiang rights abuse', *Financial Times*, 13 December 2023. https://www.ft.com/content/46b37a15-054e-4d40-b42b-f31a0e3a07c3?shareType=nongift

35   Victoria Waldersee, 'Volkswagen in talks over future of Xinjiang site as pressure mounts', Reuters, 14 February 2024. https://www.reuters.com/business/autos-transportation/volkswagen-talks-with-jv-partner-over-future-business-activities-xinjiang-china-2024-02-14/

36   William Boston and Bertrand Benoit, 'Volkswagen Under Pressure to Ditch Its China Joint Venture as U.S. Impounds Vehicles', *The Wall Street Journal*, 15 February 2024. https://www.wsj.com/business/autos/volkswagen-eyes-march-delivery-for-cars-delayed-at-u-s-ports-over-part-tied-to-customs-issues-eebd1f3b

37   Elisabeth Braw, 'Your Business in China May Be Uninsurable', *The Wall Street Journal*, 7 August 2023. https://www.wsj.com/articles/your-china-business-may-be-uninsurable-political-risk-coverage-222f15dd

38 The full text of President Ursula von der Leyen's 30 March 2023 speech to the Mercator Institute for China Studies is available on the European Commission's website. https://ec.europa.eu/commission/presscorner/detail/en/speech_23_2063

39 Xin Ping, 'From "decoupling" to "de-risking": Playing with words simply does not work', *Global Times*, 2 August 2023. https://www.globaltimes.cn/page/202308/1295517.shtml

40 A full English language translation of the July 2023 document, 'Strategy on China of the Government of the Federal Republic of Germany', can be accessed at https://www.auswaertiges-amt.de/blob/2608580/49d50fecc479304c3da2e2079c55e106/china-strategie-en-data.pdf

41 Arne Delfs and Josefine Fokuhl, 'Scholz Rebuffs Cabinet to Allow China Bridgehead at Hamburg Port', Bloomberg, 25 October 2022. https://www.bloomberg.com/news/articles/2022-10-25/germany-may-allow-china-s-cosco-to-buy-24-9-of-hamburg-port

42 Erika Solomon, 'German Businesses Bet Big on China, and They're Starting to Worry', *The New York Times*, 10 July 2023. https://www.nytimes.com/2023/07/06/world/europe/germany-china-business-economy.html#:~:text=But%20major%20brands%20like%20Volkswagen,investment%20in%20China%20this%20year. See also, Alexander Hübner and John Revill, 'Siemens to spend 1 billion euros in Germany as Berlin warns about China', Reuters, 13 July 2023. https://www.reuters.com/technology/siemens-spend-1-bln-euro-germany-berlin-warns-about-china-2023-07-13/

43 Bethany Dawson, 'Cleverly says UK "clear-eyed" over China disagreements', *Politico*, 30 August 2023. https://www.independent.co.uk/news/uk/politics/james-cleverly-china-uk-rishi-sunak-b2401762.html

44 Ibid.

45 Lucy Fisher and George Parker, 'British policy on China lacks clarity and coherence, say MPs', *Financial Times*, 30 August 2023. https://www.ft.com/content/9304e774-2774-4a87-9c97-be5b13b06a33

46 Max J. Zenglein and Anna Holzmann, 'Evolving Made in China 2025. China's industrial policy in the quest for global tech leadership', Mercator Institute for China Studies, 2 July 2019. https://merics.org/en/report/evolving-made-china-2025

47 Liza Lin, 'China intensifies Push to "Delete America" From Its Technology', *The Wall Street Journal*, 7 March 2024. https://www.wsj.com/world/china/china-technology-software-delete-america-2b8ea89f

48 Iori Kawate, 'Foreign investment in China turns negative for first time', *Nikkei Asia*, 4 November 2023. https://asia.nikkei.com/Economy/Foreign-investment-in-China-turns-negative-for-first-time

49 Bloomberg, 'China's Foreign Investment Gauge Declines to 25-Year Low', 8 August 2023. https://www.bloomberg.com/news/articles/2023-08-07/china-foreign-investment-gauge-at-25-year-low-amid-high-tensions?leadSource=uverify%20wall

50 'Ties between foreign businesses and China go from bad to worse', *The Economist*, 26 September 2023. https://www.economist.com/business/2023/09/26/ties-between-foreign-businesses-and-china-go-from-bad-to-worse

Chapter 13:
The Limits of 'Made in Vietnam'

1   For a detailed analysis of the February 1979 border war see David Shambaugh, *Where Great Powers Meet: America and China in Southeast Asia* (New York: Oxford University Press, 2021), pp. 49–52.

2   For an analysis of China's military strategy and the inadequacies of the PLA at the time, see Edward C. O'Dowd, *Chinese Military Strategy in the Third Indochina War: The Last Maoist War* (London and New York: Routledge, 2007).

3   Vinh Phong, 'Cross-border trade busy at Lang Son border gate', *The Voice of Vietnam*, 20 February 2023. https://vovworld.vn/en-US/current-affairs/crossborder-trade-busy-at-lang-son-border-gate-1177449.vov

4   Qiao Long and Chingman, 'Vietnamese Border Region Residents Remove China's Electrified Fence', Radio Free Asia, 21 September 2021. https://www.rfa.org/english/news/china/vietnam-border-09212021095446.html

5   Liyan Qi, 'As China Reopens Borders, Trafficking of Women and Girls Resumes', *The Wall Street Journal*, 30 June 2023. https://www.wsj.com/articles/as-china-reopens-borders-trafficking-of-women-and-girls-resumes-b1132ab1

6   'Death toll from China coach crash rises to 11, all Vietnamese', *Vietnam News*, 25 May 2023. https://vietnamnews.vn/society/1543075/death-toll-from-china-coach-crash-rises-to-11-all-vietnamese.html

7   An Minh, 'Vietnam women arrested for trafficking of minors', *VN Express*, 8 February 2023. https://e.vnexpress.net/news/news/vietnam-women-arrested-for-trafficking-of-minors-4568453.html

8   Reuters, 'Apple supplier Foxconn to invest $300 million more in northern Vietnam, state media reports', 20 August 2022. https://www..com/technology/apple-supplier-foxconn-invest-300-mln-more-northern-vietnam-media-2022-08-20/

9   Cheng Ting-Fang and Lauly Li, 'Vietnam to make Apple Watch and MacBook for first time ever', *Nikkei Asia*, 17 August 2022. https://asia.nikkei.com/Business/Technology/Vietnam-to-make-Apple-Watch-and-MacBook-for-first-time-ever

10   Jacky Wong, 'Samsung is a Case Study in How Manufacturers Leave China', *The Wall Street Journal*, 3 May 2023. https://www.wsj.com/articles/samsung-is-a-case-study-in-how-manufacturers-leave-china-5dcb2dcf

11   Ibid.

12   'Vietnam's economic moment has arrived', *Financial Times* editorial, 9 July 2023. https://www.ft.com/content/fa1db5ce-8f65-4b28-ab6d-b78730f98195?shareType=nongift

13   Agnes Alpuerto, 'Vietnam FDI in 2022: Biggest Investors and Top Recipients', Vietcetera, 29 December 2022. https://vietcetera.com/en/vietnam-fdi-in-2022-biggest-investors-and-top-recipients

14   Gary Sands, 'In Vietnam, Protests Highlight Anti-Chinese Sentiment',

The Diplomat, 12 June 2018. https://thediplomat.com/2018/06/in-vietnam-protests-highlight-anti-chinese-sentiment/

15 Francesco Guarascio, 'Analysis: Chinese suppliers race to Vietnam as COVID let-up opens escape route from Sino-U.S. trade war', Reuters, 16 March 2023. https://www.reuters.com/markets/asia/chinese-suppliers-race-vietnam-covid-let-up-opens-escape-route-sino-us-trade-war-2023-03-16/

16 For a detailed comparison of doing business in China and Vietnam, see James Kennemer, 'Manufacturing in China vs Vietnam: Guide to Vietnam and China Sourcing Pros and Cons', COSMO Sourcing, 22 May 2023. https://www.cosmosourcing.com/blog/china-vs-vietnam-manufacturing-sourcing-pros-and-cons

17 Tomoya Onishi, 'Vietnam targets China manufacturers after EU trade green light', *Financial Times*, 17 June 2020. https://www.ft.com/content/1247172b-e777-4feb-8ed5-27ac36519c5a

18 Ana Swanson and Brad Plumer, 'Chinese Solar Makers Evaded U.S. Tariffs, Investigation Finds', *The New York Times*, 2 December 2022. https://www.nytimes.com/2022/12/02/business/economy/chinese-solar-makers-tariffs.html

19 Ana Swanson and Chris Buckley, 'Chinese Solar Companies Tied to Use of Forced Labor', *The New York Times*, 28 January 2021. https://www.nytimes.com/2021/01/08/business/economy/china-solar-companies-forced-labor-xinjiang.html

20 See Robert Templer, *Shadows and Wind: A View of Modern Vietnam* (London: Penguin Books, 1999), p. 294.

21 Hans Kemp, *Bikes of Burden: Vietnam on a Bike* (Hong Kong: Visionary World, 2007; reprinted and updated 2021).

22 Kate Hodel and Jonathan Kaiman, 'At least 21 dead in Vietnam anti-China protests over oil rig', *The Guardian*, 15 May 2014. https://www.theguardian.com/world/2014/may/15/vietnam-anti-china-protests-oil-rig-dead-injured

23 The Chinese video of the battle for Johnson South Reef is still available to view on YouTube. https://www.youtube.com/watch?v=uq30CY9nWE8

24 'Da Nang condemns China's establishment on Paracel and Spratly archipelagos', Vietnamnet Global, 21 April 2020. https://vietnamnet.vn/en/da-nang-condemns-chinas-establishment-on-paracel-and-spratly-archipelagos-635259.html

25 Robert D. Kaplan, *Asia's Cauldron: The South China Sea and the End of a Stable Pacific* (New York: Random House, 2014), p. 59.

26 'US's Ronald Reagan aircraft carrier arrives in Vietnam's Danang', Al Jazeera, 25 June 2023. https://www.aljazeera.com/news/2023/6/25/uss-ronald-reagan-aircraft-carrier-arrives-in-vietnams-danang

27 Dzirhan Mahadzir, 'Carrier USS Ronald Reagan Back in the South China Sea, Details of Talisman Sabre Exercise Emerge', *USNI News*, 4 July 2023. https://news.usni.org/2023/07/04/carrier-uss-ronald-reagan-back-in-the-south-china-sea-details-of-talisman-sabre-exercise-emerge

28 Lien Hoang, 'Yellen's trip underlines rise of Vietnam as China factory hedge', *Nikkei Asia*, 20 July 2023. https://asia.nikkei.com/Spotlight/Supply-Chain/Yellen-s-trip-underlines-rise-of-Vietnam-as-China-factory-hedge

29　　Jon Emont, Catherine Lucey and Kay Stech Ferek, 'Biden Seeks Stronger Vietnam Ties in Bid to Counter China', *The Wall Street Journal*, 10 September 2023. https://www.wsj.com/world/asia/biden-seeks-stronger-vietnam-ties-in-bid-to-counter-china-605517df

30　　For more details of Vietnam's demographics, see Index Mundi's 'Vietnam Demographic Profile', July 2021. https://www.indexmundi.com/vietnam/demographics_profile.html

Chapter 14:
Apple's China Addiction

1　　Simina Mistreanu, 'Watch: Rioting workers at iPhone factory smash cameras and windows in row over pay', *The Telegraph*, 23 November 2022. https://www.telegraph.co.uk/world-news/2022/11/23/workers-iphone-city-smash-surveillance-cameras-latest-china/

2　　'China urges military veterans to work at iPhone factory', BBC Online, 17 November 2022. https://www.bbc.co.uk/news/technology-63654716

3　　'Foxconn: iPhone maker apologises after huge protests at China plant', BBC Online, 24 November 2022. https://www.bbc.co.uk/news/business-63739562

4　　Ben Jiang, Coco Feng and Iris Deng, 'Inside Foxconn's "iPhone City": how Apple's biggest contractor fell victim to China's zero-Covid policy', *South China Morning Post*, 26 November 2022. https://www.scmp.com/tech/big-tech/article/3201004/inside-foxconns-iphone-city-how-apples-biggest-contractor-fell-victim-chinas-zero-covid-policy?module=inline&pgtype=article

5　　Yang Jie and Aaron Tilley, 'Apple Plans to Move Production Out of China', *The Wall Street Journal*, 3 December 2022. https://www.wsj.com/articles/apple-china-factory-protests-foxconn-manufacturing-production-supply-chain-11670023099

6　　'Foxconn's Zhengzhou plant needs at least 10,000 workers for production resumption: insiders', *Global Times*, 11 November 2022. https://www.globaltimes.cn/page/202211/1279306.shtml

7　　Reuters, 'Chinese authorities call on retired soldiers to help Foxconn iPhone plant – SSN', 16 November 2022. https://www.reuters.com/world/china/chinese-authorities-call-retired-soldiers-help-foxconn-iphone-plant-ssn-2022-11-16/

8　　'China urges military veterans to work at iPhone factory', BBC Online, 17 November 2022

9　　Huileng Tan, 'Workers are fleeing from Foxconn, China's biggest iPhone factory, by climbing over fences and walking down highways on foot amid COVID fears, photos and videos show', *Business Insider*, 31 October 2022. https://www.businessinsider.com/workers-apple-supplier-foxconn-honahi-flee-china-zhengzhou-iphone-factory-2022-10?international=true&r=US&IR=T

10　　Yang Jie and Aaron Tilley, *The Wall Street Journal*, 3 December 2022.

11 Jenny Chan, Mark Selden and Pun Ngai, *Dying for an iPhone: Apple, Foxconn, and the Lives of China's Workers* (London: Pluto Press, 2020), pp. 89–90.

12 Ibid., pp. 69–92.

13 David Barboza, 'How China Built "iPhone City" With Billions in Perks for Apple's Partner', *The New York Times*, 29 December 2016. https://www.nytimes.com/2016/12/29/technology/apple-iphone-china-foxconn.html

14 Ibid.

15 Chan, et al., *Dying for an iPhone*, p. 90.

16 Yoko Kubota, 'Apple's Tim Cook Takes Stage in China to Welcoming Applause', *The Wall Street Journal*, 25 March 2023. https://www.wsj.com/articles/apples-tim-cook-upbeat-in-beijing-as-china-courts-global-ceos-373a6ff

17 Jay Newman, 'Apple is a Chinese company', *Financial Times*, 3 May 2023. https://www.ft.com/content/bf8e3846-2421-4f91-becf-2dfe39ec9941?shareType=nongift

18 The full supplier list for 2022, as disclosed by Apple, can be accessed via the company's website. https://www.apple.com/supplier-responsibility/pdf/Apple-Supplier-List.pdf

19 Jenny Chan, 'Foxconn's Rise and Labor's Fall in Global China', *American Affairs*, vol. IV, Number 4, Winter 2020. https://americanaffairsjournal.org/2020/11/foxconns-rise-and-labors-fall-in-global-china/

20 Brian Merchant, 'Life and death in Apple's forbidden city', *The Guardian*, 18 June 2017. https://www.theguardian.com/technology/2017/jun/18/foxconn-life-death-forbidden-city-longhua-suicide-apple-iphone-brian-merchant-one-device-extract

21 Ibid.

22 Chan, et al., *Dying for an iPhone*, pp. 87–8.

23 Ibid., pp. 94–103.

24 Charles Duhigg and David Barboza, 'In China, Human Costs Are Built Into an iPad', *The New York Times*, 25 January 2012. https://www.nytimes.com/2012/01/26/business/ieconomy-apples-ipad-and-the-human-costs-for-workers-in-china.html

25 Kathrin Hille, 'Foxconn aims to supply nearly half the world's EVs', *Financial Times*, 18 October 2022. https://www.ft.com/content/0a530586-2bfd-4f1b-ac0e-a2a2b90b7ffc

26 For example, see the annual rankings by Hurun, a media, research and investment group, 'Hurun Largest Foreign & HK/Macau/Taiwan Companies in China', accessed through Hurun's website. https://www.hurun.net/en-US/Rank/HsRankDetails?pagetype=lfcinchina

27 See the Hon Hai (Foxconn) press statement, 'Hon Hai Announces FY2022 & 4Q22 Financial Results', 15 March 2023. https://www.foxconn.com/en-us/press-center/press-releases/latest-news/1009

28 Frederik Balfour and Tim Culpan, 'The Man Who Makes Your iPhone', *Bloomberg*, 9 September 2010. https://www.bloomberg.com/news/articles/2010-09-09/the-man-who-makes-your-iphone

29 Ibid.

30 Ibid., and Chan, et al., *Dying for an iPhone*, pp. 48–9 and p. 58.

31 Rupert Wingfield-Hayes, 'Terry Gou: The Taiwan iPhone billionaire who wants to be president', BBC Online, 28 August 2023. https://www.bbc.co.uk/news/world-asia-66639012

32 John Koetsier, 'Why $74 billion Of Apple Revenue Is Suddenly At Risk', Forbes, 7 September 2023. https://www.forbes.com/sites/johnkoetsier/2023/09/07/why-74-billion-of-apple-revenue-is-suddenly-at-risk/#

33 Patrick McGee, 'How Apple tied its fortunes to China', Financial Times, 17 January 2023. https://www.ft.com/content/d5a80891-b27d-4110-90c9-561b7836f11b?shareType=nongift

34 Ibid.

35 Tripp Mickle, 'How China Has Added to Its Influence Over the iPhone', The New York Times, 7 September 2022. https://www.nytimes.com/2022/09/06/technology/china-apple-iphone.html

36 Qianer Liu, Eleanor Olcott and Demetri Sevastopulo, 'China's chip darling YMTC thrust into spotlight by US export controls', Financial Times, 14 October 2022. https://www.ft.com/content/404d36cc-9e4a-4ac6-9291-b5580c27cc05

37 Tim Bradshaw, 'Apple drops hundreds of VPN apps at Beijing's request', Financial Times, 22 November 2017. https://www.ft.com/content/ad42e536-cf36-11e7-b781-794ce08b24dc

38 Paul Mozur, 'Skype Vanishes From App Stores in China, including Apple's', The New York Times, 21 November 2017. https://www.nytimes.com/2017/11/21/business/skype-app-china.html

39 Benjamin Haas, 'Apple Removes New York Times app in China', The Guardian, 5 January 2017. https://www.theguardian.com/world/2017/jan/05/apple-removes-new-york-times-app-in-china

40 Charlie Smith, 'Apple Censoring Tibet Information in China', greatfire.org, 10 June 2019. https://en.greatfire.org/blog/2019/jun/apple-censoring-tibetan-information-china

41 Stephen Nellis and John Ruwitch, 'Apple pulls app used to track Hong Kong police, Cook defends move', Reuters, 10 October 2019. https://www.reuters.com/article/us-hongkong-protests-apple/apple-removes-police-tracking-app-used-in-hong-kong-protests-from-its-app-store-idUSKBN1WP09U

42 Jack Nicas, Raymond Zhong and Daisuke Wakabayashi, 'Censorship, Surveillance and Profits: A Hard Bargain For Apple in China', The New York Times, 17 May 2021. https://www.nytimes.com/2021/05/17/technology/apple-china-censorship-data.html

43 Jay Peters, Sean Hollister and Richard Lawler, 'Apple's $100 million settlement agreement "clarifies" App Store rules for developers, but doesn't change much', The Verge, 27 August 2021. https://www.theverge.com/2021/8/26/22643807/apple-developer-class-action-lawsuit-collect-information-ios-apps-anti-steering

44 The 2022 App Transparency Report can be accessed via Apple's website. https://www.apple.com/legal/more-resources/docs/2022-App-Store-Transparency-Report.pdf

45 The New York Times, 17 May 2021.

46 Alex Kantrowitz and John Paczkowski, 'Apple Told Some Apple TV+ Show Developers Not to Anger China', Buzzfeed News, 11 October 2019. https://www.buzzfeednews.com/article/alexkantrowitz/apple-china-tv-pro testers-hong-kong-tim-cook

47 Andy Greenberg, 'Apple's China-Friendly Censors Caused an iPhone Crashing Bug', Wired, 18 July 2018. https://www.wired.com/story/apple-china-censorship-bug-iphone-crash-emoji/

48 Ibid.

49 'Apple's new "private relay" feature to be withheld in China', The Guardian, 8 June 2021. https://www.theguardian.com/technology/2021/jun/08/apple-private-relay-feature-to-be-withheld-in-china

50 Mark Gurman, 'Apple limits File-Sharing Tool Used For Protests in China', Bloomberg, 10 November 2022. https://www.bloomberg.com/ news/articles/2022-11-10/apple-limits-iphone-file-sharing-tool-used-for-protests-in-china?sref=ExbtjcSG

51 Yoko Kubota, Yang Jie and Aaron Tilley, 'Apple's Latest China Challenge: A Crackdown That Could Shrink Its App Store', The Wall Street Journal, 29 September 2023. https://www.wsj.com/tech/ apple-china-met-to-discuss-beijings-crackdown-on-western-apps-2219afcb

52 Mikey Campbell, 'Apple CEO Tim Cook talks Chinese supply chain, censorship and more in interview', AppleInsider, 5 December 2017. https:// appleinsider.com/articles/17/12/06/apple-ceo-tim-cook-talks-chinese-supply-chain-censorship-and-more-in-interview

53 Frank Tang, 'Apple CEO Tim Cook joins influential Beijing University board as company's China woes continue', South China Morning Post, 21 October 2019. https://www.scmp.com/economy/china-economy/article/3033899/ apple-ceo-tim-cook-joins-influential-beijing-university-board

54 Chris Buckley, 'A Chinese Law Professor Criticised Xi. Now He's Been Suspended', The New York Times, 26 March 2019. https://www.nytimes. com/2019/03/26/world/asia/chinese-law-professor-xi.html

55 See MSNBC interview with Tim Cook, 'Privacy is "a human right": Apple CEO Tim Cook', 28 March 2019. https://www.msnbc.com/msnbc/watch/ privacy-is-a-human-right-apple-ceo-tim-cook-1197152323753

56 See Tim Cook's open letter to customers, 16 February 2016. https://www. apple.com/customer-letter/

57 Jenny Leonard and Debby Wu, 'China Seeks to Broaden iPhone Ban to State Firms, Agencies', Bloomberg, 7 September 2023. https://www. bloomberg.com/news/articles/2023-09-07/china-plans-to-expand-iphone-ban-to-some-state-backed-firms-in-blow-to-apple?sref=Xl91GI8N

58 Yelin Mo and Brenda Goh, 'What does Huawei's new phone series mean for Apple in China?', Reuters, 8 September 2022. https://www. reuters.com/technology/what-is-huaweis-new-smartphone-challenger-apple-2023-09-08/?taid=64fb2ffc0fbb3c0001cb5b28

59 Mark Gurman, 'Apple Risks Chinese Users Souring on iPhones Ahead of Launch', Bloomberg, 8 September 2023. https://www.bloomberg. com/news/articles/2023-09-08/apple-grapples-with-turmoil-in-china-days-before-iphone-15-launch

60   Brenda Goh, 'Apple's Cook opens new store in Shanghai to large crowds as sales fall', Reuters, 21 March 2024. https://www.reuters.com/technology/apples-ceo-cook-opens-new-store-shanghai-2024-03-21/

61   Liu Xin, Yang Sheng and Xing Xiaojing, 'GT Exclusive: Mainland tax, natural resource authorities inspect Foxconn companies in several provinces', *Global Times*, 22 October 2023. https://www.globaltimes.cn/page/202310/1300340.shtml

62   Kerry Brown, Justin Hempson-Jones and Jessica Pennisi, 'Investment Across the Taiwan Strait. How Taiwan's Relationship with China Affects its Position in the Global Economy', Royal Institute of International Affairs, November 2010. https://www.kerry-brown.co.uk/wp-content/uploads/2020/01/website-8.pdf

63   Ibid., p. 13.

64   Bonnie Glaser and Jeremy Mark, 'Taiwan And China Are Locked In Economic Co-Dependence', *Foreign Policy*, 14 April 2021. https://foreignpolicy.com/2021/04/14/taiwan-china-econonomic-codependence/

65   'China may be losing its sway over Taiwanese business', *The Economist*, 15 January 2024. https://www.economist.com/business/2024/01/15/china-may-be-losing-its-sway-over-taiwanese-business

66   Samson Hill and Argin Chang, 'Tycoon targeted by China Speaks Out Against Taiwan Independence', Bloomberg, 30 November 2021. https://www.bloomberg.com/news/articles/2021-11-30/tycoon-targeted-by-china-speaks-out-against-taiwan-independence

67   Reuters, 'Taiwan proposes tightening law to prevent China stealing technology', 29 November 2021. https://www.reuters.com/article/us-china-taiwan-idUSKBN1XE0YV

68   *The Economist*, 15 January 2015.

69   Laura He and Martha Zhou, 'Tim Cook is on a charm offensive in China to revive flagging iPhone sales', CNN, 21 March 2024. https://edition.cnn.com/2024/03/21/tech/china-apple-tim-cook-shanghai-visit-intl-hnk/index.html

70   Aaron Tilley, Liza Lin and Jeff Horwitz, 'China Orders Apple to Remove Popular Messaging Apps', *The Wall Street Journal*, 19 April 2024. https://www.wsj.com/tech/apple-removes-whatsapp-threads-from-china-app-store-on-government-orders-a0c02100

71   Rajesh Roy and Yang Jie, 'Apple Aims to Make a Quarter of the World's iPhones in India', *The Wall Street Journal*, 8 December 2023. https://www.wsj.com/tech/apple-aims-to-make-a-quarter-of-the-worlds-iphones-in-india-ab7f6342

Chapter 15:
China Rocks!

1   Lora Kolodny, 'Elon Musk says "China Rocks" while the US is full of "complacency and entitlement"', CNBC, 31 July 2020. https://www.cnbc.

com/2020/07/31/tesla-ceo-elon-musk-china-rocks-us-full-of-entitlement.
html

2 Mathew Campbell, Chunying Zhang, Haze Fan, David Stringer and Emma O'Brian, 'Elon Musk Loves China, and China Loves Him Back – For Now', Bloomberg, 13 January 2021. https://www.bloomberg.com/news/features/2021-01-13/china-loves-elon-musk-and-tesla-tsla-how-long-will-that-last

3 Ibid.

4 Jane Li, 'Elon Musk railed against US covid controls – but not Shanghai's lockdown', *Quartz*, 19 April 2022. https://qz.com/2156327/elon-musk-railed-against-us-covid-controls-but-not-shanghai-lockdown

5 'Chinese ministers meet Elon Musk, with China-US cooperation, NEVs in focus', *Global Times*, 31 May 2023. https://www.globaltimes.cn/page/202305/1291685.shtml

6 Reuters, 'Analysis: Tesla's China expansion hits speed bump amid industry overcapacity', 16 June 2023. https://www.reuters.com/business/autos-transportation/teslas-china-expansion-hits-speed-bump-amid-industry-overcapacity-2023-06-16/

7 'Tesla Global VP Grace Tao: Half of Global Delivery From Shanghai Gigafactory', *Pandaily*, 20 June 2022. https://pandaily.com/tesla-global-vp-grace-tao-half-of-global-delivery-from-shanghai-gigafactory/

8 Ibid.

9 Arjun Kharpal, 'Elon Musk wrapped up his first visit to China in years. Here's what the Tesla CEO was up to', CNBC, 1 June 2023. https://www.cnbc.com/2023/06/01/elon-musk-china-visit-heres-what-the-tesla-ceo-was-up-to.html

10 Shunsuke Tabeta, 'Bill Gates, Elon Musk and more flock to China despite U.S. rift', *Nikkei Asia*, 29 June 2023. https://asia.nikkei.com/Politics/International-relations/US-China-tensions/Bill-Gates-Elon-Musk-and-more-flock-to-China-despite-U.S.-rift

11 Qi Xijia, 'Musk concludes 44-hour intensive visit to China', *Global Times*, 1 June 2023. https://www.globaltimes.cn/page/202306/1291795.shtml

12 Martin Quinn Pollard, 'Elon Musk greeted with flattery and feasts during China trip', Reuters, 31 May 2023. https://www.reuters.com/business/elon-musk-visits-chinas-commerce-ministry-2023-05-31/

13 'Chinese ministers meet Elon Musk, with China-US cooperation, NEVs in focus', *Global Times*, 31 May 2023. https://www.globaltimes.cn/page/202305/1291685.shtml

14 Anna Edgerton, 'Musk Believes China Is on "Team Humanity" When It Comes To AI', Bloomberg, 13 July 2023. https://www.bloomberg.com/news/articles/2023-07-13/musk-believes-china-is-on-team-humanity-when-it-comes-to-ai

15 Anmar Frangoul, 'Elon Musk praises China's "very strong" A.I. credentials', CNBC, 6 July 2023. https://www.cnbc.com/2023/07/06/elon-musk-china-will-have-a-very-strong-ai-capability.html

16 Peter Hoskins and Derek Cai, 'Taiwan tells Elon Musk it is not for

sale', BBC Online, 15 September 2023. https://www.bbc.co.uk/news/world-asia-china-66816507

17   Annabelle Liang, 'Elon Musk wades into China and Taiwan tensions', BBC Online, 10 October 2022. https://www.bbc.co.uk/news/business-63196452

18   For fuller details of the AMC deal with the Chinese government, see Jim Mann, *Beijing Jeep: The Short, Unhappy Romance of American Business in China* (New York: Simon and Schuster, 1989), pp. 222–35.

19   Elaine Qiang, 'How will Elon Musk juggle running Twitter with his interests in China?', ABC News, 4 November 2022. https://www.abc.net.au/news/2022-11-05/elon-musk-twitter-china-tesla-interests-free-speech/101615936

20   Will Oremus, 'Twitter regrets and glass houses: 8 things we learned from the Musk bio', *The Washington Post*, 20 September 2023. https://www.washingtonpost.com/technology/2023/09/20/walter-isaacson-elon-musk-details/

21   Rohan Goswami, 'China's CCP warns Elon Musk against sharing Wuhan lab leak report', CNBC, 28 February 2023. https://www.cnbc.com/2023/02/28/chinas-ccp-warns-elon-musk-against-sharing-wuhan-lab-leak-report.html

22   Bloomberg, 'Dimon Says JPMorgan Will Be in China for Good and Bad Times', 31 May 2023. https://www.bloomberg.com/news/articles/2023-05-31/dimon-says-jpmorgan-will-be-in-china-for-good-and-bad-times

23   Reuters, 'JPMorgan's Dimon says US, China need "real engagement"', 31 May 2023. https://www.reuters.com/business/finance/jpmorgans-dimon-says-us-china-need-have-real-engagement-2023-05-31/

24   Hu Weijia, 'Blaming China is Washington's political game but won't heal US economic woes', *Global Times*, 17 August 2023. https://www.globaltimes.cn/page/202308/1296498.shtml

25   Rupert Neate, 'JP Morgan chief skips quarantine as he jets into Hong Kong', *The Guardian*, 16 November 2021. https://www.theguardian.com/business/2021/nov/16/jp-morgan-jamie-dimon-skips-quarantine-hong-kong

26   Cathy Chan and David Scanlan, 'Wall Street Loves China More Than Ever', Bloomberg, 5 January 2022. https://www.bloomberg.com/news/articles/2022-01-05/stock-market-wall-street-loves-china-more-than-ever-amid-political-turmoil

27   James T. Areddy, 'JP Morgan Wins Permission for Full Control of a Securities Business in China', *The Wall Street Journal*, 6 August 2021. https://www.wsj.com/articles/jp-morgan-wins-permission-for-full-control-of-a-securities-business-in-china-11628285229

28   'JPMorgan boss regrets saying bank will outlast Chinese Communist Party', BBC Online, 24 November 2021. https://www.bbc.co.uk/news/business-59409508

29   Alex Capri, 'Wall Street's Love Affair With China Is Headed For Trouble', *Forbes*, 17 September 2021. https://www.forbes.com/sites/alexcapri/2021/09/17/wall-streets-love-affair-with-china-is-headed-for-trouble/

30   Jack Pitcher and Rebecca Feng, 'Wall Street's China Dreams Slip Away', *The Wall Street Journal*, 23 August 2023. https://www.wsj.com/finance/stocks/wall-streets-china-dreams-slip-away-f68ac708

31 Bloomberg, 'Five big US banks "drawn to strong economic perform-ance like moths to a flame", increased exposure to China by 10 per cent to US$78 billion last year', *South China Morning Post*, 17 March 2021. https://www.scmp.com/business/china-business/article/3125723/five-big-us-banks-drawn-strong-economic-performance-moths

32 Anne Stevenson-Yang, 'Will The VIE Structure Die? What Hong Kong And Alibaba Have In Common', *Forbes*, 27 July 2021. https://www.forbes.com/sites/annestevenson-yang/2021/07/27/will-the-vie-structure-die-what-hong-kong-and-alibaba-have-in-common/

33 Kaye Wiggins and Will Louch, 'Goldman Sachs bought UK and US companies using Chinese state funds', *Financial Times*, 29 August 2023. https://www.ft.com/content/792fae47-8e2f-4363-99e9-176b33ccc09a?shareType=nongift

34 Heather Sommerville, 'China's Military and Surveillance Capabilities Have Been Boosted by U.S. Funds, House Report Says', *The Wall Street Journal*, 8 February 2024. https://www.wsj.com/tech/top-u-s-venture-firms-funded-blacklisted-chinese-companies-house-committee-says-d86aaf25?mod=itp_wsj,djemITP_h

35 Xie Yu and Julie Zhu, 'Exclusive: China invites global investors for rare meet-ing as economy sputters', Reuters, 14 July 2023. https://www.reuters.com/world/asia-pacific/china-invites-global-investors-rare-meeting-economy-sputters-sources-2023-07-14/

36 Ruchir Sharma, 'Boomy talk about the Chinese economy is a charade', *Financial Times*, 21 May 2023. https://www.ft.com/content/26f82e8f-654f-4bb5-b1a2-1256f7d5f46d

37 Kaye Wiggins, 'Wall Street banks are trying not to upset China on list-ings', *Financial Times*, 15 January 2024. https://www.ft.com/content/3b7125f2-8ee2-47b1-b3d6-acdee8e53991?shareType=nongift

38 Dan Southerland, 'U.S. Business Urged to Invest in China', *The Washington Post*, 16 November 1986. https://www.washingtonpost.com/archive/business/1986/11/16/us-business-urged-to-invest-in-china/3aa15de9-1e99-43f1-b691-36ed48a36af1/

39 Joe Cash and Brenda Goh, 'AstraZeneca will seek to "love the Communist Party", its China boss says', Reuters, 19 May 2023. https://www.reuters.com/business/healthcare-pharmaceuticals/astrazenecas-china-boss-says-drugmaker-will-seek-love-communist-party-2023-05-19/

40 Cheng Leng and Ryan McMorrow, 'EY China staff encouraged to wear com-munist party badges', *Financial Times*, 27 February 2023. https://www.ft.com/content/cfa55e7d-1294-4c4f-85cc-03c6ec63550a?shareType=nongift

41 Ibid.

42 Olaf Storbeck and Eleanor Olcott, 'Adidas goes local as it fights to over-come crisis in China', *Financial Times*, 24 April 2023. https://www.ft.com/content/ae53b8af-4741-43ba-bd31-a1b539728f9f

43 Andrew Cainey and Christiane Prange, *Xiconomics: What China's Dual Circulation Strategy Means for Global Business* (Newcastle-Upon-Tyne: Agenda Publishing, 2023), pp. 149–58.

44   Charles Hutzler and Lingling Wei, 'What it took to get Biden and Xi to the table', *The Wall Street Journal*, 12 November 2023. https://www.wsj.com/world/china/what-it-took-to-get-biden-and-xi-to-the-table-b7a899c9

45   Ryan McMorrow and Demetri Sevastopulo, 'UK business elite welcomes Xi Jinping with standing ovation', *Financial Times*, 16 November 2023. https://www.ft.com/content/a8633d7f-f785-4195-b0b2-0ea9506968c9

46   Musk's 16 November 2023 Twitter/X posting can be accessed at https://twitter.com/elonmusk/status/1725281372854428076?lang=en

47   Reuters, 'Tesla sues Chinese firm over tech secret infringement – Chinese state media', 5 September 2023. https://www.reuters.com/business/autos-transportation/tesla-sues-chinese-firm-over-tech-secret-infringement-chinese-state-media-2023-09-05/

48   Bloomberg, 'Musk Says Tesla Would Be Shut Down If Cars Used for Spying', 20 March 2021. https://www.bloomberg.com/news/articles/2021-03-20/tesla-s-musk-says-company-would-be-shut-if-cars-used-for-spying

Chapter 16:
Hong Kong's Descent into Tyranny

1   Sammy Heung, 'National security law in Hong Kong: 8 wanted suspects should be treated like "rats in the street", city leader John Lee', *South China Morning Post*, 7 July 2023. https://www.scmp.com/news/hong-kong/politics/article/3226973/national-security-law-hong-kong-8-wanted-suspects-should-be-treated-rats-street-city-leader-john-lee

2   'The world should study China's crushing of Hong Kong's freedoms', *The Economist*, 24 August 2023. https://www.economist.com/china/2023/08/24/the-world-should-study-chinas-crushing-of-hong-kongs-freedoms

3   Pak Yiu, 'Hong Kong squeezes activists in exile by interrogating relatives', *Nikkei Asia*, 30 August 2023. https://asia.nikkei.com/Spotlight/Hong-Kong-security-law/Hong-Kong-squeezes-activists-in-exile-by-interrogating-relatives

4   Pak Yiu, 'Hong Kong seeks to claw back reputation with busy month of events', *Nikkei Asia*, 1 March 2023. https://asia.nikkei.com/Politics/Hong-Kong-seeks-to-claw-back-reputation-with-busy-month-of-events

5   To get the full flavour of 'Happy Hong Kong', see the official website, which contains links to the various activities offered and the promotional video. https://www.happyhk.gov.hk/en/about.html

6   Som Lok Kei, 'Hong Kong therapists convicted of sedition over children's books', *The Guardian*, 7 September 2022. https://www.theguardian.com/world/2022/sep/07/hong-kong-authors-of-childrens-books-sheep-wolves-convicted-of-sedition

7   Didi Tang, 'Winnie the Pooh horror film dropped in Hong Kong after "Xi comparisons"', *The Times*, 22 March 2023. https://www.thetimes.co.uk/article/8c9bbe9e-c895-11ed-82d6-a363978c4bcb?shareToken=feda-795f2646925315a6e4349bb4a7f1

8   Didi Tang, 'Hong Kong Simpsons fans can't watch China episode', *The Times*, 6 February 2023. https://www.thetimes.co.uk/article/663ca366-a62c-11ed-9311-522a2d54b6fd?shareToken=1f8b704b88b6ef8bdb28a0eed42c00f0

9   Jessie Pang, 'Hong Kong court rejects challenge by jailed media tycoon Lai over British lawyer', Reuters, 19 May 2023. https://www.reuters.com/world/china/hong-kong-court-rejects-challenge-by-jailed-media-tycoon-lai-over-british-lawyer-2023-05-19/

10   Jessie Pang, 'Hong Kong court convicts 3 members of Tiananmen vigil group for security offence', Reuters, 4 March 2023. https://www.reuters.com/world/china/3-hong-kong-tiananmen-vigil-group-members-found-guilty-security-offence-2023-03-04/

11   Austin Ramzy, 'Hong Kong Police Seize Statue Commemorating Tiananmen Massacre', *The Wall Street Journal*, 5 May 2023. https://www.wsj.com/articles/hong-kong-police-seize-statue-commemorating-tiananmen-massacre-29cfb98a

12   Kari Soo Lindberg, 'Hong Kong Public Libraries Purge Books on Tiananmen Crackdown', Bloomberg, 16 May 2023. https://www.bloomberg.com/news/articles/2023-05-16/hong-kong-public-libraries-purge-books-on-tiananmen-crackdown

13   Kelly Ho, 'Hong Kong's John Lee unable to give concrete answer on whether mourning Tiananmen crackdown is legal', *Hong Kong Free Press*, 30 May 2023. https://hongkongfp.com/2023/05/30/hong-kongs-john-lee-unable-to-give-concrete-answer-on-whether-mourning-tiananmen-crackdown-is-legal/

14   David Rose, 'Hong Kong sends 5,000 police to crush Tiananmen Square remembrance', *The Times*, 5 June 2023. https://www.thetimes.co.uk/article/hong-kong-police-arrest-20-people-marking-anniversary-of-tiananmen-square-cf8nj9qfm

15   Hillary Leung, 'Man with white flowers arrested in Hong Kong on China's National Day holiday', *Hong Kong Free Press*, 3 October 2023. https://hongkongfp.com/2023/10/03/man-with-white-flowers-arrested-in-hong-kong-on-chinas-national-day-holiday/

16   Mia Castagnone, Enoch Yiu, Pearl Liu and Peggy Sito, 'John Lee urges global banks to "get in front" of the queue for business as Hong Kong "puts the worst" behind it', *South China Morning Post*, 2 November 2022. https://www.scmp.com/business/banking-finance/article/3198056/hkmas-financial-summit-kicks-publicly-hong-kong-today-marking-citys-reopening-global-capital

17   Ibid.

18   Nora McGreevy, 'Major Contemporary Art Museum Debuts in Hong Kong Amid Censorship Concerns', *Smithsonian Magazine*, 16 November 2021. https://www.smithsonianmag.com/smart-news/m-plus-museum-debuts-in-hong-kong-amid-censorship-concerns-180979070/

19   Vivian Wang, 'Hong Kong's M+ Museum Is Finally Open. It's Already in Danger', *The New York Times*, 12 November 2021. https://www.nytimes.com/2021/11/12/arts/design/hong-kong-m-museum-censorship.html

20 Kari Soo Lindberg and Stella Ko, 'Hong Kong's New Museum Tries to Please Art World – and Beijing', Bloomberg, 12 November 2021. https://www.bloomberg.com/news/features/2021-11-12/the-politics-of-hong-kong-s-new-modern-art-museum-m

21 Ibid.

22 Bloomberg, 'The Silencing of Hong Kong's Analysts', 23 November 2022. https://www.bloomberg.com/news/articles/2022-11-23/china-s-grip-on-hong-kong-means-analysts-are-censoring-more-of-their-own-work

23 Irene Chan, 'Over half of Hong Kong professionals considering leaving the city within 5 years, survey finds', *Hong Kong Free Press*, 14 October 2023. https://hongkongfp.com/2023/10/04/over-half-of-hong-kong-professionals-considering-leaving-the-city-within-5-years-survey-finds/

24 Chris Lau, 'This city never slept, but with China tightening its grip, is the party over?', CNN Business, 3 November 2023. https://edition.cnn.com/2023/11/03/economy/hong-kong-nightlife-china-dst-intl-hnk/index.html

25 Pak Yiu and Echo Wong, 'Multinationals turn away from Hong Kong for dispute resolution', *Nikkei Asia*, 8 June 2023. https://asia.nikkei.com/Spotlight/Hong-Kong-security-law/Multinationals-turn-away-from-Hong-Kong-for-dispute-resolution

26 Nathaniel Taplin, 'Why Hong Kong's Makeover Will Founder', *The Wall Street Journal*, 8 November 2022. https://www.wsj.com/articles/why-hong-kongs-makeover-will-founder-11667908502

27 See the online exhibition guide to 'The Road of Rejuvenation', a permanent exhibition at the National Museum of China, which captures these themes well. http://en.chnmuseum.cn/exhibition/current_exhibitions_648/201911/t20191120_171616.html

28 Chris Patten, *East and West* (London: Macmillan, 1998), p. 91.

29 Arthur R. Kroeber, *China's Economy: What Everyone Needs to Know* (New York: Oxford University Press, 2020), p. 83.

30 Tom Burgis, 'Queensbury Group probed over use of "secrecy jurisdictions"', *Financial Times*, 4 May 2015. https://www.ft.com/content/a95e8252-f015-11e4-ab73-00144feab7de

31 Thomas Fox-Brewster, 'Did China Order Hackers to Cripple the Hong Kong protest?', Motherboard, 5 November 2014. https://www.vice.com/en_us/article/539wnz/inside-the-unending-cyber-siege-of-hong-kong

32 Eli Binder, 'Hong Kong Protesters Spy a New Enemy: Lampposts', *The Wall Street Journal*, 30 August 2019. https://www.wsj.com/articles/hong-kong-protesters-spy-a-new-enemy-lampposts-11567161002

33 Noah Sin, 'Explainer: How important is Hong Kong to the rest of China?', Reuters, 5 September 2019. https://www.reuters.com/article/us-hongkong-protests-markets-explainer-idUSKCN1VP35H

34 'A new national security bill to intimidate Hong Kong', *The Economist*, 2 July 2020. https://www.economist.com/china/2020/07/02/a-new-national-security-bill-to-intimidate-hong-kong?frsc=dg%7Ce

35 'China's draconian security law for Hong Kong buries one country

two systems', *The Economist*, 1 July 2020. https://www.economist.com/leaders/2020/07/02/chinas-draconian-security-law-for-hong-kong-buries-one-country-two-systems

36 Stephen Morris and Attracta Mooney, 'HSBC and StanChart's support for Hong Kong law provokes ire', *Financial Times*, 4 June 2020. https://www.ft.com/content/9fee072d-b210-4a0b-b610-39bd25c57dab

37 Helen Davidson, 'Hong Kong's article 23: what is the new national security law and what will it mean for human rights?', *The Guardian*, 30 January 2024. https://www.theguardian.com/world/2024/jan/30/hong-kong-article-23-new-national-security-laws-explained-what-do-they-mean

38 For a comprehensive overview of Hong Kong's new security law, see Amnesty International's 22 March 2024 briefing, 'What is Hong Kong's Article 23 law. 10 things you need to know'. https://www.amnesty.org/en/latest/news/2024/03/what-is-hong-kongs-article-23-law-10-things-you-need-to-know/

39 Richard Lloyd Parry, 'Hong Kong election: Record low turnout in "patriots only" poll', *The Times*, 11 December 2023. https://www.thetimes.co.uk/article/fc36eb01-b9e6-45db-a237-24f8b5e1d2d3?shareToken=d577de55930d2003604faccb3d0f156f

40 Alan Wong, 'Prominent Hong Kong activist jumps bail to stay in Canada', Bloomberg, 4 December 2023. https://www.bloomberg.com/news/articles/2023-12-04/hong-kong-activist-seeks-asylum-in-canada-in-self-imposed-exile

41 See Elaine Yu, 'The Corporate Retreat From Hong Kong is accelerating', *The Wall Street Journal*, 24 October 2023. https://www.wsj.com/world/asia/hong-kong-china-corporate-headquarters-retreat-10454a9a. Also, Chan Ho-Him, 'How China's slowdown is deepening Hong Kong's "existential crisis"', *Financial Times*, 18 December 2023. https://www.ft.com/content/e4d8640e-91a6-4b70-aae3-6ab9a879d1dc?shareType=nongift

42 Hans Tse, 'Mainland court orders on civil, commercial matters can now be enforced in Hong Kong', *Hong Kong Free Press*, 29 January 2024. https://hongkongfp.com/2024/01/29/mainland-court-orders-on-civil-commercial-matters-can-now-be-enforced-in-hong-kong/

43 Kaye Wiggins, Leo Lewis and Joe Leahy, 'Deloitte and KPMG ask staff to use burner phones for Hong Kong trips', *Financial Times*, 27 November 2023. https://www.ft.com/content/eace699c-ce75-485b-ac14-e6c10375fdcc

Chapter 17:
The Humiliation of the World's Local Bank

1 A full video of the Foreign Affairs Committee grilling of HSBC executives can be accessed at the parliamentlive.tv website, https://parliamentlive.tv/event/index/c1b8e4f0-d3b5-4b81-8851-b738445b880c. A transcript of the session is available at https://committees.parliament.uk/oralevidence/1580/html/

2 Louisa Clarence-Smith and Ben Martin, 'Pressure grows on HSBC over Hong Kong activist Ted Hui', *The Times*, 8 February 2021. https://

www.thetimes.co.uk/article/pressure-grows-on-hsbc-over-hong-kong-activist-ted-hui-908x0vnxr

3   Helen Davidson, 'Hong Kong police raid church hours after pastor said HSBC froze accounts', *The Guardian*, 8 December 2020. https://www.theguardian.com/world/2020/dec/08/hong-kong-church-pastor-says-hsbc-froze-personal-and-charity-bank-accounts

4   Denise Tsang and Clifford Lo, 'Hong Kong church that helped protesters sees bank accounts frozen, allegedly in relation to crowdfunding campaign', *South China Morning Post*, 8 December 2020. https://www.scmp.com/news/hong-kong/politics/article/3113004/hong-kong-church-helped-protesters-sees-bank-accounts

5   Kris Cheng, '4 Hong Kong protester support group arrestees released on bail', *Hong Kong Free Press*, 20 December 2019. https://hongkongfp.com/2019/12/20/four-hong-kong-protester-support-group-arrestees-released-bail/

6   Primrose Riordan, 'HSBC and StanChart publicly back China's Hong Kong security law', *Financial Times*, 4 June 2020. https://www.ft.com/content/213c0e2c-f1c7-4637-a0b9-4c3f72709d52

7   Reuters, 'Former HK leader calls out HSBC following UK criticism of security law', 29 May 2020. https://www.reuters.com/article/us-hongkong-protests-hsbc-hldg-idUSKBN2351K3

8   HSBC's version of its history can be accessed at the company's website, 'Our history. Supporting our customers for more than 150 years'. https://www.hsbc.com/who-we-are/our-history

9   Jonathan Dimbleby, *The Last Governor: Chris Patten and the Handover of Hong Kong* (London: Little, Brown and Company, 1997), pp. 225–6.

10   Aruna Viswanatha and Brett Wolf, 'HSBC to pay $1.9 billion U.S. fine in money-laundering case', Reuters, 11 December 2012. https://www.reuters.com/article/us-hsbc-probe-idUSBRE8BA05M20121211

11   See Financial Conduct Authority (FCA) press release, 'FCA fines HSBC Bank plc £63.9 million for deficient transaction monitoring controls', 6 May 2022. https://www.fca.org.uk/news/press-releases/fca-fines-hsbc-bank-plc-deficient-transaction-monitoring-controls

12   For a more detailed breakdown of HSBC's profits by region and business, see the company's Annual Results 2022, available at https://www.hsbc.com/investors/results-and-announcements/all-reporting/annual-results-2022-quick-read

13   Stephen Morris, 'HSBC relocates top leadership from London to Hong Kong', *Financial Times*, 14 April 2021. https://www.ft.com/content/a487af1b-bea1-4b4e-865b-2f267abb10e5

14   Details of HSBC's business in mainland China are available on the company's website, 'HSBC in mainland China', at https://www.about.hsbc.com.cn/hsbc-in-china

15   Karen Freifeld and Steve Stecklow, 'Exclusive: HSBC probe helped lead to U.S. charges against Huawei CFO', Reuters, 26 February 2019. https://www.reuters.com/article/cbusiness-us-huawei-hsbc-exclusive-idCAKCN1QF1IA-OCABS

16 Ibid.
17 David Crow, Henny Sender and James Kynge, 'HSBC tells China it is not to blame for arrest of Huawei's CEO', *Financial Times*, 30 June 2019. https://www.ft.com/content/c832a476-9983-11e9-8cfb-30c211dcd229
18 Kalyeena Makortoff, 'HSBC boss John Flint resigns by "mutual agreement"', *The Guardian*, 5 August 2019. https://www.theguardian.com/business/2019/aug/05/hsbc-boss-john-flint-resigns-by-mutual-agreement
19 Sumeet Chatterjee and Engen Tham, 'How Beijing humbled Britain's mighty HSBC', Reuters, 28 June 2021. https://www.reuters.com/investigates/special-report/hsbc-china-politics/
20 Ibid.
21 Stephen Morris, Henry Sender and Laura Noonan, 'HSBC wobbles on a geopolitical tightrope', *Financial Times*, 10 June 2020. https://www.ft.com/content/cc35f8e2-83af-4225-826c-b2d99e51ee5e?shareType=nongift
22 Reuters, 28 June 2021.
23 *Financial Times*, 10 June 2020.
24 Stephen Morris and Tabby Kinder, 'HSBC installs Communist party committee in Chinese investment bank', *Financial Times*, 21 July 2022. https://www.ft.com/content/eac99fd9-0c30-4141-821a-45348f61c113
25 Ibid.
26 Chen Qingqing, 'Concern over Alibaba founder's Party membership lack of knowledge of CPC grass roots functions: experts', *Global Times* (via the *People's Daily*), 28 November 2018. http://en.people.cn/n3/2018/1128/c90000-9522707.html
27 Ibid.
28 Jennifer Hughes, 'China's Communist party writes itself into company law', *Financial Times*, 14 August 2017. https://www.ft.com/content/a4b28218-80db-11e7-94e2-c5b903247afd
29 Xi Jinping, *The Governance of China*, vol. II (Beijing: Foreign Languages Press, 2017), p. 288.
30 Keith Bradsher and Joy Dong, 'Xi Jinping Is Asserting Tighter Control of Finance in China', *The New York Times*, 5 December 2023. https://www.nytimes.com/2023/12/05/business/china-finance-xi-jinping.html?utm_source=substack&utm_medium=email
31 Michael Martina, 'Exclusive: In China, the Party's push for influence inside foreign firms stirs fears', Reuters, 24 August 2017. https://www.reuters.com/article/us-china-congress-companies-idUSKCN1B40JU
32 See HSBC's announcement of the appointment of Lord Udny-Lister, 'HSBC appoints Senior Adviser to the Group Chairman', 17 September 2021. https://www.hsbc.com/news-and-views/news/media-releases/2021/hsbc-appoints-senior-adviser-to-the-group-chairman. Also the UK Government's Office of the Advisory Committee on Business Appointments 7 December 2022 advice to Lord Udny-Lister on his appointment at https://www.gov.uk/government/publications/udny-lister-edward-special-adviser-at-no10-cabinet-office-acoba-advice/advice-letter-lord-udny-lister-senior-adviser-hsbc

33 Gabriel Pogrund and Emanuele Milolo, 'Revealed: Johnson's aide Edward Lister linked to both sides in Chinese embassy deal', *The Times*, 7 February 2021. https://www.thetimes.co.uk/article/revealed-johnsons-aide-edward-lister-linked-to-both-sides-in-chinese-embassy-deal-tswqbpz62

34 See the Chinese Embassy news release, Ambassador Liu Xiaoming Meets with Sir Edward Lister, Non-Executive Director at the Foreign & Commonwealth Office', 6 July 2018. http://gb.china-embassy.gov.cn/eng/tpxw/201807/t20180709_3145078.htm

35 Jim Pickard and Georg Hammond, 'Double life of Johnson's ally raises awkward conflict of interest questions', *Financial Times*, 30 April 2021. https://www.ft.com/content/4382aa0f-4784-4b21-a775-c87091f9ba31

36 Stephen Morris, 'HSBC shareholders reject Ping An-backed split proposal at AGM', *Financial Times*, 5 May 2023. https://www.ft.com/content/2c1815bc-77b6-48ba-9313-0ba47607fee5?shareType=nongift

37 Kelvin Soh and Denny Thomas, 'Thai group buys $9.4 billion Ping An stake from HSBC', Reuters, 5 December 2012. https://www.reuters.com/article/us-hsbc-pingan-idUSBRE8B400V20121205

38 Josh Mitchell, Julie Steinberg and Elaine Yu, 'HSBC Rift With Top Shareholder Ping An Goes Back Years', *The Wall Street Journal*, 18 February 2023. https://www.wsj.com/articles/hsbc-rift-with-top-shareholder-ping-an-goes-back-years-f3bba953

39 Jill Treaner, 'HSBC's global network "destroys £17 bn of value", says shareholder', *The Times*, 28 August 2022. https://www.thetimes.co.uk/article/hsbcs-global-network-destroys-17bn-of-value-says-shareholder-hzqdjjght

40 Primrose Riordan and Nicolle Liu, 'Hong Kong investors warn of action over HSBC dividends', *Financial Times*, 5 April 2020. https://www.ft.com/content/3681a998-8164-4fd1-a5e5-ae54f56a3b70

41 See HSBC's statement, 'HSBC response to statement by Ping An Asset Management Company', 19 March 2023, as published on the company's website. https://www.hsbc.com/news-and-views/news/media-releases/2023/hsbc-response-to-statement-by-ping-an-asset-management-company

42 Tabby Kinder and Stephen Morris, 'HSBC pledges to restore dividend to pre-pandemic levels', *Financial Times*, 1 August 2022. https://www.ft.com/content/1e271026-d19e-427c-a3df-4f9a219287de

43 For a fuller picture of Ping An's declared ownership, see the 'Major Shareholders' page of the investment relations section on the company website. https://group.pingan.com/investor_relations/major_shareholders.html#:~:text=The shareholding structure of the,nor de facto controlling party.

44 David Barboza, 'Billions in Hidden Riches for Family of Chinese Leader', *The New York Times*, 25 October 2012. https://www.nytimes.com/2012/10/26/business/global/family-of-wen-jiabao-holds-a-hidden-fortune-in-china.html. See also the *New York Times* 24 November 2012 graphic of Taihong's Ping An holdings at https://archive.nytimes.com/www.nytimes.com/interactive/2012/11/25/business/ping-ans-hidden-shareholders-friends-and-family-of-wen-jiabao.html

45 All Party Parliamentary Group on Hong Kong, 'Enquiry into British Banks Operating in Hong Kong', February 2023. https://www.hkinquiry.org/banking-report

46 Ibid.

47 Demetri Sevastopulo, Chan Ho-him and Kaye Wiggins, 'HSBC accused of siding with China in tussle over pension funds', *Financial Times*, 30 June 2023. https://www.ft.com/content/8e293ff2-25c7-4f78-8e6d-0e6d3eaa8686

48 Charles Capel and Harry Wilson, 'HSBC Hands Cowper-Coles Advisory Role After China Remarks Outcry', Bloomberg, 13 November 2023. https://www.bnnbloomberg.ca/hsbc-hands-cowper-coles-advisory-role-after-china-remarks-outcry-1.1997836

49 'UK business community says ready to deepen cooperation with China', *Xinhua*, 7 February 2024. https://english.news.cn/20240207/fd37905af8444723ae7481f489c5677a/c.html

50 Kaye Wiggins and Stephen Morris, 'HSBC shares fall most since 2020 after profits plummet by 80%', *Financial Times*, 21 February 2024. https://www.ft.com/content/05177d82-ac3b-4108-a958-e49bd482adcd?shareType=nongift

51 Ibid.

52 Shi Futian, 'China team reels from friendly fiasco', *China Daily*, 3 January 2024. https://www.chinadaily.com.cn/a/202401/03/WS6594b191a3105f21a507a3c2.html

53 Paul McNamara, 'AFC Asian Cup: Hong Kong boss Andersen hails team's "aggression" after they beat China for first time in 29 years', *South China Morning Post*, 2 January 2024. https://www.scmp.com/sport/football/article/3246926/hong-kongs-footballers-beat-china-first-time-29-years

Chapter 18:
Football Fantasy

1 'Sun Jihai an unlikely inductee into English football's hall of fame', World Soccer, 23 October 2023. https://www.worldsoccer.com/world-soccer-latest/sun-jihai-an-unlikely-inductee-into-english-footballs-hall-of-fame-365387

2 Sean Williams, 'China's own goal', *The Wire China*, 28 March 2021. https://www.thewirechina.com/2021/03/28/chinas-own-goal/

3 Rob Harris, 'Chinese investors buy Premier League club Southampton', Associated Press, 14 August 2017. https://apnews.com/chinese-investors-buy-premier-league-club-southampton-3d324e0811be46959ad065e2075fed1e

4 Sui-Lee Wee, Ryan Mcmorrrow and Tariq Panja, 'China's Soccer Push Puts a Storied Team Under Murky Ownership', *The New York Times*, 16 November 2017. https://www.nytimes.com/2017/11/16/business/dealbook/china-soccer-acmilan-ownership.html

5 Murad Ahmed and James Fontanella-Khan, 'Berlusconi to sell AC Milan to Chinese investors', *Financial Times*, 5 July 2023. https://www.ft.com/content/ed1859de-42b0-11e6-9b66-0712b3873ae1

6   The full FIFA men's rankings can be accessed online at https://www.fifa.
       com/fifa-world-ranking/men?dateId=id11027

7   An English language translation of 'The Overall Chinese Football
       Reform and Development Programme (2015)', published by the State
       Council, can be accessed at the website of Wild East Football. https://
       wildeastfootball.net/wuhan-zall/read-chinese-footballs-50-point-reform-
       plan-in-full-exclusive-translation/

8   Ibid.

9   More details of the broader national fitness strategy can be found in a
       statement, 'China to implement national fitness program', released by
       the State Council on 23 June 2016. https://english.www.gov.cn/policies/
       latest_releases/2016/06/23/content_281475378214258.htm

10   Sidney Lang, 'China's soccer-mad President Xi Jinping's passion for "the
       beautiful game" sparked while a child', *South China Morning Post*, 23
       October 2015. https://www.scmp.com/print/news/china/policies-politics/
       article/1871444/chinas-soccer-mad-president-xi-jinpings-passion

11   Chris Buckley, 'President Xi's Great Chinese Soccer Dream', *The New York
       Times*, 4 January 2017. https://www.nytimes.com/2017/01/04/world/asia/
       china-soccer-xi-jinping.html

12   Jonathan White, 'US$28 million a year China boss Marcello Lippi second only
       to Manchester United's Jose Mourinho as best paid', *South China Morning
       Post*, 25 April 2018. https://www.scmp.com/sport/soccer/article/2143222/
       us28-million-year-china-boss-marcello-lippi-second-only-manchester

13   Amy Hawkins, 'Chinese football stars and officials held in Xi's cor-
       ruption crackdown', *The Guardian*, 18 March 2023. https://www.the
       guardian.com/world/2023/mar/18/chinese-stars-officials-held-xi-jinping-
       football-corruption-crackdown

14   Robert Calcutt, 'Chinese club ditched plans to build world's largest football
       stadium likened to Sydney Opera House', talkSPORT, 31 October 2023.
       https://talksport.com/football/1624011/guangzhou-fc-worlds-largest-
       football-stadium-abandoned/

15   See the Manchester City online announcement, 'City launch football
       education programme in China', 19 December 2017. https://www.
       mancity.com/news/club-news/club-news/2017/december/manchester-
       city-extends-football-education-offering-in-china

16   'AC Milan to open new Shanghai office to expand Chinese presence',
       SportsPro, 20 May 2021. https://www.sportspromedia.com/news/ac-milan-
       office-china-academy-pacificpine-sports-franco-baresi/?zephr_sso_ott=
       LXZNCQ

17   James Porteous, 'Messi to Hebei for €100m a year the latest crazy
       China football rumour – even as state media warns clubs "don't mort-
       gage your future"', *South China Morning Post*, 16 December 2016.
       https://www.scmp.com/sport/soccer/article/2055120/messi-hebei-
       eu100m-year-latest-crazy-china-football-rumour-even-state

18   'Antonio Conte: Chelsea manager says Chinese football is a "danger for
       all teams"', BBC Sport, 16 December 2016. https://www.bbc.co.uk/sport/
       football/38345426

19   Agence France-Presse, 'Chinese President Xi Jinping "not so sure" about national football team, says they were lucky to beat Thailand', *South China Morning Post*, 19 November 2023. https://www.scmp.com/sport/football/article/3242060/chinese-president-xi-jinping-not-so-sure-about-national-football-team-says-they-were-lucky-beat

20   Liu Chen, 'Corruption "everywhere" in Chinese football, ex-head of governing body says in TV confession', *South China Morning Post*, 10 January 2024. https://www.scmp.com/news/china/politics/article/3247967/corruption-everywhere-chinese-football-ex-cfa-boss-says-tv-confession

21   Ibid.

22   Ryan Woo, 'Former China soccer head jailed for life after corruption crackdown', Reuters, 26 March 2024. https://www.reuters.com/sports/soccer/ex-head-china-football-association-sentenced-life-prison-state-media-report-2024-03-26/

23   Qin Jianhang and Kelly Wang, 'In Depth: Scandal-Ridden Chinese Soccer Gets in Foul Trouble Again', *Caixin Global*, 27 April 2023. https://www.caixinglobal.com/2023-04-27/in-depth-scandal-ridden-chinese-soccer-gets-in-foul-trouble-again-102040646.html

24   Chun Han Wong, 'Why Does China Remain Terrible at Soccer? Xi Jinping Has One Answer', *The Wall Street Journal*, 10 January 2024. https://www.wsj.com/world/china/chinese-soccer-remains-terrible-xi-says-this-is-why-be78cbd9?st=3jgswjpduugpaeg&reflink=article_email_share

25   Tariq Panja, 'China's Soccer Experiment Was a Flop. It May Be Over', *The New York Times*, 29 March 2023. https://www.nytimes.com/2023/03/29/sports/soccer/china-soccer.html

26   Hannah Beech, 'The Chinese Sport's Machine's Single Goal: The Most Golds at Any Cost', *The New York Times*, 8 August 2021. https://www.nytimes.com/2021/07/29/world/asia/china-olympics.html

27   Stefan Szymanski, 'Why China doesn't dominate soccer', *The Washington Post*, 18 June 2018. https://www.washingtonpost.com/news/global-opinions/wp/2018/06/18/why-china-doesnt-dominate-soccer/

28   '"You play football with your head, and your legs are there to help you": Johan Cruyff in quotes', *The Guardian*, 24 March 2016. https://www.theguardian.com/football/2016/mar/24/you-play-football-with-your-head-and-your-legs-are-there-to-help-you-johan-cruyff-in-quotes

29   Andreas Sten-Ziemons, 'How China wants to become a football heavyweight', Deutsche Welle, 4 November 2023. https://www.dw.com/en/how-china-wants-to-become-a-football-heavyweight/a-63652825

30   Ibid.

31   Ibid.

32   William Langley and Leo Lewis, 'Lionel Messi apologises for Hong Kong no-show after Chinese backlash', *Financial Times*, 7 February 2024. https://www.ft.com/content/70a17d5a-cbe3-44cd-879e-f30b3564cc42

Chapter 19:
Can China Innovate?

1   Dr Jamie Gaida, Dr Jennifer Wong Leung, Stephan Robin, Danielle Cave and Danielle Pilgrim, 'ASPI's Critical Technology Tracker – Sensors & Biotech Updates', Australian Strategic Policy Institute, 22 September 2023. https://www.aspi.org.au/report/critical-technology-tracker

2   'Spending on R & D in China hit new high', the State Council, The People's Republic of China, 21 January 2023. http://english.www.gov.cn/archive/statistics/202301/21/content_WS63cb3422c6d0a757729e5f13.html

3   See the latest United States entry in the OECD database, 'Gross domestic spending on R&D', covering the period 2000–2022. https://data.oecd.org/rd/gross-domestic-spending-on-r-d.htm

4   Alex Joske, 'Hunting the Phoenix: The Chinese Communist Party's global search for technology and talent', Australian Strategic Policy Institute, 20 August 2020. https://www.aspi.org.au/report/hunting-phoenix

5   James Yin Kang, 'The Thousand Talents Plan is part of China's long quest to become the global scientific leader', The Conversation, 1 September 2020. https://theconversation.com/the-thousand-talents-plan-is-part-of-chinas-long-quest-to-become-the-global-scientific-leader-145100

6   Che Pan, 'China sets out new rules for generative AI, with Beijing emphasising healthy content and adherence to "socialist values"', South China Morning Post, 13 July 2023. https://www.scmp.com/tech/big-tech/article/3227576/china-sets-out-new-rules-generative-ai-beijing-emphasising-healthy-content-and-adherence-socialist

7   For example, see Daniel Susskind, 'Generative AI will upend the professions', Financial Times, 18 June 2023. https://www.ft.com/content/96a1877f-0bbb-48c7-be8f-4fed437810e8. Also, Martin Casado, 'AI has finally become transformative', The Wall Street Journal, 2 August 2023. https://www.wsj.com/articles/ai-has-finally-become-transformative-humans-scale-language-model-6a67e641

8   Eduardo Baptista, 'Baidu's Ernie writes poems but says it has insufficient information on Xi, tests show', Reuters, 20 March 2023. https://www.reuters.com/technology/baidus-ernie-writes-poems-says-it-has-insufficient-information-xi-tests-show-2023-03-20/

9   Coco Feng, 'Chinese search giant Baidu defends AI research after its ChatGPT-like Ernie Bot draws a turkey for Turkey', South China Morning Post, 23 Match 2023. https://www.scmp.com/tech/tech-trends/article/3214566/chinese-search-giant-baidu-defends-ai-research-capabilities-after-its-chatgpt-ernie-bot-draws-turkey

10   Ryan McMorrow and Nian Liu, 'China slaps security reviews on AI products as Alibaba unveils ChatGPT challenger', Financial Times, 11 April 2023. https://www.ft.com/content/755cc5dd-e6ce-4139-9110-0877f2b90072?shareType=nongift

11   Ibid.

12   Donie Sullivan, Curt Devine and Allison Gordon, 'China is using the

world's largest known online disinformation operation to harass Americans, a CNN review finds', CNN, 13 November 2023. https://edition.cnn.com/2023/11/13/us/china-online-disinformation-invs/index.html

13   'Deepfake It Until You Make It. Pro-Chinese Actors Promote AI-Generated Video Footage of Fictitious People In Online Influence Operation', *Graphika*, February 2023. https://public-assets.graphika.com/reports/graphika-report-deepfake-it-till-you-make-it.pdf

14   Cissy Zhou, 'Baidu to ensure AI won't "hallucinate" on sensitive topics: CEO', *Nikkei Asia*, 17 May 2023. https://asia.nikkei.com/Business/China-tech/Baidu-to-ensure-AI-won-t-hallucinate-on-sensitive-topics-CEO

15   Sylvia Zhuang, 'AI, superconductor experts joined Chinese summer leadership retreat in Beidaihe', *South China Morning Post*, 9 August 2023. https://www.scmp.com/news/china/politics/article/3230540/ai-supercon ductor-experts-joined-chinese-summer-leadership-retreat-beidaihe#

16   A full explanation of the FBI's fears can be found on their website, 'The China Threat: China Talent Plans Encourage Trade Secret Theft, Economic Espionage'. https://www.fbi.gov/investigate/counterintelligence/the-china-threat/chinese-talent-plans

17   Bloomberg, 'China's thousand talents plan key to seizing US expertise, intelligence officials say', *South China Morning Post*, 22 January 2018. https://www.scmp.com/news/china/policies-politics/article/2152005/chinas-thousand-talents-plan-key-seizing-us-expertise

18   Bloomberg, 'Spy Fears Prompt China to Censor Its Own Recruitment Drive', 18 September 2018. https://www.bloomberg.com/news/articles/2018-09-19/china-censors-mentions-of-thousand-talents-as-spy-fears-grow

19   Julie Zhu, Fanny Potkin, Eduardo Baptista and Michael Martina, 'Insight: China quietly recruits overseas chip talent as US tightens curbs', Reuters, 24 August 2023. https://www.reuters.com/technology/china-quietly-recruits-overseas-chip-talent-us-tightens-curbs-2023-08-24/

20   An overview of some of the highest profile recruits can be found in 'The Chinese scientists leaving top US universities to take up high-profile roles in China, boosting Beijing in its race for global talent', *South China Morning Post*, 27 January 2024. https://www.scmp.com/news/china/science/article/3249683/chinese-scientists-leaving-top-us-universities-take-high-profile-roles-china-boosting-beijing-its

21   Stephen Chen, 'After 20 years in UK, British chair professor joins China's hypersonic programme', *South China Morning Post*, 13 May 2023. https://www.scmp.com/news/china/science/article/3220360/after-20-years-uk-british-chair-professor-joins-chinas-hypersonic-programme

22   'China to strengthen basic research to develop "stuck neck" techs', CGTN, 26 February 2021. https://news.cgtn.com/news/2021-02-26/China-to-strengthen-basic-research-to-develop-stuck-neck-techs--YczwcBhPTq/index.html

23   Dennis Normile, 'A Beijing think tank review of Beijing's technological weaknesses. Then the report disappeared', *Science*, 8 February 2022. https://www.science.org/content/article/beijing-think-tank-offered-frank-review-china-s-technological-weaknesses-then-report

24   The Global AI Talent Tracker is accessible via the MacroPolo website –
      https://macropolo.org/digital-projects/the-global-ai-talent-tracker/

25   Donna Lu, 'China overtakes the US in scientific research output', *The
      Guardian*, 11 August 2022. https://www.theguardian.com/world/2022/
      aug/11/china-overtakes-the-us-in-scientific-research-output

26   Alex Ho, 'What do China's High Patent Numbers Really Mean?', Center for
      International Governance Innovation, 20 April 2021. https://www.cigion
      line.org/articles/what-do-chinas-high-patent-numbers-really-mean/

27   'Paper Mills. Research report by COPE and STM', Committee on Publication
      Ethics (COPE), June 2022. https://publicationethics.org/sites/default/files/
      paper-mills-cope-stm-research-report.pdf

28   For a fuller account of Elisabeth Bik's investigation, see Leonid Schneider,
      'The full-service paper mill and its Chinese customers', For Better Science,
      20 January 2020. https://forbetterscience.com/2020/01/24/the-full-service-
      paper-mill-and-its-chinese-customers/

29   Dennis Normile, 'High-profile Chinese scientist cleared of fraud and pla-
      giarism charges involving more than 60 papers', *Science*, 22 January 2021.
      https://www.science.org/content/article/high-profile-chinese-scientist-
      cleared-fraud-and-plagiarism-charges-involving-more-60

30   Elizabeth Bik's Twitter/X thread on the Cao Xuetao verdict can be accessed
      at https://twitter.com/MicrobiomDigest/status/1352368977142398977

31   The Sina.com report on Cao Xuetao's appointment, which also contains
      details of his Communist Party membership, 'Cao Xuetao is the president of
      Nankai University', 3 January 2018, can be accessed (in Chinese) from Sina.
      com. http://news.sina.com.cn/o/2018-01-03/doc-ifyqcsft9643641.shtml

32   Confirmation of Cao Xuetao's military rank, awarded when he was associ-
      ate president of the Second Military Medical University, can be found on
      his profile page at the Nankai University website. https://en.nankai.edu.
      cn/2020/1226/c22845a330557/page.htm

33   Su Weichu, 'Weekend Long Read: The Panic, Worry and Despair Gripping
      Chinese Young Researchers', *Caixin Global*, 8 April 2023. https://www.
      caixinglobal.com/2023-04-08/weekend-long-read-the-panic-worry-and-
      despair-gripping-chinese-researchers-102016739.html

34   Smriti Mallapaty, 'China bans cash rewards for publishing papers', *Nature*,
      25 February 2020. https://www.nature.com/articles/d41586-020-00574-8

35   Meredith Chen, 'China universities waste millions, fail to make real use
      of research, audit finds in indictment of tech-sufficiency drive', *South
      China Morning Post*, 9 August 2023. https://www.scmp.com/economy/
      china-economy/article/3230413/china-universities-waste-millions-fail-
      make-real-use-research-audit-finds-indictment-tech

36   Ibid.

37   Zeyi Yang, 'Corruption is sending shock waves through China's chipmaking
      industry', *MIT Technology Review*, 5 August 2022. https://www.technology-
      review.com/2022/08/05/1056975/corruption-chinas-chipmaking-industry/

38   For a taste of this debate, see Simon Winchester's biography of Joseph
      Needham, *The Man Who Loved China: The eccentric scientist who unlocked*

the mysteries of the Middle Kingdom (London: Harper Perennial, 2008), pp. 259–61.

39 Yasheng Huang, *The Rise and Fall of the East: How exams, autocracy, stability, and technology brought China success, and why they might lead to its decline* (New Haven and London: Yale University Press, 2023), p. 244.

40 Ibid., p. 276.

41 Calder Walton, *Spies: The Epic Intelligence War Between East and West* (London: Abacus Books, 2023), pp. 364–5.

42 Nick Marro, 'Foreign Company R&D: In China, For China', *China Business Review*, 1 June 2015. https://www.chinabusinessreview.com/foreign-com pany-rd-in-china-for-china/#:~:text=According%20to%20a%202013%20 KPMG,grown%20significantly%20in%20recent%20years.

43 Asa Fitch, 'Nvidia Warns of Sales Hit From New U.S. Chip Licensing Requirements for China', *The Wall Street Journal*, 31 August 2022. https://www.wsj.com/articles/nvidia-warns-of-sales-hit-from-new-u-s-chip-licens ing-requirements-for-china-11661984074?mod=article_inline

44 Qianer Liu, 'Chinese companies resort to repurposing Nvidia gaming chips for AI', *Financial Times*, 10 January 2024. https://www.ft.com/content/ eeea7c4d-71f0-454f-bd16-b2445cb3bbb0

45 Yvette To, 'China chases semi-conductor self-sufficiency', East Asia Forum, 22 February 2021. https://www.eastasiaforum.org/2021/02/22/china-chases-semiconductor-self-sufficiency/

46 Cheng Ting-Fang and Lauly Li, 'The great nanometer chip race', *Nikkei Asia*, 13 December 2023. https://asia.nikkei.com/Spotlight/The-Big-Story/ The-great-nanometer-chip-race?utm_campaign=IC_asia_daily_free&utm_ medium=email&utm_source=NA_newsletter&utm_content=article_link

47 Qing Na, 'Caixin China New Economy Index Plumbs Seven-Month Low', *Caixin Global*, 2 February 2024. https://www.caixinglobal.com/2024-02-02/ caixin-china-new-economy-index-plumbs-seven-month-low-102163198. html

Chapter 20:
Carbon Capture

1 Gregory C. Allen, 'China's New Strategy for Waging the Microchip Tech War', Center for Strategic and International Studies, 3 May 2023. https:// www.csis.org/analysis/chinas-new-strategy-waging-microchip-tech-war

2 Bloomberg, 'From Cheap Cash to Tax Breaks, EVs in China Get Lots of Love', 14 September 2023. https://www.bloomberg.com/news/articles/2023-09-14/ from-cheap-money-to-tax-breaks-evs-in-china-get-a-lot-of-love

3 Zeyi Yang, 'How did China come to dominate the world of electric cars', *MIT Technology Review*, 21 February 2023. https://www.technologyreview. com/2023/02/21/1068880/how-did-china-dominate-electric-cars-policy/

4 Bloomberg, 14 September 2023.

5 Ibid.

6   Keith Bradsher, 'China's E.V. Threat: A Carmaker That Loses $35,000 a Car', *The New York Times*, 10 October 2023. https://www.nytimes.com/2023/10/05/business/nio-china-electric-vehicles.html

7   Reuters, 'As EV costs tumble in China, an export wave builds', 19 April 2023. https://www.reuters.com/business/autos-transportation/ev-costs-tumble-china-an-export-wave-builds-2023-04-19/

8   Stefan Nicola, 'BYD Got €3.4 Billion Chinese Aid to Dominate EVs, Study Says', Bloomberg, 10 April 2024. https://www.bloomberg.com/news/articles/2024-04-10/byd-got-3-4-billion-chinese-aid-to-dominate-evs-study-says

9   Bloomberg, 'China's Abandoned, Obsolete Electric Cars Are Piling Up in Cities', 17 August 2023. https://www.bloomberg.com/features/2023-china-ev-graveyards/?embedded-checkout=true

10   Li Rongqian and Denise Jia, 'BYD Orders $689 Million of Auto Transport Ships', *Caixin Global*, 29 August 2022. https://www.caixinglobal.com/2022-10-29/byd-orders-689-million-of-auto-transport-ships-101957519.html

11   Alex Irwin-Hunt, 'How China is charging ahead in the EV race', *FDI Intelligence*, 8 March 2022. https://www.fdiintelligence.com/content/feature/how-china-is-charging-ahead-in-the-ev-race-80771

12   Harry Dempsey and Edward White, 'China's battery plant rush raises fears of global squeeze', *Financial Times*, 4 September 2023. https://www.ft.com/content/b6038e51-7b5b-4f97-a5da-9202e71562fc

13   Gloria Li, 'China's CATL cements position as EV battery leader with jump in profits', *Financial Times*, 10 March 2023. https://www.ft.com/content/babc6b3d-8339-4a73-b078-c4504cad076f?shareType=nongift

14   Kenji Kawase, 'CATL tops China's corporate subsidies list, outranking oil majors', Nikkei Asia, 6 June 2024. https://asia.nikkei.com/Business/China-tech/CATL-tops-China-s-corporate-subsidies-list-outranking-oil-majors#

15   Kevin Whitelaw, Albertino Torsoli and Alberto Nardelli, 'EU Escalates China Tensions With Probe to Ward Off Cheap EVs', Bloomberg, 13 September 2023. https://www.bloomberg.com/news/articles/2023-09-13/eu-starts-anti-subsidy-probe-into-chinese-electric-vehicles

16   Philip Blenkinsop, 'EU to investigate flood of Chinese electric cars, weigh tariffs', Reuters, 13 September 2023. https://www.reuters.com/world/europe/eu-launches-anti-subsidy-investigation-into-chinese-electric-vehicles-2023-09-13/

17   Joe Leahy and Gloria Lee, 'China attacks EU's naked protectionist act on electric cars', *Financial Times*, 14 September 2023. https://www.ft.com/content/ec9e501c-77d2-40e7-9993-8a84729a021f

18   Hans Van Der Berchard, 'German carmakers "afraid" of China retaliation, economy minister warns', *Politico*, 23 September 2023. https://www.politico.eu/article/german-carmakers-afraid-of-chinese-retaliation-economy-minister-warns/

19   Gavin Mcguire, 'Column: It's a bit rich of the EU to ding China over EV subsidies', Reuters, 14 September 2023. https://www.reuters.com/markets/commodities/its-bit-rich-eu-ding-china-over-ev-subsidies-2023-09-14/

20   *Financial Times*, 14 September 2023.

21   International Energy Agency, 'Global Supply Chains of EV Batteries', July 2022. https://iea.blob.core.windows.net/assets/4eb8c252-76b1-4710-8f5e-867e751c8dda/GlobalSupplyChainsofEVBatteries.pdf

22   Mathieu Rosemain, '"Chinese storm" looming over Europe's EV sector, Renault chairman warns', Reuters, 8 July 2023. https://www.reuters.com/business/autos-transportation/chinese-storm-looming-over-europes-ev-sector-renault-chairman-warns-2023-07-08/

23   Jasper Jolly, 'China's share of Europe's electric car market accelerates as UK leads sales', *The Guardian*, 4 September 2023. https://www.theguardian.com/business/2023/sep/04/china-europe-electric-car-market-uk-sales-mg-tesla

24   Ibid.

25   Peter Campbell and George Parker, 'Chinese-owned battery group involved in Tata UK gigafactory', *Financial Times*, 4 August 2023. https://www.ft.com/content/ce2bb0fb-a84d-4ff2-b29f-75538be45a3b

26   Ibid.

27   Jonathan Ames, 'Chinese electric cars "could bring UK roads to a standstill"', *The Times*, 30 July 2023. https://www.thetimes.co.uk/article/chinese-electric-cars-could-bring-uk-roads-to-a-standstill-pkd8qs323

28   Professor Jim Saker, 'Executive View: The Chinese Trojan Horse', Automotive Management Online, 3 August 2023. https://www.am-online.com/opinion/2023/07/21/executive-view-the-chinese-trojan-horse#:~:text=The%20threat%20of%20connected%20electric,in%20the%20debate%20over%202030.

29   David Ferris, 'Chip Shortage Threatens Biden's Electric Vehicle Plans, Commerce Secretary Says', *Scientific American*, 30 November 2021. https://www.scientificamerican.com/article/chip-shortage-threatens-bidens-electric-vehicle-plans-commerce-secretary-says/

30   Cheng Ting-Fang and Shunsuke Tabeta, 'Tesla cars face more entry bans in China as "security concerns" accelerate', *Nikkei Asia*, 24 January 2024. https://asia.nikkei.com/Spotlight/Supply-Chain/Tesla-cars-face-more-entry-bans-in-China-as-security-concerns-accelerate

31   Bloomberg, 'Tesla Cars Barred From World University Games Ahead of Xi Visit', 26 July 2023. https://www.bloomberg.com/news/articles/2023-07-26/tesla-cars-barred-from-world-university-games-ahead-of-xi-visit

32   Craig Singleton, 'Are Chinese Battery Companies the Next Huawei?', *Foreign Policy*, 30 October 2023. https://foreignpolicy.com/2023/10/30/china-batteries-electric-cars-charging-networks-catl-byd-zeng-yuqun-huawei-security-risk/

33   Alex Blackburne, 'China's increasingly cheap wind turbines could open new markets', S & P Market Intelligence, 26 September 2022. https://www.spglobal.com/marketintelligence/en/news-insights/latest-news-headlines/china-s-increasingly-cheap-wind-turbines-could-open-new-markets-72152297

34   Olexsandr Fylyppov and Tim Lister, 'Russians plunder $5m farm

vehicles from Ukraine – to find they've been remotely disabled', CNN, 1 May 2022. https://edition.cnn.com/2022/05/01/europe/russia-farm-vehicles-ukraine-disabled-melitopol-intl/index.html

35   Charles Parton, 'Dealing with the threat of Chinese cellular (IoT) modules', *Britain's World*, the Council on Geostrategy's online magazine, 10 May 2023. https://www.geostrategy.org.uk/britains-world/dealing-with-the-threat-of-chinese-cellular-iot-modules/

36   Will Hazell and Dominic Penna, 'China "will use electric cars to spy on Britain"', *The Telegraph,* 5 August 2023. https://www.telegraph.co.uk/politics/2023/08/05/china-will-use-cars-to-spy-on-britain-ministers-fear/

37   Demetri Sevastopulo and Joe Leahy, 'Joe Biden says Chinese smart cars could pose US security threat', *Financial Times*, 29 February 2024. https://www.ft.com/content/40003f25-23e9-433f-83a3-a2244fb8b942?shareType=nongift

38   Sir Richard Dearlove, 'Chinese-made electric cars in UK could be jammed remotely by Beijing', *The Times*, 21 March, 2024. https://www.thetimes.co.uk/article/88b36c9b-bc45-4ca3-8409-7beed4d42c37?shareToken=-7d0a789de17934d32acbabdf32f7dffd

39   Charles Parton, *Britain's World*, 10 May 2023.

40   Lisa Jucca, 'China ban would slow, not halt, Western solar push', Reuters, 3 February 2023. https://www.reuters.com/breakingviews/china-ban-would-slow-not-halt-western-solar-push-2023-02-03/

41   The full 19 March 2014 indictment can be accessed via the US Department of Justice website. https://www.justice.gov/iso/opa/resources/512201451913235846 1949.pdf

42   See the 19 March 2014 press release from the US Department of Justice, 'U.S. Charges Five Chinese Military Hackers for Cyber Espionage Against U.S. Corporations and a Labor Organization for Commercial Advantage'. https://www.justice.gov/opa/pr/us-charges-five-chinese-military-hackers-cyber-espionage-against-us-corporations-and-labor

43   Reuters, 'Solarworld files for insolvency', 10 May 2017. https://www.reuters.com/article/solarworld-bankruptcy-idUSASM000BDII

44   Graham Allison, 'China's dominance of solar poses difficult choices for the West', *Financial Times*, 22 June 2023. https://www.ft.com/content/fd8e7175-9423-4042-a6f7-c404afdfcda4

45   Ibid.

46   Yuan Yang, Alice Hancock and Laura Pitel, 'Solar power: Europe attempts to get out of China's shadow', *Financial Times*, 23 March 2023. https://www.ft.com/content/009d8434-9c12-48fd-8c93-d06d0b86779e

47   Ibid.

48   Robert A. Rohde and Richard A. Muller, 'Air Pollution in China: Mapping of Concentrations and Sources', PloS One, 2015;10(8):e0135749. 20 August 2015 doi:10.1371/journal.pone.0135749. https://www.ncbi.nlm.nih.gov/pmc/articles/PMC4546277/

49   Tom Phillips, 'China's premier unveils smog-busting plan to "make skies blue again"', *The Guardian*, 5 March 2017. https://www.theguardian.com/

world/2017/mar/05/china-premier-li-keqiang-unveils-smog-busting-plan-to-make-skies-blue-again-air-pollution

50 He Guangwei, 'The Soil Pollution Crisis in China: A Cleanup Presents Daunting Challenge', *Yale Environment 360*, 14 July 2014. https://e360. yale.edu/features/the_soil_pollution_crisis_in_china_a_cleanup_presents_daunting_challenge

51 Javier C. Hernández, 'Tianjin Explosions Were Result of Mismanagement, China Finds', *The New York Times*, 5 February 2016. https://www.nytimes. com/2016/02/06/world/asia/tianjin-explosions-were-result-of-mismanage ment-china-finds.html

52 David Lague, 'China blames oil firm for chemical spill', *The New York Times*, 25 November 2005. https://www.nytimes.com/2005/11/25/world/asia/ china-blames-oil-firm-for-chemical-spill.html

53 This figure is taken from a China Labour Bulletin briefing paper, 'Worker Safety', 12 September 2021, which quoted from official figures and notes that 'New work hazards have emerged as the economy develops, and many employers continue to prioritise productivity and profit well above work safety.' https://clb.org.hk/en/content/work-safety

54 Dionne Searcey, Michael Forsythe and Eric Lipton, 'A Power Struggle over Cobalt Rattles the Clean Energy Revolution', *The New York Times*, 7 December 2021. https://www.nytimes.com/2021/11/20/world/china-con-go-cobalt.html

55 These figures and more are available in an Institute for Energy Research report, 'China Dominates the Global Lithium Battery Market', published 9 September 2020. https://www.instituteforenergyresearch.org/renewable/ china-dominates-the-global-lithium-battery-market/

56 Harry Dempsey, 'US enticed by Greenland's rare earth resources', *Financial Times*, 20 August 2019. https://www.ft.com/content/f418bb86 -bdb2-11e9-89e2-41e555e96722

57 Guillaume Pitron, 'Dirty Rare Metals: Digging Deeper into the Energy Transition', *Green European Journal*, 27 September 2018. https://www. greeneuropeanjournal.eu/dirty-rare-metals-digging-deeper-into-the-energy-transition/#:~:text=They%20include%20a%20class%20of, gallium%20than%20iron%20on%20Earth.

58 Wang Shou and Wang Xintong, 'Leaks on the Rise at China's Mining Waste Dumps', *Caixin Global*, 5 January 2024. https://www.caixinglobal.com/ 2024-01-05/leaks-on-the-rise-at-chinas-mining-waste-dumps-102153616. html

59 For an overview of the Minerals Security Partnership, see the June 2022 US Department of State briefing, 'Minerals Security Partnership'. https:// www.state.gov/minerals-security-partnership/#:~:text=In%20June%20 2022%2C%20the%20Minerals,mining%20event%20in%20the%20world.

60 Shunsuke Tabeta, 'China bans exports of rare-earth magnet technologies', *Nikkei Asia*, 21 December 2023. https://asia.nikkei.com/Economy/Trade/ China-bans-exports-of-rare-earth-magnet-technologies

61 Edward White, William Langley and Harry Dempsey, 'China imposes export

curbs on graphite', *Financial Times*, 20 October 2023. https://www.ft.com/content/8af8c05c-8e54-40e9-9051-5a0b2b036c32

62   Harry Dempsey, Peter Foster and Alice Hancock, 'UK watchdog proposes not classifying key battery material as toxic', *Financial Times*, 1 September 2023. https://www.ft.com/content/19772fa8-2063-4901-b4e1-0c8cf13cb7fd?shareType=nongift

63   Yuan Yang, Alice Hancock and Laura Pital, 'Solar power: Europe attempts to get out of China's shadow', *Financial Times*, 23 March 2023. https://www.ft.com/content/009d8434-9c12-48fd-8c93-d06d0b86779e

64   Ernest Scheyder, 'Insight: Western start-ups seek to break China's grip on rare earths refining', Reuters, 4 December 2023. https://www.reuters.com/sustainability/climate-energy/western-start-ups-seek-break-chinas-grip-rare-earths-refining-2023-12-04/

65   Alex Lawson, '"Breakthrough battery" from Sweden may cut dependency on China', *The Guardian*, 21 November 2023. https://www.theguardian.com/business/2023/nov/21/breakthrough-battery-from-sweden-may-cut-dependency-on-china

66   Robert Clark and Richard Norrie, 'China's presence in NHS supply chains: Why we need to protect our health service from future threat', Civitas, May 2022. https://www.civitas.org.uk/publications/chinas-presence-in-nhs-supply-chains/

67   Niharika Mandhana, 'China's shipyards are ready for a protracted war. America's Aren't', *The Wall Street Journal*, 13 February 2024. https://www.wsj.com/world/china/chinas-shipyards-are-ready-for-a-protracted-war-americas-arent-d6f004dd

68   Chan Ho-him, Oliver Telling and Song Jung-a, 'Shipping industry steers container production away from China', *Financial Times*, 2 November 2023. https://www.ft.com/content/c32c7b86-7420-4ffb-8d41-163f315ff72a?d. . .ubstack&utm_medium=email#myft:notification:instant-email:content

Chapter 21:
Autocrats United

1   Brian Spegele and Wenxin Fan, 'China's Xi Doubles Down on Belt and Road as Path to New World Order', *The Wall Street Journal*, 18 October 2023. https://www.wsj.com/world/china/chinas-xi-doubles-down-on-belt-and-road-as-path-to-new-world-order-aa8a8a5c

2   These quotes are taken from Xi Jinping's 14 May 2017 speech at the opening ceremony of the Belt and Road Forum for International Cooperation, as reprinted in *The Governance of China*, vol. II (Beijing: Foreign Language Press, 2017), pp 553–66.

3   Bruno Maçães, 'At the crossroads of the new Silk Road', *The Guardian*, 29 January 2019. https://www.theguardian.com/commentisfree/2018/jan/29/at-the-crossroads-of-the-new-silk-road#maincontent

4   Ammar A. Malik, Bradley Parks, Brooke Russell, Joyce Jiahua Lin, Katherine Walsh, Kyra Solomon, Sheng Zhang, Thai-Binh Elston and Seth Goodman, 'Banking on the Belt and Road: Insights from a new global dataset of 13,427 Chinese development Projects', AidData, September 2021. https://docs.aiddata.org/ad4/pdfs/Banking_on_the_Belt_and_Road__Insights_from_a_new_global_dataset_of_13427_Chinese_development_projects.pdf

5   'Africa is juggling rival powers like no other', *The Economist*, 2 March 2024. https://www.economist.com/international/2024/02/28/africa-is-juggling-rival-powers-like-no-other-continent

6   Sebastian Horn, Bradley C. Parks, Carmen M. Reinhart and Christoph Trebesch, 'China as an International Lender of Last Resort', Kiel Institute for the World Economy, March 2023. https://www.ifw-kiel.de/fileadmin/Dateiverwaltung/IfW-Publications/-ifw/Kiel_Working_Paper/2023/KWP_2244_China_as_an_International_Lender_of_Last_Resort/KWP_2244.pdf

7   'China's emerging Belt and Road debt crisis', *Financial Times*, 27 July 2022. https://www.ft.com/content/eb2d89f6-afd1-491e-b753-863e9727f6de

8   Marc Jones, 'Serious debt crisis unfolding across developing countries – UNDP', Reuters, 11 October 2022. https://www.reuters.com/markets/rates-bonds/serious-debt-crisis-unfolding-across-developing-countries-undp-2022-10-11/

9   Ezra Fieser, Shawn Donnan and Ramsey Al-Rikabi, 'IMF talks on Debt Deadlock Stuck Between China, Private Lenders', Bloomberg, 11 October 2023. https://www.bloomberg.com/news/articles/2023-10-11/imf-talks-on-debt-deadlock-stuck-between-china-private-lenders?leadSource=uverify%20wall

10   Simon Mundy, 'China backed port sparks Sri Lanka sovereignty fears', *Financial Times*, 23 October 2017. https://www.ft.com/content/f8262d56-a6a0-11e7-ab55-27219df83c97

11   Christine Lu, 'China Is a Loan Shark With No Legs Left to Break', *Foreign Policy*, 9 May 2023. https://foreignpolicy.com/2023/05/09/china-debt-lending-paris-club-bri-development-finance/

12   For a more detailed analysis of trade through the South China Sea, see the database maintained by China Power, 'How Much trade transits the South China Sea'. https://chinapower.csis.org/much-trade-transits-south-china-sea/

13   Sebastian Strangio, *In the Dragon's Shadow: Southeast Asia in the Chinese Century* (New Haven and London: Yale University Press, 2020), p. 150.

14   Joe Leahy, James Kynge and Benjamin Parkin, 'Ten years of China's Belt and Road: what has $1 trillion achieved?' *Financial Times*, 22 October 2022. https://www.ft.com/content/83501dd5-fe6d-4169-9d83-28a8cf46e681?shareType=nongift

15   Jack Brook, 'Cambodia's airport dreams stall as Chinese money dried up', *Nikkei Asia*, 23 February 2024. https://asia.nikkei.com/Business/Transportation/Cambodia-s-airport-dreams-stall-as-Chinese-money-dries-up

16   James Kynge, 'China's Belt and Road projects drive overseas debt fears', *Financial Times*, 7 August 2018. https://www.ft.com/content/e7a08b54-9554-11e8-b747-fb1e803ee64e

17 Richard Javad Heydarian, 'Why the Philippines is exiting the Belt and Road', *Asia Times*, 2 November 2023. https://asiatimes.com/2023/11/why-the-philippines-is-exiting-the-belt-and-road/

18 Laura Silver, Christine Huang and Laura Clancy, 'China's Approach to Foreign Policy Gets Largely Negative Reviews in 24-Country Survey', Pew Research Center, 27 July 2023. https://www.pewresearch.org/global/2023/07/27/chinas-approach-to-foreign-policy-gets-largely-negative-reviews-in-24-country-survey/

19 See Cao Zhihui, 'Nowhere to hide: Building safe cities with technology enablers and AI', July 2016, as published on Huawei's website. https://www.huawei.com/en/huaweitech/publication/winwin/ai/nowhere-to-hide

20 Jonathan Hillman and Maesea McCalpin, 'Watching Huawei's "safe cities"', Center for Strategic and International Studies, 4 November 2019. https://www.csis.org/analysis/watching-huaweis-safe-cities

21 Adrian Shahbaz, 'The Digital Silk Road and normative values', in David Gordon and Meia Nouwens (eds), *The Digital Silk Road: China's Technological Rise and the Geopolitics of Cyberspace* (Abingdon and London: Routledge for the International Institute for Strategic Studies, 2022), p. 114.

22 Alan Gross, Madhumita Murgia and Yuan Yang, 'Chinese tech groups shaping UN facial recognition standards', *Financial Times*, 2 December 2019. https://www.ft.com/content/c3555a3c-0d3e-11ea-b2d6-9bf4d1957a67

23 Jodi Xu Klein, 'Ex-Google CEO Eric Schmidt stresses "urgency" in countering China on artificial intelligence as US-China tech war continues', *South China Morning Post*, 24 February 2021. https://www.scmp.com/print/news/china/article/3122857/us-china-tech-war-former-google-ceo-eric-schmidt-stresses-urgency

24 'Britain moves to remove Chinese surveillance gear from government sites', *The Guardian*, 8 June 2023. https://www.theguardian.com/world/2023/jun/08/britain-to-remove-chinese-surveillance-gear-from-government-sites

25 Paul Seddon and Chris Vallance, 'Police use of Chinese camera tech criticised by surveillance watchdog', BBC Online, 15 February 2023. https://www.bbc.co.uk/news/uk-politics-64644692

26 Reuters, 'TikTok admits using its app to spy on reporters in effort to track leaks', *The Guardian*, 23 December 2022. https://www.theguardian.com/technology/2022/dec/22/tiktok-bytedance-workers-fired-data-access-journalists

27 Alex Hern, 'TikTok to be banned from UK parliamentary devices', *The Guardian*, 23 March 2023. https://www.theguardian.com/technology/2023/mar/23/tiktok-to-be-banned-from-uk-parliamentary-devices

28 Shiona McCullum, 'European Commission bans TikTok on staff devices', BBC Online, 23 February 2023. https://www.bbc.co.uk/news/technology-64743991

29 Jyoti Narayan and Nilutpal Timsina, 'Belgian intelligence service scrutinising Alibaba's presence at Liege airport', Reuters, 6 October 2023. https://www.reuters.com/technology/belgiums-intelligence-service-monitors-alibaba-hub-over-espionage-concerns-ft-2023-10-05/

30 Anna Gross, Alexander Heal, Demetri Sevastopulo, Kathrin Hille and Mercedes Ruel, 'China exerts control over internet cable projects in South China Sea', *Financial Times*, 13 March 2023. https://www.ft.com/content/89bc954d-64ed-4d80-bb8f-9f1852ec4eb1?shareType=nongift

31 Reuters, 'China ship New New Polar Bear is focus of pipeline damage probe, Finland says', *South China Morning Post*, 21 October 2023. https://www.scmp.com/news/world/europe/article/3238726/china-ship-newnew-polar-bear-focus-pipeline-damage-probe-finland-says

32 Maighnu Nanu, 'Watch: Xi Jinping tells Putin "change not seen in 100 years" is coming', *The Telegraph*, 22 March 2022. https://www.telegraph.co.uk/world-news/2023/03/22/watch-xi-jinping-tells-putin-change-not-seen-100-years-coming/

33 Reuters, 'China-Russia 2023 trade value hits record high of $240 bln – Chinese customs', 12 January 2024. https://www.reuters.com/markets/china-russia-2023-trade-value-hits-record-high-240-bln-chinese-customs-2024-01-12/

34 Graham Allison, 'Xi and Putin Have the Most Consequential Undeclared Alliance in the World', *Foreign Policy*, 23 March 2023. https://foreignpolicy.com/2023/03/23/xi-putin-meeting-china-russia-undeclared-alliance/

35 Han Wei, 'US Blacklists 12 Chinese Companies Over Alleged Russia Ties', *Caixin Global*, 14 April 2023. https://www.caixinglobal.com/2023-04-14/us-blacklists-12-chinese-companies-over-alleged-russia-ties-102018546.html

36 Hal Brands, 'Ukraine Is Now a World War. And Putin Is Gaining Friends', *Bloomberg*, 12 May 2024. https://www.bloomberg.com/opinion/features/2024-05-12/china-russia-iran-have-made-ukraine-a-world-war-against-us-europe

37 Tessa Wong, 'Zelensky accuses Russia and China of undermining summit', BBC Online, 2 June 2024. https://www.bbc.co.uk/news/articles/c722q4dn7e1o

38 Mara Hvistendahl and Alexey Kovalev, 'Hacked Russian Files Reveal Propaganda Agreement With China', *The Intercept*, 30 December 2022. https://theintercept.com/2022/12/30/russia-china-news-media-agreement/

39 For a more detailed history of this period, see Michael S. Green, 'The Sino-Soviet Border Conflict: Deterrence, Escalation, and the Threat of Nuclear War in 1969', Center for Naval Analyses, US Department of Defense, November 2010. https://www.cna.org/reports/2010/d0022974.a2.pdf

40 Reuters, 'China, Russia, Iran conduct four-day naval exercises in Gulf of Oman', 15 March 2023. https://www.reuters.com/world/china-russia-iran-conduct-four-day-naval-exercises-gulf-oman-2023-03-15/

41 For an overview of the emerging narrative of autocracy versus democracy, see Richard Youngs, 'Autocracy Versus Democracy After the Ukraine Invasion: Mapping a Middle Way', Carnegie Europe, July 2022. https://carnegieeurope.eu/2022/07/20/autocracy-versus-democracy-after-ukraine-invasion-mapping-middle-way-pub-87525

42 Tony Munroe, Andrew Osborn and Humeyra Pamuk, 'China, Russia partner

up against West at Olympics summit', Reuters, 4 February 2022. https://
www.reuters.com/world/europe/russia-china-tell-nato-stop-expansion-
moscow-backs-beijing-taiwan-2022-02-04/

43   Agence France-Presse (via France24), 'Blinken dismisses China's "marriage
of convenience" with Russia', 22 March 2023. https://www.france24.com/
en/live-news/20230322-blinken-says-china-has-not-crossed-line-on-lethal-
aid-to-russia

44   'US no longer capable of maintaining mafia-style "rules-based order"', *Global
Times*, 11 July 2023. https://www.globaltimes.cn/page/202307/1294153.
shtml

45   Gideon Rachman, 'Is there such a thing as a rules-based international
order?', *Financial Times*, 20 April 2023. https://www.ft.com/content/
664d7fa5-d575-45da-8129-095647c8abe7

46   Agence France-Presse (via France24), 22 March 2023.

47   Barack Obama, *A Promised Land* (New York: Crown, 2020), p. 474.

48   Robert Wihtol, 'Does China wield excessive influence in the Asian
Infrastructure Investment Bank?' *The Interpreter*, 16 June 2023. https://
www.lowyinstitute.org/the-interpreter/does-china-wield-excessive-influ
ence-asian-infrastructure-investment-bank

49   Jaya Josie, 'Ten years of inclusive multilateralism', *The China Daily*, 18
October 2023. http://www.chinadaily.com.cn/a/202310/18/WS652f294aa
31090682a5e91cf.html

50   David Ljunggren, 'Canada freezes ties with China-led AIIB, probes allegations of Communist domination', Reuters, 14 June 2023. https://www.
reuters.com/business/finance/canada-freezes-ties-with-china-led-aiib-probes-
allegations-communist-domination-2023-06-14/

51   James Kynge, 'China's blueprint for an alternative world order', *Financial
Times*, 22 August 2023. https://www.ft.com/content/8ac52fe7-e9db-48a8-b
2f0-7305ab53f4c3?shareType=nongift

52   Oliver Stuenkel, 'BRICS expansion would be a sign of China's growing
influence, says Oliver Stuenkel', *The Economist*, 18 August 2023. https://
www.economist.com/by-invitation/2023/08/18/brics-expansion-would-be-
a-sign-of-chinas-growing-influence-says-oliver-stuenkel

53   Bloomberg, 'China's Yuan Replaces Dollar as Most Traded in Russia', 4
April 2023. https://www.bloomberg.com/news/articles/2023-04-03/china-s-
yuan-replaces-dollar-as-most-traded-currency-in-russia

54   Drew Bernstein, 'Could China's Digital Yuan Challenge U.S. Dollar
Dominance?' *Forbes*, 23 August 2023. https://www.forbes.com/sites/drew
bernstein/2023/08/23/could-chinas-digital-yuan-challenge-us-dollar-
dominance/

Chapter 22:
The Vampire State

1   Mariko Oi, 'Evergrande: Crisis-hit Chinese property giant ordered to

liquidate', BBC Online, 29 January 2024. https://www.bbc.co.uk/news/business-67562522

2   Wang Jing, Zhou Yongqin and Ding Yi, 'China Monthly New Property Sales Plunge to Five-Year Low', *Caixin Global*, 2 February 2024. https://www.caixinglobal.com/2024-02-02/china-monthly-new-property-sales-plunge-to-five-year-low-102163223.html

3   Reuters, 'Exclusive: China authorities ask Ping An to take controlling stake in Country Garden', 8 November 2023. https://www.reuters.com/world/china/china-authorities-ask-ping-an-take-controlling-stake-country-garden-sources-say-2023-11-08/

4   Bloomberg, 'China Merges Hundreds of Rural Banks as Financial Risks Mount', 31 January 2024. https://www.bloomberg.com/news/articles/2024-01-31/china-merges-hundreds-of-rural-banks-as-financial-risks-mount

5   Jeremy Mark, 'There's less to China's housing bailout than meets the eye', Atlantic Council, 22 May 2024. https://www.atlanticcouncil.org/blogs/econographics/theres-less-to-chinas-housing-bailout-than-meets-the-eye/

6   Ibid.

7   Reuters, 'China wants to grow its economy. So why is it halting construction?' *The Christian Science Monitor*, 19 January 2024. https://www.csmonitor.com/World/Asia-Pacific/2024/0119/China-wants-to-grow-its-economy.-So-why-is-it-halting-construction

8   He Huifeng, 'China jobs: suspended production, extended unpaid leave embody woes with private businesses under pressure', *South China Morning Post*, 18 December 2023. https://www.scmp.com/economy/economic-indicators/article/3245207/china-jobs-suspended-production-extended-unpaid-leave-embody-woes-private-businesses-under-pressure

9   Iori Kawate, 'Net outflow of funds from China hits 7-year high in September', *Nikkei Asia*, 25 October 2023. https://asia.nikkei.com/Business/Markets/Net-outflow-of-funds-from-China-hits-7-year-high-in-September#

10 Neil Callanan and Ainslie Chandler, 'China's Property Crisis Is Starting to Ripple Across the World', Bloomberg, 9 February 2024. https://www.bloomberg.com/news/articles/2024-02-09/china-s-real-estate-crisis-is-starting-to-ripple-across-the-world?leadSource=uverify%20wall

11 Sun Yu, 'Moody's advised staff to work from home ahead of China outlook cut', *Financial Times*, 7 December 2023. https://www.ft.com/content/d488bcb8-1ac1-4551-bb8f-49fe6c990ce2

12 Ibid.

13 'China's banking regulator says property market is biggest "grey rhino"', Reuters, 30 November 2020. https://www.reuters.com/article/us-china-banking-idUSKBN28A1SY

14 'Why Chinese mourn Li Keqiang, their former prime minister', *The Economist*, 2 November 2023. https://www.economist.com/china/2023/11/02/why-chinese-mourn-li-keqiang

15 See the International Monetary Fund's China country focus, 'IMF Survey: China's Difficult Rebalancing Act', 12 September 2007. https://www.imf.org/en/News/Articles/2015/09/28/04/53/socar0912a

16 *The Economist*, 2 November 2023

17   John B. Knight, 'China as a Development State', *The World Economy*, vol. 37, Issue 10, October 2014, pp. 1335–47. https://onlinelibrary.wiley.com/doi/10.1111/twec.12215

18   Xi Jinping, *The Governance of China*, vol. II (Beijing: Foreign Languages Press, 2017), p. 455.

19   Ibid., p. 449.

20   'What Does China Really Spend on Defence?', *The Wall Street Journal*, 9 July 2023.   https://www.wsj.com/articles/china-defense-spending-senate-bill-angus-king-dan-sullivan-u-s-beijing-military-c3b64ba

21   Kathrin Hille, 'China's military budget outpaces other spending in shift to security', *Financial Times*, 5 March 2023. https://www.ft.com/content/66790beb-bd5b-4025-b12e-5d0e7dd8bbfb

22   'Efforts must be made to accelerate modernization of national defense and armed forces', *PLA Daily*, 13 July 2021. http://eng.chinamil.com.cn/2021special/2021-07/13/content_10061116.htm

23   Edward White and Sun Yu, 'Xi Jinping's dream of a Chinese military-industrial complex', *Financial Times*, 19 June 2023. https://www.ft.com/content/6f388e4b-9c4e-4ca3-8040-49962f1e155d?shareType=nongift

24   Ibid.

25   Reuters, 'China wants to mobilise entire nation in counter-espionage', 2 August 2023. https://www.reuters.com/world/china/china-wants-mobilise-entire-nation-counter-espionage-2023-08-01/?

26   Phoebe Zhang, 'China to tighten its state secrets law in biggest revision in a decade', *South China Morning Post*, 27 October 2023. https://www.scmp.com/news/china/politics/article/3239340/china-tighten-its-state-secrets-law-biggest-revision-decade

27   Wang Xintong, 'Chinese comedian canceled for PLA pun', *Nikkei Asia*, 19 May 2023. https://asia.nikkei.com/Spotlight/Caixin/Chinese-comedian-canceled-for-PLA-pun

28   'China lacks a credible policy to meet its own growth target', *Financial Times*, 6 March 2024. https://www.ft.com/content/9e2b59be-1f06-4001-bf68-91974951ec59?shareType=nongift

29   Kohei Fujimura, Shunsuke Tabeta and Iori Kawate, 'China congress report mentions "security" record 29 times', *Nikkei Asia*, 6 March 2024. https://asia.nikkei.com/Politics/China-People-s-Congress/China-congress-report-mentions-security-record-29-times

30   See the 23 August 2023 press release from the US Department of Commerce's Bureau of Industry and Security, 'Commerce adds seven Chinese entities to entity list for supporting China's military modernisation efforts'. https://www.bis.doc.gov/index.php/documents/about-bis/newsroom/press-releases/3121-2022-08-23-press-release-seven-entity-list-additions/file

31   Mariko Oi, 'US-China chip war: Beijing unhappy at latest wave of US restrictions', BBC Online, 18 October 2023. https://www.bbc.co.uk/news/business-67141987

32   Kevin Klyman, 'Biden Takes Measured Approach on China Investment

Controls', *Foreign Policy*, 19 August 2023. https://foreignpolicy.com/2023/08/19/biden-approach-china-economy-investment-control/

33 'China is a "ticking time bomb" because of economic woes, Joe Biden warns', *The Guardian*, 11 August 2023. https://www.theguardian.com/us-news/2023/aug/11/joe-biden-china-economy-time-bomb

34 Jennifer Welch, Jenny Leonard, Maeva Cousin, Gerard DiPippo and Tom Orlik, 'Xi, Biden and the $10 Trillion Cost of War Over Taiwan', Bloomberg, 9 January 2024. https://www.bloomberg.com/news/features/2024-01-09/if-china-invades-taiwan-it-would-cost-world-economy-10-trillion

35 Vincent Ni, 'Beijing orders "stress test" as fears of Russia-style sanctions mount', *The Guardian*, 4 May 2022. https://www.theguardian.com/world/2022/may/04/beijing-orders-stress-test-as-fears-of-russia-style-sanctions-mount

36 Jamie McGeever, 'China slips away from Treasuries but sticks with dollar bonds', Reuters, 23 February 2023. https://www.reuters.com/markets/asia/china-slips-away-treasuries-sticks-with-dollar-bonds-2023-02-22/

37 Momoka Matsumoto and Noriyuki Doi, 'China gold purchases soar 30% on economic anxieties', *Nikkei Asia*, 1 February 2024. https://asia.nikkei.com/Economy/China-gold-purchases-soar-30-on-economic-anxiety#:~:text=China%2C%20along%20with%20India%2C%20is,up%20028%25%20to%20280%20tonnes.

38 Lingling Wei, 'Xi Prepares China for "Extreme" Scenarios, Including Conflict with the West', *The Wall Street Journal*, 12 June 2023. https://www.wsj.com/articles/chinas-xi-jinping-plays-up-possibility-of-worsening-tensions-with-the-west-aac2dff8

39 'China warns of artificial intelligence risks, calls for beefed up national security', Associated Press, 31 May 2023. https://apnews.com/article/china-artificial-intelligence-national-security-00a38e550ef6b4ac12cd1f-d418363d2b

40 Tracy Qu, 'China Offers Support to Accelerate EV Makers' Global Push', *The Wall Street Journal*, 7 February 2024. https://www.wsj.com/business/autos/china-offers-support-to-accelerate-ev-makers-global-push-9ae498ff

41 Michelle Toh, 'Mexico could help this huge Chinese car maker crack the US market', CNN, 19 January 2024. https://edition.cnn.com/2024/01/19/cars/byd-hungary-mexico-global-domination-intl-hnk/index.html

42 Kathrin Hille and Cheng Leng, 'China removes defence minister two months after disappearance', *Financial Times*, 24 October 2023. https://www.ft.com/content/2608c117-98e1-4b07-8a92-dd8a5251cbb8

43 'Protests are soaring, as China's workers demand their wages', *The Economist*, 8 February 2024. https://www.economist.com/china/2024/02/08/protests-are-soaring-as-chinas-workers-demand-their-wages

44 George Magnus, 'China cannot allow jobless young to lie flat', *Financial Times*, 21 July 2023. https://www.ft.com/content/bcfb650a-e9ab-427d-baac-e22a06547e29

45 Amy Hawkins, 'Free college and IVF help: China hunts for ways to raise its birthrate', *The Guardian*, 10 March 2023. https://www.theguardian.com/world/2023/mar/10/free-college-and-ivf-help-china-hunts-for-ways-to-raise-its-birthrate

46   Pak Yiu, Grace Li, C. K. Tan and Mitsuru Obe, 'China's aging popula-
     tion threatens a Japan-style lost decade', *Nikkei Asia*, 22 March 2023.
     https://asia.nikkei.com/Spotlight/The-Big-Story/China-s-aging-popu
     lation-threatens-a-Japan-style-lost-decade
47   Dudley L. Poston Jr, 'China needs immigrants', *The Conversation*, 18 July
     2023. https://theconversation.com/china-needs-immigrants-208911
48   Ibid.
49   Lingling Wei, 'China Wants to Move Ahead, but Xi Jinping Is Looking
     to the Past', *The Wall Street Journal*, 28 December 2024. https://www.
     wsj.com/world/china/china-wants-to-move-ahead-but-xi-jinping-is-look
     ing-to-the-past-cf2e076b?st=ojnca98izvifecm&reflink=article_email_share

Index